BROOKINGS PAPERS ON EDUCATION POLICY

2006/2007

Tom Loveless
Frederick M. Hess

Editors

Sponsored by
the Brown Center on
Education Policy

BROOKINGS INSTITUTION PRESS
Washington, D.C.

Copyright © 2007
THE BROOKINGS INSTITUTION
1775 Massachusetts Avenue, N.W., Washington, DC 20036

Library of Congress Catalog Card No. 98-664027
ISSN 1096-2719
ISBN 978-0-8157-1184-1

Authorization to photocopy items for internal or personal use or the internal or personal use of specific clients is granted by the Brookings Institution for libraries and other users registered with the Copyright Clearance Center Transactional Reporting Service, provided that the basic fee is paid to the Copyright Clearance Center, 222 Rosewood Drive, Danvers, MA 01923. For more information, please contact CCC at 978/750-8400 and online at www.copyright.com. This authorization does not extend to other kinds of copying, such as copying for general distribution, or for creating new collective works, or for sale. Specific written permission for such copying must be obtained from the Permissions Department, Brookings Institution Press, 1775 Massachusetts Avenue, N.W., Washington, DC 20036; fax 202/536-3623; e-mail: permissions@brookings.edu.

BROOKINGS PAPERS ON EDUCATION POLICY
2006/2007

Introduction: What Do We Know about School Size and Class Size?   1
TOM LOVELESS AND FREDERICK M. HESS

Is Small Really Better? Testing Some Assumptions   15
   about High School Size
BARBARA SCHNEIDER, ADAM E. WYSE, AND VENESSA KEESLER

School Consolidation and Inequality   49
CHRISTOPHER BERRY

The Effects of School Size on Parental Involvement   77
   and Social Capital: Evidence from the ELS: 2002
THOMAS S. DEE, WEI HA, AND BRIAN A. JACOB

Optimal Context Size in Elementary Schools: 99
   Disentangling the Effects of Class Size and School Size
DOUGLAS E. READY AND VALERIE E. LEE

Class Size and School Size: Taking the Trade-Offs Seriously   137
DOUGLAS N. HARRIS

High School Size, Organization, and Content: 163
   What Matters for Student Success?
LINDA DARLING-HAMMOND, PETER ROSS,
   AND MICHAEL MILLIKEN

What Have Researchers Learned from Project STAR?   205
DIANE WHITMORE SCHANZENBACH

Policy from the Hip: Class-Size Reduction in California 229
PETER SCHRAG

International Evidence on Expenditures and Class Size: 245
  A Review
LUDGER WÖßMANN

The Relative Influence of Research on Class-Size Policy 273
JAMES S. KIM

THE BROOKINGS INSTITUTION

The Brookings Institution is a private nonprofit organization devoted to research, education, and publication on important issues of domestic and foreign policy. Its principal purpose is to bring the highest quality independent research and analysis to bear on current and emerging policy problems. The Institution was founded on December 8, 1927, to merge the activities of the Institute for Government Research, founded in 1916, the Institute of Economics, founded in 1922, and the Robert Brookings Graduate School of Economics and Government, founded in 1924. Interpretations or conclusions in Brookings publications should be understood to be solely those of the authors.

Board of Trustees
John L. Thornton
Chair
Strobe Talbott
President
Robert J. Abernethy
Zoë Baird
Alan R. Batkin
Richard C. Blum
Geoffrey T. Boisi
Arthur B. Culvahouse Jr.
Alan M. Dachs
Kenneth W. Dam
Vishakha N. Desai
Thomas E. Donilon
Mario Draghi

Kenneth M. Duberstein
Lawrence K. Fish
Cyrus F. Freidheim Jr.
David Friend
Ann M. Fudge
Jeffrey W. Greenberg
Brian L. Greenspun
Teresa Heinz
Samuel Hellman
Glenn H. Hutchins
Joel Z. Hyatt
Shirley Ann Jackson
Kenneth M. Jacobs
Suzanne Nora Johnson
Harold Hongju Koh

William A. Owens
Frank H. Pearl
John Edward Porter
Steven Rattner
Edgar Rios
Haim Saban
Leonard D. Schaeffer
Lawrence H. Summers
David F. Swensen
Larry D. Thompson
Andrew H. Tisch
Laura D'Andrea Tyson
Antoine W. van Agtmael
Beatrice W. Welters
Daniel Yergin

Honorary Trustees
Leonard Abramson
Elizabeth E. Bailey
Rex J. Bates
Louis W. Cabot
James W. Cicconi
A. W. Clausen
William T. Coleman Jr.
D. Ronald Daniel
Robert A. Day
Bruce B. Dayton
Charles W. Duncan Jr.
Walter Y. Elisha
Robert F. Erburu
Bart Friedman
Henry Louis Gates Jr.
Robert D. Haas
Lee H. Hamilton
William A. Haseltine

F. Warren Hellman
Robert A. Helman
Roy M. Huffington
James A. Johnson
Ann Dibble Jordan
Michael H. Jordan
Vernon E. Jordan Jr.
Breene M. Kerr
Marie L. Knowles
James T. Lynn
Jessica Tuchman Mathews
David O. Maxwell
Donald F. McHenry
Robert S. McNamara
Mary Patterson McPherson
Arjay Miller
Mario M. Morino
Maconda Brown O'Connor

Samuel Pisar
J. Woodward Redmond
Charles W. Robinson
James D. Robinson III
Judith Rodin
Warren B. Rudman
B. Francis Saul II
Ralph S. Saul
Henry B. Schacht
Michael P. Schulhof
Joan E. Spero
Vincent J. Trosino
John C. Whitehead
Stephen M. Wolf
James D. Wolfensohn
Ezra K. Zilkha

BROOKINGS PAPERS ON EDUCATION POLICY contains the edited versions of papers and comments that were presented at the ninth Brookings conference on education policy, held on May 22–23, 2006. The conference gives federal, state, and local policymakers an independent, nonpartisan forum to analyze policies intended to improve student performance. Each year Brookings convenes some of the best-informed analysts from various disciplines to review the current situation in education and to consider proposals for reform. This year's issue addresses class size and school size. The conference and journal were funded by the Smith Richardson Foundation and the George R. Brown Chair in Educational Studies at Brookings.

The papers in this volume have been modified to reflect some of the insights contributed by the discussions at the conference. In all cases the papers are the result of the authors' thinking and do not imply agreement by those attending the conference. Nor do the materials presented here necessarily represent the view of the staff members, officers, or trustees of the Brookings Institution or Smith Richardson Foundation.

Ordering Information

For information on subscriptions, standing orders, and individual copies, contact Brookings Institution Press, P.O. Box 465, Hanover, PA 17331-0465. Or call 866-698-0010. E-mail brookings@tsp.sheridan.com. Visit Brookings online at http://www.brookings.edu/press.

Brookings periodicals are available online through Online Computer Library Center (contact the OCLC subscriptions department at 800/848-5878, ext. 6271) and Project Muse (http://muse.jhu.edu).

Staff Tom Loveless, editor
Frederick M. Hess, editor
Paul DiPerna, Brown Center Assistant Director
Katharyn Field, Brown Center Coordinator
Eileen Hughes, Editorial Associate
Elizabeth Forsyth, Editorial Associate

Contributors Christopher Berry, *University of Chicago*
Linda Darling-Hammond, *Stanford University*
Thomas S. Dee, *Swarthmore College*
Wei Ha, *Harvard University*
Douglas N. Harris, *University of Wisconsin–Madison*
Brian A. Jacob, *Harvard University*
Vanessa Keesler, *Michigan State University*
James S. Kim, *Harvard Graduate School of Education*
Valerie E. Lee, *University of Michigan*
Michael Milliken, *Stanford University*
Douglas D. Ready, *Columbia Teachers College*
Peter Ross, *Stanford University*
Diane Whitmore Schanzenbach, *University of Chicago*
Barbara Schneider, *Michigan State University*
Peter Schrag, Sacramento Bee
Ludger Wößmann, *University of Munich and Ifo Institute for Economic Research*
Adam E. Wyse, *Michigan State University*

Introduction: What Do We Know about School Size and Class Size?

TOM LOVELESS
FREDERICK M. HESS

The world of education is never hurting for new reforms. For decades, one new proposal after another—in areas ranging from pedagogy to governance to school finance—has been championed by enthusiastic backers. The most successful of these have been embraced by researchers, policymakers, or influential philanthropists and become part of the fabric of schooling. Unfortunately, the track record of most reforms has been disappointing. Many highly touted proposals—site-based governance, whole language, alternative schools, and mastery learning, just to name a few—had their brief moment in the sun, then receded into the background with little evidence that they had improved education.

Today, two of the more prominent reforms on the agenda address the question of size. For more than a decade, an influential camp of education experts has argued that smaller classes are a promising way to boost student achievement. Ambitious, costly class-size reduction policies have been adopted in trendsetting states like California and Florida. Influential organizations, including the National Education Association, have made class-size reduction a favored policy proposal.

More recently, the criticism has arisen that contemporary high schools are too big and too impersonal to educate today's students effectively. One reform strategy, supported aggressively in the early 2000s by the influential Bill and Melinda Gates Foundation, has been to break up these large institutions and replace them with smaller, more intimate schools. The "small schools" strategy—which has been an organizing principle of high school improvement efforts in closely watched urban districts like New York City and San Diego and in heralded charter schools in cities like Providence and Boston—has attracted much notice and some criticism. While the Gates Foundation has gradually backed away from the small schools focus in the past year or two, it remains a popular tack for high school reformers across the land.

What are we to make of these reforms? What do we know about their benefits and costs or about how they actually affect the lives of students, teachers, and parents?

Both small classes and small schools would seem to be an easy sell. Smaller classes offer teachers more time to address the individual needs of each student. Smaller schools foster a more personal, tightly knit environment in which adults know individual students well. Most people believe that smaller, intimate educational settings provide structure, safety, and discipline that larger, bureaucratized settings cannot provide.

Of course, smallness is not cost free, whether it means reducing the size of schools or the size of classes. Both forms of downsizing incur direct costs—it costs money to shrink classes by hiring more teachers or to shrink schools by adding new campuses or subdividing existing schools—and indirect costs can develop downstream from the additional organizational changes precipitated by going small. However, researchers, politicians, philanthropists, and school reformers often tout the potential benefits of small schools and classes while giving scant attention to either the cost or difficulty of downsizing. A political environment in which costs are downplayed or ignored presents a real challenge for policymakers.

Class-size reductions are wildly popular. Doug Harris notes in this volume that 88 percent of parents reportedly support class-size reduction. Teachers also strongly endorse it; both major national teacher unions have made class-size reduction central to their school reform agendas. The American Educational Research Association (AERA), the professional association of the nation's educational researchers, issued a policy brief in 2003 that advised public officials and educators that "in the stockpile of educational policy initiatives that are worth finding resources for, small classes rank near the top of the list." The AERA brief declared, "There is no doubt that small classes can deliver lasting benefits, especially for minority and low-income students," but also admitted that "unintended consequences are possible" and that reducing class size "may not always be the best use of scarce resources."[1]

Buffeted by such research and advice, policymakers face difficult decisions. In this volume, we offer guidance on how to think through the popular calls for smaller classes and smaller schools. In the spring of 2006, we invited some of the nation's most esteemed education researchers to examine ten different facets of the school- and class-size debate at a two-day conference at the Brookings Institution in Washington. Participants heard papers presented by each of the authors and vigorously discussed the findings of the ten chapters constituting this volume.

Two issues loom largest when discussing the "smallness" strategies—or, really, any proposed school reform. One is the quality of the research documenting the benefits and the costs of the strategy in question. The second is the "trade-offs" posed by the reform: the resources that policymakers and practitioners must sacrifice, whether money or time or opportunities, in order to adopt a given course of action. Both of these themes run repeatedly through the contributions to this volume.

To introduce the essential questions and highlight both the value and the limitations of scholarly inquiry, we begin by quickly reviewing the most influential study ever conducted on either class size or school size: the Tennessee STAR class-size experiment. After discussing STAR, we proceed to sketch out some of the potential trade-offs that frame the discussion in this volume. Economists like to remind us that there is no such thing as a free lunch, and that is as true when it comes to school reform as anywhere else. What are the potential downsides of these two strategies and how might a thoughtful policymaker or educator weigh them when deciding whether to launch class- or school-size reduction program?

STAR's Costs and Benefits

The Tennessee STAR class-size experiment may be the most famous educational experiment conducted to date. As Diane Whitmore Schanzenbach discusses at length and Jimmy Kim and Doug Harris touch upon as well, the results have proved enormously influential in the class-size debate, fueling two decades of discussion about the virtues and limitations of "randomized field trials" in education. Between 1985 and 1989, the Tennessee STAR experiment examined the impact of class size on student learning by randomly assigning thousands of Tennessee students to either "regular" or "small" classes. The study involved students in kindergarten through third grade at more than seventy schools scattered across the state. The experiment compared "small" classes consisting of thirteen to seventeen students to "regular" classes of twenty-two to twenty-five students.

Researchers found significant achievement gains for students in small classes in kindergarten relative to students in larger classes; they also found additional gains in first grade, especially for black students. While there was no evidence of additional gains in second or third grade, the benefits of attending small classes during K-3 persisted through middle school, with a long-term effect on achievement of about 4.4 percentile points. The black-white test score gap also contracted. Those results were crucial in convincing California legislators to enact a dramatic statewide K-3 class-size reduction program.

It is important to acknowledge what the STAR findings do not say. They do not say anything about the value of reducing average class size by two or three students, nor do they say anything about whether the benefits are replicable on a broad scale, when hiring an enormous number of new teachers may be necessary, as was the case in California. The STAR results show that a reduction in class size from 23.5 to 15 students was associated with significant gains in kindergarten and first grade but do not provide evidence that reductions in later grades yield gains.

Implementing the small-scale STAR experiment cost $12 million during 1985–89. Diane Schanzenbach calculates an internal rate of return on that investment of 5 to 10 percent, with the caveat that several assumptions must be made to produce the return. The numbers may also change when class-size reduction is attempted on a large scale. An example of how this plays out in practice is provided by Peter Schrag, who examines California's multibillion-dollar statewide class-size reduction program of the 1990s and reports that it had mixed effects, at best. The pool of high-quality teachers in California was not large enough to accommodate the sudden demand for teachers, so the state hired thousands of inexperienced and quickly trained teachers to staff the new classrooms created by the program. The limitations of STAR's findings and the question of whether STAR's gains can be reproduced in larger settings should be weighed by policymakers deliberating the class-size issue.

Policy Trade-Offs

Trade-offs are made because resources are limited. Schools never have all the money, all the facilities, or all the high-quality teachers that they might desire. For that reason, the question is not whether a given proposal has promise but *whether it constitutes a better investment of resources than the alternatives*. For instance, a superintendent might think that it would be better to increase the pay of a district's existing workforce or provide more professional development opportunities than hire more teachers to reduce class or school size.

Class-size reduction involves at least three important trade-offs. First, resources devoted to smaller classes cannot be used elsewhere. Reducing class size directs resources into hiring rather than into raising skill levels, rewarding teacher quality, or investing in research, curricula, assessment, or other tools that might help teachers become more effective. The United States has more than doubled after-inflation school spending since 1970. Why? Much of the increase stems from class sizes having shrunk by 40 percent, meaning that new teachers have been hired at a rate that outstrips the rate at which enrollment has grown. Hanushek and Rivkin calculated that 85 percent of the increase in instructional costs between 1970 and 1990 was the result of shrinking class size.[2] The calculation is straightforward. If a district has a current average class size of twenty-four students per teacher, reducing that to an average of sixteen per teacher would require the district to increase its classroom teaching force by 50 percent and the number of classrooms by the same amount. In a district of 5,000 students, where teacher salary and benefits carry an average cost of $47,500 a year, the cost in added salary and benefits would be an additional $9.9 million a year. Some of those costs could be offset by reassigning supplemental teachers or reducing the number of teacher aides. Of course, such a calculation does not take into account the cost of modifying facilities or acquiring additional space.

Second, hiring additional teachers makes it harder to find good ones and so is likely to dilute the quality of the teaching force. The problem will be particularly pressing in less appealing schools, since high-quality teachers may leave those schools for new openings in more attractive schools and districts. In other words, class-size reduction may worsen the teacher-quality problem at low-performing or low-income schools.

Third, class-size reduction necessarily entails a school improvement strategy premised on training, hiring, and managing additional numbers of people. In most knowledge-based sectors (including medicine, law, engineering, and so on), improvements in productivity and performance have been achieved by using technology to reduce the size of the workforce, allowing employers to be more selective in hiring; investing more resources in each employee; and helping employees specialize and enhance their skills. A class-size reduction strategy adopts the opposite approach, making it more difficult to be selective in hiring or to invest in personnel.

Class-size reduction is most likely to work with teachers who find their performance significantly enhanced when teaching small classes. For that to be the case, either teachers must have mastered teaching stratgeies that take advantage of smaller classes or they must benefit significantly from the reduced management and disciplinary burden of working with fewer students. That calculus suggests that class-size reduction may well prove sensible for some students, subjects, schools, and grade levels but not as an across-the-board policy. For instance, Ludger Wößmann notes in his chapter that international evidence suggests that smaller class size seems to boost student achievement in nations that have a low-quality teaching force—presumably because their teachers are less able to manage large classes—but has no effect in nations where teachers are better paid and more educated.

Ultimately, class-size reduction may pose something of a "prisoner's dilemma": it may make sense for a given school or a small district, but the benefits may vanish if others also embrace the strategy. For particular schools, especially those with minority or low-achieving populations, there is some evidence that reducing class size may help and, aside from consuming educational dollars, little reason to imagine it will have an adverse impact. However, when the *widespread* adoption of class-size reduction creates a voracious appetite for new teachers, it is likely to reduce teacher quality in some schools by siphoning teachers off to more attractive schools and communities. This is a thorny puzzle that admits no obvious answers other than to design policies carefully.

When considering reductions in school size, policymakers should consider at least four potential trade-offs. First, again, is the simple question of cost. Smaller schools mean that expenditures on facilities and school administration are going to be spread over fewer students, yielding a higher per-pupil cost. For example, it is much less costly for a district to have one principal lead a school of 2,000 than to have five principals each lead a school of 400. The same calculation applies with regard to school nurses, gym teachers, guidance counselors, and so on. Proponents of smaller schools counter such concerns by arguing that small schools can be designed in ways that minimize additional costs or allow schools to operate with a smaller administrative staff—and that they may be so effective that the costs are worth paying. Such claims deserve consideration but should be regarded with appropriate scrutiny.

Second, the case made for comprehensive high schools by former Harvard University president James Bryant Conant in the 1960s was that they could provide complete facilities and specialized teachers. Smaller schools do not find it cost effective to construct full athletic or musical facilities, to offer a full array of extracurricular activities or language courses, to offer advanced courses that may attract only a small percentage of students in a given school (like calculus or physics) or less popular subjects (like art history or economics), to assemble a faculty that is large enough to allow teachers to specialize in the areas that they teach, or to have full-time school nurses or guidance counselors on staff. Obviously, schools might jointly offer athletic teams or courses of instruction and they can find ways to share faculty, but such arrangements—even when feasible—come at the cost of additional expense and logistical challenges.

Third, teachers may have to wear multiple hats in such schools. In order for the schools to avoid becoming more expensive on a per-pupil basis, teachers typically need to pick up responsibilities for administrative tasks and guidance counseling, among others. That increases their workload and may lead to their being asked to perform roles for which they are ill-equipped. It may also serve to increase teacher fatigue or reduce the quality of services provided. Of course, small-school proponents reply that administration and guidance counseling in comprehensive high schools leave much to be desired and that the personal touch produced by involving faculty more than offsets any negatives. Such claims have merit; the challenge for policymakers and educators is to sensibly weigh the downsides.

Fourth, there is the question of facilities. Whether school-size reduction is achieved by constructing additional school buildings or by modifying existing schools to facilitate "small school" arrangements, it requires both dollars and disruption. Adding new schools requires finding new sites, ensuring compliance with codes, building or altering facilities, and finding temporary quarters during construction. Converting existing schools to "schools within a school" requires leaving the school vacant during construction and then restarting the school—with no guarantee that such an approach will replicate whatever benefits are observed in conventional small schools.

Ultimately, as the analyses in this volume make clear, it is difficult to determine whether reducing class size or school size is the best way to spend limited educational resources. There is good reason to think that such strategies hold promise in certain times and places; there is also cause to think that pursuing either strategy in a blanket fashion is likely to prove shortsighted and wasteful. Deciding when and where reduction may be useful is the rub—and where passion and political appeals tend to crowd out careful analysis. Our hope is that the analyses offered here provide guidance to policymakers and educators seeking firmer ground.

Chapter Summaries

Barbara Schneider, Adam E. Wyse, and Venessa Keesler address a pivotal question in the school-size debate by asking whether small is really better. Schneider and her colleagues acknowledge the widespread support for smaller high schools among the public and such prominent foundations as that of Bill and Melinda Gates, but they also are concerned about the paucity of evidence that recent downsizing efforts have paid off in any tangible benefits. And they note that many important questions—such as whether student expectations for postsecondary education are affected by school size—have largely gone unexamined by researchers.

Schneider and colleagues employ hierarchical linear modeling (HLM) to model the multilevel nature of education effects and use HLM with propensity scoring to address the potential for selection bias as students are sorted nonrandomly into schools of different sizes. The models are used to analyze math achievement and postsecondary aspirations. No effect was found for math achievement—students in large and small schools achieved at comparable levels—and small schools actually seemed to depress college expectations. Attending a small school decreased the likelihood that students would say that they intended to go to college; at the same time, however, students in small high schools were more likely to apply to college and to a four-year rather than a two-year college. Thus, the evidence is mixed, and school size did not appear to make a marked difference in the postsecondary plans of high school students.

Christopher Berry examines whether the increasing school size brought about by school consolidation in mid-twentieth-century America affected the earnings of those who attended those schools. Berry notes that there was a massive and often unremarked effort to reduce the number of schools between 1930 and 1970, resulting in a large increase in average school size. Two-thirds of all schools that existed in 1930 were gone by 1970, while average daily attendance per school grew from 87 to 440 students. In 1927, 60 percent of all schools had only one teacher; by 1970, such schools were almost gone. Using a sample from the 1980 census, Berry was able to examine 994,000 white men born in the lower forty-eight states during 1920–49 and how the average school size of their native state related to their lifetime earnings.

Berry tests the thesis that larger schools might affect the degree of future variation in earnings among graduates, either by making it easier to overlook some students or by providing services that make for a uniformly stronger educational experience. Berry finds little evidence that school size affected the variation in future earnings. He notes that larger schools seem to be associated with a reduction in inequality among those who drop out and an increase in inequality among college graduates, but he concludes that the results generally do not reveal a significant relationship between school consolidation and adults' wage inequality. However, Berry notes the limits of the analysis, including its focus on white men only and the limitations imposed by the data.

He wonders whether more precise data or research that examined inequality among minorities might yield a different result. One argument for increasing school size is that it will ensure the wide availability of resources needed to equalize opportunity, while a key argument for shrinking schools claims that it will equalize opportunity by ensuring more personal attention to students. Berry's historical look finds that school size in mid-century America did not seem to have much impact, one way or the other.

Tom Dee, Wei Ha, and Brian Jacob examine the impact of school size on parental involvement. Though parental involvement is widely seen as an important determinant of school quality, they note that it is rarely discussed in research on school size. They note that it is important not only as a means to improve school quality but also because the "social capital" generated by school and community interaction is beneficial for both parents and students. They use the Education Longitudinal Study of 2002, sponsored by the National Center for Education Statistics, to examine how school size affected four measures of parental school involvement and seven measures of parental social capital. The authors were able to analyze parental data for more than 8,000 students.

They note that smaller schools might affect parental involvement and social capital either through their promotion of stronger bonds and tighter communities or through their lack of the expansive, organized social networks found in larger schools. They find that parents in smaller schools were significantly more likely to participate in parent-teacher activities or to volunteer at school and were more likely to know the parents of their children's friends, interact with those parents, and feel connected to their community. The authors conclude that the findings "provide some tentative evidence that small schools are more effective in promoting parental involvement in schools as well as engagement with the broader community." However, the authors note that the observed effects were concentrated in rural communities. They did not find those effects in suburban schools, and they note that their urban sample was too small to permit them to reach any conclusions. It appears that small schools can boost parental involvement and social capital, but it is not clear whether that effect is more than a rural phenomenon. While other chapters suggest that the academic benefits from small schools are uncertain, Dee and his colleagues find evidence that small schools can deliver civic benefits in certain contexts.

What are the best sizes for classes and schools? One methodological challenge to answering that question is that small classes tend to be clustered in small schools. Surprisingly, most researchers have not addressed the possibility that the effects of school and class size are confounded in their analyses. Douglas D. Ready and Valerie E. Lee tackle this problem in attempting to estimate the optimal school and class size at the elementary level. Although other methodological difficulties in evaluating small-class and school-size policies have been debated, a statistical untangling of the effects of small schools and small classes remains curiously absent from the discussion.

As Ready and Lee note, the research on class size has tended to be limited to elementary grades, while school-size research has been confined mostly to high schools. Ready and Lee focus on elementary schools. They examine a large database of elementary schools and classes, estimate the effects of both small schools and classes net of other size characteristics, evaluate the distribution of effects over different socioeconomic status (SES) levels, and assess whether the effects differ between kindergarten and first grade or between reading and mathematics.

Ready and Lee find that both smaller classes and smaller schools were associated with more learning. The effects for class size were stronger than the effects for school size and fell equally across SES levels. An important consideration for policymakers is that medium-size and small classes produced similar benefits for students. The disadvantage related to large classes and schools was what really mattered. A student who had been enrolled in a large class in a large school completed first grade about 1.5 months behind the typical student. Given those findings, class-size initiatives should concentrate on creating classes with fewer than twenty-six students. Reducing them further, a costly proposition, would yield only a minimal additional benefit, in first grade reading achievement.

Douglas Harris assesses the trade-offs presented by class-size and school-size policies but points out that with respect to policymaking, the costs and benefits of the two reforms appear to be less relevant than political considerations. Harris points out that class size has shrunk 40 percent since 1970, while school size has increased 9 percent since 1980. He explains three approaches that can help in weighing the merits of these developments: cost-benefit, cost effectiveness, and optimization. Each approach offers an alternative for determining whether resources devoted to class size or school size are being invested wisely. He notes that class-size reduction absorbs resources that might otherwise be used to boost teacher salaries or improve school quality and may increase expenditures on facilities and bureaucracy—which is why most cost-function studies find increasing returns to scale.

Turning to an examination of the existing research, Harris concludes that "broad-based class-size reduction would be inefficient, even in the elementary grades, where the evidence of benefits is strongest." He adds that the evidence regarding the ratio of benefits to costs "does not provide much support for small schools" but that "there is good evidence that it would be optimal to make [schools of more than 2,000 students] smaller." However, Harris notes that such determinations are overly broad and that actual results may vary immensely depending on the local context. Finally, he turns to the question of political appeal, observing that parents like class-size reduction because it is tangible, immediate, and attractive and that teachers like it because it improves working conditions. Meanwhile, small schools hold less appeal for both parents and teachers and pose headaches related to school construction or modification. Ultimately, though Harris thinks the evidence supports some targeted efforts to reduce class size and school size, political considerations favor adoption of poorly designed class-size reduction proposals while making school-size reduction unlikely.

Linda Darling-Hammond, Peter Ross, and Michael Milliken review the literature on small high schools. They note that a large number of quantitative and qualitative studies have attempted to discern whether school size matters in educational outcomes and under what conditions small schools can be expected to produce particular results. The qualitative literature fleshes out the story of schools trying to downsize and offers context for understanding how schools experience organizational change. Since no randomized trials have been conducted, the quantitative studies are confined to uncovering correlational relationships. Like all correlational research, such studies cannot nail down causality; they are merely suggestive and can neither control for the effects of unobserved variables nor mitigate the potential for selectivity bias. On balance, the studies indicate that smaller schools are associated with more positive student attitudes and a more wholesome school climate. The relationship between smallness and enhanced academic achievement, however, is only modest.

Overall, the literature does not allow conclusions about effects, but it does generate hypotheses concerning the characteristics of small schools that might prove to be the most important. Darling-Hammond and her colleagues join Ready and Lee in believing that smallness by itself does not have a direct impact on outcomes. Both chapters distinguish between schools that are small by design and schools that are small by default. Most small schools are small by default, with size determined by enrollment patterns beyond their control. Darling-Hammond and her colleagues argue that schools that are small by design are crafted to take advantage of organizational smallness. Often they feature small classes in which personalized teacher-student relationships are encouraged, a school culture emphasizing academic success, a strong core curriculum, instruction that is responsive to student learning, and opportunities for teachers to work together collegially and to improve their practice of teaching.

Diane Whitmore Schanzenbach asks what we have learned from Project STAR. Schanzenbach carefully examines several shortcomings of the STAR data (for example, baseline achievement tests were not administered) and finds that they do not seriously undermine the validity of findings. Researchers employing various analytical strategies with the STAR data consistently find a small-class benefit of about 0.15 standard deviations. When the results are disaggregated by race, blacks appear to benefit about twice as much as whites (0.24 versus 0.12 standard deviations). Follow-up studies have shown the benefits to persist into eighth grade. A positive effect also has been seen on the SAT scores and SAT test-taking rates of students in high school. Although the impact of small classes on noncognitive outcomes (for example, crime, teen pregnancy) remains inconclusive, it is a promising area for further research.

Are the gains worth the cost of reducing class size? Schanzenbach calculates a return on investment and concludes that the benefits are sizable and long lasting, especially for black students, and that the overall benefits outweigh the costs. One caveat: Schanzenbach notes that the positive effects on test scores are more pronounced in classes staffed by experienced teachers and in fact fall to statistically insignificant levels in classes instructed by inexperienced teachers. If the positive effects of small classes are contingent upon experienced teachers, that may explain the disappointing results from the massive California Class-Size Reduction program (CSR).

Peter Schrag tells that story. In the spring of 1996, Governor Pete Wilson pushed a plan through the legislature to limit all classes in grades K–3 to twenty students. At the time, California was surpassed only by Utah in having the largest classes in the country. Wilson had earlier opposed efforts to reduce class sizes. Why the change of heart? Voters had passed a constitutional requirement mandating that a set percentage of state revenue be spent on education, and, not wanting the new money to go unrestricted to local school districts, where Wilson feared it would be allocated to salary increases for teachers, he reversed his position and pushed for smaller classes.

CSR went into effect practically overnight, initially in first and second grade, then in kindergarten and third grade. The sudden demand for more classrooms meant that thousands of underqualified teachers were hired; classrooms were squeezed into utility closets, lunchrooms, and other makeshift spaces; and costs escalated to $1.7 billion a year (estimate for 2005). Did CSR boost academic achievement? As Schrag explains, the answer to that question is far from certain. The only major evaluation of the program, conducted by a research consortium headed by RAND, concluded that it was impossible to attribute changes in the state's test scores to any one cause. At the same time that class sizes were being reduced, California overhauled its curricula in both reading and math and implemented a new testing and accountability program. Despite its hefty price tag and uncertain effects, the class-size program enjoys the support of parents and teachers. Schrag ends asking whether education policies that have dubious effectiveness but widespread political support can ever be amended or repealed.

Ludger Wößmann examines the international evidence on class size. While he notes that international research comparable to that conducted in the United States is largely lacking, he was able to use data from the 1995 TIMSS test to explore the relationship of class size and student performance in western Europe. Wößmann notes that school policies, community characteristics, and parent decisions can bias results, so it is vital to carefully model and analyze causal relationships when studying class size. For instance, a simple regression finds that larger classes are correlated with higher test scores in twelve of seventeen west European nations before proper statistical controls are introduced. However, Wößmann finds that to be a by-product of bias.

In order to properly control for the tendency of schools to put high-achieving students in larger classes, Wößmann employs two quasi-experimental approaches: natural cohort fluctuation (random variation in the size of a grade level from one year to the next) and rule-induced discontinuities (produced by laws that cap class sizes at certain levels). The analysis finds that class size had a modest effect in one country (Iceland) and may have had an effect in a second (Norway) but had no statistically significant effect in the other nations. Wößmann concludes "that class size does not seem to be a major force in shaping performance in lower secondary school in the countries considered." He notes that research suggests that class size has an impact only in nations where teacher pay and education are low. He speculates that relatively capable teachers may do as well teaching large classes as small ones and that class size may matter only when the quality of the teaching force is relatively low. In that event, the trade-off between class size and teacher pay may be exceedingly stark; it may make sense to invest in only one or the other.

James Kim examines the politics of class-size policy, observing that the significance of social science research always depends on its interaction with the political process. He begins with a brief look at the Tennessee STAR experiment. Kim notes that the findings were used by proponents of class-size reduction in creating Tennessee's targeted and relatively effective Project Challenge in 1989. He compares that with the relatively unfocused class-size reduction efforts launched by Indiana and California in the 1980s and 1990s and Wisconsin's SAGE program—which was narrowly targeted initially but after showing promising results was rapidly expanded.

Kim takes several lessons from the four case studies. He finds that when policies enjoy a broad base of political support there is little incentive for public officials to carefully consider evaluation of the program's effectiveness. He observes that untargeted class-size policies generally lack provisions for careful evaluation, making it likely that evaluations will produce ambiguous findings; he also notes that political decisions can directly influence the quality of social science research. Finally, he observes that scholars are rarely in a position to provide definitive answers to pressing policy questions.

Kim's work reminds us, as do several other chapters in this book, that social science research does not operate in a vacuum. Its impact may depend as much on political considerations as on technical merit—and that technical merit itself may be a product of political decisions. This creates a thicket of challenges for anyone interested in carefully weighing the evidence on class size and school size—whether a policymaker deciding how to allocate public resources, a voter choosing between two candidates' positions on education reform, or parents selecting a school for their child to attend among several schools with different organizational characteristics. We hope that this book provides some practical tools for making such difficult decisions.

Notes

1. "Counting Students Can Count," *Research Points* 1, no. 2 (American Educational Research Association, 2003).

2. Eric A. Hanushek and Steven G. Rivkin, "Understanding the Twentieth Century Growth in U.S. School Spending," *Journal of Human Resources* 32, no. 1 (1997): 35–68.

Is Small Really Better? Testing Some Assumptions about High School Size

BARBARA SCHNEIDER, ADAM E. WYSE,
AND VENESSA KEESLER

Several years ago, I was in a meeting with a group of Chicago public school coaches and physical education teachers who were discussing the negative implications of one of Chicago's recent reform initiatives, the construction of smaller high schools. Much like other urban areas, Chicago had begun dismantling some of its large high schools to form smaller entities, with an "optimal" enrollment of 600 students. The coaches were deeply concerned that the small school movement was fostering the elimination of school-sponsored athletic teams, which sometimes acted as a magnet for marginal students, encouraging them to complete high school and in some instances enroll in college. From their perspective, intramural teams were unable to fill the void left by school-sponsored teams, which had helped some students obtain postsecondary scholarships and promoted a high school identity that instilled pride in the student body.

Reflecting on their comments, I was struck by how my work and that of others had championed small schools. Could we have been wrong? Small schools were generally viewed as places that fostered a strong sense of community and encouraged academic achievement and attainment. But many of us had not explored whether small schools were better for all types of students. More specifically, would the consequences of creating small-school environments prove to be detrimental, especially for low-income minority students enrolled in urban high schools?

The case for small schools has been made in educational research since the 1960s, when scholars such as Barker and Gump argued that smaller schools provided students with greater opportunities for participation in various extracurricular activities.[1] Within a smaller student body, the average adolescent would have a better chance of being on a team, taking a leadership position in the school, and developing stronger relationships with teachers and other adults in the school. The value of small schools was further supported in the 1980s by research on public and private schools that showed that smaller religious schools produced higher graduation rates and lower dropout rates than public schools.[2] Analyses of the National Education Longitudinal Study of 1988 in the 1990s also showed that smaller public schools produced substantial gains in mathematics achievement for high school students.[3] By 2000, the results of those studies were often used as evidence by policymakers and school administrators to support proposals to decrease school size as a strategy for increasing student achievement.

However, initial results from small-school reforms have been inconsistent.[4] In light of those results and reviews of earlier work, serious questions are being raised regarding the methodological techniques used to study the effects of school size.[5] Several concerns center on the use of inappropriate research designs for assessing causal effects, such as correlational analyses rather than random clinical trials. These concerns have led several educational researchers to revisit propensity score methods for using observational data to approximate experimental designs, methods formalized by Donald Rubin more than thirty years ago.[6] As I reviewed my own work and that of my colleagues, it became increasingly clear to me that many of the reforms being advocated, particularly in today's high schools, had rarely been studied using Rubin's methods. Many of the cornerstones of high school reform, including better academic preparation programs, peer tutoring, and use of mentors, often lacked a rigorous evaluation component.

Uncertain of what we might find, my two colleagues, Adam Wyse and Venessa Keesler, and I decided to estimate the effects of high school size using Rubin's methods and conventional hierarchical models. This paper describes our efforts, using observational data from the National Education Longitudinal Study, to approximate an experiment on the effects of school size for several student outcomes: mathematics achievement, postsecondary expectations, college attendance plans after high school graduation, and number and type of colleges to which students applied.

Constructing an Experiment

To test whether school size makes a difference in student achievement and college plans, ideally one would randomly assign students to large and small schools. However, to conduct such an experiment would be difficult. How could students be randomly assigned to schools that varied only in size? Instead, it would be more reasonable to match students on a set of characteristics and then to estimate statistically the effect of being in one environment or the other. The reason that matching becomes so important with respect to estimating school-size effects is that students who attend small schools and those who attend large schools may have very different background characteristics. We cannot assume that the treatment (in this case, school size) will have the same effect on students who have different characteristics. By using a matching strategy that achieves balance on the pretreatment differences in student characteristics, we can determine that any remaining differences among the students should be attributable to the effect of the treatment.

The Treatment

High schools originally grew in size through the twentieth century in order to accommodate larger numbers of students and provide the diverse course offerings required of a comprehensive high school.[7] One of the proponents of larger schools was James Conant, who in 1959 argued that high schools should have a graduating class of at least 100 students in order to implement a curriculum suitable to the comprehensive high school as he envisioned it.[8] What Conant envisioned as "large" was considerably smaller than many of the high schools of today, some of which have 6,000 students. Many of these high schools more closely resemble small colleges than even the largest schools of Conant's time.

What the optimal high school size should be is a matter of debate. One advocate of small schools was Valerie Lee, who investigated the impact of school size on student mathematics achievement. Lee and Smith found that schools that enroll between 600 and 900 students have better student outcomes in mathematics than do schools with larger enrollments.[9] Although large high schools have the advantage of offering more courses, Lee argued that such course differentiation leads to negative outcomes for some students who are not permitted to enroll in certain courses that may be useful for entering college, such as high-level mathematics courses.[10] More recently, Lee has argued that another benefit of smaller schools is increased student participation in extracurricular activities.[11]

The Effects of High School Size

In contrast to the effect of high school size on achievement, the effect of size on other outcomes, such as student expectations for postsecondary education, does not seem to have received the same level of attention in recent literature. From a more sociological perspective, student expectations are significant because of the link between expectations, educational attainment, and the wage differentials associated with higher levels of education. Having educational expectations that match the type of job one expects to obtain in adulthood, referred to as having aligned ambitions, has been shown to be related to postsecondary plans.[12] Having aligned ambitions also increases the likelihood that students will develop effective plans for realizing their expectations, including plans to apply to colleges consistent with their occupational interests.[13] Establishing the relationship between school size and ambition is an important first step in furthering understanding of the relationship between school organization factors such as leadership, parent-teacher relationships, teacher collegiality, and openness to innovation and student educational expectations.

It is important to determine whether high school size is useful in assisting students with different background characteristics to achieve their ambitions. Although Lee and Smith suggest that the effect of school size does not vary across socioeconomic groups, we suspect that that claim cannot be made based on the type of analysis used by many researchers.[14] It is likely that the students who attend small high schools and those who attend large high schools have different background characteristics. Moreover, until quite recently most small schools were located outside large urban school districts.

A key concern in the study of school size is the issue of differences in schools and in schools as organizations. Schools often are considered the unit of reform for new innovations.[15] Recognizing the unique organizational character of individual schools, this view suggests that change must be specific to the school and occur in the school itself. Applying this idea to school size, it is easy to see that schools can be very similar in size but very different in organization, outcomes, and norms. For example, Bryk and Schneider found that to be the case in their study of Chicago elementary schools, in which they matched schools of similar sizes and found that the schools were very different with respect to achievement outcomes and school organizational factors.[16]

Schools are not merely collections of students; they are intricate organizational structures that both define and are defined by those who attend them. Much of the research in this area has focused on the correlation between school size and learning outcomes. In this paper, we offer a different approach to conceptualizing and evaluating school size. We are not suggesting that this study will provide a definitive answer on the "best" school size, but rather that it will address several statistical issues inherent in many previous studies of school size.

Testing Assumptions about Size

In this section, both hierarchical linear modeling (HLM) and propensity score matching techniques are explored to investigate the impact of school size on twelfth-grade mathematics achievement, student expectations, college plans immediately after high school, the type of college students planned to attend, and the number of schools to which a student applied. The HLM models present analyses as they have traditionally been conducted, whereas the propensity score models represent a different approach to studying the effects of high school size that attempts to account for the selection effects present in the data. In that respect, propensity score models offer some advantages over the HLM models and might present a clearer picture of the effect of smaller schools on each of the outcome measures. For the hierarchical linear models, it was expected that students in smaller schools would experience more positive outcomes than students in larger schools. In the propensity score models, students from the largest schools (2,000 or more students) were matched with students in schools of 800 to 1,199 students. It was expected that if small schools were better for students in larger schools, then there would be positive average treatment effects for each of the propensity score models. Both strategies are illustrated with the most recent nationally representative large-scale data available, the Education Longitudinal Study of 2002.

Data and Sample

The Education Longitudinal Study of 2002 (ELS: 2002), which was conducted by the National Center for Education Statistics (NCES), is the most recent in a series of studies examining the organizational structure of high schools; student achievement, attitudes, and social behaviors; and student transition to postsecondary education.[17] ELS: 2002 is a nationally representative study covering 16,543 students in 757 high schools. We used information from both the initial survey and the first follow-up but focused primarily on data collected when students were seniors. Many prior analyses of school size used the National Education Longitudinal Study of 1988 (NELS: 88).[18] The ELS has a similar design but has the advantage of providing more recent data.

For this analysis, only students who completed surveys at both tenth and twelfth grade are included in the sample, which includes between 10,917 and 12,489 students in 660 schools. The sample size changed because we excluded respondents who had legitimate skips on all outcome variables. For missing data, we chose to impute values using an EM algorithm.[19] This algorithm is useful for imputing missing values when they can be determined by other values in the data set. Four imputed data sets were constructed for missing data and used in the analyses that follow. This strategy is more reliable than simple listwise deletion, although the results may still be an underestimation compared with those obtained by using a complete data set.[20]

Characteristics of Small Schools

In the ELS data set, the smallest schools—those with fewer than 399 students—are more heavily concentrated in rural areas (which contain 38 percent of the smallest schools) and in the Midwest (41 percent). In the smallest schools, 78 percent of the students are white, while in the largest schools, only 36 percent are white. Larger schools are more frequently urban and suburban. Schools in the "optimal" size category (800–1,199 students) are more frequently suburban schools (57 percent), have relatively high concentrations of white students (63 percent), and do not have large concentrations of low-income students. In other words, the average student in the "optimal" size school is more likely to be white and middle class and to attend high school in a suburban area. These differences in the background characteristics of the students suggest that there is a selection effect. Accordingly, we chose to investigate the effect of school size on student mathematics achievement and postsecondary expectations and plans using a series of models that attempt to adjust for selection effects (see table 1).

Estimating the Effects of School Size Using Hierarchical Linear Modeling

The use of hierarchical linear modeling is common and has largely replaced other types of modeling for estimating nested data. HLM represents a dra-

Table 1. School Descriptive Statistics
Percent

	\multicolumn{5}{c}{Students}
Characteristic	1–399	400–799	800–1,199	1,200–1,999	2,000 or more
Urbanicity					
Urban	29	30	29	38	39
Suburban	33	47	57	50	50
Rural	38	23	14	12	11
Region					
Northeast	18	17	24	12	13
Midwest	41	28	25	27	13
South	29	42	35	41	40
West	12	13	16	20	34
Race					
White	78	71	63	51	36
Black	6	11	14	17	12
Hispanic	7	10	10	13	30
Asian/Pacific Islander	2	4	8	13	17
Mutiracial	6	4	5	6	4
Sector					
Public	48	61	78	94	97
Catholic	17	27	19	4	2
Other private	35	12	3	2	1
Low income					
Less than 50 percent	80	88	79	86	77
Greater than 50 percent	20	12	21	14	23
College atendance rate					
Less than 50 percent, four-year college	40	43	49	48	62
Greater than 50 percent, four-year college	60	57	51	52	38

matic improvement over the use of ordinary least squares regression models. It is the preferred technique for analyses of this type because school effects studies are multilevel in nature—that is, there is variation in outcomes that is accounted for by both student differences and school differences.[21] Those differences can be effectively captured by a multilevel model. The "standard" model for investigating the effect of school size uses mathematics and reading achievement as the outcome measures. Previous findings using this model are striking: students in smaller schools have higher levels of mathematics and reading achievement.[22] Based on these results, Lee and Smith developed a measure of optimal high school size (between 600 and 900 students).[23]

Using an approach similar to that of Lee and Smith, we estimated the effects of school size on mathematics achievement in twelfth grade using HLM.[24] We also examined twelfth-grade students' postsecondary expectations, whether they planned to enroll in college, what types of postsecondary schools they planned to enroll in, and the number of colleges to which they applied. Unlike the outcome measure for twelfth-grade mathematics achievement, these measures are categorical; therefore a set of multinomial, multilevel models was employed in estimating these outcomes.[25]

We constructed a set of dummy variables to investigate the impact of school size as it relates to each outcome measure. For this analysis, five categories of school size were created (1–399, 400–799, 800–1,199, 1,200–1,999, and 2,000 or more). Those categories were selected because the number of students in each category was approximately the same. The size category of 800–1,199 students was excluded from each analysis; it serves as the reference category for these models.

In each model, we included controls at both the school and student level. Traditionally, school-level controls include such factors as percentage of the school that is minority; average socioeconomic status (SES) of the school; whether a school is Catholic, public, or private; and school urbanicity.[26] Average SES was treated as continuous. Dummy variables were constructed for Catholic, private, high-minority, urban, and rural schools. Student-level controls included student SES, composite test score, and dummy variables for female, Asian, black, and Hispanic students and students from other minority racial groups, such as Alaskan, American Indian, and multiracial (see appendix for description of variables).[27]

Twelfth-Grade Mathematics Achievement

To investigate the relationship between school size and mathematics achievement with the ELS: 2002 data set, we constructed a two-level model. Contrary to previous findings, our findings did not show that school size had an effect on overall twelfth-grade mathematics achievement. The only significant effect of school size was found on the composite test score slope ($p \leq .05$) for students in schools that had 2,000 or more students, suggesting that there may not be substantial differences in mathematics achievement across the school size categories (see table 2).[28]

This model does suggest that attending a private, Catholic, or higher SES school is associated with significant gains in mathematics achievement. Being enrolled in an urban school is associated with a decrease in mathematics achievement. Black students had lower mathematics achievement than white students, while Asian students performed better than the other racial and ethnic groups. Males outperformed females in mathematics. If one looks at the

Table 2. HLM Model for Twelfth-Grade Math Achievement

Effect	Coefficient	SE
On between-school gains (intercept)		
Base estimate	45.484	0.505***
Average SES	2.517	0.616***
Catholic school	4.076	0.735***
Other private school	2.619	0.918**
High minority	0.381	0.469
Urban	-1.259	0.438**
Rural	-0.107	0.525
School size		
1–399	-0.120	0.684
400–799	-0.287	0.585
1,200–1,999	-0.732	0.556
2,000 or more	0.288	0.629
On relationship between tenth-grade composite test score and gains (slope)		
Base estimate	1.264	0.046***
Average SES	-0.090	0.053†
Catholic school	-0.019	0.070
Other private school	-0.232	0.084**
High minority	-0.045	0.042
Urban	0.029	0.041
Rural	0.066	0.050
School size		
1–399	0.080	0.066
400–799	0.057	0.057
1,200–1,999	0.064	0.053
2,000 or more	0.132	0.059*
On relationship between SES and gains (slope)		
Base estimate	3.634	0.638***
Average SES	0.397	0.705
Catholic school	-2.126	0.897*
Other private school	-0.523	1.117
High minority	-1.426	0.563**
Urban	0.190	0.545
Rural	-0.900	0.705
School size		
1–399	-0.324	0.880
400–799	-0.481	0.760
1,200–1,999	0.209	0.728
2,000 or more	-0.848	0.803
Female	-1.398	0.277***
Black	-0.781	0.516†
Hispanic	-0.586	0.515
Asian	4.949	0.566***
Others	-0.495	0.644
HLM computed standard deviation	2.792	(intercept)
	0.127	(test score)
	2.058	(SES)
	15.103	(Level 1)

† ≤ .10; * $p ≤ .05$; ** $p ≤ .01$; *** $p ≤ .001$; SE = standard error.

gain slope for the tenth-grade composite test score, having higher family socioeconomic status or being enrolled in a private non-Catholic school was related to slightly lower mathematics achievement ($p \leq .10$ and $.05$, respectively). The gain slope for student SES was significantly lower for students in Catholic schools ($p \leq .05$) or in high- minority schools ($p \leq .01$).

Student Postsecondary Expectations

The model for student postsecondary expectations was based on a categorical variable that asked students how much education they expected to obtain. This variable was collapsed into four categories that were included in a multinomial, multilevel logistic regression model.[29] The categories were as follows: individuals who did not know what their future plans were or who expected to obtain less than a high school diploma; individuals who aspired to graduate from high school or attend some college but not to obtain a four-year college degree; individuals who expected to attain a four-year college degree; and individuals aspiring to a graduate or professional degree.[30] The category representing students who expected to graduate from high school or attend some college was used as the referent category (see table 3).

For each of the categories, there were no significant differences between students in schools with more than 1,199 students and students in schools with 800–1,199 students. The only effects were found for students in the smallest schools, where students were slightly more likely to say that they did not know their college plans and had slightly higher gains in their test score composite slope. Across the comparisons, students who had higher socioeconomic status and those who attended Catholic schools or other private schools were more likely to aspire to a four-year degree or graduate degree or to say that they did not know their plans than individuals who did not have those background characteristics. Black students were 1.5 times more likely to say that they did not know their college plans, 1.7 times more likely to say that they wanted a four-year degree, and 3.1 times more likely to say that they wanted a professional degree than white students. The likelihood that Asian students aspired to a four-year or graduate degree was similar to the likelihood for black students. Hispanics were 1.5 times more likely to say that they did not know their future plans than whites. Females were 1.5 times more likely to aspire to a college degree than just to graduate from high school, and they were 2.3 times more likely to expect to obtain a graduate degree than males.

Table 3. HLM Model for Student Expectations

Effect	Don't know about future plans vs. HS grad, but no four-year college degree			Four-year college degree vs. HS grad, but no four-year college degree			Graduate degree vs. HS grad, but no four-year college degree		
	Coefficient	SE	Odds ratio	Coefficient	SE	Odds ratio	Coefficient	SE	Odds ratio
On between-school gains (intercept)									
Base estimate	-1.368	0.132***	0.255	0.179	0.087*	1.196	-0.404	0.094***	0.668
Average SES	0.344	0.161*	1.410	0.522	0.114***	1.686	0.574	0.120***	1.775
Catholic school	0.559	0.199**	1.748	0.915	0.142***	2.496	0.935	0.149***	2.548
Other private school	0.171	0.237	1.187	0.366	0.166*	1.441	0.502	0.177**	1.653
High minority	0.161	0.122	1.175	0.015	0.085	1.015	0.083	0.090	1.087
Urban	-0.011	0.119	0.990	0.017	0.084	1.017	0.117	0.086	1.124
Rural	-0.203	0.136	0.816	-0.142	0.089	0.867	-0.158	0.096	0.854
School size									
1–399	0.330	0.180†	1.391	0.103	0.125	1.108	-0.040	0.133	0.961
400–799	0.164	0.155	1.179	0.036	0.105	1.037	0.023	0.111	1.023
1,200–1,999	0.065	0.149	1.068	0.063	0.099	1.065	0.027	0.104	1.027
2,000 or more	0.089	0.171	1.093	0.130	0.114	1.138	0.136	0.119	1.146
On relationship between tenth-grade composite test score and gains (slope)									
Base estimate	-0.014	0.012	0.986	0.066	0.009***	1.068	0.105	0.009***	1.111
Average SES	0.041	0.015**	1.041	0.014	0.011	1.014	0.037	0.012**	1.037
Catholic school	0.017	0.022	1.017	0.025	0.016	1.025	0.021	0.017	1.021
Other private school	0.004	0.024	1.004	-0.007	0.018	0.993	-0.040	0.019*	0.961
High minority	0.020	0.011†	1.020	-0.001	0.008	0.999	0.006	0.009	1.006
Urban	-0.007	0.024	0.993	-0.001	0.008	0.999	-0.005	0.009	0.995
Rural	-0.018	0.011	0.983	0.016	0.009†	1.016	0.019	0.010†	1.019
School size									
1–399	0.031	0.017†	1.031	0.001	0.013	1.001	0.017	0.014	1.017
400–799	0.023	0.014	1.024	0.011	0.011	1.011	0.015	0.012	1.015
1,200–1,999	0.013	0.013	1.013	0.013	0.010	1.013	0.006	0.011	1.006
over 2,000	0.003	0.015	1.003	-0.015	0.011	0.985	0.007	0.012	1.007

(continued)

Table 3. HLM Model for Student Expectations (continued)

Effect	Don't know about future plans vs. HS grad, but no four-year college degree			Four-year college degree vs. HS grad, but no four-year college degree			Graduate degree vs. HS grad, but no four-year college degree		
	Coefficient	SE	Odds ratio	Coefficient	SE	Odds ratio	Coefficient	SE	Odds ratio
On relationship between SES and gains (slope)									
Base estimate	0.379	0.169*	1.461	0.754	0.120***	2.126	1.127	0.126***	3.087
Average SES	0.209	0.194	1.232	0.124	0.144	1.132	0.266	0.148	1.305
Catholic school	0.326	0.289	1.385	0.002	0.213	1.002	-0.398	0.218	0.970
Other private school	0.268	0.334	1.307	-0.146	0.242	0.864	-0.030	0.249	1.180
High minority	-0.018	0.146***	0.982	-0.271	0.108*	0.763	-0.398	0.112*	0.672
Urban	0.057	0.143	1.058	0.046	0.107	1.048	0.118	0.110	1.125
Rural	0.017	0.173	1.017	0.038	0.126	1.039	-0.159	0.134	0.853
School size									
1–399	-0.102	0.231	0.903	0.032	0.174	1.032	0.081	0.183	1.084
400–799	-0.308	0.202	0.735	-0.155	0.148	0.857	-0.110	0.154	0.896
1,200–1,999	-0.295	0.186	0.745	-0.215	0.135	0.807	-0.145	0.141	0.865
2,000 or more	-0.216	0.202	0.806	-0.165	0.148	0.848	-0.193	0.154	0.825
Female	0.116	0.073	1.123	0.401	0.053***	1.494	0.853	0.057***	2.348
Black	0.424	0.126**	1.527	0.533	0.096***	1.703	1.134	0.101***	3.108
Hispanic	0.374	0.123***	1.454	0.099	0.095	1.104	0.490	0.101	1.632
Asian	0.560	0.165**	1.750	0.742	0.120***	2.101	1.156	0.124***	3.177
Other	0.407	0.154**	1.502	0.120	0.121	1.128	0.198	0.130	1.219
HLM computed standard deviation	0.361		(intercept)	0.292		(intercept)	0.330		(intercept)

† ≤ .10; * p ≤ .05; ** p ≤ .01; *** p ≤ .001; SE = standard error.

College Attendance Immediately after High School Graduation

The next model explored whether students who graduate from high school plan to go to college after graduation. The outcome measure for this analysis included the following options: not planning to attend college after high school; not knowing about college after high school; or planning to attend college right after high school. In this model, the comparison group was students who answered that they planned to attend college in the fall after high school graduation in the spring.

Overall, it appears that students across all schools were likely to say that they were planning to attend college immediately after high school graduation. Those in schools with 1,200 to 1,999 students were more likely to say that they did not plan to attend college after high school than those in schools with 800 to 1,199 students ($p \leq .10$). In high schools with 2,000 or more students, students were less likely to say they did not know their future plans ($p \leq .05$). As average student socioeconomic status rose, students were more likely to report that they would attend college immediately after high school graduation ($p \leq .10$) (see table 4).

Female, black, and Asian students were more likely to say that they would attend college than to respond "no" or "don't know." Being in a Catholic school or having a family with greater socioeconomic status was similarly associated with students being more likely to respond that they were planning to attend college immediately after high school graduation. An increase in the student test score composite slope also was related to greater likelihood of planning to attend college.

Number of Schools to Which Students Applied

In addition to student expectations, several other measures were considered for estimating the effects of school size. The variable "number of schools to which a student applied" was selected because it provides evidence regarding actual steps taken by a student to secure a college education and may be a more accurate measure of expectations than a student's statement of how far in school he or she expects to go. This outcome measure included the following categories: one school, two to four schools, and five or more schools, with no schools as the reference category.

Again, school size did not appear to be related in any systematic way to the number of schools to which a student applied. Students in the smallest schools

Table 4. HLM Model for College Going Immediately after High School

Effect	No college after HS vs. Yes college			Don't know about college after HS vs. Yes college		
	Coefficient	SE	Odds ratio	Coefficient	SE	Odds ratio
On between-school gains (intercept)						
Base estimate	-2.428	0.138***	0.088	-1.329	0.159***	0.265
Average SES	-0.279	0.165†	0.756	-0.276	0.199*	0.757
Catholic school	-0.529	0.197**	0.589	-1.253	0.256***	0.286
Other private school	-0.029	0.229	0.971	-0.539	0.283**	0.583
High minority	0.124	0.125	1.131	-0.072	0.150	0.930
Urban	0.096	0.119	1.101	0.004	0.147	1.004
Rural	0.102	0.140	1.107	-0.002	0.164	0.998
School size						
1–399	0.023	0.189	1.024	-0.024	0.226	0.976
400–799	0.080	0.161	1.083	0.019	0.192	1.019
1,200–1,999	0.272	0.152†	1.312	0.040	0.179	1.041
2,000 or more	-0.140	0.180	0.869	-0.289	0.137*	0.749
On relationship between tenth-grade composite test score and gains (slope)						
Base estimate	-0.071	0.012***	0.932	-0.050	0.010***	0.951
Average SES	-0.017	0.015	0.983	-0.017	0.018	0.983
Catholic school	-0.008	0.022	0.992	-0.052	0.022*	0.949
Other private school	0.019	0.024	1.020	-0.003	0.029	0.997
High minority	0.003	0.011	1.003	0.002	0.013	1.002
Urban	0.010	0.011	1.010	0.005	0.013	1.005
Rural	-0.003	0.013	0.997	-0.024	0.011*	0.977
School size						
1–399	0.001	0.017	1.001	0.004	0.020	1.004
400–799	0.017	0.015	1.017	-0.004	0.017	0.996
1,200–1,999	0.005	0.014	1.005	0.000	0.016	1.000
2,000 or more	0.011	0.016	1.012	-0.001	0.019	0.999
Effects on relationship between SES and gains (slope)						
Base estimate	-0.473	0.182**	0.623	-0.729	0.211***	0.483
Average SES	-0.130	0.204	0.878	-0.050	0.247	0.951
Catholic school	0.187	0.293	1.205	-0.107	0.385	0.899
Other private school	0.125	0.327	1.133	-0.058	0.408	0.944
High minority	0.079	0.155	1.082	0.274	0.122**	1.316
Urban	0.039	0.152	1.039	-0.028	0.186	0.972
Rural	-0.183	0.188	0.832	-0.018	0.216	0.983
School size						
1–399	-0.328	0.249	0.720	0.004	0.294	1.004
400–799	-0.358	0.217†	0.699	0.096	0.256	1.101
1,200–1,999	-0.111	0.198	0.895	-0.123	0.233	0.884
2,000 or more	0.116	0.224	1.123	0.093	0.267	1.098
Female	-0.544	0.079***	0.581	-0.835	0.094***	0.434
Black	-0.748	0.146***	0.473	-0.716	0.170***	0.489
Hispanic	0.070	0.131	1.073	-0.297	0.131**	0.743
Asian	-0.766	0.182***	0.465	-1.087	0.226***	0.337
Others	0.031	0.172	1.031	0.118	0.132	1.125
HLM computed standard deviation	0.345		(intercept)	0.395		(intercept)

† ≤ .10; * $p \leq .05$; ** $p \leq .01$; *** $p \leq .001$; SE = standard error.

(fewer than 399 students) applied to one school instead of no schools at a significantly higher rate ($p \leq .05$).

Students in the same schools who had higher average socioeconomic status also applied to one school instead of no schools at a higher rate ($p \leq .01$). Those effects were found only in the smallest schools. In addition, we found that students in both the 1,200–1,999 and the 2,000 or more categories were less likely to apply to five or more schools than to apply to no schools ($p \leq .001$ and $p \leq .10$, respectively) (see table 5).

Female students applied to two or more colleges more frequently than they applied to no colleges ($p \leq .001$), while black and Asian students applied to any number of colleges more frequently than they applied to no colleges ($p \leq .01$ and .001). Hispanic students were more likely to apply to one college than to no colleges ($p \leq .01$). Those findings suggest that, controlling for school size and other demographic variables in a multilevel model, minority students and female students are more likely to apply to multiple colleges than their white male counterparts.

Type of College to Which Students Applied

This outcome measure includes the following categories: two-year college, vocational/technical college, and four-year college (the reference category). As in the other models, there did not appear to be a distinct effect for school size. Students in the largest schools applied to two-year colleges at a higher rate than students in schools of other sizes ($p \leq .05$). Those with higher test scores in schools that had 400 to 799 and 1,200 to 1,999 students were less likely to apply to vocational/technical colleges than to four-year institutions ($p \leq .05$ and .10, respectively). Female students were less likely to enroll in vocational/technical institutions than their male counterparts. Similarly, black, Hispanic, and Asian students all were less likely to enroll in vocational/technical institutions than white students, and blacks, Asians, and other ethnic minorities were less likely to enroll in two-year colleges than whites (see table 6).

This sequence of HLMs highlights several issues. The first is that we did not find a clear size effect in these models with this data set. Second, due to the fact that there appeared to be selection bias issues in the data, we were concerned that simply controlling for factors such as school and student socioeconomic status would not capture the effects of school size on student learning and expectations. To address these issues, we used propensity score matching.

Table 5. HLM Model for Number of Schools to Which Student Applied

Effect	One school v. none			Two to four schools v. none			Five or more schools v. none		
	Coefficient	SE	Odds ratio	Coefficient	SE	Odds ratio	Coefficient	SE	Odds ratio
On between-school gains (intercept)									
Base estimate	-0.273	0.103*	0.761	0.165	0.099†	1.179	-1.783	0.162***	0.168
Average SES	0.168	0.130	1.183	0.415	0.124**	1.515	1.109	0.188***	3.030
Catholic school	0.501	0.155*	1.650	0.786	0.149***	2.194	1.098	0.222***	2.998
Other private school	0.028	0.188	1.028	0.319	0.179†	1.376	0.565	0.277*	1.759
High minority	-0.181	0.098†	0.834	-0.117	0.093	0.890	0.492	0.148***	1.664
Urban	0.190	0.094*	1.209	0.180	0.090*	1.197	0.376	0.137**	1.457
Rural	0.032	0.104	1.032	0.055	0.102	1.056	-0.246	0.182	0.782
School size									
1–399	0.317	0.145*	1.373	0.016	0.142	1.016	-0.123	0.226	0.884
400–799	0.146	0.122	1.157	-0.081	0.119	0.923	-0.308	0.189	0.735
1,200–1,999	-0.027	0.116	0.973	-0.131	0.112	0.877	-0.596	0.179***	0.551
2,000 or more	-0.029	0.132	0.971	-0.185	0.126	0.831	-0.326	0.196†	0.722
On relationship between tenth-grade composite test score and gains (slope)									
Base estimate	0.042	0.010***	1.043	0.062	0.009***	1.063	0.089	0.013***	1.093
Average SES	0.025	0.012**	1.025	0.014	0.011	1.014	0.029	0.014*	1.029
Catholic school	0.020	0.017	1.020	0.021	0.016	1.021	0.026	0.019	1.027
Other private school	-0.007	0.019	0.993	-0.024	0.017	0.976	-0.025	0.022	0.975
High minority	-0.015	0.009	0.986	-0.009	0.008	0.991	-0.010	0.012	0.990
Urban	0.001	0.009	1.001	-0.004	0.008	0.996	-0.006	0.011	0.994
Rural	0.013	0.010	1.013	0.007	0.009	1.007	0.002	0.016	1.002
School size									
1–399	-0.005	0.014	0.995	0.009	0.013	1.010	-0.002	0.019	0.998
400–799	0.003	0.012	1.003	0.012	0.011	1.012	0.014	0.016	1.014
1,200–1,999	0.010	0.011	1.010	0.006	0.010	1.006	0.024	0.015	1.024
2,000 or more	0.023	0.012†	1.023	0.011	0.011	1.011	0.018	0.016	1.018

	\multicolumn{4}{c}{}	\multicolumn{4}{c}{}	
On relationship between SES and gains (slope)								
Base estimate	0.412	0.134**	1.510	0.567	0.120***	1.763	1.035	0.167***	2.814
Average SES	0.407	0.159*	1.502	0.468	0.146**	1.596	0.631	0.183**	1.879
Catholic school	-0.294	0.217	0.745	-0.172	0.199	0.842	-0.151	0.237	0.860
Other private school	-0.273	0.256	0.761	-0.312	0.233	0.732	-0.490	0.288†	0.613
High minority	-0.178	0.121	0.837	-0.190	0.109	0.827	-0.355	0.146*	0.701
Urban	-0.045	0.117	0.956	-0.018	0.106	0.982	-0.203	0.136	0.816
Rural	-0.235	0.139†	0.791	-0.163	0.128	0.850	-0.218	0.207	0.804
School size									
1–399	0.324	0.193†	1.383	0.229	0.179	1.257	0.294	0.237	1.342
400–799	0.171	0.163	1.186	-0.065	0.149	0.937	-0.008	0.197	0.992
1,200–1,999	0.102	0.154	1.107	0.135	0.137	1.144	0.134	0.187	1.143
2,000 or more	-0.120	0.169	0.887	0.037	0.150	1.038	-0.143	0.197	0.867
Female	0.403	0.060***	1.497	0.514	0.055***	1.671	0.850	0.077***	2.340
Black	-0.031	0.116	0.970	0.767	0.099***	2.153	1.205	0.139***	3.336
Hispanic	-0.266	0.109*	0.770	0.046	0.098	1.047	0.199	0.138	3.716
Asian	0.354	0.132**	1.424	0.721	0.119***	2.057	1.313	0.146***	1.220
Others	-0.170	0.141	0.843	0.026	0.127	1.026	0.445	0.169**	1.561
HLM Computed standard deviation	0.5184		(intercept)	0.4513		(intercept)	0.9919		(intercept)

† ≤ .10; * $p ≤ .05$; ** $p ≤ .01$; *** $p ≤ .001$; SE = standard error.

Table 6. HLM Model for Type of College Student Plans to Attend

| | Vocational college vs. four-year college ||| Two-year college vs. four-year college |||
Effect	Coefficient	SE	Odds ratio	Coefficient	SE	Odds ratio
On between-school gains (intercept)						
Base estimate	-1.652	0.140***	0.192	-1.021	0.103***	0.360
Average SES	-0.861	0.203***	0.423	-0.587	0.126***	0.556
Catholic school	-0.848	0.252**	0.428	-0.353	0.150*	0.703
Other private school	-0.774	0.315*	0.461	-0.140	0.183	0.870
High minority	0.111	0.144	1.117	0.183	0.095†	1.201
Urban	-0.251	0.147†	0.778	-0.336	0.092**	0.715
Rural	0.036	0.149	1.036	-0.046	0.106	0.955
School size						
1–399	-0.001	0.206	0.999	0.081	0.143	1.084
400–799	-0.187	0.178	0.830	-0.072	0.123	0.931
1,200–1,999	-0.234	0.171	0.791	0.125	0.117	1.133
2,000 or more	0.039	0.187	1.040	0.316	0.129*	1.372
On relationship between tenth-grade composite test score and gains (slope)						
Base estimate	-0.099	0.012***	0.906	-0.086	0.009***	0.918
Average SES	-0.049	0.018**	0.953	-0.033	0.011**	0.967
Catholic school	-0.027	0.027	0.974	-0.033	0.015*	0.968
Other private school	0.034	0.033	1.035	0.013	0.018	1.013
High minority	0.004	0.012	1.004	-0.002	0.008	0.998
Urban	0.024	0.013†	1.024	0.009	0.008	1.009
Rural	-0.014	0.013	0.987	-0.019	0.010†	0.982
School size						
1–399	0.011	0.019	1.011	0.006	0.013	1.006
400–799	-0.032	0.016*	0.969	0.001	0.011	1.001
1,200–1,999	-0.028	0.015†	0.973	-0.008	0.010	0.992
2,000 or more	0.011	0.016	1.011	0.005	0.011	1.005
On relationship between SES and gains (slope)						
Base estimate	-0.978	0.181***	0.376	-0.601	0.119***	0.548
Average SES	-0.517	0.243	0.596	-0.335	0.140*	0.713
Catholic school	0.022	0.359	1.022	0.338	0.185†	1.402
Other private school	0.634	0.447	1.885	0.291	0.222	1.338
High minority	0.189	0.172	1.209	0.243	0.105*	1.275
Urban	0.036	0.177	1.037	-0.044	0.102	0.957
Rural	-0.002	0.189	0.998	0.006	0.126	1.006
School size						
1–399	-0.157	0.265	0.855	-0.054	0.171	0.948
400–799	0.212	0.226	1.236	-0.052	0.147	0.949
1,200–1,999	0.017	0.214	1.017	-0.028	0.136	0.972
2,000 or more	0.289	0.231	1.335	0.143	0.144	1.154
Female	-0.925	0.085***	0.397	-0.087	0.053	0.917
Black	-0.978	0.146***	0.376	-0.877	0.099***	0.416
Hispanic	-0.333	0.145*	0.717	-0.098	0.095	0.907
Asian	-1.381	0.211***	0.251	-0.726	0.112***	0.484
Others	-0.210	0.182	0.810	-0.326	0.126**	0.722
HLM computed standard deviation	0.4584		(intercept)	0.5789		(intercept)

† ≤ .10; * p ≤ .05; ** p ≤ .01; *** p ≤ .001; SE = standard error.

Estimating the Effects of School Size by Using Propensity Score Matching

To fully understand and isolate the effect of school size on student performance and outcomes, we would need to randomly assign students to schools of various sizes, then evaluate the impact of school size on their outcomes. For obvious reasons, that is not possible. In this analysis, we estimated a set of propensity scores in order to approximate an experimental design. We used propensity scores to match individuals with similar characteristics so that any potential benefit of being in one group or another could be assessed.[31] Propensity scores offer distinct advantages with large-scale data sets in that they allow for more direct comparison of groups of students who have the same characteristics and a similar likelihood of receiving the "treatment" (that is, being part of whatever treatment group is being studied).

For this analysis, we began by performing a series of tests in order to approximate the best student matches. We added different matching criteria to sort the sample into ten separate strata of students whose propensity of being in a very large school (2,000 or more students) was the same as their propensity of being in an "optimal" size school (800–1,199 students).[32] Matching was conducted on sixty-eight pretreatment covariates[33] that included questions about student and family demographics, student motivation, extracurricular activities, and tenth-grade test scores.[34] The variables included in this matching strategy were selected because they were assumed to be primarily a function of the student, not the school attended.

The propensity scores were then sorted into ten separate strata, which were used in a regression equation to estimate the potential effect of being in an optimal size school. We did five separate matches, one for each outcome measure. The total number of students ranged from 3,910 to 4,465. We found a 95 percent balance on the sixty-eight pretreatment covariates that were used to construct each match, indicating that sufficient balance had been achieved.[35] In addition, we examined the balance of the logit of the propensity score within each stratum for both the mean and standard deviation. That also indicated that adequate balance had been achieved.

Table 7 indicates that students in the tenth stratum were most likely to attend a small school and those in the first stratum were most likely to attend a large school. In the models below, separate within-stratum regression models were constructed for each stratum by using a set of dummy variables. That allowed us to estimate the potential effect of going to a small school for students in each stratum. Further, we used an across-strata regression controlling for each stra-

Table 7. Balance of Logit of Propensity Score

	2,000 or more students			800 to 1,199 students		
Stratum	N	Mean	SD	N	Mean	SD
Student expectations and math achievement						
1	382	-2.01	0.49	64	-1.92	0.37
2	338	-1.16	0.16	109	-1.11	0.16
3	289	-0.68	0.11	157	-0.65	0.11
4	254	-0.33	0.09	193	-0.33	0.09
5	238	-0.02	0.08	208	-0.01	0.07
6	215	0.26	0.08	232	0.26	0.08
7	173	0.54	0.09	274	0.55	0.08
8	142	0.83	0.09	304	0.85	0.09
9	81	1.17	0.11	366	1.19	0.11
10	56	1.81	0.36	390	1.85	0.36
Plans to go to college						
1	352	-2.00	0.53	56	-1.92	0.36
2	302	-1.11	0.15	106	-1.08	0.17
3	265	-0.65	0.12	144	-0.62	0.11
4	219	-0.31	0.09	189	-0.30	0.09
5	226	0.00	0.08	183	0.02	0.08
6	192	0.28	0.08	216	0.29	0.08
7	155	0.57	0.09	254	0.57	0.09
8	119	0.86	0.09	289	0.89	0.09
9	79	1.19	0.11	330	1.23	0.11
10	50	1.85	0.37	358	1.90	0.37
Type of college						
1	330	-2.04	0.62	60	-1.85	0.40
2	298	-1.10	0.15	93	-1.06	0.14
3	255	-0.65	0.12	136	-0.62	0.11
4	205	-0.30	0.09	186	-0.30	0.09
5	217	-0.01	0.08	174	0.01	0.08
6	187	0.27	0.08	204	0.27	0.08
7	144	0.56	0.09	247	0.56	0.09
8	124	0.83	0.09	267	0.85	0.08
9	77	1.16	0.11	314	1.19	0.11
10	48	1.83	0.35	343	1.84	0.36
Number of schools applied to						
1	332	-2.01	0.59	59	-1.86	0.38
2	295	-1.10	0.15	96	-1.06	0.14
3	258	-0.65	0.12	133	-0.62	0.11
4	205	-0.30	0.09	186	-0.30	0.09
5	214	-0.01	0.08	177	0.01	0.09
6	186	0.27	0.08	205	0.28	0.08
7	147	0.55	0.09	244	0.56	0.08
8	122	0.83	0.08	269	0.85	0.08
9	77	1.17	0.11	314	1.19	0.11
10	49	1.81	0.36	342	1.84	0.36

Table 8. OLS Within-Stratum Propensity Score Regression for Math Achievement[a]

Stratum	2,000 or more students Mean	800 to 1,199 students Mean	Mean difference	SE
1	46.447	49.329	2.882	2.298
2	47.245	47.507	0.226	1.794
3	46.887	45.253	-1.635	1.538
4	47.773	48.928	1.155	1.505
5	47.717	45.969	-1.749	1.464
6	48.731	49.912	1.181	1.438
7	49.809	49.295	-0.515	1.385
8	50.616	49.704	-0.912	1.544
9	51.084	51.863	0.779	1.825
10	53.465	51.823	-1.641	2.046
Average treatment effect			-0.162	0.514

Note: SE = standard error.
a. None of the findings are statistically significant.

tum to estimate the overall average treatment effect of being in a school of 800 to 1,199 students.[36]

Twelfth-Grade Mathematics Achievement

For this model, 4,465 students were sorted into ten strata based on their propensity scores. A set of dummy variables representing the size of the school that a student attended was used in each within-stratum ordinary least squares regression equation. Table 8 shows the average effect of being in each stratum for the ten strata as well as the overall treatment effect of attending a small school in terms of twelfth-grade mathematics achievement.

The overall average effect across strata is slightly negative and nonsignificant. This finding indicates that the benefits of attending a small school do not seem to accrue for mathematics achievement. In this case, as with the HLM models, we cannot conclude that attending small schools would have the desired effect for students attending schools of 2,000 or more students. In other words, this finding indicates that students attending very large high schools do not uniformly stand to benefit from attending a smaller school.

Looking across the different strata, we find no statistically significant coefficients. If small schools had a benefit with respect to mathematics achievement, we would expect to find that all students experience an increase in their mathematics achievement from attending a small school. That was not the case. For example, students in the first stratum, those who were the most dissimilar to students currently enrolled in small schools, could have significantly higher scores if they were enrolled in small schools. The same cannot be said of students in the tenth stratum, where the opposite might occur. Specifically, those in stratum 10 who were currently enrolled in large schools (mean = 53.465) should have lower mathematics achievement scores than those in small schools (mean = 51.823), but that did not occur.

Student Postsecondary Expectations

A multinomial logistic regression model was estimated for student postsecondary expectations for each stratum. This model compares the effects of school size on postsecondary expectations of students expecting to graduate from high school or attend some college with the effects for students in the other three categories (not knowing about the future, aspiring to attend a four-year college, or aspiring to obtain a graduate or professional degree). Results are presented in table 9.

From these results, it seems that the average student would not have had higher educational expectations if he or she had been in a small school. In the first multinomial logistic regression, comparing "expect to obtain less than a high school degree" with "expect to graduate from high school," we find that the average treatment effect (−.091) is not significant. That finding suggests that school size is not significant for this comparison. Moving to the next set of comparisons, we find that the average treatment effect may be an adverse effect, with smaller schools having lower expectations. When we look at the comparison of "expect to attend a four-year college" and "expect to complete some college," attending a small school is associated with decreased likelihood that students will expect to seek a four-year college degree (−.189, $p \leq .05$). Similarly, when we compare coefficients for students who expect to obtain a graduate degree and those for students who expect to complete some college, we find again that students in small schools are less likely to seek advanced degrees.

Comparing across strata we find significant results for stratum 3 in the first and second comparisons. The second comparison shows that the effect of small schools is negative for students in this stratum (−.684, $p \leq .01$) In the last comparison, for students in stratum 8 and stratum 10, we find that small schools have a negative effect on students' expectations to obtain an advanced degree (−.617, $p \leq .05$ and −.924, $p \leq .05$ respectively).

If small schools had a positive significant effect on educational expectations, we would have found that the average treatment effect was positive.

Table 9. Multinomial Logistic Regression with Propensity Scores for Student Expectations

	2,000 or more students	800 to 1,199 students			Log odds
	Coeff	Coeff	MD	SE	diff
Less than high school/don't know vs. high school/some college only					
1	-0.621	0.182	0.803	0.463 †	2.232
2	-0.599	-0.821	-0.222	0.413	0.801
3	-0.971	-1.928	-0.957	0.445 *	0.384
4	-0.940	-1.142	-0.202	0.379	0.817
5	-0.806	-0.395	0.411	0.351	1.508
6	-0.740	-1.466	-0.727	0.390 †	0.484
7	-1.358	-0.821	0.537	0.453	1.711
8	-0.606	-1.005	-0.398	0.426	0.671
9	-1.482	-1.409	0.073	0.550	1.076
10	-1.946	-1.288	0.658	1.094	1.931
Average treatment effect			-0.091	0.137	0.913
Four-year college vs. high school/some college only					
1	0.168	0.531	0.363	0.423	1.437
2	0.215	0.113	-0.101	0.318	0.904
3	0.483	-0.201	-0.684	0.255 **	0.505
4	0.198	0.227	0.030	0.258	1.030
5	0.593	0.361	-0.232	0.265	0.793
6	0.506	0.000	-0.506	0.259 †	0.603
7	0.488	0.693	0.205	0.276	1.228
8	0.821	0.401	-0.420	0.298	0.657
9	0.087	0.321	0.234	0.326	1.263
10	0.999	0.447	-0.552	0.463	0.576
Average treatment effect			-0.189	0.094 *	0.828
Graduate/professional vs. high school/some college only					
1	0.327	0.916	0.589	0.398	1.802
2	0.679	0.588	-0.091	0.289	0.913
3	0.321	-0.143	-0.464	0.254 †	0.629
4	0.307	0.427	0.120	0.250	1.127
5	0.593	0.346	-0.247	0.265	0.781
6	0.560	0.292	-0.268	0.250	0.765
7	0.721	0.713	-0.008	0.269	0.992
8	0.969	0.352	-0.617	0.299 *	0.540
9	0.310	0.368	0.058	0.312	1.059
10	1.421	0.497	-0.924	0.443 *	0.397
Average treatment effect			-0.195	0.091 *	0.823

† ≤ .10; * p ≤ .05; ** p ≤ .01; *** p ≤ .001; SE = standard error; MD = mean difference.

Furthermore, we would expect to find that students who were most dissimilar to small school students—that is, those in strata 1 through 3—would experience the greatest benefit if enrolled in small schools. We did not find that to be the case.

Table 10. Multinomial Logistic Regression with Propensity Scores for Plans to Go to College

	2,000 or more students	800 to 1,199 students			
	Coeff	Coeff	MD	SE	Log odds diff
No college after high school vs. Yes college					
1	-2.541	-3.239	-0.697	0.753	0.498
2	-2.761	-3.379	-0.618	0.641	0.539
3	-2.499	-2.548	-0.049	0.424	0.952
4	-2.254	-2.342	-0.088	0.362	0.916
5	-2.314	-2.169	0.145	0.362	1.156
6	-2.714	-3.390	-0.676	0.519	0.509
7	-3.541	-2.403	1.138	0.561*	3.121
8	-3.546	-2.613	0.932	0.637	2.540
9	-3.121	-2.901	0.220	0.647	1.245
10	-3.871	-2.537	1.334	1.033	3.796
Average treatment effect			0.072	0.163	1.075
Don't know about college after high school vs. Yes college					
1	-2.066	-2.833	-0.767	0.619	0.464
2	-2.037	-1.769	0.268	0.335	1.307
3	-2.057	-1.749	0.308	0.315	1.360
4	-2.254	-2.160	0.095	0.347	1.099
5	-1.946	-1.646	0.300	0.297	1.350
6	-2.404	-1.716	0.688	0.331*	1.990
7	-2.632	-2.398	0.234	0.359	1.264
8	-2.160	-1.758	0.402	0.350	1.494
9	-2.140	-1.872	0.268	0.409	1.308
10	-3.871	-1.889	1.982	1.023 †	7.258
Average treatment effect			0.309	0.117**	1.362

† ≤ .10; * p ≤ .05; **p ≤ .01; *** p ≤ .001; SE = standard error; MD = mean difference.

College Plans Immediately after High School Graduation

The overall treatment effect for propensity score models exploring college plans after high school graduation suggests that if students in large schools were to enroll in small schools there would be an increase in the number of students who respond either that they do not know their future plans or that they do not plan to go to college immediately after high school.[37] Specifically, if a student attends a small school he or she is 1.362 times more likely to be uncertain about his or her future plans. However, most students aspire to attend college after graduation, as indicated by the fact that across both comparisons all coefficients for each stratum are negative. Those coefficients support the commonly held notion that most students aspire to attend college, but it appears that for students in large schools, attending a small school results in a decrease in plans to attend college (see table 10).

In within-stratum comparisons for both models, the only significant coefficients are found for stratum 7 in the first model and stratum 6 in the second. In both instances attending a small school would be associated with a negative effect on students' college plans.

Number of Schools to Which Students Applied

In the next model we see a benefit for small schools. The overall positive average treatment effect suggests that students in large schools probably would be more likely to apply to college if they had attended a small school. In the case of applying to one school compared with applying to none at all, a student attending a small school was 1.355 times more likely to apply to college. These results may point to a difference in resources within small-school communities; small-school environments may be better equipped to help students align their ambitions with actual plans of action (see table 11).

Across all the comparisons, we find positive effects for stratum 3 in the first comparison and stratum 8 in the third. In the first comparison, students in small schools are more likely to apply to one college than to no college; in the third comparison, students are more likely to apply to five or more colleges than to no college. However, there are some significant negative effects for small schools, specifically in stratum 1 in model 2 and stratum 10 in model 3. In those strata, being enrolled in a small school is associated with a greater tendency to apply to no college at all.

Type of College to Which Students Applied

In this multinomial logistic regression model, we explored the potential effect of attending a small school on the types of colleges to which students applied (see table 12). Overall, students were more likely to choose a four-year college than another option when applying to postsecondary institutions, as indicated by the fact that coefficients under both large schools and small schools are always negative. In general, that finding suggests that if students apply to college, they tend to apply to four-year colleges more than to others. It is still important to look at the average treatment effects, since there might be further increases or decreases associated with attending small schools. In these data, it appears that attending a small school results in a greater desire to apply to a four-year college than a two-year college ($-.191$, $p \leq .05$). These findings, much like those for the number of schools applied to, suggest that small schools may be better equipped to align students' aspirations with a course of action.

Table 11. Multinomial Logistic Regression with Propensity Scores: Number of Schools Applied To

	2,000 or more students	800 to 1,199 students			
	Coeff	Coeff	MD	SE	Log odds diff
One vs. none					
1	-0.466	0.054	0.520	0.369	1.682
2	-0.511	-0.336	0.174	0.342	1.191
3	-0.899	0.000	0.899	0.324 **	2.457
4	-0.676	-0.327	0.349	0.325	1.418
5	-0.606	-0.525	0.082	0.326	1.085
6	-0.714	-0.640	0.074	0.339	1.076
7	-0.644	-0.633	0.012	0.343	1.012
8	-1.129	-0.552	0.576	0.402	1.780
9	-0.480	0.084	0.564	0.398	1.757
10	1.179	0.379	-0.800	0.600	0.449
Average treatment effect			0.304	0.112 **	1.355
Two to four vs. none					
1	-0.187	-1.792	-1.605	0.642 *	0.201
2	-0.365	-0.624	-0.259	0.362	0.772
3	-0.523	-0.102	0.421	0.315	1.523
4	-0.364	-0.296	0.069	0.310	1.071
5	-0.424	-0.560	-0.136	0.320	0.873
6	-0.108	-0.076	0.032	0.285	1.033
7	-0.470	-0.247	0.223	0.317	1.250
8	-0.231	-0.298	-0.067	0.319	0.935
9	-0.847	-0.018	0.830	0.441 †	2.292
10	0.916	0.457	-0.459	0.619	0.632
Average treatment effect			0.062	0.110	1.064
Five or more vs. none					
1	0.072	0.054	-0.018	0.359	0.982
2	0.163	0.164	0.002	0.296	1.002
3	0.000	0.373	0.373	0.281 †	1.452
4	0.240	0.621	0.381	0.257	1.464
5	0.525	0.371	-0.154	0.252	0.857
6	0.342	0.241	-0.101	0.260	0.904
7	0.422	0.406	-0.017	0.269	0.984
8	0.386	0.564	0.178	0.271 *	1.195
9	0.482	0.891	0.410	0.319	1.506
10	1.705	1.030	-0.675	0.568 *	0.509
Average treatment effect			0.088	0.091	1.092

† ≤ .10; * p ≤ .05; ** p ≤ .01; *** p ≤ .001; SE = standard error; MD = mean difference.

Table 12. Multinomial Logistic Regression with Propensity Scores for Type of College

	2,000 or more students	800 to 1,199 students			
	Coeff	Coeff	MD	SE	Log odds diff
Vocational/technical vs. four-year college					
1	-2.249	-3.091	-0.842	0.758	0.431
2	-2.459	-2.132	0.327	0.477	1.387
3	-2.217	-2.377	-0.161	0.432	0.851
4	-2.003	-2.118	-0.115	0.370	0.892
5	-2.324	-2.035	0.289	0.392	1.335
6	-2.147	-1.883	0.265	0.353	1.303
7	-2.408	-2.120	0.288	0.453	1.333
8	-2.554	-2.033	0.521	0.446	1.683
9	-2.043	-2.455	-0.412	0.464	0.662
10	-3.714	-2.201	1.512	1.012	4.538
Average treatment effect			0.121	0.142	1.129
Two-year college vs. four-year college					
1	-0.593	-1.145	-0.552	0.329 †	0.576
2	-0.677	-0.782	-0.105	0.264	0.901
3	-0.643	-1.174	-0.530	0.250 *	0.588
4	-0.709	-1.279	-0.570	0.242 *	0.565
5	-0.869	-0.961	-0.092	0.235	0.912
6	-1.394	-1.121	0.273	0.257	1.314
7	-1.050	-1.233	-0.183	0.253	0.833
8	-1.204	-1.321	-0.117	0.270	0.890
9	-1.216	-1.340	-0.124	0.319	0.884
10	-1.922	-1.406	0.516	0.463	1.675
Average treatment effect			-0.191	0.087 *	0.826

† $\leq$ .10; * $p \leq$ .05; ** $p \leq$ .01; *** $p \leq$ .001; SE = standard error; MD = mean difference.

Only in the second comparison of this model do we find significant coefficients for strata 3 and 4. The coefficients for those strata suggest that students in large schools would be more likely to apply to four-year colleges if they were to attend small schools.

Conclusions and Limitations

School size is a pressing educational policy concern; therefore it is important to use the most rigorous methods to estimate the effects of school size on student outcomes. Results of these analyses suggest that perhaps the burden of proof is on small schools, as we do not find consistent benefits for smaller schools and in some cases find that the average effect for small schools might be the opposite of the intended effect. In fact, small schools may have detrimental effects for certain groups of students. More detailed experiments or analyses focusing on particular types of students need to be conducted. For example, it would be prudent to conduct specific analyses focusing on the groups of students most likely to be placed into newly constructed small-school environments. Typically, such students are found in large urban areas. Since we did not find consistently positive and significant results in the stratum that represents students most likely to come from these large-school environments, it seems warranted to investigate further what the effects of small schools would be for these students and in which circumstances small schools would be beneficial.

One of the major limitations of this study is that we were able to compare only the effects of moving from the largest schools (2,000 or more students) to an "optimal"-size school (800–1,199 students). It is possible that we did not isolate the best comparison group. Perhaps decreasing school size from 2,000 or more students to 1,500 students would be beneficial. In addition, some high schools have well over 2,000 students, but the data set does not allow us to identify such schools. Despite the limitations of our work, we maintain that high school reforms need to be tested with the most rigorous methods available. Given the resources and policy choices being made on the basis of size, our results should give policymakers considerable pause.

What we find is that on some of the most pressing accountability measures, such as test scores and college aspirations, school size does not appear to make a marked difference. As those are the strongest predictors of college success, it is indeed problematic that we did not find a small-school effect for them. However, with respect to students taking action on college plans—for example, by applying to college—small schools appear to have a positive impact. These increases with respect to students taking action on their college plans are resource issues. Perhaps one mechanism for increasing matriculation rates of students in large urban high schools would be to offer more hands-on experiences with the college application process.

What makes small schools successful is not just the size of the schools but the resources of the parents and communities in which they are located. Large high schools, particularly those in urban areas, do not have the same resources as small schools, whose social capital, both in and out of the school, can reinforce norms about college attendance. These differences seem to be present in our results, in that we find that on average, small schools seem to be better at aligning students' ambitions with an actual course of action. Our results are not able to substantiate specifically that social capital and resource discrepancies are the cause of these observed differences, but that seems to be a likely explanation. However, large schools have other resources, such as multiple athletic teams for girls and boys and more course options. Reducing the size of large urban high schools does not guarantee that students in those schools will experience the same benefits as students in small schools in other locations, such as small towns or suburban locations. Paradoxically, if urban students were to attend small schools they would be likely to lose some resources that were available to them in larger schools. Optimal school size appears "optimal" only for a selective group of students, not all students—and especially not for some students found in urban high schools.

Appendix: Description of Variables

Variable	Description	Mean	SD
Dependent variable			
Student expectations	Variable based on the question "How far in school do you expect to get?" asked of high school seniors. Range is 1 to 4, where 1 = *don't know*, 2 = *four-year degree*, 3 = *graduate degree*, and 4 = *high school diploma, no degree*	2.73	0.91
Number of schools	Students indicated number of schools to which they applied. Range is 1 to 4, where 1 = *five or more schools*, 2 = *one school*, 3 = *two to four schools*, and 4 = *no schools*.	2.71	1.00
Type of college	Students indicated what type of postsecondary institution they planned to attend. Range is 1 to 3, where 1 = *vocational/technical school*, 2 = *two-year college,* and 3 = *four-year college*.	2.63	0.61
College plans right after high school	Students indicated whether they planned to go to college right after high school. Responses were *don't know* (coded 1), *no* (coded 2), and *yes* (coded 3).	2.75	0.57
Math/reading achievement	Composite measure included in the ELS:2002 data set. This score is the average of the math and reading standardized scores, re-standardized to a national mean of 50.0 and a standard deviation of 10.0. The standardized *t* score is a norm-referenced measurement of achievement. It provides information on status compared with that of peers (as distinguished from the IRT-estimated number-right score, which represents status with respect to achievement on a particular criterion set of test items). Range is 20.91 to 81.04.	51.27	9.85

Variable	Description	Mean	SD
Independent variable			
School size	Total school enrollment from administrator questionnaire. Recoded into five size categories where 1 = 1–399 students, 2 = 400–799 students, 3 = 800–1,199 students, 4 = 1,200–1,999 students, and 5 = 2,000 or more students.		
1–399 students		0.17	0.38
400–799 students		0.2	0.40
800–1,199 students		0.18	0.38
1,200–1,999 students		0.27	0.44
2,000 or more students		0.18	0.38
Control variable for HLM[a]			
Level 1 predictor:			
Female	Respondent is female.		
Black	Respondent is black.		
Hispanic	Respondent is Hispanic.		
Asian	Respondent is Asian.		
Other	Respondent is another race/ethnicity. Respondent is white (the omitted category).		
Test score composite	Composite test score measure of math and reading scores included in ELS:2002 data set. Also used as outcome variable.		
Student socioeconomic status	Composite variable in ELS:2002. SES calculated by family income, mother and father education, and parent occupation. Range is -2.12 to 1.97.		
Level 2 predictor:			
Average school socioeconomic status	Average SES for every student in each school. Range is -1.01 to 1.41.		
Minority concentration	1 if school has on average more than 40 percent minority students, 0 if school has less than 40 percent minority students.[b]		
Sector	Dummy variable for Catholic and other private schools, with public schools as reference.		
Urbanicity	School is urban, suburban, or rural.		
Region	Region of the country (Northeast, Midwest, South, West).		

a. Contact author for means and standard deviations, as they differed across HLM models due to changing sample sizes.
b. This follows the procedure used in Lee and Smith (1997).

Notes

1. Roger G. Barker and Paul V. Gump, *Big School, Small School: High School Size and Student Behavior* (Stanford University Press, 1964).

2. James Coleman and Thomas Hoffer, *Public and Private High Schools: The Impact of Communities* (New York: Basic Books, 1987).

3. Valerie E. Lee and Julia B. Smith, "High School Size: Which Works Best and for Whom?" *Educational Evaluation and Policy Analysis* 19, no. 3 (1997): 205–28; Valerie E. Lee, "Using Hierarchical Linear Modeling to Study Social Contexts: The Case of School Effects," *Educational Psychologist* 35, no. 2 (2000): 125–41. The positive effects that Lee and Smith found were based on hierarchical linear modeling.

4. Joseph Kahne, Susan Sporte, and Marisa de la Torre, "Small Schools on a Large Scale: Comparing Teacher Contexts, Student Contexts, and Student Outcomes in CHSRI and Non-CHSRI Schools," paper presented at the Steering Committee Meeting of the Consortium on Chicago School Research, Chicago, January 2006; Emil J. Haller, David H. Monk, and Lydia T. Tien, "Small Schools and Higher Order Thinking Skills," *Journal of Research in Rural Education* (Fall 1993): 66–73; Patricia Wasley and others, *Small Schools: Great Strides: A Study of New Small Schools in Chicago* (New York: Bank Street College of Education, 2000); G. Alfred Hess and Solomon Cytrynbaum, "The Effort to Redesign Chicago High Schools: Effects on Schools and Achievement," in *Reforming Chicago's High Schools: Research Perspectives on School and System Level Change,* edited by Valerie Lee (Chicago: Consortium on Chicago School Research at the University of Chicago, 2002), pp. 19–49; Diane Ravitch, "Bill Gates, the Nation's Superintendent of Schools," *Los Angeles Times,* July 30, 2006.

5. Midwestern Regional Educational Laboratory, "Still at Risk: The U.S. High School," paper presented at "Research on Improving High Schools: A Forum for Advancing the Research Agenda," Washington, May 5, 2005.

6. See, for example, Paul R. Rosenbaum and Donald B. Rubin, "The Central Role of the Propensity Score in Observational Studies for Causal Effects," *Biometrika* 70, no. 1 (1983):41–55; Donald B. Rubin, "Using Multivariate Matched Sampling and Regression Adjustment to Control Bias in Observational Studies," *Journal of the American Statistical Association* 74 (1979): 318–28; and Donald B. Rubin and Neal Thomas, "Combining Propensity Score Matching with Additional Adjustments for Prognostic Covariates," *Journal of the American Statistical Association* 95 (2000): 573–85. The National Science Foundation (NSF) charged the American Educational Research Association (AERA) Grants Board to explore how observational studies can be used to evaluate various research designs for estimating causal effects: American Educational Research Association Grants Board, "Estimating Causal Effects Using Experimental and Observational Designs: A Think Tank White Paper" (San Francisco: AERA Grants Board, forthcoming).

7. Valerie Lee, "School Size and the Organization of Secondary Schools," in *Handbook of Sociology of Education,* edited by Maureen Hallinan (New York: Kluwer/Academic Plenum Publishers, 2000).

8. James B. Conant, *The American High School Today: A First Report to Interested Citizens* (New York: McGraw-Hill, 1959).

9. Lee and Smith, "High School Size," pp. 205–28.

10. Lee, "School Size and the Organization of Secondary Schools."

11. Ibid. See also Kathleen Cotton, "School Size, School Climate, and Student Performance," *Close-Up* 20 (Portland, Ore.: Northwest Regional Educational Laboratory, 1996) for an extensive review of research on small schools and their impact on student outcomes.

12. Barbara Schneider and David Stevenson, *The Ambitious Generation: America's Teenagers, Motivated but Directionless* (Yale University Press, 1999); David H. Kim and Barbara Schneider,

"Social Capital in Action: Alignment of Parental Support in Adolescents' Transition to Postsecondary Education," *Social Forces* 84, no. 2 (2006): 1181–1206.

13. Schneider and Stevenson, *The Ambitious Generation.*

14. Lee and Smith, "High School Size."

15. David L. Stevenson, "The Fit and Misfit of Sociological Research and Educational Policy," in *Handbook of the Sociology of Education,* edited by Hallinan.

16. Anthony S. Bryk and Barbara L. Schneider, *Trust in Schools: A Core Resource for Improvement* (New York: Russell Sage Foundation, 2002).

17. National Center for Education Statistics, Education Longitudinal Study of 2002 (U.S. Department of Education) (http://nces.ed.gov/surveys/els2002/ [October 26, 2006]).

18. National Center for Education Statistics, National Education Longitudinal Study of 1988 (U.S. Department of Education) (http://nces.ed.gov/surveys/nels88 [October 26, 2006]).

19. Arthur P. Dempster, Nan Laird, and Donald B. Rubin, "Maximum Likelihood from Incomplete Data via the EM Algorithm," *Journal of the Royal Statistical Society,* series B, vol. 39, no. 1 (1977):1–38. The EM algorithm is a general purpose iterative algorithm for computing maximum likelihood (ML) estimates for incomplete data. On each iteration of the algorithm, there is an expectation step (E-step) and a maximization step (M-step), and iterations continue until convergence is reached. This produces imputed values for the missing data.

20. Joseph L. Schafer, *Analysis of Incomplete Multivariate Data* (New York: Chapman and Hall, 1997); Roderick J. A. Little and Donald B. Rubin, *Statistical Analysis with Missing Data* (New York: John Wiley & Sons, 1987); Paul D. Allison, *Missing Data* (Thousand Oaks, Calif.: Sage, 2002).

21. Stephen W. Raudenbush and Anthony S. Bryk, *Hierarchical Linear Models: Applications and Data Analysis Methods* (Sage Publications, 2002); Lee, "Using Hierarchical Linear Modeling to Study Social Contexts."

22. Lee and Smith, "High School Size."

23. Ibid.

24. Our models are similar to those of Lee and Smith in "High School Size" but differ in the way that the dummy variables for the school size categories are defined. This difference was primarily due to the fact that we used the categorical variable for school size given in the ELS data set, whereas Lee and Smith constructed their own set of dummy variables from a continuous variable. We also did not use the weights that Lee and Smith used because our data set did not include students who were sampled in eighth grade and followed throughout high school.

25. Composite test scores and SES were fixed, as their slopes varied (nonrandomly) across the multinomial multilevel logistic models.

26. The construction of the variable for percentage of minority students and average SES of the school is identical to that in Lee and Smith, "High School Size." In the case of percent minority, a dummy variable was created that indicated whether a school had more than 40 percent minority students.

27. The variables representing composite test score and SES were grand mean centered to produce the adjusted school mean for each school. This is the standard centering recommended in Raudenbush and Bryk, *Hierarchical Linear Models.*

28. The lack of significant difference across school size may be a function of the coding of the dummy variables used in these analyses.

29. This strategy was used after it was determined that the original variable that contained nine categories resulted in a set of level-1 residuals that was not normally distributed. Several transformations of the original variable were performed, but the problem of lack of normality persisted.

30. The two categories representing students who expected to obtain less than a high school degree and students who expected to obtain a high school GED had very few members. Several different models were run. No statistical differences in the significance of coefficients were found

for whether they were included in the "don't know" category or the reference category. On that basis we included students who expected to obtain a high school GED in the reference category and those who expected to obtain less than a high school degree in the "don't know" category.

31. Rosenbaum and Rubin, "The Central Role of the Propensity Score in Observational Studies for Causal Effects."

32. This optimal size category is slightly different from the one suggested by Lee and Smith in "High School Size," but it is consistent with the theoretically ideal small-school size.

33. Please contact the authors for a list of the covariates used in these analyses.

34. We also tried matching on student and family characteristics only and on student and family characteristics including student motivation, extracurricular activities, and student employment. We found that matching only on student and family characteristics did not provide sufficient balance. However, matching on demographics, student motivation, extracurricular activities, and student employment did provide balance.

35. The differences of means across the stratum were not different in 95 percent of the cases. That is what is expected, assuming a 5 percent error rate, because 5 percent of the means will differ by chance alone.

36. We use weighted least squares (WLS) to estimate the overall treatment effects because it was determined that there was heteroscedasticity across the different groups. In these cases, conclusions based on OLS estimates are not minimum variance and the overall significance of the result cannot be adequately determined from the estimates. WLS is a common solution to this problem when the variances can be estimated, as was done with these data.

37. It is important to note here that these comparisons of uncertainty are different from those discussed in the previous model—that is, here the "don't know" response is based on a variable that is different from the one in the models in table 9. The comparison in this case is to "definitely going to college (yes)" versus the other two categories.

School Consolidation and Inequality

CHRISTOPHER BERRY

One of the most remarkable yet least remarked upon accomplishments in American public education in the twentieth century is the success of the school consolidation movement. Between 1930 and 1970, nine out of every ten school districts were eliminated through consolidation. Nearly two-thirds of schools that existed in 1930 were gone by 1970. These and related reforms transformed the small, informal, community-controlled schools of the nineteenth century into centralized, professionally run educational bureaucracies. The American public school system as we know it was born during this brief, dynamic period. While school consolidation represents what may be the most profound reform movement in twentieth-century education, almost nothing is known about its consequences for students.

In earlier work on the consolidation movement, Martin West and I found that students educated in systems with larger schools earn significantly lower wages as adults.[1] Like many others who have studied the relationship between school attributes and student outcomes, we focused our attention on *average* outcomes. However, there is good reason to suspect that school consolidation influenced the *variation* in student outcomes as well. In particular, by dramatically cutting the number of schools and districts, consolidation reduced an important source of between-school and between-district variation in educational quality. At the same time, however, consolidation was motivated by a desire to increase instructional specialization, which could be achieved by substantially increasing the size of schools and districts. Thus within-school and within-district variation in education quality may have risen as schools and districts became larger and instruction more specialized. This paper investigates

The author is grateful to Jens Ludwig, Marcos Rangel, and Martin West for helpful comments.

the relationship between changes in school and district size and variation in student outcomes, as measured by adult wage inequality.

The paper is organized as follows. The first section provides background information on the consolidation movement and related trends in the organization of public education. The second reviews the related literature about the effect of school and district size on student outcomes and about the contribution of education to wage inequality. The third describes the estimation strategy and data. The fourth section presents the results of the analysis, and a final section concludes.

Background: The School Consolidation Movement

The movement for school consolidation must be seen as part of a larger trend toward the professionalization of education that began in the late nineteenth century.[2] To the "administrative progressives" of the time, the concentration of authority over schooling in the hands of professional educators was seen as a cure for both the corruption of city school systems and the parochialism of rural systems. Consolidation came first to urban areas, where one of the cornerstones of the progressive attack on rule by political machines was the formal organization of schooling under the leadership of professional superintendents. Reformers then turned their attention to rural areas, where they decried the inefficient, unprofessional, and "backward" practices of small community schools. In their vision of a professionally run school, reformers drew their inspiration from the modern corporation, with its principles of "scientific" management by experts.

At the center of this reform movement was a push for larger schools. The leading education reformer of the early twentieth century, Ellwood P. Cubberley, pressed three primary arguments in favor of school consolidation.[3] First, in small schools, many of which had only one teacher, the ratio of administrators and school officials to teachers was unnecessarily high. Larger schools allowed for more efficient, centralized administration. Second, at a time when many small schools did not even divide children by grade level, consolidation held the promise of highly specialized instruction. Teachers in large schools could specialize not only by grade but also by subject area. In addition, reformers sought to provide specialized training to students destined for different roles in the labor force. Third, a consolidated school could provide better facilities at lower cost. For instance, Cubberley's plan for a model elementary school building included—in addition to classrooms—a manual training room,

Figure 1. Number of Public Schools, 1869–1999[a]

Number of schools (thousands)

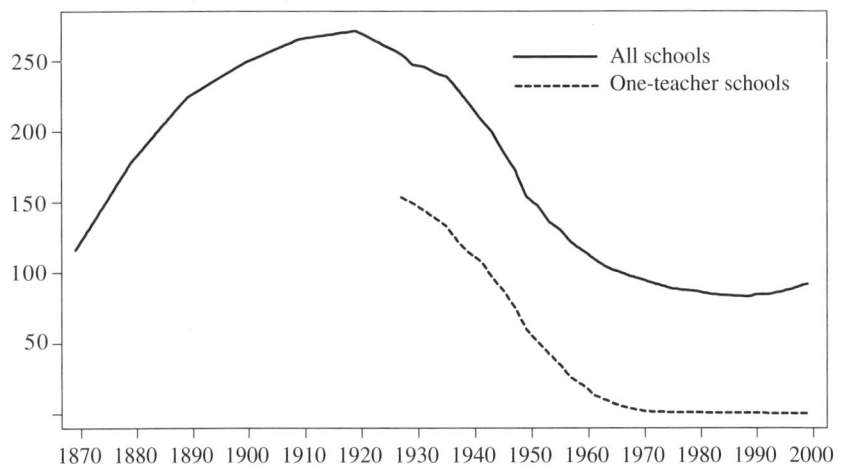

[Graph showing number of all schools and one-teacher schools from 1870 to 2000]

Source: Data for years before 1960, *Biennial Survey of Education*; data for 1960 onward, *Digest of Education Statistics*.
a. Data for one-teacher schools only available after 1927.

a library, an assembly hall, a domestic science room, and a science laboratory.[4] Supporting these facilities required the concentration of students and resources. In sum, consolidated schools, in the view of Cubberley and other reformers, provided economies of scale in administration, instruction, and facilities.

The success of Cubberley and his progressive colleagues can be seen in the precipitous decline in the number of U.S. schools beginning in the 1920s, as shown in figure 1.[5] After proliferating since the founding of the first colonies, the number of public schools reached a peak of 217,000 in 1920. The number of schools declined rapidly over the succeeding fifty years. The pace of decline slowed in the 1970s, and the number of schools reached a nadir in the late 1980s at around 83,000. Also notable over the period was a pronounced shift away from one-teacher schools. In 1927, the first year for which data on one-teacher schools are available, they composed 60 percent of all public schools. By 1970, one-teacher schools had all but died out; only about 400 remained in 1999.

While schools were being consolidated, the number of pupils in attendance was on the rise. Average daily attendance (ADA) in public elementary and secondary schools roughly doubled from 1929 to 1969, rising from approximately 21 million to 42 million.[6] The dwindling number of schools, coupled with rising attendance, led average school size to expand dramatically during the middle twentieth century. Figure 2 shows the average size of schools over the period for

Figure 2. Average School Size, 1869–1999

Average daily attendance per school (thousands)

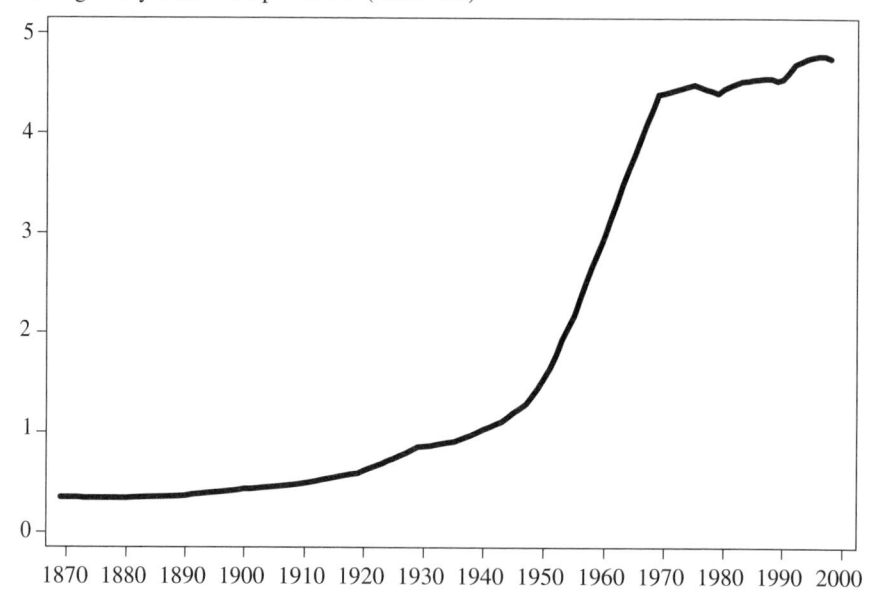

Source: Data for years before 1960, *Biennial Survey of Education*; data for 1960 onward, *Digest of Education Statistics*.

which data are available. During the period of rapid consolidation, 1930 to 1970, ADA per school increased from 87 to 440. In other words, the average school was five times larger in 1970 than in 1930. Schools witnessed their most rapid burst of growth in the years from 1950 to 1970, as increasing attendance rates, the baby boom, and institutional consolidation coincided.

The desire to consolidate schools was linked directly with the necessity to consolidate districts. It was the general opinion of Cubberley and other reformers of the day that one consolidated school should be created in place of five to seven existing schools, on average.[7] The average school district at the time, however, had only two schools, and most districts in rural areas operated only a single school. Thus consolidating five to seven schools usually would require consolidating school districts as well. In Cubberley's view, therefore, the district system of school governance was "the real root of the matter." He contended, "To have a fully organized school board in every little school district in a county, a board endowed by law with important financial and educational powers is wholly unnecessary from any business or educational point of view and is more likely to prevent progressive action than to secure it."[8] A central aim of the consolidation movement, therefore, was to change the gov-

Figure 3. Number of School Districts, 1931–99

Number of school districts (thousands)

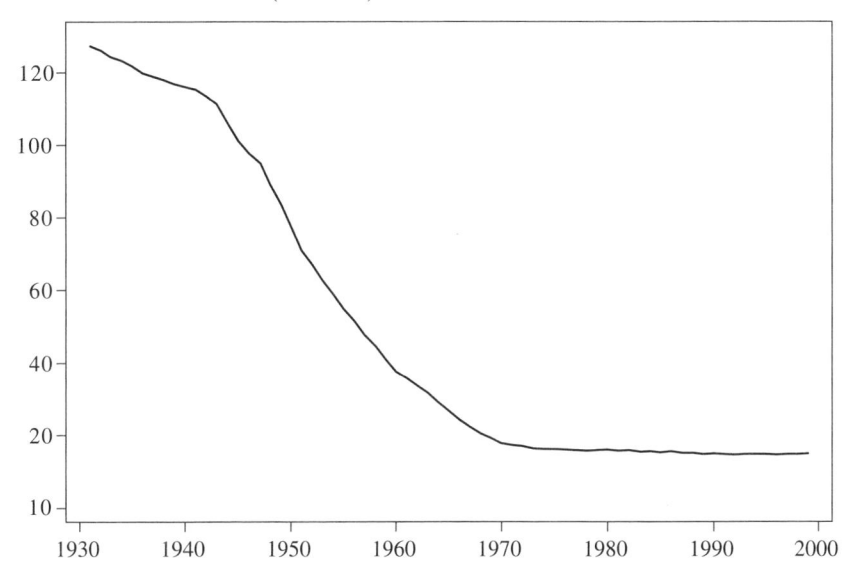

Source: Data for years before 1960, *Biennial Survey of Education*; data for 1960 onward, *Digest of Education Statistics*.

ernance of education, placing authority at higher levels, such as township, county, or state governments.

For these reasons, the consolidation of districts ran apace with the consolidation of schools, as indicated in figure 3. The informal nature of school districts early in the twentieth century is evidenced by the fact that many states did not even keep a count of the number of districts prior to 1930.[9] The 1931–32 edition of the *Biennial Survey of Education* was the first to report statistics of school districts in each state.[10] As figure 3 shows, the data soon revealed a decline in the number of districts. The number of districts fell by half between 1931 and 1953, as more than 60,000 districts were dissolved by consolidation. The number of districts declined by half again between 1953 and 1963 and roughly half again between 1963 and 1973. The number of districts stabilized in the early 1970s and has not changed appreciably over the last thirty years. Coupled with rising attendance, ADA per school district increased from approximately 170 to 2,300 students between 1930 and 1970, an increase of fourteen times, as shown in figure 4.

State governments took an active role in consolidation. Professional educators linked to state departments of education often spearheaded initiatives to

Figure 4. Average District Size, 1931–99

Average daily attendance per district (thousands)

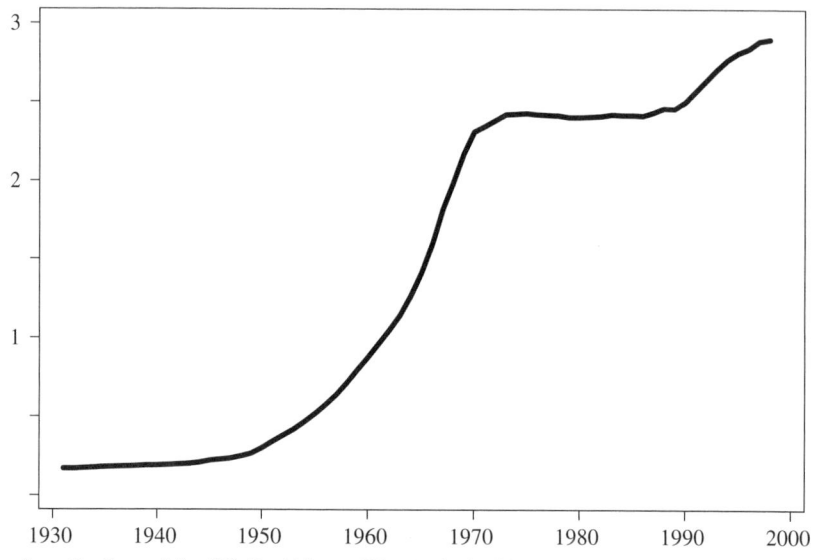

Source: Data for years before 1960, *Biennial Survey of Education*; data for 1960 onward, *Digest of Education Statistics*.

consolidate local schools, as part of broader efforts to expand state control over public education. Although local resistance to consolidation was often fierce, state governments induced consolidation through fiscal incentives or forced consolidation by legislatively redrawing district boundaries.[11] Gradually, local control over education was weakened by the elimination of most locally elected school boards, and the authority of the remaining boards was eroded as state governments gradually extended their authority over previously locally controlled issues, such as accreditation, curriculum, and teacher certification.[12] In short, as schools became larger, school boards became more distant from local communities and lost authority relative to professional administrators and state government officials.

The expanding role of state governments in public education is demonstrated by the rapid centralization of school funding that occurred over the same period. As demonstrated in figure 5, the state share of funding for public education grew considerably from about 1930 to 1950 and made a smaller jump again in the late 1970s. The local share of revenue, meanwhile, declined from more than 80 percent early in the century to less than half by the mid-1970s. For about the last twenty-five years, state and local governments have contributed nearly equal shares of public education funding. The federal share

Figure 5. Sources of Public Education Funding, 1919–98

Share of revenue (percent)

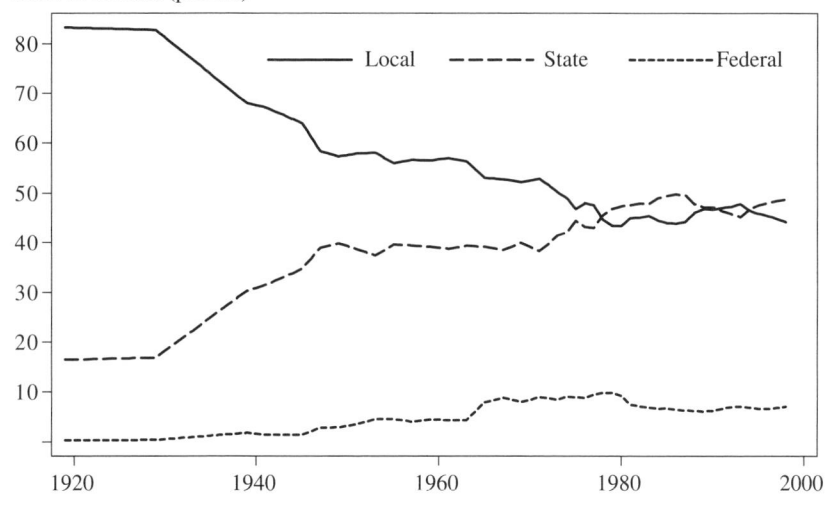

[Figure: Line graph showing Local, State, and Federal shares of public education funding from 1920 to 2000. Local share declines from ~83% in 1920 to ~45% by 2000; State share rises from ~17% to ~48%; Federal share remains below 10% throughout.]

Source: Data for years before 1960, *Biennial Survey of Education*; data for 1960 onward, *Digest of Education Statistics.*

of education funding has risen noticeably from its starting point of next to nothing in 1920 but still remains at less than 10 percent.

The aim of this paper is to investigate the impact of institutional changes associated with the school consolidation movement on the variance of student outcomes, as measured by wages. Theoretically, the consolidation movement would appear to have had two, possibly countervailing, effects on the within-state variance in educational quality. On the one hand, by greatly reducing the number of independent districts and individual schools, consolidation should have increased the uniformity of education received within states. That is, by creating ever larger districts and schools, consolidation should have reduced between-district and between-school variation in educational quality. On the other hand, one of the reformers' avowed motives for creating larger schools and districts was to facilitate the specialization of instruction within schools. Whereas a small one-room school provided essentially the same educational experience for every student, large consolidated schools could tailor instruction to students' age, ability, interest, and career track. Thus the consolidation movement presents a trade-off between reduced between-school and between-district variation in education and increased within-school and within-district variation. Although available data do not permit a separate analysis of these two components of variation, the remainder of the paper attempts to assess the net effect of consolidation on the variation in students' adult wages.

Related Literature

I am not aware of any existing study of school consolidation and the variance of student outcomes. The topic, however, is at the intersection of two large related literatures: one on the effects of school quality on average student outcomes, the other on the relationship between educational attainment and wage inequality. The school quality literature is too vast and controversial to review in any detail here.[13] Rather, I focus on a handful of studies dealing specifically with school and district size. The most closely related study is by Berry and West, who investigate the effects of changing school and district size associated with consolidation on average adult wages for white men born between 1920 and 1949.[14] Using several different identification strategies, the authors find that students educated in systems with larger schools earn significantly lower wages as adults. They focus on mean wages and do not investigate the variance in outcomes.

Andrews, Duncombe, and Yinger review the literature on school and district size for more recent cohorts.[15] Of the seven studies of school size and student performance reviewed by these authors, only one, by Kenny, finds increasing returns to scale.[16] The remaining six studies find decreasing returns to scale. Four of these studies also identify constant returns to scale over at least some range of the data, suggesting that returns to scale in school size are nonlinear. Summers and Wolfe find that African American students are particularly harmed by large school size, while Lee and Smith find that students of low socioeconomic status do particularly poorly in large schools.[17] Both of these results imply a positive relationship between school size and the variation in student outcomes, although this relationship is not the focus of either paper. Although the reasons for the superior performance of small schools have not been definitively identified, explanations have focused on nonacademic factors, such as greater sense of community belonging among students, closer interaction with adults, and greater parental involvement.[18]

The empirical literature on the effects of *district* size on student outcomes is smaller and less consistent in its findings. Two studies—one by Walberg and Fowler and one by Ferguson—find a negative relationship between student achievement and district size, controlling for student and teacher characteristics, in New Jersey and Texas, respectively.[19] In contrast, Sebold and Dato find increasing returns to district size for California high schools, while Ferguson and Ladd find increasing returns to district size for elementary schools in Alabama.[20] Unfortunately, as each of these studies focuses on a different state, it is difficult to identify the reasons for the discrepancies in their conclusions. Hoxby takes a different approach, focusing on competition among districts rather than size per se.[21] In a study of metropolitan areas nationwide, she finds a negative relationship between student achievement and the concentration of enrollment in a small number of school districts.

A second branch of related literature examines the growth in wage inequality beginning in the 1970s. This extensive literature is reviewed by Levy and Murnane and by Katz and Autor.[22] A central theme is that wage differentials by education have increased dramatically—in particular the college–high school wage premium—and represent an important component of overall increases in wage inequality.[23] At the same time, however, residual wage inequality—that is, wage dispersion within groups of workers with the same level of education and experience—has also increased substantially and accounts for a large part of the total increase in wage inequality.[24] While Katz and Autor suggest variation in school quality as a potential explanation for growing wage inequality, I am not aware of any study that tests this proposition directly.[25] Thus, while education plays a prominent role in the inequality literature, no one has yet provided evidence of a connection between school quality and wage inequality, much less a relationship between the school consolidation movement and inequality.

Empirical Strategy and Data

The basic question of this paper is whether there is a relationship between the institutional changes associated with the school consolidation movement and the variance in student outcomes. Direct measures of academic performance, such as standardized test scores, are not available across states for the period under investigation. Instead, I rely on students' adult wages as the measure of performance. To the extent that the labor market rewards educational quality, variation in wages for students educated in school systems with different institutional characteristics, all else equal, should reflect variation in school quality associated with those characteristics. By the same token, the inequality in wages for students educated in different school systems should reflect the unevenness of educational quality within those systems, holding other factors constant.

I use data from the Public Use Microdata Sample (PUMS), A Sample, of the 1980 census.[26] Cases are restricted to white men born in the forty-eight mainland states between 1920 and 1949, which produces a sample of 994,000 individuals.[27] The analysis proceeds in two stages. In the first, I divide the sample into state-of-birth by year-of-birth cells. With forty-eight states by thirty years of birth, this yields 1,440 cells. The average cell size is 688 observations; the median is 485. The largest cell has 5,100 observations; the smallest has 17, and 90 percent of cells have at least 110 observations.[28] Within each cell, I compute four measures of inequality: the standard deviation of log weekly wages, the difference between the ninetieth and the tenth percentile of the log weekly wage distribution, the difference between the ninetieth and the fiftieth percentile, and the difference between the fiftieth and the tenth percentile. The first two indexes reflect overall variation in wages; the 90-50 differential reflects variation at the upper end of the distribution, while the 50-10 differential reflects variation at the lower end.[29]

The average value of each of these inequality measures across states is presented by year-of-birth in table 1. Clearly, wage inequality increases steadily with age, as those born most recently have the lowest level of wage inequality across all four measures. Certainly much of this pattern is explained by growing wage dispersion with age and experience. The second-stage analysis seeks to determine whether any of the difference in average inequality across birth-years can be associated with differences in school characteristics related to consolidation. In other words, is any of the reduction in wage variation among men educated more recently attributable to the fact that they generally were educated in larger schools, within larger districts, with more centralized funding?

In the second stage, these indexes of inequality are regressed against average school size, average district size, and state share of funding for education. All of the school attributes are derived from the *Biennial Survey of Education*. For each cell, the quality measures are averaged over the years in which someone born in a given year would have been in school, assuming a starting school age of six and allowing for a maximum of twelve years in public school. So, for instance, the cell of individuals born in Ohio in 1930 would be matched with the average school characteristics in Ohio from 1936 to 1947.[30] The second-stage models also include state-of-birth and year-of-birth fixed effects. Identification in the second-stage models is thus based on variation within states over time in the deviation from the national level of inequality for a given year of birth. Cells are weighted by sample size, and standard errors are clustered by state of birth.

Using this method, differences in wage inequality associated with school quality could arise for two reasons. First, a given attribute of a state's school system might affect the variation in educational attainment. Second, a given attribute might affect the variation in the return to a year of education. Either

Table 1. Average Within-State Wage Inequality, by Year of Birth[a]

Year of birth	Standard deviation of log wage	90-10	90-50	50-10
1920	0.587	1.373	0.635	0.739
1921	0.577	1.355	0.629	0.726
1922	0.573	1.333	0.622	0.711
1923	0.576	1.342	0.625	0.717
1924	0.563	1.319	0.625	0.694
1925	0.566	1.311	0.603	0.708
1926	0.565	1.308	0.606	0.702
1927	0.565	1.321	0.614	0.706
1928	0.556	1.297	0.609	0.689
1929	0.557	1.296	0.604	0.692
1930	0.551	1.277	0.592	0.685
1931	0.543	1.263	0.584	0.679
1932	0.549	1.274	0.587	0.687
1933	0.545	1.260	0.588	0.672
1934	0.543	1.258	0.587	0.671
1935	0.546	1.263	0.580	0.682
1936	0.539	1.234	0.567	0.667
1937	0.532	1.215	0.563	0.652
1938	0.530	1.218	0.567	0.651
1939	0.530	1.209	0.551	0.658
1940	0.529	1.206	0.556	0.650
1941	0.518	1.185	0.542	0.643
1942	0.521	1.177	0.535	0.642
1943	0.515	1.168	0.524	0.644
1944	0.516	1.168	0.511	0.657
1945	0.505	1.142	0.496	0.646
1946	0.505	1.138	0.484	0.654
1947	0.499	1.129	0.481	0.647
1948	0.495	1.119	0.481	0.639
1949	0.494	1.122	0.478	0.644
Total	0.534	1.226	0.556	0.670

Source: Data are from the 1980 PUMS.
a. Observations represent state-of-birth by year-of-birth cells for white men born in the forty-eight mainland states between 1920 and 1949. Each row provides the average of the forty-eight state-level inequality measures, weighted by sample size. Inequality measures are based on log weekly wages.

of these effects would influence the within-cell variation in observed wages. In an effort to disentangle effects on educational attainment from effects on the return to education, I present an additional analysis based on state-of-birth by educational attainment cells. Specifically, I divide the sample into four educational classes: those with less than twelve years of education, those with exactly twelve years, those with thirteen to fifteen years, and those with sixteen or more years of education. In order to prevent cells from becoming too small, I use ten-year birth cohorts rather than individual year-of-birth cells; that is, cohort one, born 1920–29; cohort two, born 1930–39; and cohort three, born 1940–49. This approach produces 576 cells for each cohort for state-of-birth by education class, with an average size of 1,719 and median size of 1,055. Finding a relationship between school attributes and within–education class wage inequality would suggest that the effect of school quality on wage inequality operates at least partly through the return to education.

The average value of each of these inequality measures across states is presented by education class and cohort-of-birth in table 2. An interesting finding is that there is no apparent difference in inequality between the older and younger cohorts for the least-educated group of workers. Again, the second stage of analysis seeks to ascertain whether any of the within-education group differences in inequality across cohorts can be attributed to differences in school characteristics associated with consolidation.

As discussed above, school consolidation must be seen as part of a broader movement of educational reform. Over the same period, for example, the school term grew longer and class sizes grew smaller. In a related paper, Card and Krueger argue that these measures of school quality exert a positive effect on returns to education for the same cohort of men observed in the 1980 PUMS.[31] Although the authors do not investigate the effects of these school quality measures on wage inequality, I include class size and term length in the models estimated below to eliminate this potential source of omitted variable bias. State average measures of term length and the ADA-based ratio of pupils to teachers over time are derived from the *Biennial Survey of Education*.[32] In addition, to control for the state's resources, I include state per capita income and percent of the state's population that is rural.[33] The annual income data are from the Regional Economic Information System of the Bureau of Economic Analysis, and the percent rural is from the decennial census, with linear interpolation for intervening years. Each of the control variables is averaged over the years an individual with a given year of birth could have been in school, as described above.

Summary statistics for the state-of-birth by year-of-birth cells and for the state-of-birth by cohort-of-birth cells are presented in table 3.

Results

Table 4 presents models of the standard deviation of the log weekly wage within state-of-birth by year-of-birth cells. The quality attributes are introduced individually and then jointly, with percent rural, per capita income, and state-

Table 2. Average Within-State Wage Inequality, by Education Class and Birth Cohort[a]

Years of education and birth cohort	Standard deviation of log wage	Percentile of log wage distribution		
		90-10	90-50	50-10
Less than 12 years				
1920–29	0.525	1.199	0.513	0.686
1930–39	0.518	1.204	0.508	0.696
1940–49	0.528	1.251	0.537	0.713
Total	0.524	1.214	0.518	0.696
Exactly 12 years				
1920–29	0.504	1.117	0.470	0.647
1930–39	0.471	1.034	0.442	0.593
1940–49	0.463	1.036	0.437	0.600
Total	0.476	1.057	0.447	0.610
13 to 15 years				
1920–29	0.550	1.251	0.574	0.677
1930–39	0.507	1.142	0.516	0.626
1940–49	0.488	1.088	0.465	0.623
Total	0.506	1.137	0.502	0.635
16 or more years				
1920–29	0.580	1.370	0.665	0.705
1930–39	0.538	1.229	0.617	0.612
1940–49	0.524	1.173	0.553	0.619
Total	0.540	1.230	0.594	0.635

Source: Data are from the 1980 PUMS.
a. Observations represent state-of-birth by cohort-of-birth by education group cells for white men born in the forty-eight mainland states between 1920 and 1949. Each row provides the average of the forty-eight state-level inequality measures, weighted by sample size. Inequality measures are based on log weekly wages.

of-birth and year-of-birth effects used as controls in all the models. Of the five school-quality variables examined, only term length demonstrates a significant relationship with wage inequality. The results also indicate that individuals from cells with a larger rural population have greater variation in adult wage inequality. However, the relationship between ruralness and wage inequality is no longer significant when term length is included. It is not surprising that there is a significant correlation between term length and percent rural across cells of −0.61, an indication that school terms historically are shorter in states with more rural populations. It appears from equations 5 and 6 of table 4 that term length, rather than ruralness per se, is related to wage inequality. One interpretation of this result is that longer average terms result from a reduction in the differential between rural and urban terms, with a resulting decrease in the associated adult wage differential. Substantively, the effect of term length on

Table 3. Summary Statistics[a]

Variable	Mean	Median	Standard deviation	Minimum	Maximum
State-of-birth by year-of-birth data					
Standard deviation of log wages x 100	53.40	53.07	3.92	39.96	87.97
90-10 wage differential	1.23	1.21	0.12	0.71	2.38
90-50 wage differential	0.56	0.55	0.07	0.23	1.21
50-10 wage differential	0.67	0.66	0.07	0.39	1.66
Average ADA per school[b]	211.37	189.05	120.33	25.51	562.02
Average ADA per district[b]	1,626.18	694.32	2,500.85	31.91	23,721.21
State share of education funding	0.35	0.36	0.16	0.01	0.91
Average ADA per teacher	24.65	24.88	2.79	14.40	32.37
Average term length	177.12	178.29	6.57	135.38	187.29
Percent rural population	0.38	0.33	0.18	0.08	0.83
Income per capita (1967 dollars)[c]	1,981.71	2,016.20	634.95	425.25	3,326.11
State-of-birth by cohort-of-birth data					
Standard deviation of log wages x 100	53.71	53.55	3.10	47.98	61.91
90-10 wage differential	1.24	1.23	0.10	1.04	1.48
90-50 wage differential	0.56	0.55	0.06	0.46	0.69
50-10 wage differential	0.68	0.67	0.05	0.57	0.85
Average ADA per school[b]	211.37	178.97	116.85	25.86	512.50
Average ADA per district[b]	1,626.18	722.71	2,483.15	32.79	19,730.08
State share of education funding	35.36	35.19	16.27	1.12	90.70
Average ADA per teacher	24.65	24.89	2.77	14.60	31.76
Average term length	177.12	178.61	6.43	138.86	186.91
Percent rural population	0.38	0.33	0.18	0.08	0.81
Income per capita (1967 dollars)[c]	1,981.71	2,002.74	617.34	537.94	3,098.74

Source: Data sources are described in the appendix.
a. Cells are weighted by sample size.
b. In the analyses in the text, school and district size are expressed as the natural log of ADA in thousands.
c. In the analyses in the text, per capita income is expressed in thousands of constant 1967 dollars.

inequality is modest, with the coefficient in model 6 indicating that a 1 standard deviation increase in term length is associated with a decrease of about one-eighth (0.121) of a standard deviation in wage inequality.

Income per capita also becomes statistically significant when term length is controlled for in models 5 and 6. Individuals from cells with higher income during their school years demonstrate lower wage inequality as adults. The effect of income is substantial, with the coefficient in equation 6 indicating that a 1 standard deviation increase in per capita income is associated with nearly a 0.5 standard deviation decline in adult wage inequality. In addition, class size is marginally significant in the omnibus model 6, with a negative coefficient suggesting that smaller classes are associated with greater wage inequality. The negative relationship between class size and inequality may result from increased sorting of students by ability in school systems with smaller classes,

Table 4. Standard Deviation of Log Wage, State-of-Birth by Year-of-Birth Cells[a]

Variable	(1)	(2)	(3)	(4)	(5)	(6)
School size	0.0092 (0.5556)					-0.2345 (0.7598)
District size		0.2651 (0.2220)				0.4009 (0.2795)
State share of funding			-1.4654 (2.5752)			-0.0625 (2.3894)
Pupil-teacher ratio				-0.1401 (0.1129)		-0.1837* (0.1067)
Term length					-0.064*** (0.022)	-0.072*** (0.023)
Percent rural	6.892*** (2.329)	7.198*** (2.111)	6.952*** (2.290)	5.808*** (2.182)	2.618 (2.603)	0.858 (2.597)
Income per capita	-1.5508 (1.4760)	-1.7529 (1.3610)	-1.6520 (1.3869)	-1.4167 (1.3744)	-2.8420* (1.4889)	-3.0325** (1.4071)
Number of observations	1,440	1,440	1,440	1,440	1,440	1,440
R^2	0.64	0.64	0.64	0.64	0.64	0.64

Source: Wage data are from the 1980 PUMS, school characteristics are from the *Biennial Survey of Education*, percent rural is from the census, and income per capita is from the Bureau of Economic Analysis. Data sources are described further in the data appendix.
* Significant at the 10 percent level.
** Significant at the 5 percent level.
*** Significant at the 1 percent level.
a. Observations represent state-of-birth by year-of-birth cells for white men born in the forty-eight mainland states between 1920 and 1949. The dependent variable is the within-cell standard deviation of log weekly wages in 1979 multiplied by 100. Observations are weighted by sample size. All models include state-of-birth and year-of-birth fixed effects. Robust standard errors, with clustering on state of birth, are reported in parentheses. The independent variables are state-of-birth specific averages over the years in which an individual born in a given year could have been in school, assuming a school starting age of six and a maximum of twelve years of schooling. School size and district size are measured as the log of average daily attendance in thousands. Income per capita is measured in thousands of constant 1967 dollars.

although I have no direct evidence that this is the case for the period under consideration here. Finally, it is worth noting that the variables included in the model explain relatively little of the total variation in wage inequality across cells. A model including only state-of-birth and year-of-birth dummies (not shown) yields an R^2 of 0.631. Meanwhile, model 6, which includes all quality variables and controls, yields an R^2 of 0.642.

Table 5 presents models of three additional measures of inequality based on differentials between percentiles of the within-cell log wage distribution. The 90-10 differential captures overall wage inequality, and in this model term length, income, and class size all demonstrate negative effects, consistent with the results from table 4. Term length appears to exert its effect primarily at the

Table 5. Log Wage Percentiles, State-of-Birth by Year-of-Birth Cells[a]

	Percentile of log wage distribution		
Variable	90-10	90-50	50-10
School size	0.0267	0.0086	0.0181
	(0.0237)	(0.0151)	(0.0181)
District size	0.0011	-0.0064	0.0075
	(0.0098)	(0.0064)	(0.0064)
State share of funding	-0.0715	-0.0546	-0.0169
	(0.0731)	(0.0461)	(0.0607)
Pupil-teacher ratio	-0.0065*	-0.0020	-0.0045*
	(0.0038)	(0.0024)	(0.0024)
Term length	-0.0024***	-0.0007	-0.0017***
	(0.0009)	(0.0007)	(0.0006)
Percent rural	0.0449	-0.1835**	0.2284***
	(0.1061)	(0.0760)	(0.0683)
Income per capita	-0.1266**	-0.0581*	-0.0685*
	(0.0495)	(0.0333)	(0.0364)
Number of observations	1,440	1,440	1,440
R^2	0.64	0.67	0.33

Source: Wage data are from the 1980 PUMS, school characteristics are from the *Biennial Survey of Education*, percent rural is from the census, and income per capita is from the Bureau of Economic Analysis. Data sources are described further in the appendix.
* Significant at the 10 percent level.
** Significant at the 5 percent level.
*** Significant at the 1 percent level.
a. Observations represent state-of-birth by year-of-birth cells for white men born in the forty-eight mainland states between 1920 and 1949. The dependent variables are differences between percentiles of the within-cell log weekly wage distribution. Observations are weighted by sample size. All models include state-of-birth and year-of-birth fixed effects. Robust standard errors, with clustering on state of birth, are reported in parentheses. The independent variables are state-of-birth specific averages over the years in which an individual born in a given year could have been in school, assuming a school starting age of six and a maximum of twelve years of schooling. School size and district size are measured as the log of average daily attendance in thousands. Income per capita is measured in thousands of constant 1967 dollars.

lower end of the wage distribution, as its coefficient for the 50-10 differential is larger and highly significant, whereas for the 90-50 differential it is not. In other words, longer terms are associated with less variation at the low end of the wage distribution, perhaps because the increases in term length are concentrated in rural areas. Income per capita, meanwhile, appears to have roughly equivalent effects throughout the wage distribution. An interesting finding is that the percent rural variable produces a significant, positive coefficient in the 50-10 equation and a significant, negative coefficient in the 90-50 equation. Apparently, individuals from cells with larger rural populations experience greater wage variation at the low end of the distribution, but less variation at the top end, as adults.

Overall, the results of tables 4 and 5 do not provide much evidence of a connection between the school consolidation movement and variation in student outcomes, as measured by adult wages. Of the school-quality variables examined, only term length exhibits a strongly significant relationship with wage inequality, with class size demonstrating a marginally significant association. Neither term length nor class size is necessarily related to consolidation, although changes in them tend to occur contemporaneously with consolidation, as explained above.

The models in tables 4 and 5 can be thought of as reduced-form models, in that they subsume effects operating through both changes in educational attainment and changes in the return to education. In other words, increasing term length may reduce wage variation by either reducing the variation in completed years of education or by reducing the variation in the return to a year of education. In order to untangle these two effects, the next series of models examines wage variation within cells defined by educational attainment. Four education categories are examined: less than twelve years of education, exactly twelve years of education, thirteen to fifteen years of education, and sixteen or more years of education. Within each education category, I compute wage variation within state-of-birth by cohort-of-birth cells, where cohorts are defined as those born from 1920 to 1929, from 1930 to 1939, and from 1940 to 1949. For each educational group, therefore, 144 cells represent three cohorts by forty-eight states of birth. Tables 6 through 9 present models of each of the four measures of log wage inequality for each educational class.

Models of wage inequality for men with less than a high school degree are presented in table 6. Term length again shows a negative relationship with wage inequality and is significant in all of the models except the one for the 90-50 wage differential. Even in the lowest education group, then, the effects of increasing term length are concentrated at the bottom of the wage distribution. School size is significant for the first time and also demonstrates a negative relationship with wage inequality. In other words, men of low education from states and cohorts with larger schools experience diminished wage inequality. For example, a 1 standard deviation increase in school size is associated with a 0.5 standard deviation reduction in the 90-10 log wage differential. District size, however, appears to work in the opposite direction, as the coefficient indicates that a 1 standard deviation increase in district size is associated with a 0.5 standard deviation *increase* in the 90-10 wage differential among this category of men with less than a high school degree.

For those with a high school degree and those with some college, presented in tables 7 and 8, respectively, term length consistently demonstrates a significant, negative relationship with wage inequality, with disproportionate effects for the 50-10 wage differential. School size and district size, while retaining, respectively, their negative and positive signs, do not attain statistical signifi-

Table 6. Log Wage Inequality, Less than High School Degree, State-of-Birth by Cohort-of-Birth Cells[a]

Variable	Standard deviation of log wage	Percentile of log wage distribution		
		90-10	90-50	50-10
School size	-2.5969*	-0.0899**	-0.0568**	-0.0332
	(1.5105)	(0.0406)	(0.0251)	(0.0331)
District size	1.4462***	0.0388***	0.0140	0.0247**
	(0.4891)	(0.0132)	(0.0090)	(0.0103)
State share of funding	0.0505	0.0015*	0.0005	0.0010
	(0.0308)	(0.0009)	(0.0006)	(0.0008)
Pupil-teacher ratio	-0.1013	0.0017	0.0030	-0.0013
	(0.1606)	(0.0049)	(0.0031)	(0.0034)
Term length	-0.0956**	-0.0035**	-0.0008	-0.0028***
	(0.0443)	(0.0016)	(0.0011)	(0.0008)
Percent rural	17.0653***	0.3410**	0.0172	0.3238***
	(5.4168)	(0.1576)	(0.1045)	(0.1013)
Income per capita	0.8148	0.0712	-0.0398	0.1110*
	(2.1235)	(0.0680)	(0.0493)	(0.0639)
Number of observations	144	144	144	144
R^2	0.37	0.41	0.28	0.36

Source: Wage data are from the 1980 PUMS, school characteristics are from the *Biennial Survey of Education*, percent rural is from the census, and income per capita is from the Bureau of Economic Analysis. Data sources are described further in the data appendix.
* Significant at the 10 percent level.
** Significant at the 5 percent level.
*** Significant at the 1 percent level.
a. Observations represent forty-eight state-of-birth by three cohort-of-birth cells for white men born in the forty-eight mainland states between 1920 and 1949. The three cohorts are composed of men born from 1920 to 1929, 1930 to 1939, and 1940 to 1949. The dependent variables are standard deviations and differences between percentiles of the within-cell log weekly wage distribution. Observations are weighted by sample size. All models include state-of-birth and cohort-of-birth fixed effects. Robust standard errors, with clustering on state of birth, are reported in parentheses. The independent variables are state-of-birth specific averages over the years in which an individual born in a given cohort could have been in school, assuming a school starting age of six and a maximum of twelve years of schooling. School size and district size are measured as the log of average daily attendance in thousands. Income per capita is measured in thousands of constant 1967 dollars.

cance at conventional levels for any of the models in tables 7 and 8. The consolidation-related variables thus demonstrate no relationship with educational inequality for the modal educational group, high school graduates, or for individuals with some college.

Results for men with sixteen or more years of education are presented in table 9. Term length proves to be negative and significant in every model, consistent with findings for the other education groups. School size shows a negative effect for the 50-10 differential, but a positive effect for the 90-50 differential, although only the latter is significant. The positive relationship between school size and the 90-50 differential is the opposite of the negative relationship observed for the group with less than a high school education in table 6. Moreover, the estimated effect is substantial; the coefficient suggests

Table 7. Log Wage Inequality, High School Graduates, State-of-Birth by Cohort-of-Birth Cells[a]

Variable	Standard deviation of log wage	Percentile of log wage distribution		
		90-10	90-50	50-10
School size	-0.5721	-0.0220	-0.0225	0.0005
	(1.6445)	(0.0412)	(0.0211)	(0.0414)
District size	0.6317	0.0229*	0.0087	0.0142
	(0.5104)	(0.0138)	(0.0068)	(0.0123)
State share of funding	0.0087	-0.0000	-0.0001	0.0001
	(0.0273)	(0.0008)	(0.0004)	(0.0010)
Pupil-teacher ratio	-0.0009	-0.0005	0.0015	-0.0020
	(0.1386)	(0.0044)	(0.0023)	(0.0040)
Term length	-0.0954*	-0.0026**	0.0001	-0.0027***
	(0.0530)	(0.0011)	(0.0006)	(0.0010)
Percent rural	-0.8966	-0.0513	-0.0400	-0.0113
	(5.4491)	(0.1336)	(0.0684)	(0.1368)
Income per capita	-1.9152	-0.0248	-0.0452	0.0205
	(2.8146)	(0.0660)	(0.0348)	(0.0664)
Number of observations	144	144	144	144
R^2	0.76	0.70	0.56	0.52

Source: Wage data are from the 1980 PUMS, school characteristics are from the *Biennial Survey of Education*, percent rural is from the census, and income per capita is from the Bureau of Economic Analysis. Data sources are described further in the data appendix.
* Significant at the 10 percent level.
** Significant at the 5 percent level.
*** Significant at the 1 percent level.
a. See note to table 6.

that a 1 standard deviation increase in school size is associated with nearly a two-thirds (0.640) standard deviation increase in the 90-50 differential for college graduates. Finally, district size registers a significant positive relationship with the 50-10 wage differential, although it does not attain statistical significance in any of the other models in table 9.

Discussion

In conclusion, I discuss the estimated effects of consolidation on adult wage inequality, as well as the effects of term length, which was not the primary focus of the paper but yielded interesting results nonetheless.

Consolidation

Overall, the analysis presented above provides little evidence that the school consolidation movement has had important effects on the variance of out-

Table 8. Log Wage Inequality, Some College, State-of-Birth by Cohort-of-Birth Cells[a]

Variable	Standard deviation of log wage	Percentile of log wage distribution		
		90-10	90-50	50-10
School size	-0.7259	-0.0023	0.0033	-0.0057
	(2.2001)	(0.0454)	(0.0329)	(0.0309)
District size	0.3792	0.0049	-0.0040	0.0089
	(0.6980)	(0.0132)	(0.0107)	(0.0128)
State share of funding	0.0027	-0.0005	0.0004	-0.0008
	(0.0622)	(0.0010)	(0.0006)	(0.0010)
Pupil-teacher ratio	-0.1315	0.0009	-0.0042	0.0051
	(0.2370)	(0.0053)	(0.0034)	(0.0049)
Term length	-0.1280**	-0.0034**	0.0008	-0.0041***
	(0.0512)	(0.0016)	(0.0011)	(0.0010)
Percent rural	-10.2049	-0.1147	0.0270	-0.1417
	(6.5009)	(0.1508)	(0.1001)	(0.0964)
Income per capita	-3.5269	-0.1327*	0.0377	-0.1704***
	(2.7131)	(0.0764)	(0.0612)	(0.0533)
Number of observations	144	144	144	144
R^2	0.75	0.83	0.79	0.51

Source: Wage data are from the 1980 PUMS, school characteristics are from the *Biennial Survey of Education*, percent rural is from the census, and income per capita is from the Bureau of Economic Analysis. Data sources are described further in the data appendix.
* Significant at the 10 percent level.
** Significant at the 5 percent level.
*** Significant at the 1 percent level.
a. See note to table 6.

comes, as measured by wages, for most students. For the group with the lowest educational attainment, being educated in a state and cohort with larger schools is associated with lower inequality in adult wages. This finding may indicate that state-cohort cells with larger schools provide a more uniform standard of education for low-achieving students, possibly by reducing the variation in school quality in rural areas, where one-room schools were the norm prior to consolidation. At the same time, school size is shown to have a positive relationship with wage inequality for college graduates, although only for the 90-50 log wage differential. One interpretation of this finding is that larger schools provide more specialized instructional opportunities, which are especially relevant for college-bound students. However, I am hesitant to make much of this finding, both because it is counterintuitive and because school size is significant in only one of the four models for college graduates.

The positive association between district size and wage inequality among those who did not complete high school is also a puzzle. To the extent that within-district quality is more uniform than between-district quality, district consolidation would be expected to reduce variation in student outcomes. However, it is possible that larger districts systematically provide different

Table 9. Log Wage Inequality, College Graduates, State-of-Birth by Cohort-of-Birth Cells[a]

Variable	Standard deviation of log wage	Percentile of log wage distribution		
		90-10	90-50	50-10
School size	-0.2825	0.0216	0.0650**	-0.0434
	(1.8176)	(0.0498)	(0.0300)	(0.0341)
District size	0.8351	0.0126	-0.0162	0.0288***
	(0.5652)	(0.0170)	(0.0121)	(0.0109)
State share of funding	-0.0140	-0.0005	-0.0011	0.0007
	(0.0483)	(0.0017)	(0.0011)	(0.0010)
Pupil-teacher ratio	0.0332	0.0020	0.0055*	-0.0035
	(0.1675)	(0.0071)	(0.0030)	(0.0058)
Term length	-0.1372**	-0.0064***	-0.0023*	-0.0041***
	(0.0600)	(0.0020)	(0.0013)	(0.0013)
Percent rural	-8.0646	-0.2653	-0.1965	-0.0688
	(6.4896)	(0.2085)	(0.1625)	(0.1145)
Income per capita	-4.1669	-0.2705***	-0.1666***	-0.1038
	(3.5109)	(0.0992)	(0.0553)	(0.0643)
Number of observations	144	144	144	144
R^2	0.78	0.81	0.78	0.69

Source: Wage data are from the 1980 PUMS, school characteristics are from the *Biennial Survey of Education*, percent rural is from the census, and income per capita is from the Bureau of Economic Analysis. Data sources are described further in the data appendix.
* Significant at the 10 percent level.
** Significant at the 5 percent level.
*** Significant at the 1 percent level.
a. See note to table 6.

opportunities for students with lower educational attainment. Additional research using contemporary data may shed light on this question.

Notably, the state government's share of education funding registers no significant effect at conventional levels in any of the estimated models. By this account, greater centralization of spending has not historically produced the equalizing effects sought by many of today's school finance reformers. Although not an indicator of consolidation per se, class size shows a negative relationship with inequality, which is significant at the 10 percent level in several models. It is possible that smaller classes provide greater opportunities for sorting students by ability or background, which ultimately exacerbates variation in achievement.

While the results generally do not reveal a significant relationship between school consolidation and adult wage inequality, it is important to emphasize that my analysis is restricted to white men. A valuable extension of this research would be to include women and minorities in the analysis. It is possible that consolidation had important effects on between-group rather than within-group inequality. For instance, if school consolidation brought blacks and whites into unified schools and districts that were previously segregated, inequality between races may have been affected even if inequality among whites was not. If so, then consolidation may have had very important consequences for inequality that are missed in the present analysis.

Finally, in general the estimates for the consolidation-related variables are statistically insignificant because they are imprecisely estimated, not necessarily because they are small in magnitude. For example, if the estimates of table 5 are converted to standardized beta coefficients, the impact of school size in the three models is 0.14, 0.08, and 0.17 for the 90-10, 90-50, and 50-10 income ratios, respectively. The estimates for district size are 0.01, –0.12, and 0.15; for the state share of funding, they are –0.10, –0.12, and –0.04. These standardized coefficients are of the same order of magnitude as the (standardized) estimates of term length, which are –0.13, –0.06, and –0.16. This pattern of variation in the estimates suggests that there is more variation across states in the effects of the three consolidation-related variables than in the effect of term length. With additional research, it may be possible to identify the sources of the variation across states in the effects of consolidation and, in so doing, to produce more precise estimates of the impact of consolidation on inequality.

Term Length

Of all the variables examined, term length evinces the most robust relationship with wage inequality, although it is not the major focus of this paper. For the total sample of state- and year-of-birth cells, and for each of the education groups, term length is negatively associated with wage inequality. Moreover, for the total sample and each of the subgroups, term length exhibits its largest effect on inequality at the lower end of the wage distribution, as indicated by the 50-10 wage differential. That term length produces an effect for every category of educational attainment suggests that its overall impact on wage inequality must arise at least partly through a reduction in the variation in returns to education. Although I do not have data on within-state variation in term length, it is likely that increases in average term length were achieved by increasing school terms in rural districts, which historically lagged urban districts in the length of the school year. It is also plausible that increasing terms for rural schools produced more even educational quality between rural and urban districts, which was later reflected in reduced variation in adult wages.

An important caveat is that nearly all of the variation in term length in the sample is observed in southern states. While average term length for southern cohorts increased from approximately 157 days in 1920 to 176 in 1950, average term length in other regions was relatively unchanged. Although the state fixed effects should account for unobserved but time-invariant regional factors, it is important to consider other regional factors that may have changed over the study period, such as the migration of blacks to the North. Because term length is not the primary focus of this paper, I do not pursue these issues here. Nevertheless, future research focusing on the connection between term length and inequality should pay attention to the identification issues related to regional variation in the timing of increases in term length.

It is tempting to conclude that increasing term length is a proven strategy for reducing inequality that ought to be emulated in current policy reforms. Indeed, there are those who champion "year-round" or "extended-time" schooling even today.[34] I am cautious about making inferences for contemporary policy reforms based on the analysis presented here because the entire sample is composed of men born before 1950. Much has changed. Nevertheless, extending the school term may be a promising reform and one that is relatively easy to implement. In addition, changes in school terms are amenable to randomized trials, which would generate more compelling evidence of a causal relationship than the design used in this paper. Finally, while reducing inequality is a laudable policy goal, reforms should be based on their expected effects on average outcomes, not inequality alone.

Data Appendix

1980 Census Data

The sample is constructed from the 5 percent Public Use A file, which is a self-weighting sample of the U.S. population. I limit my analysis to white men born between 1920 and 1949 in the forty-eight mainland states, with years of birth estimated from information on birth quarter and age. Cases with imputed data for age, race, sex, education, weeks worked, or earnings are dropped. Individuals who reported no weeks of work, annual wage and salary income of less than $101, or average weekly wage and salary income of less than $36 or more than $2,500 are also excluded.

School Characteristics

Data on average daily attendance, the number of public schools, the number of school districts, and the state share of funding for public education are from various issues of the *Biennial Survey of Education* and, after 1960, the *Digest of Education Statistics*. Data on term length and the average-daily-attendance-based pupil-teacher ratio are derived from the same sources and were provided to me by Petra Todd, whose assistance I gratefully acknowledge. Because data from the *Biennial Survey* are available only every two years, I code each estimate to the odd year of the issue and linearly interpolate values for the even year. For instance, the values reported in the 1931–32 and 1933–34 editions are assigned to 1931 and 1933, respectively. The value for 1932 is then computed as the average of these values.

Other Variables

Annual state per capita income beginning in 1929 is from the state personal income estimates of the Bureau of Economic Analysis. I use the consumer price index to convert all of the estimates into 1967 dollars.

The percent of the population classified as rural is from the 1920, 1930, 1940, 1950, and 1960 U.S. censuses. Values for intervening years are linearly interpolated.

Year-of-Birth Aggregates

Each year of birth is assigned the average of the school characteristics, per capita income, and percent rural over the period during which people born in that year would have attended school, assuming a maximum twelve years of schooling. For instance, a high school graduate born in 1920 would have entered school in 1926 and graduated in 1937, so school characteristics were averaged over 1926–37 for individuals born in 1920. When a variable is not available for a given year—for instance, per capita income for 1926–28—values are averaged over the years for which data are available.

Notes

1. Christopher Berry and Martin West, "Growing Pains: The School Consolidation Movement and Student Outcomes," Working Paper (University of Chicago, Harris School of Public Policy, 2005).
2. The discussion in this paragraph is based on David Tyack, *The One Best System: A History of American Urban Education* (Harvard University Press, 1974).
3. This discussion draws from Ellwood P. Cubberley, *A Brief History of Education* (Boston: Houghton-Mifflin, 1922), especially ch. 10.
4. Ibid., p. 253.
5. The *Biennial Survey of Education* was the federal government's first publication to systematically track statistics related to state and local education. The *Biennial Survey* began publication in 1869, changed title to become the *Digest of Education Statistics* in 1960, and has been published under that name to this day. These two publications are the source of data for all the figures presented in this paper. See Department of Education, National Center for Education Statistics (nces.ed.gov/programs/digest [October 2006]).
6. Average daily attendance is a better indicator of size than is enrollment. Early in the century, there were often substantial discrepancies between the number of students nominally enrolled in schools and those attending regularly. Today, the two are nearly identical. For a comparison of the average daily attendance and enrollment over time, see James Heckman, Anne Layne-Farrar, and Petra Todd, "Human Capital Pricing Equations with an Application to Estimating the Effect of School Quality on Earnings," *Review of Economics and Statistics* 78, no. 4 (1996): 562–610.
7. Cubberley, *Brief History of Education,* p. 227.
8. Ibid., p. 186.
9. Although data on the number of school districts are not available prior to 1931, if districts followed a trajectory comparable to schools, we can infer that the number of districts was at its apex around that time.
10. Department of Education, *Biennial Survey of Education, 1931–32.*

11. Clifford Hooker and Van Mueller, *The Relationship of School District Reorganization to State Aid Distribution Systems,* Special Study 11 (National Education Finance Project, 1970).

12. David Strang, "The Administrative Transformation of American Education: School District Consolidation, 1938–1980," *Administrative Science Quarterly* 32, no. 3 (September 1987): 352–66.

13. Hanushek provides a useful review of the literature. See Eric A. Hanushek, *The Evidence on Class Size,* Occasional Paper 98-1 (Rochester, N.Y.: W. Allen Wallis Institute of Political Economy, 1998). The contributors to Gary Burtless, ed., *Does Money Matter? The Effect of School Resources on Student Achievement and Adult Success* (Brookings, 1996), demonstrate its controversies.

14. Berry and West, "Growing Pains."

15. Mathew Andrews, William Duncombe, and John Yinger, "Revisiting Economies of Size in American Education: Are We Any Closer to a Consensus?" *Economics of Education Review* 21, no. 3 (June 2002): 245–62.

16. Andrews, Duncombe, and Yinger restrict their survey to studies that meet minimum standards of methodological rigor. Lawrence Kenny, "Economies of Scale in Schooling," *Economics of Education Review* 2, no. 1 (1982): 1–24.

17. Anita A. Summers and Barbara L. Wolfe, "Do Schools Make a Difference?" *American Economic Review* 67, no. 4 (1977): 639–52; V. E. Lee and J. B. Smith, "High School Size: Which Works Best and for Whom?" *Educational Evaluation and Policy Analysis* 19, no. 3 (Fall 1997): 205–27.

18. For example, see Kathleen Cotton, "School Size, School Climate, and Student Performance," School Improvement Research Series (Office of Educational Research and Improvement, 1996).

19. Herbert J. Walberg and William J. Fowler, "Expenditure and Size Efficiencies of Public School Districts," *Educational Researcher* 16, no. 7 (1987): 5–13. Ronald Ferguson, "Paying for Public Education: New Evidence on How and Why Money Matters," *Harvard Journal on Legislation* 28, no. 2 (Summer 1991): 465–98.

20. Ronald F. Ferguson and Helen F. Ladd, "Additional Evidence on How and Why Money Matters: A Production Function Analysis of Alabama Schools," in *Holding Schools Accountable: Performance-Based Reform in Education,* edited by Helen F. Ladd (Brookings, 1996). Frederick D. Sebold and William Dato, "School Funding and Student Achievement: An Empirical Analysis," *Public Finance Quarterly* 9, no. 1 (January 1981): 91–105.

21. Caroline Hoxby, "Does Competition among Public Schools Benefit Students and Taxpayers?" *American Economic Review* 90, no. 5 (2000): 1209–38.

22. Frank Levy and Richard J. Murnane, "U.S. Earnings Levels and Earnings Inequality: A Review of Recent Trends and Proposed Explanations," *Journal of Economic Literature* 30, no. 3 (September 1992): 1333–81. Lawrence Katz and David Autor, "Changes in the Wage Structure and Earnings Inequality," in *Handbook of Labor Economics,* volume 3A, edited by Orley Ashenfelter and David Card (Amsterdam: Elsevier Science, 1999).

23. For example, Lawrence Katz and Kevin Murphy, "Changes in Relative Wages, 1963–1987: Supply and Demand Factors," *Quarterly Journal of Economics* 107 (January 1992): 35–78.

24. For example, Chinhui Juhn, Kevin M. Murphy, and Brooks Pierce, "Wage Inequality and the Rise in Returns to Skill," *Journal of Political Economy* 101, no. 3 (June 1993): 410–42.

25. Katz and Autor, "Changes in the Wage Structure and Earnings Inequality," pp. 1497–98.

26. Census Bureau, Public Use Microdata Sample (PUMS), A Sample, 1980 (www.census.gov/main/www/pums.html [September 2006]).

27. The focus on white men is necessary because of the rapid and geographically uneven changes in the labor market opportunities for women and blacks during the period. Additional details on case selection are provided in the data appendix.

28. In the analyses presented below, I weight cells by sample size. Eliminating the cells with fewer than 100 observations does not change the results importantly.

29. Katz and Autor, "Changes in the Wage Structure and Earnings Inequality."

30. It is possible to match each individual to the specific years he was in school, using information on year of birth and years of education. However, for a cell of individuals born in the same year, this conflates educational quality with years of education. This issue is discussed further below.

31. David Card and Alan Krueger, "Does School Quality Matter? Returns to Education and the Characteristics of Public Schools in the United States," *Journal of Political Economy* 100 (February 1992): 1–40.

32. I am grateful to Petra Todd for providing me with the term length and pupil-teacher data.

33. I would much prefer to have data on the within-state *variation* in resources by year of birth, such as lagged state-level wage inequality. Unfortunately, the data necessary to make consistent comparisons of wage structure are not available prior to 1940, which leaves out much of the period under consideration here. See Katz and Autor, "Changes in the Wage Structure and Earnings Inequality." Lack of controls for inequality at the time of birth is a significant limitation, and I hope to find an alternative approach for a future version of the paper.

34. For example, Patricia Gandara and Judy Fish, "Year-Round Schooling as an Avenue to Major Structural Reform," *Educational Evaluation and Policy Analysis* 16, no. 1 (Spring 1994): 67–85. Also see, for instance, the National Association for Year-Round Education and its associated website (www.nayre.org [May 2006]) and publications.

The Effects of School Size on Parental Involvement and Social Capital: Evidence from the ELS:2002

THOMAS S. DEE, WEI HA, AND BRIAN A. JACOB

Recent state and federal policies designed to improve American public schools have generally focused on introducing standards (for example, No Child Left Behind) or choice (for example, charter schools and vouchers). However, another increasingly prominent approach to reform has emphasized the possible benefits of creating smaller schools as well as small, focused learning communities within schools, particularly at the high school level.[1] The growing national interest in the small-schools movement has been catalyzed largely by private foundations (most notably, the Bill and Melinda Gates Foundation) rather than by explicit state and federal action.[2] Regardless of its origin, this reform agenda has brought renewed attention to a long-standing research literature that examines the effects of school size on the organizational character and performance of schools.

This literature focuses on how school size influences both costs and outcomes (for example, test scores and educational attainment). However, it also emphasizes how school size may change the nature of educationally relevant social interactions among students, teachers, and administrators. In particular, the apparent consensus in this literature is that the increased formalization of interactions in larger schools harms school quality by fostering alienation and a loss of organizational focus among students and staff.[3] However, there appears to be little corresponding evidence on how school size influences patterns of parental involvement in schools. This is somewhat surprising in light of the fact that constructive parental engagement with schools is widely seen as an important determinant of school quality.[4]

Furthermore, the effects of school size on parents may also matter for an important reason that is wholly unrelated to the direct objectives of schools. Public schools are often viewed as vital community institutions that can deepen social networks and promote a variety of welfare-enhancing social norms (for example, trust and reciprocity). The role of public schools in promoting this broad group of outcomes, which researchers currently group under the heading "social capital," has important implications both for the optimal design of schools as well as for the proper division between the public and private sectors.[5] The size of a public school, for example, could quite conceivably influence the amount of social capital within a community through its effects on parental interactions.

In this study, we present new empirical evidence on whether the size of public high schools influences measures of parental involvement and social capital. This analysis is based on nationally representative data from the base year of the Education Longitudinal Study of 2002 (ELS:2002). In addition to examining novel measures of outcome based on recent data, our study also engages a substantive methodological concern. Any inferences about the causal effects of school size are likely to be complicated by the fact that the unobservable traits that influence a parent's pattern of civic engagement (for example, the enjoyment a parent derives from interacting with others) may also influence the size of the public school the family chooses. The conventional approach to addressing this concern is to exploit a plausible natural experiment that influences school size.[6] However, in the absence of a compelling experiment, we adopt an approach developed in a recent study by Altonji, Elder, and Taber on the effects of Catholic schools.[7] Following their lead, we attempt to establish bounds on the causal effects of school size by using the differences in observed traits across parents connected to smaller and larger schools as a guide to the size and direction of their potentially confounding unobserved traits.

The paper is organized as follows. The next section provides brief discussions of the school-size literature and the possible relationships between school size and the engagement of parents. This is followed by a discussion of the ELS:2002 data, a presentation of our baseline, multivariate analysis of these data, and a presentation of the results of our bounding exercise. A final section concludes.

School Size and Parents

Questions about the appropriate size of American public schools are far from new. In particular, the late nineteenth and most of the twentieth century witnessed a purposeful and aggressive consolidation movement, which increased the size of schools nationwide. This stunning reorganization of American education reflected a progressive-era impulse toward "scientific" management by experts. David B. Tyack characterizes the "administrative progressives" who promoted consolidation as business and professional elites who wanted to have the organization of schools emulate that of the modern business corporation and to delegate almost total administrative power to an expert superintendent and staff. These reformers saw in small, locally controlled schools "only corruption, parochialism, and vestiges of an outmoded village mentality."[8]

A more explicit argument made in favor of larger schools was that larger schools would improve school quality by facilitating a more diverse and targeted curriculum. For example, James B. Conant, a former president of Harvard University, wrote an influential report advocating the elimination of small high schools, which he characterized as unable to offer a sufficiently comprehensive curriculum.[9] Similarly, proponents of larger schools alleged that considerable cost savings would accrue from capturing economies of scale in school administration and facilities.

However, the current research literature indicates that the size of many larger public schools has negative consequences. In particular, recent reviews suggest that high schools of 600 to 900 students balance economies of size with the negative consequences of larger schools.[10] Some commentators argue that the distinct advantages of smaller, autonomous schools are rooted in their governance, student-faculty relations, parental involvement, and accountability.[11] In particular, drawing on basic sociological theory, Lee, Bryk, and Smith argue that the increased formalization of larger schools can harm group cohesion and create static roles that promote alienation and attenuate organizational focus.[12] A number of empirical studies have reported supporting evidence indicating that larger schools alienate teachers and students from educational goals.[13]

However, relatively little evidence examines how the size of public schools influences the prevalence and character of parental involvement.[14] Similarly, although local public schools are often viewed as vital community institutions, we know of no empirical evidence that assesses whether smaller schools are more effective than larger schools in this role.[15] However, anecdotal descriptions of the local opposition to forced school closures, which often stress concerns about civic identity and social cohesion, suggest that this is the case.

Similarly, in discussing anthropological evidence that community schools integrate people into social networks and civic and cultural life, Tyack writes, "Thus, they became institutions valued in themselves, quite apart from the goal of teaching students certain skills and knowledge."[16]

Contemporary scholars describe the social cohesion, trust, and civic engagement ostensibly promoted by smaller schools and districts as examples of "social capital." Over the last three decades, the concept of social capital has achieved a wide currency across the social sciences. The definitions used by researchers vary somewhat, but, in general, social capital refers to social norms (for example, trust) and social networks that are thought to provide strong complements to a variety of important social and economic outcomes.[17] One of the most prominent topics in the recent literature on social capital is the evidence that it has been declining in the United States. The influential work of Robert Putnam suggests that these declines are due to the isolating effects of television and the aging of the "civic" generations born between 1910 and 1940.[18] One prominent type of evidence for the decline in social capital is the decline of membership in local parent-teacher associations (PTAs).[19]

Should we expect larger public schools to discourage the involvement of parents in groups like the PTA or to reduce other types of social capital? Such an expectation would be consistent with some of the seminal, theoretical work on public goods. For example, James Buchanan argues that voluntary compliance with behavioral sanctions and the provision of public goods like social capital are more likely in small communities than in large ones.[20] Similarly, Mancur Olson hypothesizes a negative relationship between group size and the voluntary provision of public goods.[21] However, larger schools could conceivably increase the social capital in their communities by promoting expanded social networks and amplifying the rewards and sanctions for community engagement. Similarly, an expansion of social networks could also attenuate distrust of others. In light of these possibilities, the effects of school size on social capital should be viewed as an empirical question.

Education Longitudinal Study of 2002

The ELS:2002 is the most recent in a series of nationally representative, longitudinal studies of secondary school students sponsored by the National Center for Education Statistics (NCES). The target for the baseline sample in ELS:2002 consisted of high school sophomores in the spring of 2002. The sample design reflected a two-stage selection process.[22] In the first stage, schools were selected with probabilities proportional to their size and within strata defined by census region, urbanicity, and control of the school (that is, public, Catholic, other private). Within participating schools, approximately twenty-six sophomores were selected within strata defined by race and ethnicity.[23] This procedure oversampled private schools and students who were Asian or Hispanic.

The base-year respondents consisted of 15,362 high school sophomores from 752 schools. In addition to surveying students, ELS:2002 gathered information from a number of other sources, including school records, teachers, parents, and administrators. The parent survey elicited a variety of information about the student's family background. However, it also included questions, which are discussed in more detail below, about the parents' interactions and engagement with their school and their community. Initially, the parent survey, which was available in both English and Spanish, was mailed to the student's home with instructions that it should be completed by the parent or guardian who was most familiar with the student's educational experiences. Follow-up requests allowed parents to respond to either a written questionnaire or a computer-assisted telephone interview (CATI).

Our analytical sample consists of approximately 8,000 individual respondents (see table 1). The reduction in sample size is due, in part, to the exclusion of private and Catholic schools (more than 3,323 observations), public schools with unusual grade spans (those that did not begin with the ninth or tenth grade, 1,470 cases), and students who had completed ninth grade in a foreign country (89 cases). The restricted-use version also includes a variable that distinguishes between comprehensive schools and other types of schools, such as magnets, charters, and other schools that may be small by design. Unfortunately, very few schools are not classified as comprehensive, making a separate analysis of them infeasible. However, as a robustness check, we estimated models including only comprehensive schools and found results comparable to those reported here.

The remaining reductions to our sample reflect both the unwillingness of some parents to complete the survey and, to a lesser extent, the fact that some schools were unwilling to provide home addresses for some or all of the sampled students.[24] To assess whether the patterns of nonresponse to each question vary with school size, we examine auxiliary regressions in which a dummy variable for a missing response to a particular question is the dependent variable.[25] Our results suggest that, conditional on our other controls, nonresponse is not related to school size for ten of our eleven dependent variables. However, smaller schools are 1 percentage point more likely to have nonresponders to a question about volunteering in school.

Table 1. Summary Statistics[a]

Variable	Number of observations	Mean	Standard deviation
Dependent variables			
Belong to PTA	8,248	0.231	0.422
Attend PTA meetings	8,256	0.327	0.469
Take part in PTA activities	8,202	0.251	0.434
Act as a volunteer at the school	8,197	0.249	0.434
Belong to other organization with parents from school	8,268	0.284	0.451
Parent knowledge about child's friends' parents	7,823	2.327	0.674
Friends' parent gave advice	8,183	0.302	0.459
Friends' parent did favor	8,169	0.638	0.481
Friends' parent received favor	8,148	0.691	0.462
Friends' parent supervised on field trip	8,132	0.307	0.461
Feelings of connectedness in the community	8,279	0.754	0.431
Independent variables			
Whether enrolled in a small school (enrollment fewer than 800)	8,431	0.168	0.374
School enrollment			
1–399	8,431	0.043	0.203
400–799	8,431	0.125	0.331
800–1,199	8,431	0.176	0.381
1,200–2,199	8,431	0.42	0.494
More than 2,200	8,431	0.236	0.425

Source: Authors' calculations based on ELS:2002 data.
a. This extract is based on high-school sophomores in the spring of 2002 who attended public schools, whose lowest grade was ninth or tenth, who did not complete ninth grade in a foreign country, and whose parents had valid responses to the parent survey.

Our measures of school size are based on an enrollment question from the survey of school administrators. In particular, we rely on the administrator's report about the tenth-grade enrollment rather than total school enrollment because the latter question was not included on an abbreviated questionnaire to which some administrators responded. Regardless, the reported grade-level enrollments correspond quite closely to the school-level reports. We use the enrollment data to characterize each school as belonging to one of five categories of size. In some specifications, our measures of school size are dummy variables representing each of these categorical responses. However, in other specifications, our measure is a "small-school" dummy variable, which is equal to 1 for schools where the administrator reported tenth-grade enrollment of 799 students or fewer. This small-school indicator effectively identifies schools with fewer than 600 to 800 students. This margin is of interest given the prior evidence suggesting that this is the optimal size of enrollments.

Our dependent variables reflect parents' responses to four questions about their involvement in their child's high school as well as seven questions related to social capital. More specifically, the first two parental-involvement questions involve whether the parent (or their spouse or partner) attends or belongs to the school's parent-teacher organization. The remaining two parental-involvement questions address more intensive involvement with the school (that is, taking part in PTA activities and volunteering at the school).

The first social capital question asks whether the parent belongs to any neighborhood or religious organizations with other parents from the child's school. The second social capital variable is based on the parent's knowledge of three of their child's close friends and their parents. Specifically, for each of the student's three close friends, the questionnaire inquires whether the parent knows the friend, the friend's mother, and the friend's father (yes = 1, no = 0). We sum the three binary responses (1 = yes) for each of the three friends and then average the variables across friends to create a measure that varies from 0 to 3.

The next four social capital variables are binary responses to questions about the parent of a child's friend giving advice about teachers and courses, giving and receiving favors from such a parent, and whether such a parent has supervised an educational outing or field trip. The final social capital variable directly captures the responding parent's perception of his or her community. More specifically, it identifies whether the parent feels that he or she is part of a neighborhood or community or that it is "just a place to live."

Our analysis exploits as controls the detailed variables that are available in ELS:2002 on the observable traits of students, parents, families, and their high schools. Our most parsimonious specification simply includes as controls eleven dummy variables for interactions between each school's census region and its urbanicity (that is, urban, suburban, and rural), where suburban-Northeast is the omitted category. However, in a second specification, we introduce a broad array of controls for observables at the student, family, and school levels, which could be reasonably viewed as exogenous. These include separate demographic controls for the student and the reporting parent (race-ethnicity, gender, age, and English as a native language). Other variables in this group reflect the educational attainment of the parent, the marital structure of the student's family, family size (number of dependents and its square), labor force status of the parent (full-time, part-time, not working), parental occupation (six categories), and family income (linear, quadratic, and cubic terms along with a dummy variable for top-coded income).

This group also includes nine separate variables that identify (on a scale of 1 to 4) the amount of time the parent spends with the child in various, non-school activities (for example, talking, attending religious services, concerts, sporting events). At the parent level, we also include interactions of educational attainment with gender and with native-language status. School-level controls include a dummy variable indicating whether the school begins at grade nine, the number of days in the school's academic year, the lowest and highest salaries paid to full-time teachers, the percentage of full-time and part-time teachers who teach "out of field," three dummy variables for the level of crime in the school's neighborhood, and linear and quadratic terms for the percentage of the school's students on free or reduced-price lunch. We also set the values of all the variables described here to 0 when missing and include separate dummy variables that identify whether each variable is missing among our control variables. Furthermore, we experimented with additional controls that are more likely to be viewed as possibly endogenous with respect to school size and quality (for example, controls for students who have repeated a grade, have learning disabilities, or have behavior problems). We found that the results conditioned on these variables are similar to those reported here.

Baseline Results

The conventional approach to evaluating the effects of school size has been to construct regression-adjusted comparisons that exploit the cross-sectional variation in school size. In table 2, we characterize the geographic distribution of school size in ELS:2002 across twelve categories defined by interacting census region (West, South, Northeast, and Midwest) with urbanicity (urban, suburban, and rural). The results indicate that smaller high schools (those with fewer than 800 students) are particularly uncommon in urban areas. Furthermore, while small high schools are more common in rural and suburban communities, rural communities are particularly likely to have the very smallest high schools (those with fewer than 400 students). Because the communities within these region-urbanicity categories are likely to have distinct and unobserved cultural and economic traits that influence parental involvement and social capital, our results condition on dummy variables unique to each of these categories.

This baseline specification implies that our inferences are based effectively on comparing outcomes among respondents who are *within* a given region-urbanicity cell but involved with schools of different sizes. Nonetheless, the nonrandom sorting of families across schools within these areas could still complicate the inferences based on this approach. The notion that parents "vote with their feet" in response to the quality of local public schools is well docu-

Table 2. Distribution of Respondents, by School Size, Urbanicity, and Census Region

Urbanicity and region	Percent of respondents	Fewer than 400	400–799	800–1,199	1,200–2,199	More than 2,199
Urban						
West	7.8	0.00	0.00	8.11	35.35	56.54
South	10.2	0.54	6.59	10.88	52.06	29.93
Northeast	3.3	5.62	1.60	12.87	26.79	53.12
Midwest	5.4	0.00	4.58	15.13	64.75	15.55
Rural						
West	2.8	27.71	0.00	6.19	46.59	19.50
South	8.9	10.31	25.90	21.70	31.01	11.08
Northeast	3.0	6.68	10.71	32.83	49.79	0.00
Midwest	3.8	35.57	29.02	14.41	8.79	12.22
Suburb						
West	13.9	1.01	10.38	12.85	39.03	36.73
South	15.5	1.80	15.24	18.86	44.61	19.48
Northeast	11.4	1.65	22.03	26.78	40.96	8.58
Midwest	14.1	1.52	10.57	22.72	47.57	17.62

Source: Authors' calculations based on ELS:2002 data.

mented. This raises the concern that the unobserved characteristics associated with school selection may also be associated with outcomes such as parental involvement or community attachment.

To explore the relationship between observed characteristics and attendance at a small school, we regress a binary indicator for schools with fewer than 800 students on dummy variables specific to each region-urbanicity cell as well as the student-, parent-, and school-level controls described in the previous section. While no obvious patterns emerge, several of the control variables have a statistically significant effect associated with small-school attendance. For example, the children of skilled and unskilled laborers are more likely than the children of professionals to attend small schools. However, Hispanic students and those from larger families are less likely to attend small schools. Interestingly, the R^2 for this regression is 0.24, which indicates that a substantial amount of the variation in small-school attendance is not explained by the extensive set of controls.

Nonetheless, the partial correlation between some observables and small-school attendance suggests that omitted variables could lead to inconsistent estimates of the school-size effect. The following set of equations formalizes these fundamental concerns:

(1) $$y_{ij} = \alpha\left(small_j\right) + \mathbf{X}_{ij}\gamma + e_{ij},$$

(2) $$small_j = \mathbf{X}_{ij}\beta + u_{ij},$$

where i indexes parents and j indexes schools. Most empirical studies of school size estimate single-equation models that resemble equation 1. In these studies, the identifying assumption is that corr($e, u \mid \mathbf{X}$) = 0. Researchers typically hope that the vector of control variables, $\mathbf{X}$, is sufficiently detailed that the assumption is largely correct.

In our analysis, we start by following this standard practice in the literature. The tables below present weighted estimates that reflect the sampling design in the ELS. The standard errors shown account for arbitrary correlation within schools. Unless otherwise noted, the estimates presented come from ordinary least squares (OLS) models. In the case of binary outcome variables, probit estimates yield comparable results, and so OLS estimates are presented for ease of interpretation. In the following section, we conduct additional analyses to bound the potential selection bias following the strategy outlined in Altonji, Elder, and Taber.[26]

Table 3 presents the main results for parental involvement. Several interesting patterns emerge across the four outcomes. For example, the results in the first column suggest that parents affiliated with the largest high schools are significantly *more* likely to belong to a PTA. One explanation for this counterintuitive result is that larger schools are more formal and highly organized institutions, which are simply more likely to have a PTA and to have effective recruiting practices. Regardless, these estimates are much smaller and statistically insignificant in the second specification, which conditions on the student, teacher, and school observables. The results for the next dependent variable indicate that parents whose children attend a larger high school are *less* likely to take part in PTA activities. However, while the estimated effects associated with larger schools are almost uniformly negative, the only statistically significant effect occurs in schools that have 1,200 to 2,199 students. The parents associated with those schools are 4.6 to 6.8 percentage points less likely to attend PTA meetings than the parents affiliated with the smallest schools.

The remaining results in table 3 focus on more intensive forms of parental involvement: taking part in PTA activities and volunteering at the school. The results from these regressions indicate that these forms of parental involvement are significantly less likely to occur in larger schools. For example, parents whose children attend schools with 800–1,199 students are 6.9 percentage points, or nearly 24 percent, less likely to take part in PTA activities when compared with parents whose children attend schools with fewer than 400 students. Overall, these results imply that smaller schools may not enhance formal PTA membership, but they do foster a more intensive type of involvement. The estimated effects of larger schools on intensive parental involvement become larger (in absolute value) in the second specification with the student, parent, and school controls. This pattern suggests that the observables predicting attendance at a smaller school are also associated with reduced parental involvement.

The results in table 3 also provide fairly consistent evidence that intensive parental involvement declines monotonically as school size increases. For example, parents in schools with 400–799 students are 8.6 percentage points less likely to volunteer than parents associated with the smaller schools. However, parents in schools with more than 2,200 students are 12.3 percentage points less likely to volunteer. While the magnitude of some of the difference in point estimates between moderately and extremely large schools is not trivial, the estimates for most indicators of school size for categories above 400 students are not statistically distinguishable from each other.

Table 4 presents the main results for the social capital outcomes. Mirroring the parental involvement results, these results indicate that school size is negatively associated with social capital among parents. Specifically, parents whose children attend larger high schools are less likely to report that they belong to an organization with other parents from the school or to know the parents of their child's friends; they also are less likely to report that these parents ever gave them advice or supervised their child on a field trip. Moreover, those parents whose children attend larger high schools are roughly 6–9 percentage points (that is, 7–11 percent) less likely to report that they feel connected to their community, relative to parents whose children attend schools with fewer than 400 students.

In general, these results are highly statistically significant. However, the effect of size varies across the outcome measures. For example, the estimated effect of the largest schools on the probability of belonging to a neighborhood or religious organization with another parent is approximately 19 percent of the mean in the control group. Parents whose children attend the largest schools have knowledge of the parents of their child's friends that is 0.22 of a standard deviation lower than that of parents whose children attend schools with fewer than 400 students. Finally, while there is some indication that the negative effects increase with school size, the difference between categories of schools with more than 400 students is not always statistically distinguishable.

Table 3. Estimated Effects of School Size on Parental Involvement

Independent variable	Belong to PTA (1)	Belong to PTA (2)	Attend PTA meetings (1)	Attend PTA meetings (2)	Take part in PTA activities (1)	Take part in PTA activities (2)	Volunteer at the school (1)	Volunteer at the school (2)
School enrollment								
400–799	0.034	-0.024	-0.019	-0.037	-0.026	-0.057**	-0.053	-0.086**
	(0.032)	(0.026)	(0.026)	(0.027)	(0.030)	(0.028)	(0.032)	(0.028)
800–1,199	0.055*	-0.024	-0.013	-0.033	-0.045	-0.069**	-0.042	-0.080**
	(0.033)	(0.026)	(0.024)	(0.024)	(0.030)	(0.027)	(0.032)	(0.027)
1,200–2,199	0.125**	0.012	-0.046**	-0.068**	-0.046*	-0.079**	-0.054*	-0.108**
	(0.033)	(0.027)	(0.022)	(0.024)	(0.027)	(0.026)	(0.031)	(0.027)
More than 2,200	0.137**	0.022	0.036	-0.011	-0.061**	-0.096**	-0.087**	-0.123**
	(0.040)	(0.029)	(0.026)	(0.027)	(0.029)	(0.028)	(0.036)	(0.030)
Control group mean (standard deviation)	0.134 (0.341)		0.300 (0.459)		0.293 (0.456)		0.322 (0.468)	
p value for F statistics	0.000	0.218	0.002	0.003	0.243	0.019	0.145	0.001
Number of observations	8,248	8,248	8,256	8,256	8,202	8,202	8,197	8,197
R^2	0.029	0.176	0.023	0.114	0.004	0.119	0.012	0.139

Source: Authors' calculations based on ELS:2002 data.
* Significant at 10 percent.
** Significant at 5 percent.
a. Standard errors, adjusted for school-level clustering, are reported in parentheses. All regression estimates are weighted. The p value refers to an F test of the null hypothesis that the four school-size coefficients are equal. Specification 1 includes eleven dummy variables unique to each region-urbanicity cell. Specification 2 adds to the prior model more than eighty controls reflecting the observed characteristics of students, parents, families, and schools. See the text for a more detailed description.

Table 4. Estimated Effects of School Size on Social Capital[a]

Independent variable	Belong to other organization with parents from school (1)	(2)	Parent knowledge about child's friends' parents (1)	(2)	Friends' parent gave advice (1)	(2)	Friends' parent did a favor (1)	(2)	Friends' parent received a favor (1)	(2)	Friend's parent supervised a field trip (1)	(2)	Feelings of connectedness in community (1)	(2)
School enrollment														
400–799	−0.025 (0.035)	−0.059** (0.026)	−0.069 (0.043)	−0.098** (0.042)	−0.025 (0.031)	−0.042 (0.028)	0.024 (0.031)	−0.005 (0.026)	0.015 (0.031)	−0.016 (0.028)	−0.067** (0.029)	−0.080** (0.028)	−0.046* (0.026)	−0.062** (0.025)
800–1,199	−0.015 (0.033)	−0.050** (0.024)	−0.095** (0.045)	−0.113** (0.042)	−0.012 (0.029)	−0.031 (0.027)	0.033 (0.030)	−0.000 (0.026)	0.018 (0.031)	−0.015 (0.027)	−0.081** (0.029)	−0.082** (0.029)	−0.065** (0.026)	−0.079** (0.025)
1,200–2,199	−0.006 (0.033)	−0.054** (0.024)	−0.148** (0.042)	−0.170** (0.043)	−0.035 (0.027)	−0.069** (0.026)	0.019 (0.029)	−0.034 (0.026)	0.027 (0.030)	−0.027 (0.028)	−0.113** (0.027)	−0.120** (0.028)	−0.062** (0.025)	−0.080** (0.026)
More than 2,200	−0.045 (0.038)	−0.062** (0.027)	−0.149** (0.046)	−0.149** (0.047)	−0.066** (0.029)	−0.087** (0.028)	0.004 (0.031)	−0.016 (0.028)	−0.003 (0.033)	−0.019 (0.030)	−0.141** (0.028)	−0.142** (0.031)	−0.102** (0.027)	−0.094** (0.028)
Control group mean (standard deviation)	0.323 (0.468)		2.474 (0.577)		0.335 (0.472)		0.647 (0.478)		0.698 (0.460)		0.394 (0.489)		0.832 (0.374)	
p value for *F* statistics	0.451	0.164	0.002	0.001	0.056	0.006	0.712	0.210	0.653	0.848	0.000	0.000	0.004	0.018
Number of observations	8,268	8,268	7,823	7,823	8,183	8,183	8,169	8,169	8,148	8,148	8,132	8,132	8,279	8,279
R^2	0.014	0.201	0.013	0.124	0.006	0.091	0.010	0.124	0.009	0.133	0.009	0.067	0.018	0.123

Source: Authors' calculations based on ELS:2002 data.
* Significant at 10 percent.
** Significant at 5 percent.
a. Standard errors, adjusted for school-level clustering, are reported in parentheses. All regression estimates are weighted. The *p* value refers to an *F* test of the null hypothesis that the four school-size coefficients are equal. Specification 1 includes eleven dummy variables unique to each region-urbanicity cell. Specification 2 adds to the prior model more than eighty controls reflecting the observed characteristics of students, parents, families, and schools. See the text for a more detailed description.

All of the results in tables 3 and 4 control for the unobservable determinants unique to the rural, suburban, and urban communities within each census region. Nonetheless, the vast majority of small high schools (that is, those with fewer than 800 students) are located in rural areas, and very few small, public high schools are located in urban areas. This means that the small-school effects discussed above are likely to be driven by rural and, to a lesser extent, suburban location. Yet the policy interest currently surrounding small schools focuses overwhelmingly on poor urban districts. In table 5, we examine the extent to which the estimated effects of small schools are similar across urban, suburban, and rural communities. More specifically, table 5 reports the estimated effects of small schools (fewer than 800 students) on each of the eleven outcomes for separate urban, suburban, and rural samples.

The results in table 5 indicate that the beneficial effects of smaller schools on parental involvement and social capital appear to be almost exclusively concentrated in rural communities. Given that only about 6.1 percent of urban students in the ELS:2002 attend schools with fewer than 800 students, we do not have much statistical precision for this sample. In suburban communities, roughly 15–20 percent of students attend schools with fewer than 800 students, providing a reasonable amount of variation in school size. However, the results in table 5 indicate that parental involvement and social capital are no different in small suburban schools than in larger suburban schools. With only one exception, the point estimates are very close to zero and statistically insignificant.

Selection on Observables

The estimates suggest that school size has modest effects on parental involvement and social capital in rural schools, but no significant or substantial effects in urban or suburban schools. It is still the case, however, that selection on unobservables may be present, leading us to misestimate the impact of school size. In the absence of a randomized experiment or other source of exogenous variation in school size, one can never be certain to have eliminated all omitted variables. In recent work, however, Altonji, Elder, and Taber (hereafter referred to as AET) have developed a strategy for examining the extent of selection on unobservables using information on the selection on observables.[27]

The basic intuition is that the degree of selection on observables can serve as a measure of the extent to which there may be selection on unobservables. Recall that the potential selection bias stems from the fact that the unobserved components of equations 1 and 2 may be correlated. Hence one can determine

Table 5. Estimated Effects of Small School, by Urbanicity

Dependent variable	Urban	Suburban	Rural
Parental involvement			
Belong to PTA	0.100*	-0.027	0.001
	(0.051)	(0.027)	(0.025)
	[0.224]	[0.237]	[0.270]
Attend PTA meetings	0.009	0.009	0.038
	(0.038)	(0.024)	(0.025)
	[0.392]	[0.321]	[0.290]
Take part in PTA activities	0.056*	0.012	0.079**
	(0.032)	(0.023)	(0.025)
	[0.234]	[0.249]	[0.243]
Volunteer at the school	0.061	0.005	0.094**
	(0.076)	(0.022)	(0.031)
	[0.193]	[0.254]	[0.251]
Social capital			
Belong to other organization with parents from school	-0.077**	0.006	0.071**
	(0.035)	(0.022)	(0.029)
	[0.211]	[0.286]	[0.308]
Parent knowledge about child's friends' parents	-0.106	0.063**	0.173**
	(0.071)	(0.026)	(0.043)
	[2.209]	[2.314]	[2.356]
Friends' parent gave advice	0.001	0.005	0.042
	(0.061)	(0.021)	(0.036)
	[0.259]	[0.306]	[0.298]
Friends' parent did favor	-0.014	0.002	0.039*
	(0.047)	(0.020)	(0.023)
	[0.559]	[0.640]	[0.658]
Friends' parent received favor	-0.040	-0.012	0.058**
	(0.048)	(0.019)	(0.028)
	[0.625]	[0.687]	[0.701]
Friends' parent supervised on field trip	-0.018	0.021	0.099**
	(0.032)	(0.020)	(0.033)
	[0.296]	[0.303]	[0.310]
Feelings of connectedness in community	0.007	0.016	0.112**
	(0.035)	(0.017)	(0.025)
	[0.670]	[0.752]	[0.770]

Source: Authors' calculations based on ELS:2002 data.
* Significant at 10 percent.
** Significant at 5 percent.
a. Standard errors, adjusted for school-level clustering, are reported in parentheses. All regression estimates are weighted and based on specification 2 from tables 3 and 4. The bracketed number is the mean of the dependent variable in the control group.

the extent of the bias under various assumptions regarding $\rho = \text{corr}(e, u)$. More important, AET develop a model whereby, under a set of explicit assumptions, the maximum possible correlation is calculated as

$$(3) \qquad 0 \leq \rho \leq \frac{\text{Cov}(\mathbf{X}'\beta, \mathbf{X}'\gamma)}{\text{Var}(\mathbf{X}'\gamma)}.$$

Three key assumptions underlie this model: first, the observable covariates, **X**, are chosen at random from the full set of factors that determine the outcome, *y*; second, the number of observable and unobservable factors is large; and third, the part of the outcome variable that is related to the observables has the same relationship to the endogenous variable as the part of the outcome that is related to the unobservables. While these are strong assumptions that will not be met fully in any empirical application, AET provide a compelling case that they are at least as plausible as the standard assumptions underlying regression analysis.

Table 6 presents the results of an AET-inspired bounding exercise for the relationship between school size and our outcomes. To simplify the analysis and presentation, we consider a single indicator of school size that takes on a value of 1 for all schools with fewer than 800 students. We choose 800 since it coincides with the optimal high school size, although, as the results from tables 3 and 4 suggest, our results are not particularly sensitive to choosing another cutoff for our definition of small schools. Moreover, to facilitate the comparison between our baseline estimates and the bounding exercise, we estimate unweighted OLS regressions that make no adjustment for heteroskedasticity. This does not change the results in any meaningful way (comparison tables are available upon request). Finally, for the sake of parsimony, we present a limited set of outcome variables.

We conduct this exercise separately for rural, suburban, and urban schools, and our baseline specification conditions on dummy variables for each census region. In effect, we acknowledge that region and urbanicity act as proxies for relevant structural factors that influence both school size and the outcome variables. But we rely on the detailed student, parent, and school observables as a guide to the possibly confounding influence of the unobservables in this analysis.

The top panel presents the results for rural schools. Comparing the first and second rows, we see that the estimated impact of small schools actually becomes more positive when one controls for the detailed set of student, family, and school variables. This suggests that the simple OLS estimates are biased downward, unlike what one would expect if parents who were more inclined to become involved in their child's school sought out smaller learning environments. When the OLS estimates appear to be biased downward, the magnitude of this bias seems relatively small given the slight differences between these estimates. This is reflected in the small maximum correlations for this panel, which range from –0.054 to –0.099.

Despite the relatively small degree of selection on observables, the range of estimates shown in the bottom two rows of table 6 can be somewhat large. For example, if one assumes the maximum potential selection on unobservables,

Table 6. Sensitivity of Small-School Estimates to Various Assumptions Regarding the Degree of Selection on Unobservables

Assumption	Take part in PTA activities	Act as volunteer at the school	Parent knows parents of child's friends	Feelings of connectedness to the community
Rural				
Small-school estimate with region-urbanicity controls	0.055** (0.024)	0.081** (0.024)	0.127** (0.035)	0.078** (0.022)
Small-school estimate with region-urbanicity indicators and parent and student controls	0.077** (0.028)	0.105** (0.029)	0.150** (0.042)	0.088** (0.026)
Implied direction of bias	Downward	Downward	Downward	Downward
max ρ = corr (e, u)	−0.090	−0.099	−0.072	−0.054
R^2 from regression of outcome on all covariates	0.167	0.171	0.157	0.139
Control group mean (standard deviation)	0.243 (0.429)	0.251 (0.434)	2.356 (0.650)	0.770 (0.421)
Small-school estimate assuming				
$\rho = 0.5 *$ max ρ	0.126** (0.027)	0.161** (0.028)	0.209** (0.041)	0.116** (0.025)
$\rho =$ max ρ	0.176** (0.027)	0.217** (0.028)	0.267** (0.041)	0.144** (0.025)
Suburban				
Small-school estimate with region-urbanicity controls	0.021 (0.018)	0.005 (0.018)	0.111** (0.028)	0.040** (0.017)
Small-school estimate with region-urbanicity indicators and parent and student controls	0.019 (0.018)	0.009 (0.018)	0.063** (0.029)	0.022 (0.018)
Implied direction of bias	Upward	Downward	Upward	Upward
max ρ = corr (e, u)	0.010	−0.021	0.201	0.112
R^2 from regression of outcome on all covariates	0.119	0.131	0.113	0.123
Control group mean (standard deviation)	0.249 (0.432)	0.254 (0.435)	2.313 (0.686)	0.752 (0.432)
Small-school estimate assuming				
$\rho = 0.5 *$ max ρ	0.013 (0.018)	0.021 (0.018)	−0.125** (0.029)	−0.044** (0.018)
$\rho =$ max ρ	0.008 (0.018)	0.034* (0.018)	−0.320** (0.029)	−0.110** (0.018)
Urban				
Small-school estimate with region-urbanicity controls	0.073* (0.039)	0.028 (0.036)	−0.162** (0.071)	−0.058 (0.043)
Small-school estimate with region-urbanicity indicators and parent and student controls	0.066 (0.041)	0.068* (0.037)	−0.075 (0.075)	−0.008 (0.045)
Implied direction of bias	Upward	Downward	Downward	Downward
max ρ = corr (e, u)	0.026	−0.143	−0.168	−0.169
R^2 from regression of outcome on all covariates	0.147	0.154	0.139	0.124
Control group mean (standard deviation)	0.234 (0.424)	0.193 (0.395)	2.209 (0.745)	0.670 (0.470)
Small-school estimate assuming				
$\rho = 0.5 *$ max ρ	0.041 (0.040)	0.191** (0.037)	0.202** (0.074)	0.167** (0.044)
$\rho =$ max ρ	0.017 (0.040)	0.315** (0.037)	0.486** (0.074)	0.345** (0.045)

Source: Authors' calculations based on ELS:2002 data.
** Significant at the 5 percent level.
* Significant at the 10 percent level.
a. In all models, small schools are defined as those with fewer than 800 students. In order to facilitate comparison with the bounding exercise, all estimates in this table are based on unweighted regressions with standard errors that have not been adjusted to account for heteroskedasticity. Weighting the estimates introduces only minor changes in the small-school estimate. Weighted estimates are available from the authors upon request. The student and parent controls included in the models above are from the middle specifications in tables 3 and 4. The maximum correlation is calculated using the formulas outlined in AET and is described in the text.

the impact of small schools on taking part in PTA activities would be 17.6 percentage points, which is more than twice as large as the OLS estimate of 7.7 percentage points and large relative to the baseline mean of 24.3 percent. The primary reason for this is that the available covariates explain a relatively small fraction of the variation in our outcome measures. The R^2 terms, for example, range from 0.139 to 0.171. Given the same degree of correlation with the unobservables, the higher the R^2, the lower the selection bias in the outcome equation. The intuition for this result is that a larger amount of residual variation means that a relatively small degree of selection can have larger effects on the coefficient estimates.

Despite the imprecision of the bounding exercise, the direction of selection suggests that small schools in rural communities have a strong positive effect on parental involvement and social capital. In contrast, the results for suburban schools, shown in the second panel, suggest that small schools in these areas have no positive effects on our outcomes. For three of the four outcomes shown in table 6, the OLS estimates appear to be biased upward, although the maximum implied correlation is modest in each case. Given the low explanatory power of our covariates, however, the AET bounds indicate that the true effect of size on the two social capital measures might even be negative. For the one outcome where there appears to be some downward bias (whether parents volunteer at the school), the magnitude of the bias is so small that even the most extreme assumption about correlated errors implies only a marginally significant 3.4 percentage point effect, or less than 10 percent given the baseline of 25.4 percent.

The urban school results, shown in the third panel, are mixed and, as indicated above, not very precise. For example, the naïve OLS estimate for perceived connectedness to the community is 0 (–0.008). However, the AET bound based on $\rho = -0.169$ is 34.5 percentage points, an effect that is nearly half of the baseline mean of 67.0 percent. We do not view the results of this bounding exercise as suggesting that small schools clearly have such large effects. Instead, taken together, we view these results as underscoring the uncertainty about the effects of small schools in urban communities.

Discussion

Proponents of the small-school movement argue that autonomous and appropriately sized schools are more effective than large schools at promoting student achievement. In particular, the literature on school size suggests that small schools are better because they have positive effects on the engagement and social interactions of students and staff. The analysis presented here explores another area in which small schools may influence children—namely, the enhanced involvement of their parents in the school and the promotion of social capital in the larger community.

The results presented here provide tentative evidence that small schools are more effective in promoting parental involvement in schools as well as engagement with the broader community. Specifically, we find that in rural communities smaller high schools not only increase the probability that parents take part in PTA activities and volunteer at the school, but also promote some measures of social capital (for example, knowledge of other parents and community identification). The policy relevance of this evidence turns, in part, on the contributions that parental involvement may make to school quality. But, given the widely held view that social capital provides a vital complement to economic advancement, these results also suggest that smaller schools can benefit at-risk communities in ways that extend beyond the schoolhouse door.

However, several important qualifications to these conclusions should be noted. For example, while we find consistent, strong, and positive impacts of small schools in rural communities, we find no such evidence in suburban communities. Although this may be due, in part, to the lower precision in suburban communities, the effects associated with school size seem to be noticeably larger in rural communities. Unfortunately, there are so few small schools in the urban communities in our data that we cannot say much about the influence of school size in these contexts. Taken as a whole, our results suggest that there may be some beneficial effects of small schools on the outcomes we consider, but there may also be cultural or economic features unique to rural communities that limit the external validity of these results for other areas.

A final caveat is that the literature on school size appears to have paid relatively little attention to the thorny problem of identifying the causal effects of smaller schools. This perennial empirical problem is exacerbated in this setting by the general lack of compelling natural experiments. With respect to some of our results, we have tentatively expressed more confidence in some causal interpretations by using the evidence from bounding exercises that rely on how the selection into small schools relates to the selection on other observables that influence parental involvement and social capital. However, more definitive evidence on the true effects of small schools is likely to emerge from ongoing randomized experiments. Our results suggest that a fruitful direction for future research would be to consider how small schools influence the engagement of parents both in and outside their child's school.

Notes

1. Nahal Toosi, "Small Schools Changing Shape of Nation's Largest School System," Associated Press, May 13, 2006.
2. Anne D. Lewis, "Washington Commentary: High Schools and Reform," *Phi Delta Kappan* 85, no. 8 (April 2004): 563; Tom Vander Ark, "The Case for Small High Schools," *Educational Leadership* 59, no. 5 (February 2002): 55–59.
3. Valerie E. Lee, Anthony S. Bryk, and Julia B. Smith, "The Organization of Effective High Schools," in *Review of Research in Education*, edited by Linda Darling-Hammond (Washington: American Educational Research Association, 1993), pp. 171–267; Mark A. Royal and Robert J. Rossi, "Schools as Communities," *ERIC Digest* 111 (March 1997).
4. See Lee, Bryk, and Smith, "The Organization of Effective High Schools." When asked about serious problems at their school, public school teachers participating in the 1999–2000 Schools and Staffing Survey chose "lack of parental involvement" more frequently than all problems other than "students come unprepared to learn." See Thomas D. Snyder, Alexandra G. Tan, and Charlene M. Hoffman, *Digest of Education Statistics 2005*, NCES 2006-030 (Government Printing Office, 2006), especially table 71.
5. For example, in a recent study, William A. Fischel argues that voters consistently reject voucher plans because they recognize that local public schools promote the development of community-specific social capital. See William A. Fischel, "An Economic Case against Vouchers: Why Local Public Schools Are a Local Public Good," Working Paper 02-01 (Dartmouth College, Economics Department, October 20, 2002).
6. For example, a recent study by Ilyana Kuziemko on the achievement consequences of school size exploits the variation in school size generated by school openings, closings, and mergers in Indiana. See Ilyana Kuziemko, "Using Shocks to School Enrollment to Estimate the Effect of School Size on Student Achievement," *Economics of Education Review*, vol. 25, no. 1 (2006): 63–75.
7. Joseph G. Altonji, Todd E. Elder, and Christopher R. Taber, "Selection on Observed and Unobserved Variables: Assessing the Effectiveness of Catholic Schools," *Journal of Political Economy* 113, no. 1 (2005): 151–84.
8. David B. Tyack, *The One Best System: A History of American Urban Education* (Harvard University Press, 1974), p. 127.
9. James Bryant Conant, *The American High School Today* (New York: McGraw-Hill, 1959).
10. Karen Irmsher, "School Size," *ERIC Digest* 113 (July 1997); Matthew Andrews, William Duncombe, and John Yinger, "Revisiting Economies of Size in American Education: Are We Any Closer to a Consensus?" *Economics of Education Review* 21, no. 3 (June 2002): 245–62. The average enrollment of regular, public high schools during the 2002–03 school year was 813 students. National Center for Education Statistics (NCES), *2004 Digest of Education Statistics* (Department of Education, 2004), table 94.
11. Deborah Meier, "The Big Benefits of Smallness," *Educational Leadership* 54, no. 1 (September 1996): 12–15.
12. See Lee, Bryk, and Smith, "The Organization of Effective High Schools"; Max Weber, *The Theory of Social and Economic Organization*, translated by A. M. Henderson and T. Parsons (Glencoe, Ill.: Free Press, 1947).
13. Anthony S. Bryk and Mary Erina Driscoll, "The High School as Community: Contextual Influences and Consequences for Students and Teachers," ED 302 539 (University of Wisconsin, National Center on Effective Secondary Schools, 1988); Valerie E. Lee and Susanna Loeb, "School Size in Chicago Elementary Schools: Effects on Teachers' Attitudes and Students' Achievement," *American Educational Research Journal* 37, no. 1 (Spring 2000): 3–31; Robert Crosoe and Monica Kirkpatric Johnson, "School Size and the Interpersonal Side of Education: An Examination of

Race-Ethnicity and Organizational Context," *Social Science Quarterly* 85, no. 5 (December 2004): 1259–74.

14. For example, James Griffin presents evidence that larger elementary schools are associated with lower levels of parental involvement. However, these inferences are based on only one suburban school district. See James Griffin, "The Relation of School Structure and Social Environment to Parent Involvement in Elementary Schools," *Elementary School Journal* 99, no. 1 (September 1998): 53–80.

15. However, Fischel presents a cross-state regression ($N = 48$), which indicates that an index of "social capital" is lower in states where more students are in "big" school districts. See Fischel, "An Economic Case against Vouchers," table 1.

16. See Tyack, *The One Best System*.

17. See Steven N. Durlauf and Marcel Fafchamps for a comprehensive and critical review of the theoretical and empirical literature on social capital. See Steven N. Durlauf and Marcel Fafchamps, "Social Capital," Working Paper 10485 (Cambridge, Mass.: National Bureau of Economic Research, May 2004).

18. See Robert Putnam, *Bowling Alone: The Collapse and Revival of American Community* (New York: Simon and Schuster, 2000). A recent study by Costas and Kahn suggests that the declines in social capital are overstated and that much of the decline since 1970 is due to increases in female labor force participation and growing income inequality. See Dora Costas and Matthew E. Kahn, "Understanding the American Decline in Social Capital, 1952–1988," *Kyklos* 56, no. 1 (2003): 17–46.

19. See Putnam, *Bowling Alone*, p. 55.

20. See James M. Buchanan, "Ethical Rules, Expected Values, and Large Numbers," *Ethics* 76 (October 1965): 1–13.

21. Mancur Olson Jr., *The Logic of Collective Action* (Harvard University Press, 1965). However, Sandler notes that this relationship depends on a number of modeling assumptions (for example, the utility function, the technology of the public good supply, and the nature of strategic interactions). See Todd Sandler, *Collective Action: Theory and Applications* (University of Michigan Press, 1992).

22. See Steven J. Ingels, Daniel J. Pratt, James E. Rogers, Peter H. Siegel, and Ellen S. Stutts, *Education Longitudinal Study of 2002: Base Year Data File User's Manual*, NCES 2004.405, project officer: Jeffrey A. Owings (Department of Education, National Center for Education Statistics, 2004).

23. Ibid.

24. Ibid.

25. The econometric specification is described in more detail in the next section.

26. Altonji, Elder, and Taber, "Selection on Observed and Unobserved Variables."

27. Wei Pan and Kenneth A. Frank present a related procedure that uses observables to identify a reference distribution that can be used to estimate the probability of "retaining causal inference" (that is, rejecting the null hypothesis of no effect) in the presence of an omitted variable. Wei Pan and Kenneth A. Frank, "A Probability Index of the Robustness of a Causal Inference," *Journal of Educational and Behavioral Statistics* 28 (2003): 315–37.

Optimal Context Size in Elementary Schools: Disentangling the Effects of Class Size and School Size

DOUGLAS D. READY AND VALERIE E. LEE

Young children's learning—and how their learning is distributed by social background—may be influenced by the structural and organizational properties of their school. This study focuses on one important structural dimension of these educational contexts: *size*. Over the past several decades, various elements of the size of educational contexts have become a major focus of researchers, politicians, and corporate leaders. Billions of public and private dollars have been invested in reforms to reduce the size and scope of both classrooms and schools. Unlike many educational reform initiatives, these downsizing efforts have found support from virtually every quarter. A united front of stakeholders has coalesced behind the notion that "smaller is better." Although size-reduction policies are well intentioned, their effectiveness is unclear, and some efforts have produced unintended and even undesirable consequences. Moreover, their cost-effectiveness has seldom been considered.

Based on results from the famous Tennessee class-size experiment, California invested billions of dollars encouraging its schools to limit classes in the early grades to no more than twenty students. Quite recently, the push to reduce the size of high schools has been accompanied by enormous financial support from foundations and the federal government in an effort to encourage schools-within-schools, small learning communities, and small stand-alone schools. Curiously, these important policy initiatives—reduced class size and reduced school size—have not been simultaneously considered within elementary school contexts. However, the effects of class size may be a function of school size, the effects of school size may be a function of class size, or both. The lack of research that simultaneously considers these potentially related elements of size is somewhat surprising.

Despite the groundswell of public support for smaller educational settings, the empirical base regarding the confounding effects of various components of elementary school size remains quite sparse, particularly if only methodologically sound studies are considered. Moreover, crafting size-reduction polices that faithfully reproduce the findings of experimental and quasi-experimental studies is a challenging task. In short, efforts to reduce various elements of size in elementary schools may be an instance where policy is far in front of research.

Background

Determining how the size of educational contexts may influence student outcomes can be conceptualized and measured at multiple levels. Decisions regarding the appropriate unit of analysis are important, as each level may uniquely influence student learning. It seems logical to assume that the social and structural consequences of size would be strongest where they most directly affect the daily activities of teaching and learning. For example, at the elementary school level, a focus on class size seems most reasonable. Unlike high school students, elementary school students spend more time in a single classroom. However, non- and quasi-experimental studies of elementary school class size rarely account for school size—clearly a problem, as class size may be a function of school size. Moreover, as most high schools contain the same grades (nine through twelve), examining the effects of school size on student outcomes in those contexts seems quite appropriate. Conversely, the grade spans that elementary schools include vary widely, with K–3, K–6, and K–8 schools all relatively common. If elementary schools contain fewer grades (K–3, for example), each grade is likely to include more students and classes. Thus grade size may be an additional element of context size in elementary schools.

Unfortunately, the research on these separate (yet related) elements of elementary school size is generally quite weak. Apart from the recent class-size experiments in Tennessee and Wisconsin, research in this area generally employs small and nonrepresentative samples, relies on cross-sectional data, and suffers from numerous other methodological limitations. Moreover, the theoretical justifications behind these studies often rest on literature reviews. One strange result is a circular chain, wherein literature reviews often cite other literature reviews rather than solid empirical studies. In one sense this is understandable, given the scarcity of high-quality research on the topic. Our review focuses on class size in elementary schools, as the research on other components of elementary school context is limited in both quality and quantity.

Research on Class Size

In 1985 Tennessee initiated a longitudinal class-size reduction experiment that would serve as the foundation for similar efforts across the country.[1] The experiment, titled Project STAR (Student/Teacher Achievement Ratio), randomly assigned several thousand kindergartners to one of three within-school experimental conditions: a small class enrolling between thirteen and seventeen children, a large class enrolling between twenty-two and twenty-six children with a single teacher, or a large class with a teacher and an aide. At the end of kindergarten, the achievement of children in small classes was almost one month ahead of the achievement of children in the other two classroom conditions; by the end of first grade, the same children were almost two months ahead (ES = 0.2–0.25 standard deviation).

Although Project STAR is generally considered the premier educational study with a randomized design in contemporary educational research, the study has garnered some criticism.[2] Because participation in STAR required at least three classrooms at each grade level—a small class, a large class, and a large class with an aide—only larger schools participated in the study. Moreover, student attrition from the treatment group was substantial and potentially nonrandom: only 48 percent of the original treatment group participated through third grade, and children who left the sample may have been lower achieving.[3] Teachers with smaller classes were also aware that they were part of the intervention group. Not only did many teachers enter the study already convinced that smaller classes were superior, but the state was simultaneously considering universal class-size reductions.[4] In this sense, such teachers may have induced experimenter expectancies.[5] However, class-size effects may be *under*estimated in the Tennessee experiment, as "large" classrooms enrolled only twenty-six students. The nationally representative ECLS-K data we employ in this study indicate that a substantial proportion of U.S. elementary schools offer classes enrolling more than twenty-six students.

In 1996 Wisconsin launched a similar (although more modest) class-size reduction experiment titled SAGE (Student Achievement Guarantee in Education). Unlike STAR, the SAGE design was randomized between, not within, schools. Kindergarten through third-grade classrooms in SAGE schools enrolled only fifteen students, compared to classrooms of twenty-one to twenty-five in the control schools.[6] Wisconsin's program differed from Tennessee's in another way: it targeted low-income schools—both SAGE and control schools enrolled substantial numbers of children living in poverty. Despite these differences in design and study participants, findings from the SAGE program are comparable to those from the Tennessee study: children in SAGE schools experienced higher achievement gains than their control school counterparts (ES = 0.2 standard deviation).[7]

In 1996 California used the STAR findings to justify a program that offered districts $650 for every child enrolled in a classroom with twenty or fewer students. In general, evaluations of California's efforts have been formative rather than summative. Unlike the evaluations of the class-size initiatives in Tennessee and Wisconsin, the California design was not experimental. All districts were permitted to receive funds and reduce class sizes simultaneously, rendering meaningful evaluation virtually impossible, as comparison groups were not available. For example, on average, by the end of third grade, children in the "treatment group" were enrolled in smaller classes for only one year more than those in the "control group." Moreover, selection bias was quite apparent, in that low-income schools were the last to implement smaller classes, despite the financial incentives for doing so. Even if these critical design flaws are ignored, estimating the relationship between student learning and class size would not be possible—the data permit only cross-sectional comparisons, as students' cognitive skills were not assessed in the early grades. Although evaluators report class-size "effects," we agree with their judgment that findings regarding student achievement are "inconclusive."[8]

As policy interest in the size of educational contexts increases, it is important to evaluate size-reduction efforts on two additional criteria: cost and unintended consequences. First, as class-size reduction programs are quite expensive, school districts and taxpayers are (rightly) interested in whether such costly investments are educationally sound.[9] California currently spends more than $1.6 billion a year on its efforts to reduce class enrollments below twenty—a number still larger than the ideal class size identified in the Tennessee and Wisconsin experiments. Although policies that seek to reduce class size are very popular among teachers and parents, the educational return on such a substantial investment remains unclear.

Second, several unintended and undesirable consequences accompanied California's class-size-reduction policy. By definition, large-scale, class-size-reduction programs require many more teachers, and California did not have a surplus of qualified teachers. As such, many districts hired teachers lacking full credentials to staff new classrooms, a practice that runs counter to the "highly qualified teacher" provisions within the federal No Child Left Behind legislation. Prior to class-size reduction, only 1.8 percent of California's K–3 public school teachers were uncertified; by the second year of the program, 12.5 percent lacked full credentials. Moreover, schools serving socioeconomically disadvantaged students were disproportionately forced to hire uncertified and inexperienced teachers.[10]

Another unintended, but serious, consequence in California flowed from the need to create 18,000 additional classrooms virtually overnight. Already crowded low-income districts often had inadequate facilities to accommodate new classrooms.[11] Many schools and districts not only adopted year-round calendars, but also transformed teacher lounges, gymnasiums, auditoriums, libraries, labs, special education facilities, and even storage rooms into classrooms. Again, these issues are not particular to California. Almost 60 percent of large school districts nationally that received federal class-size-reduction funds reported difficulty locating adequate classrooms for their new teachers.[12]

Research on School Size

Extant and relevant empirical studies of school size are typically characterized by a host of problems—defined in terms of level, outcomes, design, and quality. Regarding the first problem—level—almost all school-size studies have focused on high schools. It is unclear whether research findings regarding high school size are generalizable to elementary schools. The second problem—outcomes—refers to the fact that most research on size is not longitudinal, relying on simple correlations between school size and student achievement status, rather than achievement growth over time. Achievement status is quite different from learning.

A third general problem concerns study design. Not only are the majority of school-size studies cross-sectional rather than longitudinal, but most assume that the relationship between school size and student outcomes is linear. In our own research, we document a distinctly nonlinear relationship between high school size and student learning.[13] Another common, but fundamental, design flaw is that almost no research on school size recognizes that questions regarding school size and student outcomes are multilevel. Thus the large majority of school-size research examines the relationship with aggregate data (that is, size effects on school-average achievement). This approach ignores the fact that size may differentially influence learning, based on students' social background. Moreover, size effects may interact with such basic school characteristics as racial or social class composition.[14]

Using multilevel methods and a longitudinal design, Lee and Smith conclude that achievement gains are largest in medium-size high schools (600–900 students), although schools with somewhat smaller enrollments are more equitable, in terms of the relationship between social background and achievement gains.[15] Although the same size range is ideal in schools differentiated by their concentration of minorities and socioeconomic status (SES), size has stronger effects on student learning in schools educating less-advantaged populations. In another study, we explore how the size of Chicago's K–8 elementary schools influences achievement gains for seventh and eighth graders, both directly and through teachers' attitudes. That study finds favorable effects for smaller elementary schools (below 400 students) but no differences between medium and large schools (more than 750 students).[16] Moreover, teachers' willingness to take responsibility for their students' learning is greater in smaller schools. A more thorough and complete review of the literature on school size is available in the paper by Darling-Hammond, Ross, and Milliken in this volume.

Research on Grade Span

Another area that has received little empirical scrutiny is grade span, a concept that describes how many and which grades are included within a single school. There are both structural and philosophical reasons arguing for narrow versus broad grade spans. Much of the literature on grade span focuses on middle and junior high schools, neglecting elementary school configurations, where the construct is equally valid. The decision about what grades to include in which schools is generally guided by matters of practical necessity rather than educational value. The size of existing buildings, enrollments, and fiscal resources determines grade spans more often than thoughtful attention to children's social and academic needs.[17]

Our interest in grade span is twofold. First, grade configurations influence the social and academic characteristics of schools. Socially, broader grade spans within schools create opportunities for older children to act as role models for younger peers.[18] These opportunities may occur both informally (for example, at recess and in the cafeteria) and formally (for example, through "reading buddy" and other activities). Academically, school principals craft goals for their school based partly on the grades the school serves. Principals in K–8 and K–12 schools are more likely to stress higher-order thinking over basic skills than principals in schools enrolling lower grades.[19] Moreover, broader grade spans facilitate teacher communication across grades, matching pedagogical strategies and expectations to children's developmental stages.[20]

Second, the grade configuration of elementary schools influences the number of children within each grade. Schools serving fewer grades typically have more students and classes per grade (for example, K–3); schools serving many grades typically have fewer students per grade (for example, K–8 and K–12). The same mechanisms may link school size and grade size to student outcomes. For example, schools that enroll more students per grade are more likely to sort students into tailored academic programs or even academically homogeneous classrooms, thus increasing the odds that children's learning will be stratified academically and socially. Indeed, some research uses grade size as a proxy for school size.[21] However, we choose to maintain an important distinction between these two elements of elementary school size.

Summary of Research on Size

In general, extant research favors smaller educational contexts, defined both in terms of school size and class size. However, the strands of research examining class size and school size are curiously independent and seldom combined into a single study. Despite extensive literature on school size in high schools and class size in elementary schools, these bodies of research do not inform one another. Research on *school* size focuses almost exclusively on secondary schools, whereas research on *class* size focuses entirely on elementary schools (and really at the lowest grades). It seems reasonable to assume that these size elements are related in U.S. elementary schools, despite the paucity of research exploring the connection.

Although policymakers have recently embraced a strong advocacy of small high schools (not necessarily with empirical support), research on high school size may not be applicable to elementary schools. And despite the well-designed Tennessee experiment, many nagging issues challenge the documented relationship between several elements of organizational size and student learning in elementary school. Although teachers at all levels favor smaller classes, basic issues of educational cost and efficiency cannot be ignored. In the policy arena, the size dimensions we consider in this study are amenable to direct policy manipulation. People who work in schools should recognize how the various elements of size work together—rather than thoughtlessly embrace the mantra that smaller is better. School practitioners, policymakers, and taxpayers may rightly ask, Better for whom? How small is "small"? Possibly better for some but harmful for others? In this study we bring together what are currently quite disparate strands of research to address some of these questions.

Research Questions

Our exploration of these issues differs from extant studies linking size to student outcomes in four important respects. First, we focus on elementary school size. Second, we conceptualize the size of educational contexts quite broadly, focusing on the relative impacts of *class size* and *school size,* while simultaneously accounting for *grade span*. Third, we explore the effects of these structural characteristics of elementary schools on both learning and the equitable distribution of that learning by children's social background, particularly race or ethnicity and socioeconomic status. Fourth, our research design provides considerable methodological leverage with which to disentangle the confounding effects on student learning of student background and the size of elementary school contexts.

The paper is organized around three research questions:

—*Effects on learning trajectories.* How can we characterize the relationship between elementary class size, school size, and student learning in reading and mathematics over the kindergarten and first-grade years? Of particular interest is whether class size is related to student learning once we account for school size, and vice versa.

—*Size effects on the social distribution of learning.* Do the effects of school and class size differ for children of different social backgrounds? If so, are smaller classes and schools more important for more disadvantaged students?

—*Changes in size effects over time and subject.* To what extent do the effects of these various elements of size differ between kindergarten and first grade and between learning in literacy and in mathematics? In other words, are certain elements more important in kindergarten than in first grade or for the development of literacy rather than mathematics skills?

Method of Research

This study is located within a type of research called "school effects," which investigates how school characteristics influence student outcomes. Most school-effects research centers on high schools. However, this type of research in elementary schools flows from a seminal study by Barr and Dreeben.[22] A few recent studies also focus on elementary school effects.[23] The school-effects tradition capitalizes on a basic notion in education: nesting. That is, students are nested in classrooms, and classrooms are nested in schools. At each level of nesting, different policies and practices influence students' experiences. In this study, we conceptually and analytically nest students within schools. Although we could logically have the classroom as the unit of analysis, we do not pursue this approach for three reasons. First, two of the three size dimensions (school size and grade span) are school-level phenomena. Second, class size is typically a function of school enrollments and district policies; class sizes within schools vary little. Third, the structure of the data we use does not support the classroom as a separate unit of analysis.

Data

In this study, we employ data from the Early Childhood Longitudinal Study, Kindergarten Cohort (ECLS-K). Sponsored by the National Center for Education Statistics (NCES), these data are ideal for studying how organizational size influences children's learning, particularly with the statistical methods discussed below. The ECLS-K collection of base-year (1998) data followed a stratified design structure. The primary sampling units were geographic areas consisting of counties or groups of counties from which about 1,000 public and private schools offering kindergarten programs were selected. A target sample of about twenty-four children was then drawn from each school. In this chapter, we employ the first four data waves of ECLS-K, which include information on the same children in the fall and spring of kindergarten (waves 1 and 2) and the fall and spring of first grade, with a random subsample in the fall (waves 3 and 4). Beyond testing children with one-on-one untimed achievement tests at each wave, data were also collected from parents through structured telephone interviews, from each child's teacher, and from schools.[24] These rich data allow researchers to capture a longitudinal picture of a recent, large, and nationally representative cohort of young children as they move through elementary school.

Growth Curves within an HLM Framework

We employ hierarchical linear modeling (HLM) within a three-level growth-curve framework.[25] Specifically, we nest learning trajectories within children, who are nested within schools. Our level-1 HLM models estimate children's individual learning trajectories. At level 2, we model these learning trajectories as functions of children's social and academic background. At level 3—the focus of this study—we estimate the effects of organizational size on children's learning.

AN ALTERNATE GROWTH-CURVE APPROACH. Quantitative researchers traditionally have used analysis of covariance (ANCOVA) or gain-score models to measure change over time within individuals. Over the past several decades, however, social scientists have concluded that estimating change based on only two data points is inherently inadequate.[26] Myriad statistical and substantive issues have driven this methodological shift, although one central concern is shared: traditional approaches assume that variance in the outcome remains steady over time. This assumption *itself* implies that growth trajectories among individuals are perfectly parallel, "an entirely unrealistic state of affairs [that] is obvious even at the most casual glance."[27]

As an alternative approach, educational researchers are increasingly using three or more data points to model growth rates and learning trajectories. Such analyses entail both within-individual and between-individual components.[28] The first analytic phase estimates the growth rates of individuals, while the second phase focuses on the detection and *explanation* of systematic variance in individual growth rates.[29] An endless array of potential explanatory covariates exists, including the characteristics of individual children, their classrooms and teachers, schools, peers, and neighborhoods.[30] Our examination of the relationship between components of elementary school size and cognitive growth falls within this relatively new analytic framework.

CONCEPTUALIZING TIME. The ECLS-K data present a unique challenge to researchers interested in modeling children's cognitive growth over time. Longitudinal studies of student learning generally consider the timing of events as constant across cases (that is, "third grade" represents an identical value or construct). However, the dates on which the ECLS-K cognitive assessments were administered vary considerably across children, both within and between schools. This is understandable given the enormity of the data collection involved with ECLS-K and the time required for each one-on-one assessment. In addition to variability in testing dates, the starting and ending dates of academic years vary across schools.

The result of this variability in school exposure at each assessment is that children's opportunities to learn differed both within and between schools. For example, the time children were in school between the fall and spring kindergarten assessments ranged from almost four to over eight months, averaging about six months (although the school year is nine months). For some children, the fall assessments took place months into the school year and the spring assessments occurred several months before the end of the school year. As such, the assessments do not represent comparable events in time across children. Further complicating the analyses, children were in school for approximately half of the "summer vacation" between the spring kindergarten and fall first-grade assessments. Considering the rapid learning rates among young children, researchers who employ the ECLS-K data must take these concerns into account.[31]

Despite these analytic challenges, the structure of the ECLS-K data provides a unique methodological opportunity. Our level-1 models include three time-varying covariates that indicate individual children's exposure to school at each assessment: months of exposure to kindergarten, months of exposure to summer between kindergarten and first grade, and months of exposure to first grade. For example, at the time of the first assessment the average child had been "exposed" to more than two months of kindergarten, but zero months of summer and zero months of first grade. With the second assessment, the average child had experienced more than eight months of kindergarten but had not been exposed to summer or first grade. At the third assessment, the average child had been exposed to 9.5 months of kindergarten (a full year), 2.7 months of summer (the traditional summer vacation), and more than a month of first grade. At the point of the fourth and final assessment, the average child had been exposed to 9.5 months of kindergarten, 2.7 months of summer, and more than eight months of first grade.

These three measures of school exposure—each linked to the four assessment dates—allow us to model four distinct parameters: *initial status*, or children's achievement as they began kindergarten (literally, predicted achievement with exposure to zero days of kindergarten, zero days of summer, and zero days of first grade). Rather than initial *status*, the three remaining parameters are linear *learning* rates or slopes over *the kindergarten year*, *the summer between kindergarten and first grade*, and *the first-grade year*. Again, the variability in testing dates permits this "slopes as outcomes" approach, where the slopes are adjusted for exposure to school. An additional benefit of this approach is that at each analytic level, all coefficients are in an easily interpretable metric: points of learning *per month* in kindergarten, summer, and first grade. We also present our class-size and school-size estimates in effect-size (standard deviation) units. In this chapter, we focus on the estimates obtained from the kindergarten and first-grade parameters, which address our questions regarding the influence of educational size on student learning.[32]

LEARNING PATTERNS IN ECLS-K. As our focus in this study is on learning rather than achievement, we explore learning patterns from children's entry into kindergarten to the end of first grade. Figure 1 displays young children's observed learning trajectories during this period. As these learning trajectories are constructed from test scores, in the metric of the IRT (item response theory)-equated number-right scores available in ECLS-K, the scales differ for reading and math. Panel A depicts learning in reading; panel B depicts learning in mathematics. On average, the first testing occurred in late October 1998, the second in early May 1999, the third in early October 1999, and the fourth in early May 2000. Thus the observed trajectories begin and end on those dates.

The panels in figure 1 suggest three similar trends for both subjects. First, we see a pattern of continual growth (or learning). Young children's achievement in these subjects increases steadily. Second, we see a slight decline in the learning slope over the summer between kindergarten and first grade, more so in reading than in math. Third, we see a slightly higher learning slope in first grade than in kindergarten. These slope variations are more noticeable in reading than in math.

Recall that our basic HLM growth-curve models estimate four learning parameters in each subject: initial status, monthly achievement gain over the kindergarten year, monthly gain over the summer, and monthly gain over the first-grade year. Figure 2 displays these patterns, in which achievement growth is adjusted for differences between when schools actually opened and closed and when the tests were administered to each child. The slopes of the lines in figure 2 may be expressed in a monthly learning metric.

Estimates of the four parameters of interest—initial status and the three gain slopes—from figure 2 indicate that results in figure 1 are misleading in three ways. First, initial status (achievement at entry into kindergarten) is overestimated in figure 1, as the first testing was nearly two months (sometimes more) into the school year. Estimated initial status in September, from figure 2, is a few test points lower than the observed achievement several weeks later. Second, the time gap between the second and third assessments in figure 1 is too wide to isolate true summer learning (that is, only those months when school is not in session), as both assessments were made during the school year. In figure 2, learning trajectories extend across the entire kindergarten and first-grade school years, coinciding with the average time of school closing at the end of kindergarten and opening at the beginning of first grade. In-school time periods average 9.5 months; summer averages 2.7 months. Third—and most important—the slopes of the lines for the three growth parameters in figures 1 and 2 are different, especially during the summer. The estimated learning slopes are slightly steeper for the in-school periods in figure 2 than in figure 1. The most striking comparison shows that the estimated summer learning slope

Figure 1. ECLS-K Overall Learning Trajectories Based on Average Testing Times

Panel A. Reading achievement (HLM estimated scores)

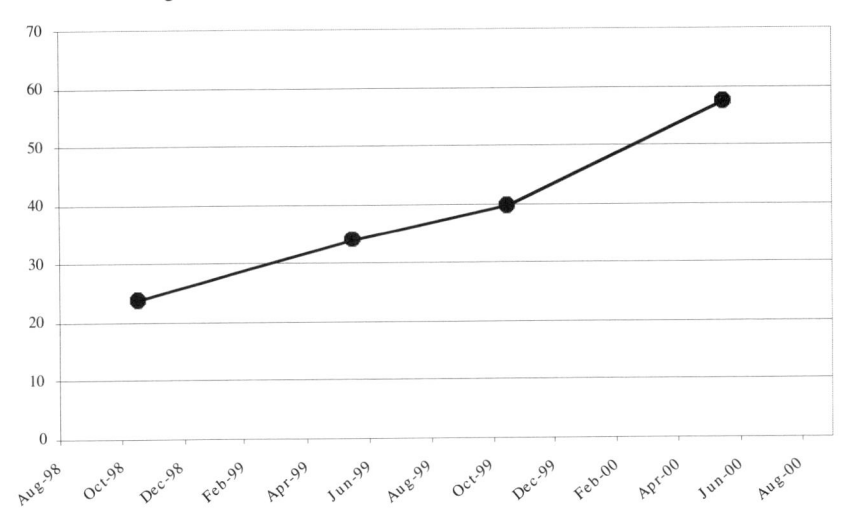

Panel B. Math achievement (HLM estimated scores)

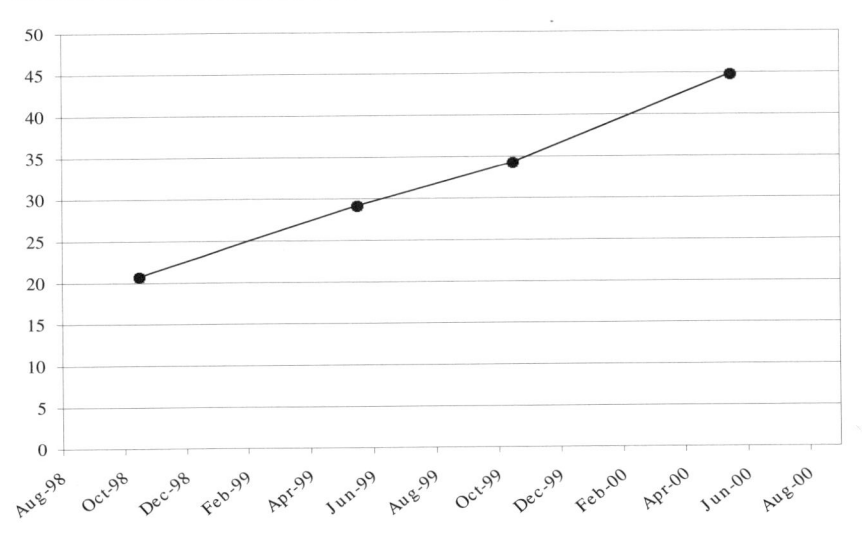

Source: Authors' calculations using ECLS-K data.
HLM = hierarchical modeling.

Figure 2. Estimated Overall Learning Trajectory, in School and out of School

Reading achievement (HLM estimated scores)

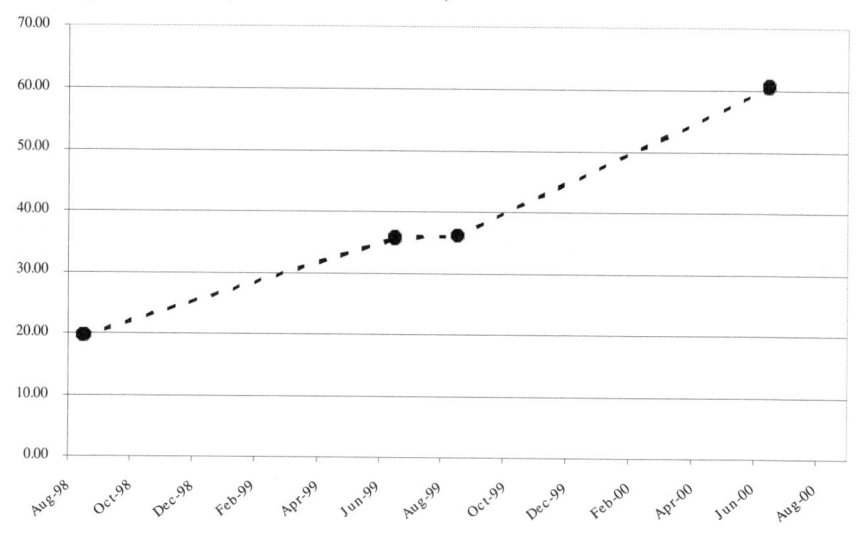

Math achievement (HLM estimated scores)

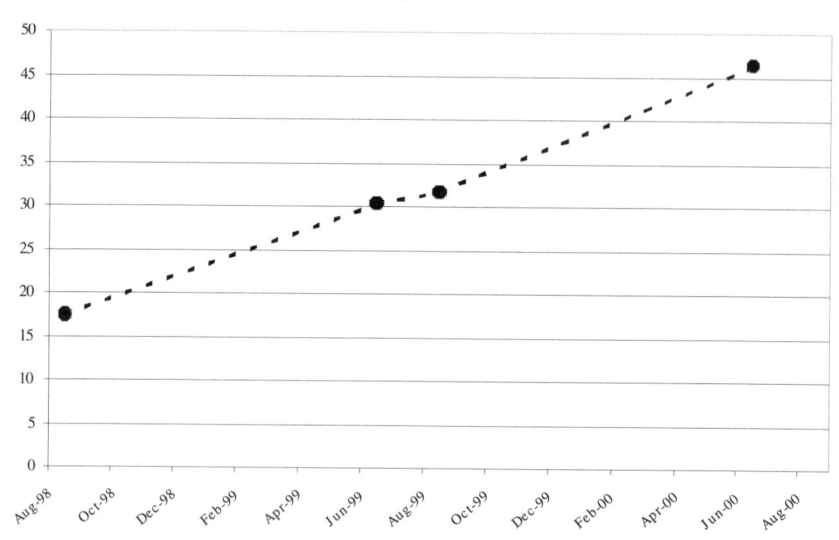

Source: Authors' calculations using ECLS-K data.
HLM = hierarchical modeling.

for reading in figure 2 is nearly flat when we model true out-of-school learning (rather than learning between the two assessment time points).

WEIGHTS. Because ECLS-K used a multistage stratified sampling design, the data include a series of design weights. As with other longitudinal NCES data sets, analyses using ECLS-K require the use of weights to compensate for unequal probabilities of selection within and between schools (for example, the intentional oversampling of Asian and Pacific Islander children) and nonresponse effects. Although our growth-curve models consider achievement at four waves of the ECLS-K data, the "1234" panel ECLS-K weights are only defined for children in the sample at time 3. Hence the use of those weights automatically restricts the sample to that small subgroup of children and schools with data at the beginning of first grade. Instead, these analyses employ the "124" panel weights, which retain the larger sample. Our descriptive and analytic analyses employ a child-level weight (C124CW0) to compensate for differential sampling both within and between schools. We use the ECLS-K school-level weight (S2SAQW0) with our school-level descriptive and multilevel analyses. Both weights are normalized to a mean of 1 to reflect the actual (smaller) sample sizes.

ANALYTIC SAMPLE. From the full ECLS-K sample, we constructed our analytic sample in two stages. First, we selected children who had a nonmissing weight, remained in the same school in kindergarten and first grade, advanced to the first grade following the 1998–99 kindergarten year, had complete data on gender, race or ethnicity, and socioeconomic status, and had test scores for at least three of the four literacy and mathematics assessments. We then selected schools that had a nonmissing weight, were not year-round schools, were public schools that offered kindergarten and first grade, and enrolled at least five ECLS-K children.[33] Our final analytic sample includes 25,545 literacy and 25,545 mathematics test scores nested within 7,740 children, who are nested within 527 public schools. An analysis of missing data revealed that our subsample is somewhat more socioeconomically advantaged than the full ECLS-K sample, with fewer language-minority children and fewer children from the lowest SES quintile. The loss of lower-SES and language-minority children mostly occurred when the sample was restricted by available test scores, as all testing was in English.

Measures

A central task of this study is to consider the most fruitful way to conceptualize various elements of public elementary school size. Although we had intended to include grade cohort size as a separate element, we found that kindergarten and first-grade cohort size was highly correlated with school size ($r = 0.75$). This is reasonable, given that elementary schools with larger enrollments generally enroll more students at each grade. However, this finding means that grade cohort and school size are not independent constructs. The focus of our study is on the effects of class size and school size on children's learning in the early grades.

CLASS SIZE. Because ECLS-K sampled only a modest number of children per school, most within-classroom sample sizes are quite small. This sampling design precluded our ability to conceptualize the classroom as a separate unit of analysis. Using an HLM fully unconditional model, we found that the vast majority (over 85 percent) of variance in class size is between (rather than within) schools. That is, classes at the same grade within the same school were very likely to enroll close to the same number of children. Thus we decided to consider class size as school-level aggregates (that is, separate averages of the kindergarten and first-grade class sizes in each school). Based on the Tennessee class-size parameters, we designated classes enrolling seventeen or fewer children as "small classes." For reasons discussed below, we designated classes enrolling twenty-five or more children as "large classes." In our multivariate HLM analyses, we compare schools with these large and small classes to those with medium-size classes (between seventeen and twenty-five students).

Neither the Tennessee nor the Wisconsin class-size experiments examined medium-size classrooms. Classrooms with enrollments between seventeen and twenty-two did not participate in Project STAR, and Wisconsin's SAGE program involved no classrooms enrolling between fifteen and twenty-one students. This is quite understandable, in that these evaluations sought to maximize their ability to identify class-size effects. However, the nationally representative ECLS-K data we employ in this study indicate that, in roughly half of all public schools, medium-size kindergarten and first-grade classrooms (enrollments between seventeen and twenty-five students) are the norm. Moreover, the Tennessee and Wisconsin experiments suffered from restricted class-size ranges: no classrooms in either experiment enrolled more than twenty-six students. The ECLS-K data again indicate that a considerable number of U.S. public school students in kindergarten and first grade are enrolled in classrooms larger than this. As such, the parameters of the "large" classrooms in this study are somewhat larger than those in either the Tennessee or the Wisconsin experiments.

SCHOOL SIZE. For three reasons, we chose not to employ a continuous measure of school size in our statistical models. First, the variable measuring elementary school size is positively skewed, with many more small than large schools. This non-normal distribution precludes its use as a continuous measure in our multivariate analyses, which assume normal distributions. Second, our previous research on school size suggests nonlinear relationships between school size and student learning.[34] Third, in addressing issues of interest to policymakers and school administrators, it is helpful to offer results that have clear substantive meaning. Although we could have transformed our school size measure using the natural logarithm, describing results in terms of "log size" can be a cumbersome venture. Thus we have constructed a series of dummy variables that identify small schools (fewer than or equal to 275 children), medium-small schools (276–400), medium-size schools (401–600), medium-large schools (601–800), and large schools (more than 800 students). In our multivariate analyses, medium-size schools are the uncoded comparison group.

DEPENDENT MEASURES: COGNITIVE ASSESSMENTS. Each ECLS-K cognitive assessment was administered individually, with an adult assessor spending fifty to seventy minutes with each child at each testing wave.[35] The literacy assessment at each wave was designed to measure both basic literacy skills (print familiarity, letter recognition, beginning and ending sounds, rhyming sounds, word recognition) as well as more advanced reading comprehension skills (initial understanding, interpretation, personal reflection, and ability to demonstrate a critical stance). These advanced literacy skills, which were assessed through verbal dialogue between the child and the assessor, measured children's ability to identify the main points of a passage and connect text to their own personal experiences and assessed their critical thinking skills and ability to distinguish real versus imaginary content. Mathematics assessment items were designed to measure conceptual and procedural knowledge and problem solving, with items equally divided between number sense and measurement. The scores on both the reading and mathematics assessments at each wave were equated separately using item response theory, in order to make them appropriate measures of change over time. Our analyses use the IRT-scale scores.[36]

SOCIAL AND ACADEMIC BACKGROUND. Children's socioeconomic status is captured with a composite measure of parents' income, education, and occupational prestige (a z score; $M = 0$, $SD = 1$). Our analyses also employ a dummy-coded gender measure (girls = 1, boys = 0) and a measure indicating whether the child was a member of a traditionally underperforming racial or ethnic group (Hispanic, African American, Native American, and multiracial children = 1, white and Asian children = 0). The models further account for children's age (in months), whether the child lived in a single-parent home (yes

= 1, no = 0), and whether a language other than English was the primary home language (yes = 1, no = 0). Academic background is captured by whether the child was repeating kindergarten (yes = 1, no = 0) and attended full-day kindergarten (yes = 1, no = 0).

SCHOOL CHARACTERISTICS. The focus of this research is our level-3 (between-school) HLM models. In addition to the average class-size and school-size measures discussed above, to capture grade span we use a set of dummy-coded indicators to identify primary (K–3) schools, K–8 schools, and K–12 schools, which are each compared to elementary (K–6) schools in our multivariate HLMs. Our school-level models also incorporate composition controls for school-average SES (a z score) and high-minority enrollment (a dummy variable indicating non-white and non-Asian enrollments above 33 percent). Due to documented associations between urbanicity and school size, we include dummy-coded indicators of school location (large city, medium city, rural–small town, each compared to suburbs–urban fringe).

Results

We present both descriptive and multivariate results. Our descriptive results provide information about both children and schools, organized by the size of their classes and schools. We tested group mean differences for statistical significance with t tests (for continuous variables) and cross-tabulations (for categorical variables). We present our within-school and between-school multivariate and multilevel HLM results separately. Our within-school results describe the relationships between child-level characteristics and student learning. Our between-school models explore the effects of elementary school organizational size on student learning—the focus of this paper. All HLM results in tables are presented in the test score points per month (ppm) metric described earlier, although we also convert some to effect sizes (ES) and annual test-score point differences.

Descriptive Results

Table 1 presents information about schools and students organized by school size. A linear relationship is evident between school size and average kindergarten and first-grade class size, although the differences are small and mostly not statistically significant. We find stronger evidence of a (curvilinear) relationship between average-SES and school size. A 0.4 standard deviation

Table 1. Descriptive Statistics for Schools and Students, by School Size[a]

Indicator	Small school	Medium-small school	Medium-size school	Medium-large school	Large school
Schools (N = 527)					
Sample size	110	128	171	80	38
Average kindergarten class size	19.3	20.2	20.7	21.5	22.2
	(5.9)	(4.6)	(4.8)	(3.9)	(3.7)
Average first-grade class size	18.2***	19.3	20.4	21.4	21.2
	(4.8)	(3.0)	(3.2)	(3.1)	(4.2)
Average socioeconomic status[b]	−0.3*	−0.1	0.1	0.1	−0.2*
	(0.7)	(0.9)	(1.1)	(1.0)	(1.0)
Percent high-minority school[c]	18.2**	24.2	33.1	33.8	44.7
Percent primary school (K–3)	18.2***	6.3	4.6	5.0	2.6
Percent elementary school (K–6)	64.5***	82.7	83.9	82.5	86.8
Percent K–8 school	11.8	7.9	6.3	10.0	10.5
Percent K–12 school	5.5	3.1	5.2	2.5	0.0
Percent large city	9.1	7.0	10.9	21.3*	18.4
Percent medium-size city	20.9	22.6	24.6	17.5	13.2
Percent suburban or urban fringe	20.0***	32.8	38.9	48.8	50.0
Percent small town or rural	50.0***	32.6	25.3	12.5*	18.4
Students (N = 7,740)					
Sample size	1,004	1,510	2,733	1,615	878
Socioeconomic status[b]	−0.2***	−0.1***	0.0	0.1	−0.1*
	(0.9)	(1.0)	(1.0)	(1.0)	(0.9)
Age (months)	66.1	66.1	66.1	66.4	66.2
	(4.2)	(4.2)	(4.2)	(4.2)	(4.3)
Percent female	51.3	46.3	49.2	47.7	48.8
Percent full-day kindergarten	49.2	48.9	51.0	59.2***	71.9***
Percent minority (non-white or non-Asian)	24.0***	28.5	31.3	33.4	34.5
Percent English as a second language	3.6***	3.2***	6.7	7.6	8.0
Percent single-parent family	23.3	23.6	22.5	23.8	22.4
Percent repeating kindergarten	4.8*	2.7	3.1	4.9**	2.7

Source: Authors' calculations using ECLS-K data.
* $p < 0.05$; ** $p < 0.01$; *** $p < 0.001$.
a. Unweighted $N = 7,740$ children nested within 527 public schools. Small schools are up to 275 students; medium-small schools are 276–400 students; medium-size schools are 401–600 students; medium-large schools are 601–800 students; large schools are more than 800 students. All significance tests are compared to medium-size schools; standard deviations are in parentheses.
b. Measure is z scored (M = 0, SD = 1).
c. School enrollment is at least 33 percent non-white, non-Asian.

average SES gap separates small and medium-size schools ($p < 0.05$), and a 0.3 standard deviation gap separates large and medium-size schools. As subsequent results suggest, small schools tend to be rural (and lower SES) and large schools tend to be urban (and also lower SES). In short, public schools at both ends of the size continuum tend to serve socioeconomically disadvantaged students. Indeed, half of the small schools in our sample are located in small towns and rural areas, compared to only one-quarter of medium-size schools

($p < 0.001$). Further reflecting the small-town and rural character of these schools, less than one-fifth (18.2 percent) of small schools have high-minority enrollments, compared to almost one-third of medium-size schools ($p < 0.01$). In terms of grade span, compared to medium-size schools, small schools are less likely to be primary schools and more likely to be elementary schools ($p < 0.001$).

Mirroring these school-level descriptive statistics, the results in table 1 indicate that children in small, medium-small, and large schools tend to come from less-advantaged families than children in medium-size schools. Minority children are less likely to attend small compared to medium-size schools ($p < 0.001$). Children in medium-large and (especially) large schools are more likely to attend full-day kindergarten ($p < 0.001$). This may reflect the fact that many urban public schools (which tend to be larger) offer full-day kindergarten as a compensatory program. Children in small and medium-large schools are more likely to be kindergarten repeaters than those in medium-size schools. Children's age, gender, and single-parent status are not related to the size of the school they attend.

Table 2 presents information about schools and students organized by average class size in kindergarten and first grade. Although the sociodemographic relationships are similar to those found in table 1, there are some clear differences. Most notably, the relationship between school size and average class size becomes even more evident. Schools with small kindergarten and first-grade classes enroll roughly 130 fewer students than schools with medium-size kindergarten and first-grade classes ($p < 0.001$). Moreover, schools with large first-grade classes enroll almost 100 students more than those with medium-size first-grade classes ($p < 0.05$). Schools with large kindergarten and first-grade classrooms are also considerably more likely to enroll high proportions of minority students ($p < 0.05$) and to be located in large cities ($p < 0.01$). Conversely, schools with small classes are quite likely to be located in small towns and rural areas ($p < 0.01$) and in suburban and urban fringe communities ($p < 0.01$). Indeed, more than two-thirds of schools with small classes are located in these areas (40.2 and 29.0 percent of small kindergarten classes; 42.5 and 23.9 percent of small first-grade classes).

A curvilinear relationship between class size and socioeconomic status is evident. Children attending schools with small *and* large class sizes are less socially advantaged compared to those attending schools with medium-size classes ($p < 0.001$). Almost half of the children attending schools with large kindergarten (43.4 percent) and first-grade classrooms (45.9 percent) are members of racial or ethnic minority groups ($p < 0.001$). As with SES, schools with

Table 2. Descriptive Statistics for Schools and Students, by Class Size[a]

Indicator	Kindergarten			First grade		
	Small classes[a]	Medium-size classes	Large classes	Small classes	Medium-size classes	Large classes
Schools (N = 527)						
Sample size	107	341	80	113	374	40
Average enrollment	359.0***	484.2	473.2	344.9***	478.9	572.6*
	(156.7)	(212.8)	(265.9)	(188.4)	(206.2)	(272.9)
Average socioeconomic status[b]	−0.2*	0.1	−0.3**	−0.4***	0.1	−0.2*
	(0.8)	(1.0)	(0.9)	(0.8)	(1.0)	(1.0)
Percent high-minority school[c]	18.7*	29.1	41.3*	23.9	27.9	51.3*
Percent primary school (K–3)	4.7	9.0	7.5	6.2	9.0	2.6
Percent elementary school (K–6)	72.0**	83.4	70.0**	77.9	79.6	82.1
Percent K–8 school	15.0***	5.2	16.5***	9.7	8.0	15.4
Percent K–12 school	7.5*	2.3	6.3*	7.1*	3.4	0.0
Percent large city	4.9*	11.4	24.1**	5.3*	12.2	28.2**
Percent medium-size city	27.1	24.4	8.9**	28.3*	20.7	22.5
Percent suburban or urban fringe	29.0**	38.4	33.8	23.9**	39.4	35.0
Percent small town or rural	40.2**	25.9	32.9	42.5**	27.6	12.8*
Students (N = 7,740)						
Sample size	1,295	5,352	1,093	1,289	5,749	702
Socioeconomic status[b]	−0.1***	0.0	−0.2***	−0.2***	0.0	−0.1***
	(1.0)	(1.0)	(1.1)	(0.9)	(1.0)	(1.1)
Age (months)	66.3	66.2	66.1	66.6**	66.1	66.0
	(4.4)	(4.2)	(4.2)	(4.4)	(4.2)	(4.2)
Percent female	46.4	49.1	47.6	47.2	48.6	49.8
Percent full-day kindergarten	38.3***	56.8	62.9***	57.2	53.4	63.9***
Percent minority (non-white or non-Asian)	27.0	29.2	43.4***	30.6	29.2	45.9***
Percent English as a second language	3.2***	6.0	9.2***	4.0**	5.9	10.8***
Percent single-parent family	27.3***	21.2	28.8***	24.2*	22.4	27.7**
Percent repeating kindergarten	3.7	3.5	3.9	3.7	3.7	2.3

Source: Authors' calculations using ECLS-K data.
* $p < 0.05$; ** $p < 0.01$; *** $p < 0.001$.
a. Unweighted $N = 7,740$ children nested within 527 public schools. Small classes are up to seventeen students; medium-size classes are between seventeen and twenty-five students; large classes are more than twenty-five students. All significance tests are compared to schools with medium-size classes; standard deviations are in parentheses.
b. Measure is z scored (M = 0, SD = 1).
c. School enrollment is at least 33 percent non-white, non-Asian.

small *and* large classrooms also enroll greater proportions of children from single-parent homes and children for whom English is not the primary home language. Almost two-thirds of children in public schools with large kindergarten and first-grade classrooms receive full-day kindergarten, compared to slightly more than half of students in schools with medium-size classrooms ($p < 0.001$). Despite their relative socioeconomic disadvantage, children attending schools with small kindergarten classrooms are less likely to receive full-day kindergarten ($p < 0.001$); only 38.3 percent of children in schools whose kindergarten classes are small attend full-day kindergarten.

In sum, our descriptive results indicate a modest, but positive, relationship between public school size and class size. Thus the effects of each measure of context size should be estimated net of the other. Smaller schools (with smaller classes) are more likely to be located in rural areas, whereas larger classes (often in larger schools) are more often located in large cities. Although schools with high concentrations of minority students are more likely to be large (and to offer large classes), the relationship between SES and school size follows a different pattern. Both the largest and the smallest schools (with larger and smaller classes) enroll disproportionate numbers of socially disadvantaged children. It is clear from these descriptive differences that our estimates of class-size and school-size effects on young children's learning must include statistical controls for social background, school composition, school location, and grade span.

Within-School Results

Our within-school HLM models explore the associations between child-level characteristics and learning in kindergarten and first grade (see table 3). We speak of "learning" because the outcomes are gains over the kindergarten and first-grade years (figure 2). Although our between-school models represent the primary focus of this study, we briefly describe our child-level results here. Over the kindergarten year, girls gain more skills in literacy (0.13 test score points per month [ppm], $p < 0.001$) and mathematics (0.04 ppm, $p < 0.05$) than their male counterparts. Children attending full-day kindergarten learn considerably more than their peers attending half-day programs (0.26 and 0.15 ppm in literacy and mathematics, respectively; $p < 0.001$). These results are similar to findings from our previous research using ECLS-K.[37]

In previous work, we describe the considerable racial and socioeconomic disparities that characterize young children's achievement as they begin kindergarten.[38] The results in table 3 indicate that these social disparities actually

Table 3. Within-School Models of Kindergarten and First-Grade Literacy and Mathematics Learning[a]

Indicator	Literacy learning	Mathematics learning
Kindergarten		
Female	0.13***	0.04*
Full-day kindergarten	0.26***	0.15***
Age (months)	0.00	0.00
Socioeconomic status[b]	0.07**	0.04**
English as a second language	0.13*	0.09*
Single-parent family	–0.05	–0.02
Repeating kindergarten	–0.14	–0.16*
Minority (non-white or non-Asian)	–0.13**	–0.12***
Intercept	1.61***	1.29***
First grade		
Female	0.03	–0.04
Full-day kindergarten	–0.27***	–0.11**
Age (months)	–0.01	–0.01***
Socioeconomic status[b]	0.06*	–0.02
English as a second language	0.10	0.01
Single-parent family	–0.06	–0.01
Repeating kindergarten	–0.38	–0.14*
Minority (non-white or non-Asian)	0.01	0.03
Intercept	2.56***	1.56***

Source: Authors' calculations using ECLS-K data.
* $p < 0.05$; ** $p < 0.01$; *** $p < 0.001$.
a. $N = 7,740$ children nested within 527 public schools. All coefficients are in a points-per-month learning metric. All measures are grand-mean centered.
b. Measure is z scored ($M = 0$, $SD = 1$).

increase during kindergarten. Even after adjusting for many other child-level covariates, minority status is associated with reduced literacy and mathematics gain during kindergarten (–0.13 ppm in literacy, $p < 0.01$; -0.12 ppm in mathematics, $p < 0.001$). Conversely, higher-SES children tend to gain more skills: a 1 standard deviation increase in SES is associated with 0.07 ppm additional learning in literacy and 0.04 ppm additional learning in mathematics ($p < 0.01$).

Children for whom English is not the primary home language gain more literacy skills during kindergarten than their English-speaking counterparts (0.13 ppm in literacy, $p < 0.05$; 0.09 ppm in mathematics, $p < 0.05$). Unlike these potentially compensatory effects associated with language-minority status and full-day kindergarten, the results in table 3 challenge the efficacy of kindergarten retention practices. Kindergarten repeaters learn less than nonrepeaters in mathematics (–0.16 ppm, $p < 0.05$) and gain literacy skills at comparable rates to nonrepeaters during their second year of kindergarten.

We turn now to within-school results for the first grade. Our results in table 3 suggest that, over the first-grade year, children who did not attend full-day kindergarten "catch up" to their counterparts who did. Indeed, the learning advantages of full-day kindergarten are significantly reversed during first grade. Another departure from the kindergarten results is that minority and nonminority students learn at similar rates during first grade (that is, their learning rates are parallel), whereas they are disadvantaged in kindergarten learning in both subjects. However, higher-SES children continue to gain more skills in literacy during first grade ($p < 0.05$), but not in math. Accounting for the other covariates, first-grade literacy and mathematics learning are not related to gender, single-parent, or language status.

We also note here the different learning rates in each subject in kindergarten and first grade (comparing the intercepts in column 1 and column 2). Particularly in literacy—but also in mathematics—on average children gain considerably more skills in first grade than in kindergarten. The literacy intercepts indicate an adjusted average monthly gain of 1.61 ppm in kindergarten, but 2.56 ppm during first grade. Although the distinction is not as stark with mathematics, children gain 0.27 ppm more in first grade than in kindergarten (1.56 versus 1.29 ppm). These differential learning rates may reflect two phenomena: a generally stronger academic focus of most first-grade classrooms and the fact that virtually all first grades are full day. One implication for this study is obvious: less variability in kindergarten learning suggests less variability that may be explained as a function of elementary school organizational size.

EXPLORING EQUITY. In the HLM level-2 models presented in table 3, all child-level variables modeling learning are grand-mean centered, and their between-school variances are fixed to 0. Our original intention, as described in the second research question, was to explore whether class size or school size was associated with equity. The equity measures we considered are captured by the relationship between SES and learning in either subject at either grade—essentially four slopes-as-outcomes (two subjects, two grades). Although in some cases, these slopes vary significantly between schools, none of the four SES-learning slopes is related to either class size or school size. In other words, the class- and school-size effects we report here are similar across race and social class background. Thus we "fix" the four SES-learning slopes in our level-2 HLM models (similar to the slopes of the other child characteristics in these models). We also explore whether class-size and school-size effects—which we discuss below—are different for schools with different minority concentrations and social class compositions. We do find some interactions, but they are inconsistent. As such, we decided to focus on our main effects, which are themselves quite complicated.

BETWEEN-SCHOOL RESULTS. The major findings from our study of class size and school size are presented in table 4. The estimates obtained from our between-school level-3 HLM models are adjusted for both the child-level characteristics in table 3 as well as the school-level measures described earlier and displayed here. As the child-level estimates presented in table 3 change very little from the level-2 HLM models, we do not present them again here. Rather, we focus on our major findings regarding the relationship between organizational size and student learning. However, it is important to understand that the learning outcomes (the intercepts) of the level-3 HLM models shown in table 4 include the full set of controls shown in table 3.

Compared to children in schools with large kindergarten classes, children in schools with small kindergarten classes gain 0.10 ppm more in literacy and 0.08 ppm more in mathematics ($p < 0.10$). Expressed in terms of the standard deviation of the subject- and grade-specific learning slopes, these represent yearly (nine-month) effect sizes of 0.14 standard deviation in literacy and 0.15 standard deviation in mathematics. More noteworthy, children in schools with medium-size classrooms gain more in literacy (0.14 ppm, ES = 0.19 SD) and mathematics (0.08 ppm, ES = 0.15 SD) than those in large kindergarten classrooms ($p < 0.05$). Because we are interested in identifying "ideal" class sizes, we also estimated effects of small compared to medium-size classrooms in other HLM models not shown here. However, we found no differences in literacy or mathematics learning between schools offering small rather than medium-size kindergarten classrooms. The interpretation of these results suggests *detrimental* effects of large kindergarten class size rather than *beneficial* effects of small classes.

These findings support the conclusions from the Tennessee and Wisconsin class-size experiments. However, we extend their important findings. By including schools with medium-size classrooms in our models—which neither the Tennessee nor the Wisconsin experiments considered—our results suggest that schools may enjoy similar advantages by decreasing enrollment from large to mid-size classrooms. Moving to even smaller classes does not appear to provide additional academic benefits, even though such a change would surely require considerable additional costs.

Table 4 also documents significant class-size effects on literacy and mathematics learning during first grade, but with somewhat different patterns. Compared to those in large first-grade classes, children attending schools with small classes gain 0.19 ppm more in literacy (ES = 0.20 SD; $p < 0.05$) and 0.12

Table 4. Between-School Models of Kindergarten and First-Grade Literacy and Mathematics Learning[a]

Indicator	Literacy learning	Mathematics learning
Kindergarten		
Small classes[b]	0.10~	0.08~
Medium-size classes	0.14*	0.08*
Small school[c]	−0.04	−0.03
Medium-small school	0.02	0.02
Medium-large school	0.02	0.00
Large school	−0.03	−0.01
Primary school (K–3)[d]	−0.07	−0.06
K–8 school	−0.09	0.03
K–12 school	−0.08	−0.08
Large city[e]	0.05	0.04
Medium-size city	0.05	−0.02
Rural-small town	−0.11~	−0.05
Average socioeconomic status[f]	0.01	−0.04~
High-minority school[g]	−0.07	−0.12*
Random effect (intercept)	1.55***	1.28***
First grade		
Small classes[b]	0.19*	0.12**
Medium-size classes	−0.07	0.09*
Small school[c]	0.03	0.13*
Medium-small school	0.07	0.08
Medium-large school	0.04	0.02
Large school	−0.17*	−0.03
Primary school (K–3)[d]	−0.08	0.01
K–8 school	0.12	0.04
K–12 school	−0.57***	−0.03
Large city[e]	−0.01	0.08
Medium-size city	0.12~	0.18***
Rural or small town	−0.12	−0.05
Average socioeconomic status[f]	0.03	−0.05*
High-minority[g]	−0.18*	−0.13*
Random effect (intercept)	2.49***	1.43***

Source: Authors' calculations using ECLS-K data.
~ $p < 0.10$; * $p < 0.05$; ** $p < 0.01$; *** $p < 0.001$.

a. $N = 7{,}740$ children nested within 527 public schools. All coefficients are in a child-level points-per-month of learning metric.
b. Small classes (up to seventeen students) and medium-size classes (between seventeen and twenty-five students) are compared to large classes (more than twenty-five students).
c. Small schools (275 students or fewer), medium-small (276–400 students), medium-large (601–800 students), and large schools (more than 800 students) are compared to medium-size schools (401–600).
d. Compared to elementary (K–6) schools.
e. Compared to suburban or urban fringe schools.
f. Measure is z scored (M = 0, standard deviation = 1).
g. School enrollment at least 33 percent non-white, non-Asian.

ppm more in mathematics (ES = 0.24 SD; $p < 0.01$). Children in schools with medium-size classrooms also learn more mathematics than their peers in schools offering large classrooms (0.09 ppm, ES = 0.18 SD; $p < 0.05$). As we do with kindergarten learning, we compare the learning rates associated with small and medium-size first-grade classrooms. Whereas we find no benefits of small compared to medium-size kindergarten classrooms, children in schools with small first-grade classrooms gain more literacy skills than those in schools with medium-size first-grade classrooms (0.12 ppm, ES = 0.13 SD; $p < 0.05$). In mathematics, however, we find no differences between schools offering small and medium-size classrooms.

Figures 3 and 4 offer simple illustrations of these class-size effects. Compared to both small and medium-size classrooms, the results shown in figure 3 indicate that children in schools with large kindergarten classes gain fewer literacy skills over the course of the kindergarten year. In first grade, however, the effects are somewhat different: schools with small classes have an advantage over schools with both medium and large classes. The results for mathematics learning presented in figure 4 are more dramatic. Children learn less in schools with large compared to both small and medium-size classrooms ($p < 0.05$), whereas the learning rates for children in schools with small and medium-size classes are similar. As explained earlier, schools with small classes have no advantage in terms of mathematics learning over those offering medium-size classes. However, clear negative effects are associated with schools offering large kindergarten and first-grade classes.

Once we take into account the types of students they enroll and other social and structural characteristics—notably average class size—we find less dramatic evidence of school-size effects on student learning in kindergarten, as shown in table 4. In first grade, however, size effects are more important. Students learn more mathematics per month in small compared to medium-size schools (0.13 ppm, ES = 0.24 SD; $p < 0.05$) and learn fewer literacy skills per month in large compared to medium-size schools (–0.17 ppm, ES = –0.18 SD; $p < 0.05$). The less dramatic findings regarding elementary school size (compared to class size) may be due to the self-contained nature of most kindergarten and first-grade classrooms, so that the classroom context may be more relevant to learning than the larger school context. As noted, unlike high school students, children's experiences in elementary school are generally influenced more by their classroom context, in which the vast majority of their experiences occur.

The findings about school-size effects on learning in literacy and mathematics in first grade may be clearer when displayed graphically. As with figures

Figure 3. Annual Literacy Learning, by Class Size and Grade

Points of learning per academic year

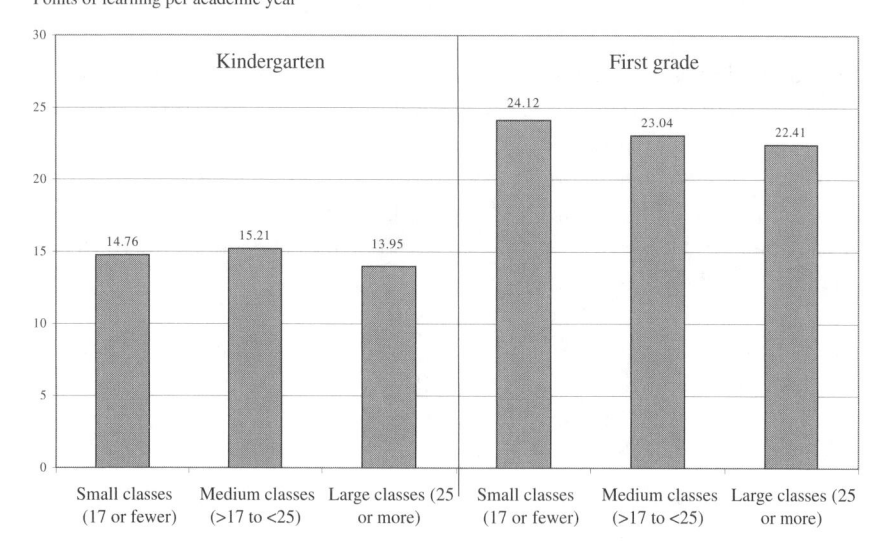

Kindergarten			First grade		
14.76	15.21	13.95	24.12	23.04	22.41
Small classes (17 or fewer)	Medium classes (>17 to <25)	Large classes (25 or more)	Small classes (17 or fewer)	Medium classes (>17 to <25)	Large classes (25 or more)

Source: Authors' calculations using ECLS-K data.

3 and 4, which document class-size effects over a full school year, figure 5 also presents annualized results.[39] Three findings are evident. First, learning in mathematics is advantaged in small schools (annual learning of 14.04 points a year versus 12.6 points a year in large schools). Second, learning in literacy is considerably disadvantaged in large schools (19.98 points a year versus 23.04 points a year in medium-small schools). Third, consistent with our earlier studies of school size in upper grades, school-size effects on learning in the lower-elementary grades are distinctly nonlinear. Given the substantial correlation between school size and average class size in this nationally representative sample of U.S. public elementary schools, as well as the association of school size with school grade span and location, we believe these findings are quite important.

Although they are not the focus of this chapter, table 4 indicates other school-level effects on student learning. In kindergarten, children in small-town and rural schools gain fewer literacy skills than their suburban counterparts (−0.11 ppm, $p < 0.10$). Another notable effect is the reduced first-grade literacy learning among children in K–12 schools compared to children in public elementary schools. Compared to those attending traditional K–6 schools, students in K–12 schools gain about 0.5 point less per month (0.57 ppm, $p < 0.001$). Moreover, children attending schools in medium-size cities

Figure 4. Annual Mathematics Learning, by Class Size and Grade

Points of learning per academic year

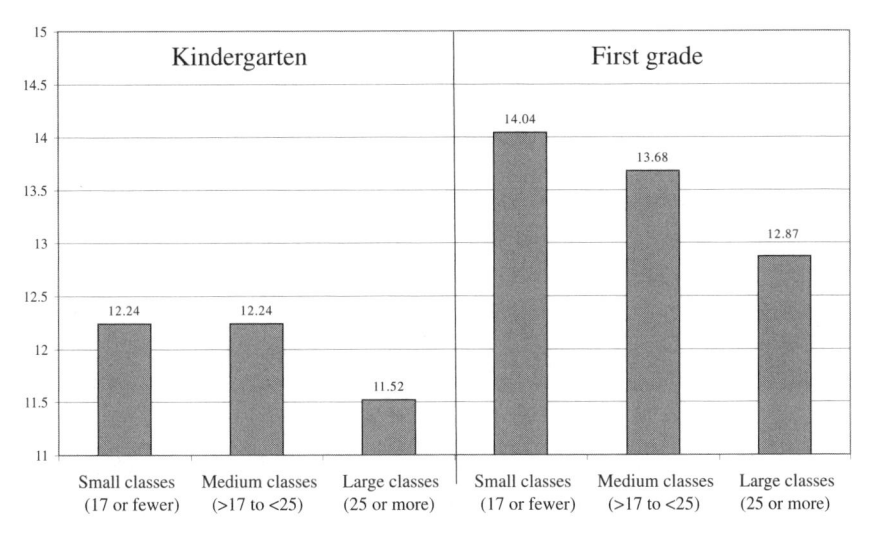

	Kindergarten			First grade		
	Small classes (17 or fewer)	Medium classes (>17 to <25)	Large classes (25 or more)	Small classes (17 or fewer)	Medium classes (>17 to <25)	Large classes (25 or more)
	12.24	12.24	11.52	14.04	13.68	12.87

Source: Authors' calculations using ECLS-K data.

learn more in literacy and mathematics than their counterparts attending schools in suburban and urban fringes ($p < 0.001$). Even after accounting for the other child- and school-level covariates, children attending high-minority-enrollment schools gain fewer skills in kindergarten (–0.12 ppm in mathematics; $p < 0.05$) and in first grade (–0.18 ppm in literacy; –0.13 ppm in math; $p < 0.05$). In kindergarten and first grade, once we account for the other child- and school-level covariates, we find a small negative relationship between school-average SES and mathematics learning.

Revisiting Our Research Questions

Early in this chapter we pose three research questions around which we designed this study. Before expanding on the larger implications of the study, we summarize our results in terms of our guiding questions. Our first research question asks how class size and school size influence young children's learning trajectories in their first two years of formal schooling. Our results here are quite straightforward. Even in models that estimate class size and school size simultaneously for separate learning trajectories and also include substantial controls for other child and school characteristics, we find effects for both measures of context size. Kindergarteners attending schools with medium-size

Figure 5. Annual First-Grade Learning Rates, by School Size and Subject

Points of learning per academic year

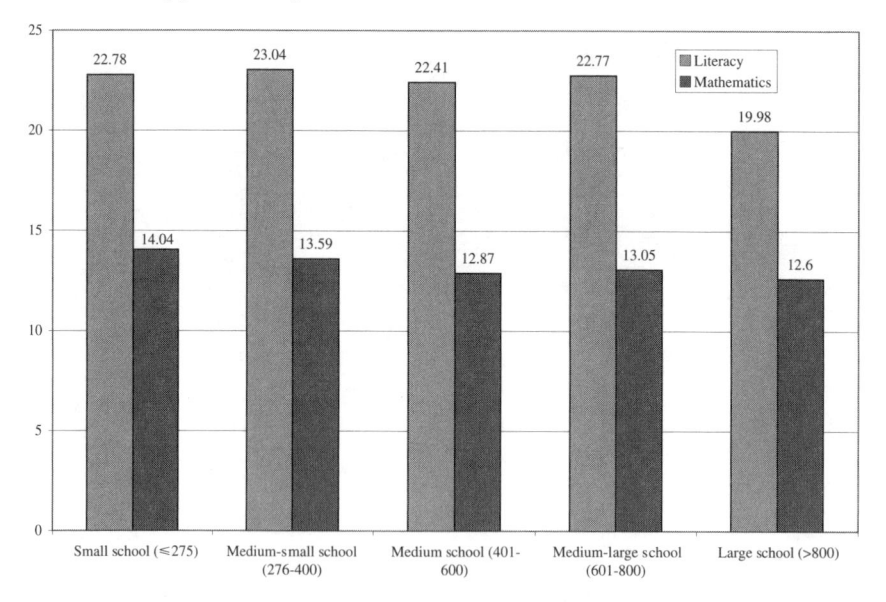

School size	Literacy	Mathematics
Small school (≤275)	22.78	14.04
Medium-small school (276-400)	23.04	13.59
Medium school (401-600)	22.41	12.87
Medium-large school (601-800)	22.77	13.05
Large school (>800)	19.98	12.6

Source: Authors' calculations using ECLS-K data.

classes learn more in both literacy and mathematics than their peers in schools with large classes. In first grade, children's learning rates are greater in schools with small compared to large classes. School-size effects, although more modest, are evident for children's learning in both subjects, but only in first grade. Mathematics learning is higher in small schools, and literacy learning is lower in the largest schools. Thus the findings for our first research question are consistent; in general, young children learn more in smaller contexts.

Our second research question focuses on the equitable distribution of learning, in particular by children's social class. Here, our findings are less satisfying but also quite consistent. We identify no relationship between either class size or school size on the equitable distribution of learning in either grade or subject.

Our third research question asks if the effects of the size of educational contexts are different for the same children's learning rates in kindergarten and first grade. In terms of findings about school size, the results do vary by grade. Although school size does not influence children's learning over the kindergarten year, we do find school-size effects on first graders' learning, generally favoring smaller schools. The class-size effects on learning also vary by grade. Kindergartners learn more in both subjects in schools with medium compared to larger classes, whereas first graders learn more in schools with small classes.

Discussion

Our results suggest robust class-size effects, net of school size, the types of students enrolled, and other school-level characteristics; the effects of both class size and school size are estimated in the same models. That is, the class-size effects we report here are independent of school size, and vice versa. To us, this says that these size effects are both real and important. In literacy and mathematics learning in both kindergarten and first grade, our study provides clear support for the findings from the Tennessee and Wisconsin class-size experiments: children learn more in small compared to large classes. However, our study adds several additional dimensions. First, we compare schools with small and large classes to those with medium-size classes—the type of classroom that elementary school students are most likely to experience. With kindergarten literacy and mathematics as well as first-grade mathematics, schools with small and medium classes do not differentially influence student learning (figures 3 and 4). Rather, schools with *large* classes are *detrimental* to student learning. Only in first-grade literacy learning do we find small class sizes to be more beneficial than medium-size classes.

Second, although our study is not an experimental one, our findings are net of a large set of statistical controls that are systematically linked with the size of school contexts: students' social background, whether they experienced full- or half-day kindergarten, school social composition, and several structural and organizational properties of schools, such as grade span and urbanicity. Third and most important is the structure of our analytic models, where class size and school-size effects are estimated simultaneously. The fourth advantage of this study over others that have considered this topic—perhaps the most important contribution—is the structure of our analysis of learning gains, where children's achievement is measured one-on-one in untimed tests of literacy and mathematics. Moreover, children's learning trajectories are estimated in a complex piecewise linear growth model that accounts for when children are in and out of school.

Are These Findings Large or Small?

As table 4 indicates, first graders in small classes learn almost 10 percent more per month in literacy than children in large classrooms (2.68 versus 2.49 ppm, ES = 0.20 SD). Translating this 0.19 monthly advantage into nine months of learning—the traditional school year—suggests that children in large compared to small classes finish first grade roughly three weeks behind (0.19 x 9 = 1.71, with an average monthly gain of 2.56), an approach we adopt in figures 3–5. Moreover, if children remained in the same elementary school for five or six years and if the class-size and school-size effects were constant over time, these differences would be very substantial: a roughly 10-point advantage for children in small over large classes by the end of sixth grade, or 4.5 months of additional learning. Our findings (particularly when presented in terms of effect sizes) are quite similar to those reported in the Tennessee and Wisconsin experiments, despite the fact that our student samples and methodological approaches differ considerably.

Our results also suggest that first-grade literacy gains are smaller in large elementary schools (those that enroll more than 800 children), and math gains are greater in small schools in the same grade. If these results were sustained over the elementary school years, they would be very large. Moreover, as indicated in table 1, large elementary schools are more likely to have large first-grade classes. This suggests that some children suffer the double disadvantage of attending large schools that offer large classes. Our estimates suggest that such children complete first grade almost 1.5 months behind children enrolled in small first-grade classrooms and schools with enrollments below 800. Again, if the double disadvantage were sustained, children's learning would be very adversely affected.

What causal mechanisms might explain the associations between class size and student learning? Teachers in smaller classes may know their students better and thus more easily tailor instruction to students' needs. Another explanation argues that, rather than instructional or pedagogical improvements, class-size effects may operate through improved classroom climate. Smaller classrooms may foster a more positive disciplinary environment, with fewer student disruptions. As a result, teachers in smaller classes may need to spend less time on classroom management, leaving more time for instruction. In this view, class size benefits may accrue from *student* rather than *teacher* changes in behavior. Future work on this topic might identify practices and processes that typify smaller classrooms. This is crucial, as class size per se may not be the issue, but rather the pedagogical approaches and classroom climates that accompany smaller classrooms.

How might large or small schools influence student learning in elementary schools? Beyond the mechanisms through which class size may influence learning, teachers in smaller schools—both across grades and within the same grade—may have more opportunity to collaborate, to discuss their instructional practices with their colleagues, and to share tips on how to best accommodate challenging children. The less complex organizational form of small schools facilitates collaboration and makes practice more transparent. Moreover, in larger elementary schools weak teachers and struggling students can "slip through the cracks." Similar to class size, we argue that school size does not have a direct effect on student learning, despite the fact that this is exactly the approach our study has, by necessity, taken.

Two Types of Small Schools

In this study, we find that organizational size—of both classes and schools—influences children's learning in literacy and mathematics in both kindergarten and first grade. However, once we account for the characteristics of students and their schools, class size plays a more consistent role than school size in young children's cognitive development. This finding raises questions that are rarely discussed by those who advocate smaller educational contexts. Why do some small schools work better than others? Some schools—both public and private—have small enrollments because they wish to (and are able to) consciously limit the number of students they serve (and frequently also the type of students they enroll). However, the vast majority of small schools are public, and many are in rural areas that must enroll all students in their catchment area. Even with the powerful trend toward consolidation, many schools have small enrollments because there are simply few students in the community (especially in rural areas and communities with declining populations). It seems quite inappropriate to confuse these two types of small schools. Some are "small by design"; others are "small by default." The first group of schools inherently possesses many advantages not shared by the latter group. Interesting as they are, small schools such as Central Park East Elementary School are incredibly different from the majority of rural and small-town small schools, even though some enroll economically disadvantaged students.[40]

Our own and others' research has led us to wonder whether "smallness" by itself is an inherently valuable characteristic, as many advocates claim. Smallness accompanied by the ability to organize a school around a special theme or ideology, to enroll only students, families, and faculty to whom this theme appeals, and to select among applicants is a special kind of smallness. This is very different from smallness experienced by the large majority of "small by default" schools. Indeed, many small elementary schools would prefer to be larger, partly because resources flow to most public schools based on student enrollment. In the context of this study, it is impossible to establish whether small classes and small schools are the product of conscious efforts to limit the size of educational contexts or simply the result of low enrollments. However, in reality such distinctions are crucial when making policy about enrollment or class size.

An Alternative to Small

Policymakers and school practitioners regularly make decisions about the size of elementary schools and classrooms, what grades to include in their school, and the total number of students in each grade. Although school professionals are often required to make such decisions based on local funding, available personnel, or demographic and enrollment projections, ideally they would also base such important decisions on high-quality empirical evidence. Although this study does not meet the current call for randomized studies that would allow very strong causal inferences, we suggest that the empirical results we have drawn from these multiwave longitudinal data and sophisticated statistical models provide a very strong base from which to extract direct policy implications.

In light of our findings, the policy-relevant question may not be whether *small* contexts are more beneficial for student learning than *large* contexts, but whether *medium*-size environments are preferable to large environments, at least in relation to class size. Earlier in this chapter we describe several problems and unforeseen consequences that arose from policies that sought to reduce class sizes in California, even though such decisions were based on very solid empirical evidence from the experimental Tennessee class-size study. With these unintended consequences of California's policy in mind—as well as ever-present concerns about funding—"small" may be unattainable or even undesirable. For example, in districts and schools where large classrooms are a reality, fiscal questions might lead decisionmakers to wonder whether moving from large to even medium-size classrooms would produce equally favorable (and less costly) results. In general, our results suggest that such a move would offer comparable learning benefits. However, our findings about school size are restricted to the extremes, rather than the middle of the distribution. First graders' literacy learning is lower in the largest schools; first graders' mathematics learning is higher in the smallest schools.

Our purpose in this study has been to provide evidence about the potentially confounding elements of elementary school size based on solid data and appropriate methodology. We hope that people who work in schools—and those who make decisions affecting them—would seriously consider how the various elements of size work together, rather than simply accept the increasingly common ideology that "small is good." The findings reported in this paper lead us away from an unquestioning allegiance to small size. Rather than the constant mantra of "small is good," our results lead us to a different proclamation: "large is bad."

Notes

1. Jeremy D. Finn and Charles M. Achilles, "Tennessee's Class Size Study: Findings, Implications, Misconceptions," *Educational Evaluation and Policy Analysis* 21, no. 2 (1999): 97–109; Alan B. Krueger, "Economic Considerations and Class Size," Working Paper 447 (Princeton University, Industrial Relations Section, 2000); Alan B. Krueger and Diane M. Whitmore, "Would Smaller Classes Help Close the Black-White Achievement Gap?" in *Bridging the Achievement Gap*, edited by John E. Chubb and Tom Loveless (Brookings, 2002), pp. 11–46; Barbara Nye and others, "Do Low-Achieving Students Benefit More from Small Classes? Evidence from the Tennessee Class Size Experiment," *Educational Evaluation and Policy Analysis* 24, no. 3 (2002): 201–18.

2. Eric A. Hanushek, "Some Findings from an Independent Investigation of the Tennessee STAR Experiment and from Other Investigations of Class Size Effects," *Educational Evaluation and Policy Analysis* 21, no. 2 (1999): 143–63; Eric A. Hanushek, "The Evidence on Class Size," Occasional Paper 98-1 (Rochester, N.Y.: W. Allen Wallis Institute of Political Economy, 1998); Caroline M. Hoxby, "The Effects of Class Size on Student Achievement: New Evidence from Population Variation," *Quarterly Journal of Economics* 115, no. 4 (2000): 1239–85.

3. Hanushek, "Some Findings from an Independent Investigation of the Tennessee STAR Experiment."

4. Ibid. See also Hoxby, "The Effects of Class Size on Student Achievement."

5. See William R. Shadish, Thomas D. Cook, and Donald T. Campbell, *Experimental and Quasi-Experimental Designs for Generalized Causal Inference* (New York: Houghton Mifflin, 2002).

6. Alex Molnar and others, "Evaluating the SAGE Program: A Pilot Program in Targeted Pupil-Teacher Reduction in Wisconsin," *Educational Evaluation and Policy Analysis* 21, no. 2 (1999): 165–77; Alex Molnar and others, "Wisconsin's SAGE Program and Achievement through Small Classes," in *Bridging the Achievement Gap*, edited by Chubb and Loveless, pp. 91–108.

7. Molnar and others, "Evaluating the SAGE Program."

8. CSR Research Consortium, *What We Have Learned about Class Size Reduction in California* (Sacramento: California Department of Education, 2002).

9. Hoxby, "The Effects of Class Size on Student Achievement"; Krueger and Whitmore, "Would Smaller Classes Help Close the Black-White Achievement Gap?"

10. CSR Research Consortium, *What We Have Learned about Class Size Reduction in California*; Christopher Jepsen and Steven Rivkin, *Class Size Reduction, Teacher Quality, and Academic Achievement in California Public Elementary Schools* (San Francisco: Public Policy Institute of California, 2002).

11. CSR Research Consortium, *What We Have Learned about Class Size Reduction in California*.

12. U.S. Department of Education, *A Descriptive Evaluation of the Federal Class-Size Reduction Program: Final Report* (Washington, 2004).

13. Valerie E. Lee and Julia B. Smith, "High School Size: Which Works Best and for Whom?" *Educational Evaluation and Policy Analysis* 19, no. 3 (1997): 205–27.

14. As we found in ibid.

15. Ibid.

16. Valerie E. Lee and Susanna Loeb, "School Size in Chicago Elementary Schools: Effects on Teachers' Attitudes and Students' Achievement," *American Educational Research Journal* 37, no. 1 (2000): 3–31.

17. Carnegie Council of America, *Turning Points: Preparing American Youth for the 21st Century* (New York: Carnegie Corporation, 1989); Joyce L. Epstein, "What Matters in the Middle Grades: Grade Span or Practices?" *Phi Delta Kappan* 71, no. 6 (1990): 438–44.

18. Epstein, "What Matters in the Middle Grades"; David Marshank, "From Teachers' Perspectives: The Social and Psychological Benefits of Multiage Elementary Classrooms," paper presented at the conference Emerging Images of Learning: World Perspectives for the New Millennium, Chicago, March 1994.

19. Epstein, "What Matters in the Middle Grades."

20. David T. Burkam, Deborah L. Michaels, and Valerie E. Lee, "School Grade Span and Academic Achievement: How Important Is the Presence of a First Grade to a Kindergartner's School Performance?" *Elementary School Journal* 107, no. 3 (2007): 287–303.

21. See, for example, Valerie E. Lee and Julia B. Smith, "Effects of School Restructuring on the Achievement and Engagement of Middle-Grade School Students," *Sociology of Education* 66, no. 3 (1993): 163–87.

22. Robert Barr and Rebecca Dreeben, *How Schools Work* (University of Chicago Press, 1983).

23. Burkam, Michaels, and Lee, "School Grade Span and Academic Achievement"; Valerie E. Lee and others, "Full-Day vs. Half-Day Kindergarten: In Which Program Do Children Learn More?" *American Journal of Education* 11, no. 2 (1996): 163–208; Valerie E. Lee, Douglas D. Ready, and Laura LoGerfo, "School Effects on Learning Rates over the Kindergarten and First-Grade Years," paper presented at the annual conference of the American Educational Research Association, San Francisco, April 2006.

24. National Center for Education Statistics (NCES), *Early Childhood Longitudinal Study: User's Manual for the ECLS-K First Grade Restricted-Use Data Files and Electronic Codebook* (Department of Education, Office of Educational Research and Improvement, 2002).

25. Stephen W. Raudenbush and Anthony S. Bryk, *Hierarchical Linear Models,* 2nd ed. (Thousand Oaks, Calif.: Sage, 2002); Judith D. Singer and John B. Willett, *Applied Longitudinal Data Analysis: Modeling Change and Event Occurrence* (New York: Oxford University Press, 2003).

26. See Raudenbush and Bryk, *Hierarchical Linear Models*; Michael H. Seltzer, Ken A. Frank, and Anthony S. Bryk, "The Metric Matters: The Sensitivity of Conclusions about Growth in Student Achievement to Choice of Metric," *Educational Evaluation and Policy Analysis* 16 (Spring 1994): 41–49; David R. Rogosa and John B. Willett, "Understanding Correlates of Change by Modeling Individual Differences in Growth," *Psychometrika* 50, no. 2 (1985): 203–08; John B. Willett, "Questions and Answers in the Measurement of Change," *Review of Research in Education* 5 (1988): 345–422.

27. John B. Willett, "Questions and Answers in the Measurement of Change," p. 377.

28. Ibid.

29. Rogosa and Willett, "Understanding Correlates of Change by Modeling Individual Differences in Growth."

30. Willett, "Questions and Answers in the Measurement of Change."

31. David T. Burkam and others, "Social-Class Differences in Summer Learning between Kindergarten and First Grade: Model Specification and Estimation," *Sociology of Education* 77, no. 1 (2004): 1–31; Lee, Ready, and LoGerfo, "School Effects on Learning Rates over the Kindergarten and First-Grade Years."

32. Our initial unconditional HLM analyses included a traditional third-degree polynomial model. This model revealed a nonlinear growth pattern between the start of kindergarten and the end of first grade in both reading and mathematics, with increasing learning in kindergarten, decreasing learning over the summer months, and increasing learning in first grade. For two reasons, however, this paper does not develop the polynomial model further. First, the complexity of such models makes them rather difficult to interpret. Second, traditional growth models assume that the temporal distance between repeated measures is constant across individuals—an assumption violated by the data structure of ECLS-K. Rather, we employ piecewise linear models, which permit us to explore the differential kindergarten and first-grade growth rates.

33. We selected only public schools and students, as we felt that decisions about school and class size, and the costs and benefits flowing from such decisions, would be fundamentally different in public and private schools.

34. See Lee and Loeb, "School Size in Chicago Elementary Schools"; Lee and Smith, "High School Size."

35. NCES, *Early Childhood Longitudinal Study*.

36. As suggested by Seltzer, Frank, and Bryk, "The Metric Matters."

37. Lee and others, "Full-Day vs. Half-Day Kindergarten"; Douglas D. Ready and others, "Explaining Girls' Advantage in Kindergarten Literacy Learning: Do Classroom Behaviors Make a Difference?" *Elementary School Journal* 106, no. 1 (2005): 21–38.

38. See Valerie E. Lee and David T. Burkam, *Inequality at the Starting Gate: Social Background Differences in Achievement as Children Begin School* (Washington: Economic Policy Institute, 2002).

39. The results in figures 3–5 are computed as follows. The intercept is first added to the monthly effect for each size category, and then the sum is multiplied by nine. This is because all results in table 4 are in the points-per-month learning metric.

40. See Deborah Meier, *The Power of Their Ideas: Lessons for America from a Small School in Harlem* (Boston: Beacon Press, 1995).

Class Size and School Size: Taking the Trade-Offs Seriously

DOUGLAS N. HARRIS

Small classes and small schools appear to have educational benefits for students. In small classes, children experience fewer disruptions and receive more personal attention and individualized instruction. Likewise, in small schools, students appear to feel safer and less likely to get "lost in the crowd" and teachers are able to provide a more coherent curriculum. There is a large research literature, including many of the papers in this volume, suggesting that these qualities of the learning environment translate into actual gains in student achievement and attainment.[1]

But nearly all previous studies on the benefits of small classes and schools ignore the other element that is of equally great interest to administrators and policymakers—the *costs*. Resources that go to small classes and small schools cannot be used to buy laptops for teachers, raise teacher salaries, increase professional development, add pre-kindergarten programs, or purchase new textbooks. That does not mean, of course, that smaller settings are necessarily unwise, but it does mean that they entail the loss of some opportunities. The purpose of this paper is to provide evidence about the benefits and costs of smaller educational settings and thereby provide guidelines for developing school resource policies that maximize educational outcomes. Below, I refer to these as the efficient or "optimal" resources, though it is important to recognize that other research on this topic, such as the paper in this volume by Ready and Lee, uses the term "optimal" even when they are excluding costs and considering only the benefits of resources.

The author wishes to thank Dale Ballou, Patrice Iatorola, Martin West, Diane Whitmore Schanzenbach, and other participants in the June 2006 BPEP conference at the Brookings Institution for useful comments. Henry Levin, Patrick McEwan, and David Plank provided valuable comment on earlier versions of this work. Jian Gao provided valuable research assistance. The author is responsible for all errors.

The first step in estimating optimal resources is to consider the actual costs of smaller classes and schools. Most of these are relatively easy to identify and measure. To reduce class size, schools must either hire more teachers or have existing teachers work longer hours; they also must reconfigure existing classroom space or provide additional space in portable structures or new buildings. In the case of small schools, facility costs also figure prominently, especially for items such as gymnasiums and offices, which generally have to be replicated in every school. Other costs that are more difficult to measure arise because small settings reduce opportunities for productive use of resources: for example, a teacher who is effective in teaching math may be less able to use that skill in a small school if he or she has to spend time teaching other subjects such as science. In large schools, teachers are better able to specialize.

Interestingly, education researchers, including economists, pay little attention to these or any other costs, and in the case of small classes and schools, the few studies that do exist do not yield entirely consistent conclusions. Part of the problem, as I show below, is that there are different ways to combine costs and benefits, and some are better than others. Costs and benefits also vary across circumstances—urban versus rural schools, elementary versus high schools—so some of the apparent contradictions are just reflections of differences in what is optimal in different situations. Through a review of past studies and additional analysis, this paper draws some tentative conclusions about class size and school size, but it also suggests that most of the important questions require future study.

The fact that there is no clear evidence supporting the value of small classes and small schools has not, however, prevented policymakers at all levels from devoting substantial resources, particularly to smaller classes. Table 1 shows that the pupil-teacher ratio has dropped from 22.3 to 16.2 since 1970.[2] Adjusting for changes in the number of pupils, that represents a nearly 40 percent increase in the number of teachers. Also, note that pupil-teacher ratios in elementary schools, which historically have been larger than those in secondary schools, actually dropped below those in secondary schools for the first time in 2000 and have remained there since. School size also has changed, but not as much. Average school size has increased by about 9 percent since 1980, although that small percentage partly reflects the disproportionate increase in the number of special schools—vocational, alternative, and combined elementary-secondary schools—which tend to be smaller than regular schools. Based on the numbers reported in table 1, the size of regular elementary and secondary schools has increased by 19 and 13 percent, respectively, in the past

Table 1. Trends in School Resource Allocation[a]

	Pupil-teacher ratio			School size (enrollment)		
Year	Elementary	Secondary	Total	Elementary	Secondary	Total
1970	24.3	19.8	22.3	n.a.	n.a.	n.a.
1980	20.4	16.8	18.7	399	719	478
1990	18.9	14.6	17.2	449	684	497
2000	16.5	16.6	16.4	477	795	519
2002	16.2	16.7	16.2	476	813	519

Source: National Center for Education Statistics, *Digest of Education Statistics*, 2000, 2004, 2005.

a. Elementary and secondary columns are based on regular schools only and therefore exclude special schools such as vocational, alternative, and mixed elementary-secondary. The total columns combine regular and special schools and,because regular schools are larger and have higher pupil-teacher ratios, are not simple averages of the elementary and secondary columns. Also, 1980 school sizes are actually from 1982.

quarter-century. In short, class size and school size are moving in opposite directions.

It is possible that the trends toward smaller classes and larger schools have improved the quality of education, but the analysis here calls that notion into question. Recent surveys indicate that both teachers and parents prefer smaller classes to other reforms, even when the large costs are considered.[3] Regarding school size, nearly half of the respondents in another recent survey said that schools were about the right size but an additional 15 percent indicated that schools were actually *too small*.[4] Those survey results mirror the actual changes in school resources shown in table 1, suggesting a strong market influence behind the recent resource trends. In the discussion below, I argue that the disproportionate popularity of small classes is driven by a combination of misperceptions about educational quality and differences between the educational objectives considered by researchers and policymakers and those of interest to parents and teachers.

In the next section, I briefly describe three methods that could be used to estimate optimal class and school sizes. Cost-effectiveness analysis and cost-benefit analysis are used most commonly, although still rarely. I also outline a method that addresses many of the limitations of these two methods—what I will call "optimization." In the section on class-size reduction, I review the few previous studies that formally compare the costs and benefits of reducing class size. Their findings suggest that the broad-based trend toward smaller classes in recent decades has probably resulted in lower student achievement than would have been possible if other uses had been made of the resources available. The trend toward larger school sizes, in contrast, has probably improved student achievement.

It is important to remember, however, that these conclusions only apply to the *average* class and school. Even if the findings above regarding broad-based trends are correct, it is possible, even likely, that reducing the size of school settings still represents the best way to improve educational outcomes in the large number of cases in which classes and schools are much larger than average. That suggests that policymakers, if they are going to reduce class and school sizes, should choose their targets carefully. They should also recognize that parents and educators might push for these changes for reasons other than the desire for higher test scores.

Analysis of Costs, Benefits, and Efficiency

Cost-benefit analysis and cost-effectiveness analysis provide the most common, basic approach to comparing educational resources, though economists tend to prefer an "optimization" approach. Below, I describe the logic of these three approaches, including the decision guidelines for policy recommendations in each case. I also provide simple examples to highlight the decision guidelines and explain why the recommended decisions vary. This section sets up the later discussion of studies that use these approaches to study class size and school size.

In cost-benefit analysis, total benefits are measured in monetary terms and subtracted from total costs to obtain the net benefits of a given intervention. When a proposal has positive net economic benefits, it improves efficiency and "passes" the cost-benefit test. This approach may sound familiar, especially to federal policymakers and analysts acquainted with environmental policies, for which government-mandated cost-benefit analyses are common.

To fully understand cost-benefit analysis and how it compares with the other approaches, it is important to distinguish the total benefits and costs from the marginal or "incremental" benefits and costs. Consider the following example. Suppose that the benefit of each additional or "incremental" unit—say, reducing class size from 23 to 22 students—is $300 per student. For simplicity, also assume that the incremental costs are $200 per student. Finally, suppose that these incremental benefits and costs are constant, so that going from 23 to 22 students per class carries the same changes in costs and benefits as going from 22 to 21 students and so on. Now, consider a school district with 1,000 students that is considering reducing average class size from 23 to 15 students. In that case, the total cost—or the sum of all the incremental costs—is $1,600,000 a year. Subtracting that figure from the total benefits, $2,400,000, yields a net benefit of $800,000. On the basis of the above decision rule, the policy should be adopted. These calculations are shown in table 2.

The second approach, cost-effectiveness analysis, differs from cost-benefit analysis in several important ways. In this case, the decision guideline is to choose the proposal with the greatest ratio of incremental benefits to incremental costs. Why might we be more interested in the ratio of benefits to costs? Suppose that we are comparing two policies, one of which requires a total investment of $1,000 per pupil and the other $100 per pupil. A cost-benefit analysis would focus on the total costs, and both might yield some dollar figure of net benefits. But the investments are of such different magnitudes, one being ten times larger than the other, that they are difficult to compare. Looking at the ratios eliminates the issue of the difference in scale. But why the ratio of *incremental* benefits and costs? In most cost-effectiveness analyses the distinction is unimportant because the incremental benefits and costs are assumed to be the same regardless of the size of the investment or the initial level of the resource. Under that assumption, the ratio of total benefits to total costs will be identical to the ratio of incremental benefits to incremental costs.

Cost-effectiveness analysis also requires the researcher to compare incremental costs and benefits across multiple resources. In table 2, I use the same incremental costs and benefits of class-size reduction as in the cost-benefit example to illustrate the difference. I also make up hypothetical—although, as the next section shows, possibly realistic—assumptions about alternative resources. For class size, the ratio equals 1.5 ($300 ÷ 200); in comparison, the hypothetical ratio for an alternative resource is 3.0. In this scenario, the larger ratio for the alternative proposal implies that the policymaker should choose it over class-size reduction, contradicting the cost-benefit approach.

The third approach, optimization, differs from the other two by allowing the incremental benefits or costs or both to vary depending on how much of a change in the resource is being considered. Economists generally assume, on the basis of empirical research, that incremental benefits decline as more of a resource is used. For example, hiring one mechanic to repair broken machines in a car manufacturing plant will probably produce a substantial benefit. Hiring a second mechanic may also help, but the second mechanic's contribution is likely to be less than that of the first. And so on.

The optimization approach also assumes that incremental costs change. For example, it may be relatively easy to hire one mechanic at a given salary, but finding another might require searching in other towns for candidates with the requisite skills, or the employer might have to hire someone from another industry or related occupation and train the person in the tasks of the specific

Table 2. Hypothetical Examples for Analyzing Costs and Benefits

Approach	Cost-benefit	Cost-effectiveness	Optimization
Decision guideline	Adopt if total benefits exceed total costs.	Adopt if ratio of incremental benefits to costs exceeds ratios for other resources.	Set all resources so that the ratio of incremental benefits to costs is the same for all resources.
Assumptions and calculations	Incremental costs = $200 per student Incremental benefits = $300 per student Total costs (23 to 15 students): $200 x 1,000 students x 8 student reduction $1,600,000 Total benefits: $300 x 1,000 students x 8 student reduction $2,400,000 Net benefits: $2,400,000 − $1,600,000 $800,000	Incremental costs = $200 per student Incremental benefits = $300 per student Ratio of incremental benefits to incremental costs for class size: $$\frac{\$300}{\$200} = 1.5$$ Ratio of incremental benefits to incremental costs for some alternative resource: $$\frac{\$300}{\$100} = 3.0$$	Incremental costs = $200 Incremental benefits vary Because of declining incremental benefits, the ratio for class size in column (2) is not fixed. Shifting resources to the alternative raises the class-size benefit-cost ratio and reduces the ratio of the alternative resources.
Recommendation	Reduce class size to 15 students.	Adopt alternative.	Raise class size until ratios are the same.

Source: Author's calculations.

job to be filled. Or, perhaps, more simply, the salary might have to be increased to attract qualified candidates. All of these options would lead to increasing incremental costs, as more mechanics are hired.

The same is true of class-size reduction. Going from 23 to 22 students may provide some benefits, but at some point the benefits will decline. At the extreme, the benefit of going from 2 students to 1 student is likely to be small— or even negative. Also, even though the above examples assume that incremental costs are the same when going from 23 to 22 and from 22 to 21 students, that is not the case. Again, consider the extremes. Suppose, for simplicity, that a school has 6 students and 2 classes, yielding an average class size of 3. Going from 3 students to 2 students would require 1 additional teacher—a 50 percent increase. But going from 2 students to 1 student would require 3 additional teachers—a 100 percent increase. The same principle of increasing incremental costs holds at more realistic class sizes as well. In addition, in some subjects and grades (especially math and science in urban and rural schools), there are shortages of teachers, so salaries need to be raised to attract additional teachers. While teacher shortages often are exaggerated, the earlier example highlights the fact that the increasing incremental cost of class-size reduction is a fact proven by basic arithmetic alone. The optimization approach, more so than cost-benefit and cost-effectiveness analysis, attempts to take into account the changes in costs and benefits.

These differences in assumptions also allow for different decision guidelines that are more in line with economic theory. The simpler case is where it is possible to assume that there is no budget constraint. While that may seem unrealistic, budgets do change and the amount of resources that schools may receive over the long term is not fixed. If we ignore the short-term budget constraints, the decision guideline involves not just picking the proposal with the greatest ratio of benefits to costs but setting the incremental benefit to *equal* the incremental cost.[5] That means, as with the cost-benefit example, that it is not necessary to consider alternative resources. Turning to column 1 in table 2, assume that benefits decline on a straight line from $300 at 23 students to $140 at 15 students. Total benefits now have declined to $1,760,000.[6] That is still greater than the total costs, and the policy therefore still passes a cost-benefit test. But is a class size of 15 optimal? No. With that decline in benefits, incremental costs equal incremental benefits at a class size of 17, not 15. While this problem does not arise in all circumstances, the larger lesson here is that cost-benefit analysis may not be the best tool for understanding resource allocation.[7] The same problem arises in two studies discussed later that applied cost-benefit analysis to class and school size.

The other case, perhaps more intuitive to school administrators, is the one with a fixed-budget constraint. Assuming that all resources have to be used in the current period, the best decision now involves setting the ratio of incremental benefits to incremental costs so that it is equal for all resources. Because it involves comparing multiple resources, this is more like the cost-effectiveness example. Now, rather than choosing the resource that has the greatest ratio, adjustments can be made so that all resources have the same ratio. Why would we want to do that? For the simple reason that if any resource had a higher ratio—a bigger "bang for the buck"—then it would make more sense to shift resources toward that resource and away from the others, until the ratios were equalized again.

When these three general approaches—cost-benefit, cost-effectiveness, and optimization—are compared, the last of the three might be viewed as ideal. But, as a practical matter, each approach has its own strengths and weaknesses. The main advantage of cost-benefit analysis is that it requires information about only one resource, though that is also its main disadvantage from the perspective of administrators who face budget constraints and who therefore have to consider the trade-offs among various options. Another disadvantage is that it requires measuring all educational benefits in monetary terms. In the examples regarding class size and school size, that has been accomplished by relating the resource to an educational outcome (for example, test scores) and then relating that outcome to future worker productivity, as measured by monetary wages. The problem is that that approach is likely to exclude other benefits that are difficult to express in monetary terms. For example, administrators and policymakers often are interested in increasing educational outcomes for their own sake or improving other outcomes, such as civic participation, that are unrelated to worker productivity.

Cost-effectiveness analysis has advantages over cost-benefit analysis in these respects. Though the examples in table 2 use monetary measures of benefits, other measures, such as student test scores or the probability of graduating from high school, are more commonly used. Also, cost-effectiveness requires comparing the costs and effects of multiple resources and therefore addresses some of the practical considerations faced by administrators. However, again, that is also the approach's disadvantage—making the comparisons requires collecting considerable information.

Cost-benefit and cost-effectiveness analyses also share some limitations. In particular, both indicate whether a specific policy option is beneficial—more of this, less of that—but neither indicates a specific policy. If the average class size is too small, how large should it be? That question can be answered, at least in theory, through the optimization approach. While modeling the changes in incremental benefits and costs requires still more information than cost-effectiveness analysis does, the approach at least illustrates the many assumptions that have to be made in order to offer concrete recommendations.

With this background on the research methods used to compare costs and benefits, it is now possible to discuss how these approaches to comparing costs and benefits have been applied in studies of class size and school size, the two school resource issues of interest in this volume.

Optimal Class Size

Very few studies consider the costs and benefits of small classes and even fewer attempt to estimate a specific optimal class size. One of these studies reviews evidence of the cost-effectiveness of various resources and concludes that putting more resources into textbooks and writing materials and changing certain instructional practices would provide the greatest effects for the associated costs. The authors also note the "puzzling" observation that "class-size reductions are even less [cost] effective than teacher salaries." That last conclusion, however, is based mainly on the results of a single study that considered only the schooling system in another country, India.[8]

Two other studies, one by economist Alan Krueger and one with his colleague Diane Whitmore, provide cost-benefit analyses of the Tennessee STAR class-size experiment, which included random assignment of students across small classes (averaging 17 students) and large classes (averaging 22 students) in grades K-3.[9] The two studies make different sets of assumptions regarding the effects of class size on student test scores and the effects of test scores on worker productivity.

In the Krueger and Whitmore study, the authors assumed that STAR produced a long-term effect on student test scores of 0.13 of a standard deviation (equivalent to about 4.4 percentile points) and, in the second study, they assumed that the effect increased to 0.2 of a standard deviation. While it is unclear why the assumption changes, it is worth considering which is more reasonable. On one hand, the lower estimates may understate the actual effects because they exclude effects on outcomes other than test scores, such as the increased probability of graduating from high school and going to college. But there also are reasons to think that the higher estimate is an overestimate. In addition to other researchers who have expressed a more skeptical view of the STAR results, I have noted previously that some of the positive effects being attributed to small classes may actually be the result of increased teacher quality.[10] As in most policy experiments, STAR focused on a sample of schools that, while more than sufficient for research purposes, was a very small percentage of the schools in the state. Therefore, the additional teachers who had to be hired to implement the small classes almost certainly came from other schools that were not involved in the experiment and, to the degree that teacher quality is a factor, the loss of quality teachers would have reduced achievement in those schools. Such negative effects on other schools, to the degree that they occurred, are not considered in most discussions of class size or in the Krueger or Krueger and Whitmore studies.

The relationship between student test scores and worker productivity is the second key part of the calculation. The Krueger study assumes that a one standard deviation increase in student test scores is associated with a 20 percent increase in students' future wages in the workforce. As the authors acknowledge in the Krueger and Whitmore study, this number probably is an overestimate because the analysis used to estimate effects did not control for years of education.[11] Because attainment is correlated with test scores and because some of the increase in wages resulting from more years of education does not reflect a true increase in productivity, the 20 percent figure is most likely an overestimate of the true effect.[12]

In a separate study, Krueger assumes instead that the effect on future wages of an increase of one standard deviation in student test scores is just 8 percent. But the Krueger study also effectively doubles that number because Krueger multiplies it by the effect on reading scores and the effect on math scores and then adds them together. To be clear, he is not asserting that STAR produced a $0.2 + 0.2 = 0.4$ standard deviation increase in test scores, but rather that the two separate test scores have independent effects on worker wages. Krueger does cite evidence that workers who have higher verbal skills may be more productive even after controlling for their quantitative skills, though it is only one study and there is generally little evidence on the topic.[13]

The differences in assumptions between the Krueger and Krueger and Whitmore studies largely cancel each other out and therefore yield similar results. The earlier study, with a moderate class-size effect and a large relationship between test scores and wages, finds an internal rate of return of 5.5 percent. The more recent study, using a larger class-size effect and a smaller relationship between test scores and wages, yields a slightly higher internal rate of return of 6.2 percent. Further, after replicating the results of these analyses myself, I also considered other combinations of assumptions that yield a range of internal rates of return of from 3 to 10 percent. The upper end of this range is above the discount rate normally used by economists, though the lower value, as well as the base values reported in the two Krueger studies, is close to the standard discount (interest) rate. This is the same as saying that STAR-type class-size reduction may pass a cost-benefit test in the sense described in table 2.[14]

But recall the limitations of cost-benefit analysis. First, as discussed in the previous section, the results in a cost-benefit analysis are sensitive to the specific class-size change that is proposed. The STAR experiment may therefore reduce class size too far. Also, these cost-benefit analyses do not compare costs and benefits with those of other resources. In other published work, I have addressed this second issue by comparing class-size reduction with higher teacher salaries.[15] As in the earlier study of India, my previous analysis suggests that increasing test scores by 0.05 of a standard deviation by reducing class size would require $1,287 in additional expenditures per pupil, much more than the apparent $163 cost per pupil of achieving the same test score increase through an increase in teacher salaries. The main limitation of this analysis is that understanding the effects of higher salaries requires a clear connection between salaries and teacher quality and effort. Several studies have tried to make that connection by using teachers' scores on college entrance exams. While several economists have found that these scores or other tests of cognitive ability are good indicators of teacher quality, more recent evidence calls that notion into question. It is now widely believed that these and other common indicators of teacher quality are not closely linked to the contributions teachers make to student learning.[16]

It also is difficult to model the complicated interactions between class size and teacher salary. Because smaller classes require hiring more teachers, higher salaries increase the (incremental) cost of class-size reduction. While I have tried to model these complex interactions, doing so requires making questionable assumptions; I therefore have relied here on simpler models that consider class size and teacher salary separately.[17] This still requires measuring teacher quality, but it does not require estimating the effect of class size on teacher quality.[18]

While the research base is relatively small, the results discussed in this section do point toward an important conclusion—and two important caveats. The apparent conclusion is that broad-based class-size reduction would be inefficient, even in the elementary grades where the evidence of benefits is strongest. The cost-benefit analyses contradict that conclusion, but the contradiction appears to be due to the limitations of the approach itself and the apparent overestimates of monetary benefits. Applying the cost-benefit approach with more realistic assumptions makes the net benefits (internal rates of return) insufficient to pass a cost-benefit test. Class-size reduction also seems to stack up poorly in the studies that compare class size with teacher salaries.

The apparent inefficiency of class-size reduction, however, is based on a very small research base, which hopefully others will try to expand in future years. In addition, even if the conclusion is correct, it applies only to the average classroom, not to individual ones. In other words, across-the-board reductions in class size probably are not warranted. But, given the remaining inequalities in overall resources across schools, districts, and states, it is likely that class-size reduction is warranted in some situations where class sizes are now very large.[19] Put differently, if incremental benefits decline as class size is reduced, then the incremental benefit may be large in schools where class-size reduction has not already taken place.

Optimal School Size

In this section, I provide a similar review of studies of small schools. There are more studies on this topic than on small classes, and I therefore focus on summarizing the basic conclusions of the research and discussing in more detail a few of the most important and recent analyses. I begin by describing a fourth approach to studying costs and benefits that is common in studies of small schools.

Cost Functions and Economies of Scale

Economists frequently study economies of scale that arise, for example, in large-scale manufacturing operations. Large car factories require substantial upfront or "fixed" costs that must be incurred before a single car can be built. Once the plant is in place, the only additional costs are the incremental costs—labor plus all of the various car components. The plant owners might decide to make only 100 cars, but the cost per car would be much lower if the plant produces more, for the simple reason that the fixed costs are now divided over more units. The larger scale may also allow workers to specialize and therefore become more productive. Whatever the reason, when increasing resources (inputs) in a facility yields proportionally greater output (and therefore, in most cases, a decline in cost per unit), economists say that there are "increasing returns to scale."[20]

At some point, however, an increase in scale may cause an increase in the cost per unit. More units could be made by having workers put in longer hours, but they may be less productive during those extra hours. Or additional workers might be hired, but they may be less productive than the existing workforce, as the employer dips deeper into the pool of candidates. When increasing resources results in less than a proportional increase in output, there are "decreasing returns to scale."

Figure 1 shows the relationship between cost per unit and scale of production and the general patterns of increasing and decreasing returns to scale. This U-shaped "cost function" includes a great deal of information about fixed costs, incremental costs, changes in worker productivity, and so on. But it also

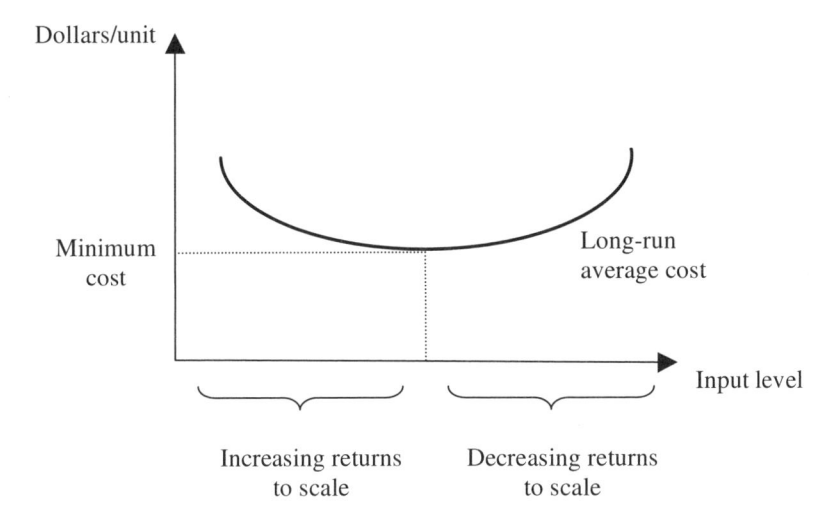

Figure 1. Increasing and Diminishing Marginal Returns to Scale

[Graph showing a U-shaped Long-run average cost curve with Dollars/unit on the vertical axis and Input level on the horizontal axis. The minimum cost point separates the region of Increasing returns to scale (left) from Decreasing returns to scale (right).]

Source: Author's illustration.

illustrates the relatively simple idea that there is a point at which average cost per unit is minimized—the optimal scale. If the cost function can be estimated accurately, it can provide information about the optimal scale.

The same reasoning applies in education. In this case, the scale is commonly viewed as the number of students in a school. Having more students in a school spreads the fixed costs across more students. In addition, teachers with specialized skills, such as in teaching math, can focus on teaching math courses. A small school, in contrast, might not have enough students to allow a teacher to teach math all day; the teacher might also teach science, a subject in which he or she is less skilled. There may be other factors, however, that make the relationship between costs and scale look the opposite. For example, large schools may require a more formal bureaucratic structure, which can be both costly and inefficient.[21] They may also be less cohesive,[22] induce lower motivation among teachers and administrators,[23] and have higher transportation costs compared with those of smaller schools.[24] If these effects are larger than those that create increasing returns to scale, then there are diminishing returns to scale and school size should be reduced.

Identifying the educational cost function involves using data to estimate the relationship between cost per student and the various factors affecting that cost. Prices of inputs, such as the salaries of teachers, are of course key aspects of costs. It is also necessary to control for the quality of output.[25] In the car example, it would make little sense to compare the cost of producing a Chevrolet and a Mercedes. Producing quality is costly, and that fact needs to be accounted for.

As with the other three methods, the cost function approach has its weaknesses. One of the most significant is that educational quality is difficult to measure. Researchers typically end up relying on student test scores, though they are now widely considered to be poor measures of school productivity, not because achievement is unimportant but because the scores themselves do not accurately reflect a school's contribution to learning. The cost of facilities is particularly important in the analysis of small schools, yet that cost frequently is not available or is excluded in favor of "operational costs" such as salaries. Other issues are discussed below within the context of specific studies.[26]

Literature Review

Somewhat greater attention has been paid to the costs of smaller schools than to those of class-size reduction. Below, I discuss several studies that have used the cost function approach.[27] There also is one study that uses a cost-benefit analysis approach similar to that used in Krueger's class-size studies.

Nearly all cost function studies find evidence of increasing returns to scale.[28] If their results are correct, that would tend to argue against school-size reduction. To see why, refer back to figure 1, which shows that increasing returns arise to the left of the optimal scale—that is, where the actual scale is lower than the optimum. It is worth noting, however, that most cost function studies do not report or attempt to estimate a specific optimal school size.[29]

Evidence from studies conducted several decades ago suggests that optimal high school sizes are consistently in the range of 1,400 to 1,800 students.[30] Three studies, focusing on high schools in the relatively rural states of Iowa, West Virginia, and Wisconsin, find optimal school sizes within that range. However, those studies, as well as much of the research literature on the topic, are more than four decades old; for that reason, they may not apply to the current context.

Urban high schools are perhaps of greatest interest given the current policy environment and the attention that the Bill and Melinda Gates Foundation has focused on reducing the size of high schools in these locations. A much more recent study by Stiefel and colleagues provides perhaps the most relevant evidence on these schools, using data on 121 small high schools in New York City.[31] In contrast to reviews of older studies, their study concludes that high schools with 600 to 2,000 students are the *least* cost effective compared with smaller and larger schools.[32] That seems to contradict the initial finding of increasing returns to scale. What explains the difference? The main reason appears to be that they gave relatively equal weight to a very small number of very small schools. They start by estimating a standard cost function and then estimate from that the predicted costs for each school. Grouping the results into four categories by school size, they find that the largest and smallest schools are most cost effective, implying the inverted-U cost curve. However, if the smallest schools (those with fewer than 600 students) are excluded, the results remain identical to those of the previous studies; that is, they find evidence of increasing returns to scale for schools of from 600 to more than 2,000 students in both parts of their analysis. It is unsurprising that the results diverge when the smallest schools are dropped because there are only eight schools in this category while eighty-four schools have more than 600 students. The conclusions in the study about medium and large schools therefore are more likely to be valid than those for the smallest schools.

That leaves an important question: are the eight very small high schools that appear to be cost effective truly cost effective? If so, that might mean that the results of other studies are misleading and that the consistent finding of increasing returns to scale is due to the fact that there simply are so few small schools in the samples that their benefits were not reflected in the results. While that is possible, it is unlikely, for the simple reason that many of the studies are based on data from decades ago, when schools already were very small. Surely Iowa, West Virginia, and Wisconsin had plenty of small high schools back in the 1950s and 1960s. That suggests that there may actually be something different about large urban locations like New York City or that there may be something quite distinctive about the small schools in the Stiefel study that are not captured in that analysis.

Cost-benefit analysis is another way to approach the issue of optimal school size. Ilyana Kuziemko uses a framework that is almost identical to that in Krueger's class-size analysis.[33] Using a relatively rich longitudinal database from Indiana, she first estimates the benefits of small elementary schools and then combines that estimate with evidence on costs from another study.[34] Using the highest reasonable cost estimate—a 50 percent decrease in enrollment size requires a 20 percent increase in per-pupil spending—she finds that the present discounted value of the net benefits is still more than $3,000 per pupil.[35]

Because the Kuziemko study is so similar to the Krueger class-size studies, many of the same caveats apply here as well. One of those caveats, regarding the lack of comparison of class size with different resource options, can also be addressed—by comparing the results of the two studies and their findings on school and class size. Because I already have replicated the Krueger class-size analyses, that is relatively easy to do. First, as Kuziemko did, I assume that the discount rate is 4 percent. I then insert this value into the base model from the first Krueger study to calculate the net benefits of the STAR experiment. Even though the investment required for small class is somewhat smaller, the net benefits are substantially larger. Put differently, the ratio of benefits to costs is larger with class-size reduction. Given the other evidence that reducing class size itself may not be a good investment, that does not provide much support for small schools.

Again, that conclusion applies only to the *average* school. Therefore, if the optimal high school size is in the 1,400–1,800 student range described earlier and the average high school has, say, 1,200 students, then it would appear that the average school is too small. But even in this case, data show that there are still more than 1,600 schools across the nation that have more than 2,000 students.[36] Therefore, if we view the problem as being confined to these extremely large high schools, then—with the exception of the Stiefel study—there is good evidence that it would be optimal to make these schools smaller.

There is also some evidence to suggest that the optimal school size varies according to school type and student characteristics. The optimal elementary school size is, of course, probably different from that of middle and high schools. The benefits also appear to be greater for students of low socioeconomic status.[37] Existing research does not allow for clear calculations of the optimal school size across all of these different situations.[38]

Actual versus Optimal: The Role of Political and Market Pressures

In this section, I consider how costs and benefits are perceived by parents and teachers and how their perceptions affect the actual levels of class and school size observed in schools, as well as the difference between the optimal and actual decisions discussed in the previous sections. This section identifies and discusses four specific pressures that might yield such an inconsistency: parental preference for tangible improvements in the educational environment over other less obvious changes that may improve educational quality; parental preference for immediate rather than long-term educational improvement; teacher preference for improvements in working conditions and a reduced workload; and high "transaction costs" related to staffing levels and school construction.

Class Size

The first section of this paper mentioned the popularity of small classes among parents. For example, one survey found that 88 percent of parents and 80 percent of the general public favor additional class-size reduction in grades K-3.[39] The results were quite similar in a separate survey in which class-size reduction and higher teacher salaries were supported by 85 percent of parents and 83 percent of the general public.[40] Even when the possibility of paying for the proposals with higher taxes was included in the question, roughly half still supported both proposals. Also, the state of Florida recently approved by majority vote a statewide referendum to create a broad-scale class-size reduction program, despite vociferous opposition from the state's popular governor, widespread publication of the financial costs, and the fact that small classes are being established in all grades, including grades 4–12, for which there is little evidence that small classes are effective. The widespread support expressed in these surveys is consistent with the substantial resources that have already been devoted to reducing class size in recent decades.

One explanation for the popularity of small classes is that parents cannot easily observe many forms of educational quality. Except for those who occasionally volunteer in the classroom, parents spend almost no time in the classroom with their children. As a result, their knowledge of educational quality comes mainly from what they hear from their children, what they might see from homework assignments and report cards, and from what they hear from other parents. They may therefore prefer changes that are more visible, such as smaller classes. In contrast, the effect of higher teacher salaries on teachers' effort and on recruitment and retention of teachers is harder to observe.

Because their children are in any given school for such a short period, parents may also prefer changes that occur quickly enough to allow their children to benefit. In addition, superintendents and school board members are under significant pressure for quick results, especially in the era of accountability when test scores and sanctions are based on short-term performance.[41] That gives another advantage to class-size reduction: it can be accomplished relatively quickly, as long as new school construction is not required. The same cannot be said for smaller schools.

Like parents, teachers also prefer class-size reduction to other reforms. They even prefer small classes to salary increases.[42] In one sense, that is not surprising. Reducing class size improves the classroom environment and lowers the workload—the number of papers and exams that they have to grade and the number of parent-teacher conferences that they have to schedule, for example. Yet it does not seem plausible that the benefits are so large that they would more than offset the desire for higher salaries. While there is evidence that teachers and other workers respond to incentives in similar ways, the survey results may largely reflect the strong sense among teachers that their own financial considerations should be unimportant.[43] That may lead them to understate the importance of salary in their answers to these types of survey questions. Whatever the reason, teachers do seem to have a strong preference for small classes.

That preference also suggests that class-size reduction is not being driven by teacher unions. As representatives of the teachers, these groups often are criticized for what are perceived as poor educational policies and practices and for the disproportionate influence that they have over political and administrative decisionmaking. The reasoning goes like this: while union members constitute a relatively small share of all voters, their share of actual school board election votes is relatively high. Indeed, one analysis found that teachers in a sample of California school districts were 1.6 to 6.4 times more likely to vote than the average registered voter.[44] Their voting power and influence on policymaking could be expanded even further if schools reduced class sizes and therefore hired more teachers. While that may be true in theory, the strong popularity of class size among teachers suggests that recent trends are not being driven by teacher unions' desire for voting power. They are simply representing the wishes of their members.

The final consideration is the ease of implementation, or lack of transaction costs. In schools that are under capacity, reducing class size often is relatively easy to accomplish. Such a policy would be paid for out of a school operating budget—or more commonly, a school district operating budget—that is controlled by school leaders (school board and administrators) in negotiation with teacher unions. Given the support from both parents and educators, such budget allocations would appear relatively easy to implement. In economic terms, the "transaction cost" of small classes is low.

The situation is somewhat different when schools already are at capacity or overcrowded, as often occurs in growing communities such as today's exterior suburbs, or "exurbs." But even in those cases, there are ways to reduce class size without building schools. Portable rooms can be purchased or rented. Existing space can be used more intensively, both by increasing the percentage of rooms used at any given time or by lengthening the school day. None of these options are costless, of course, but they are options that are considered when class-size reduction is considered a high priority.

From this discussion it is relatively easy to see why class sizes have been consistently reduced in recent decades. Small classes are popular with parents and teachers, in part or in whole, because they are perceived to be in the interest of parents, teachers, and students. Together, these groups represent a potent force in the design of educational policy.

School Size

Not all small educational settings are so popular, however. One survey of parents finds that 64 percent of parents think that schools, rather than being too large, are "about the right size" or are "too small."[45] That is quite different from the situation with class size. As I discuss below, the difference can be at least partially explained by the fact that small classes are fundamentally different from small schools—in ways that change the market and political pressures at play.

Why might parents have little preference for smaller schools? One reason may be that the benefits of small schools are less tangible. Small classes would seem to result in more personal attention and less disruption—concrete benefits that the average person can relate to. Small schools, in contrast, seem to suggest vague notions of cohesiveness and community, which parents may have difficulty observing. Also, unlike with small classes, it takes a great deal of time to reduce the size of schools. In the typical district, small schools require new school construction or at least substantial renovation. The best-case scenario is found in a district that owns and can reopen older buildings that have been closed, but even such buildings are likely to require substantial repairs (disrepair may be one of the reasons that the schools were closed to begin with). In most places, such changes would require passing a bond issue, which can take years to accomplish—and still longer for the construction or renovation to be completed. Few parents have a direct incentive to support such a policy, although they may still support it because of benefits to other children.

Teachers may prefer small schools, though they have a much smaller effect than small classes on teacher well-being. Small schools may allow for better relationships with other teachers and between teachers and students, but they also are likely to include a school principal with a more watchful eye. More important, small schools have no direct effect on teachers' workload or the quality of the classroom environment—which is where teachers spend most of their time.

A final factor affecting the popularity of small schools is the high transaction cost of small schools. Again, most schooling takes place within school buildings and nearly all school construction requires voters to approve a bond issue, separate from other sources of school operating funds. It is not only that school construction takes a great deal of time, but also that each step in the bond issue process requires a great deal of effort. School boards form committees to study possible changes and to survey local voters. Administrators have to hire and manage consultants regarding demographic projections, site location, and architecture. Site selection can be a particular challenge, especially in communities that have little open space, requiring possibly expensive land acquisition. State policies often complicate matters by requiring schools to be built in particular ways. And the list goes on. Of course, there are circumstances—notably when schools are severely overcrowded—in which new construction and renovation is a near necessity.

The recent trend toward large schools and small classes is therefore relatively easy to explain. Small schools take a great deal of time and effort to produce and have ambiguous benefits for both parents and teachers. Small classes, in contrast, can be accomplished relatively easily and with clear benefits for parents and teachers. While these conclusions are partly the result of other alterable policies, such as how school construction is financed, there also are inherent market pressures behind them.

Conclusion

This paper shows that the benefits of small classes and small schools, while they may be substantial in some cases, often are overwhelmed by the substantial costs. Research evidence, though admittedly scant, does not support the across-the-board reductions in class size that have occurred in recent decades, though research does seem to support the general trend toward larger schools. In neither case, however, does that mean that small classes or small schools are never a good idea. Indeed, the research on school size lends support to the idea of dividing extremely large schools. This suggests that proposals to reduce class and school sizes, if implemented, should target specific schools and classes.

There is strong popular demand for smaller classes, but not smaller schools. Educational markets and political institutions abhor slowness and uncertainty and reward quick and tangible change. That tendency would appear to be reinforced by the pressure of accountability, which would be ironic in this case considering that accountability was created in part to improve the efficiency of school resource use. To the degree that accountability fails to reward actual improvements in efficiency, which may be often, the questionable tendencies of the educational system will be reinforced rather than curtailed.[46] In addition to improving accountability, policymakers could alter market and political pressures by changing policies related to school construction that may promote construction of overly large schools.

Researchers, too, can play their part. Current research displays a fundamental inadequacy: it devotes almost all its attention to estimating benefits. Perhaps benefits represent the more intriguing problem to study, but it also leaves policymakers, at least those who take research seriously and read volumes such as this one, with a continuous flow of half-answers to important policy questions. Analysis of cost and benefits, as this paper shows, is not always easy, but it is not impossible either—and it is necessary for the design of sound educational policies.

Notes

1. While the literature on these topics is large, it is not completely persuasive. As Caroline Hoxby pointed out during her remarks at the conference associated with this volume, almost all of the studies on the subject are correlational and these relationships may not be causal.

2. The pupil-teacher ratio measures the number of teachers assigned to a school divided by the number of students assigned to the school, while class size is the number of students in each class. The pupil-teacher ratio is generally lower than the class size because teachers are less likely than students to be in class during every class period. The two measures differ for other reasons as well.

3. Two surveys support this conclusion: Phi Delta Kappa International, *The 30th Annual Phi Delta Kappa/Gallup Poll of the Public's Attitudes toward the Public Schools: Politics and the Public Schools* (1998) (www.pdkintl.org/kappan/kp9809-2c.htm [October 30, 2006]); and Public Agenda, *Issue Guides: Education* (2003) (www.publicagenda.org/issues/ [June 25, 2005]).

4. Phi Delta Kappa International, *The 30th Annual Phi Delta Kappa/Gallup Poll of the Public's Attitudes toward the Public Schools: Effectiveness of Public Schools* (1998) (www.pdkintl.org/kappan/kp9809-2a.htm [October 30, 2006]).

5. This assumes that the contribution of each input is independent of the levels of the other inputs. More realistically, the resources are interdependent; for example, the productivity of the teacher depends on whether he or she has a small class size.

6. The incremental benefit for the entire group of students is $300 multiplied by 1,000 students, or $300,000. If the incremental benefit were constant, that number would be the same for each one-student reduction in class size. Instead, it declines to $140 multiplied by 1,000, or $140,000. So the average incremental group benefit is halfway between the two, $220,000. Multiplying the last number by 8 yields $1,760,000.

7. Cost-benefit analysis is best applied to large projects that are relatively fixed in nature, for example, building a baseball stadium or a sewer system. The decision in these cases is to do the project or not; there is little middle ground. That is sometimes the case with small schools, especially in small school districts where small changes in school size are impossible. At the extreme, a district with only one school can reduce its average school size only by building a new school, thereby cutting the average school size in half.

8. Lant Pritchett and Deon Filmer, "What Education Production Functions Really Show: A Positive Theory of Education Expenditures," *Economics of Education Review* 18 (1999): 223–39. The quotation is from page 228 of the article. The India study that they refer to is *India: Primary Education Achievement and Challenges*, Report 15756-IN (Washington: World Bank, 1996).

9. Alan B. Krueger, "Economic Considerations and Class Size," *Economic Journal* 113 (February 2003): 34–63; Alan B. Krueger and Diane M. Whitmore, "The Effect of Attending a Small Class in the Early Grades on College Test Taking and Middle School Test Results: Evidence from Project STAR," *Economic Journal* 111 (January 2001): 1–28. For a detailed description of the STAR experiment and its effects, see the Whitmore Schanzenbach paper in this volume.

10. For a more skeptical view of the STAR study, see Eric A. Hanushek, "Some Findings from an Independent Investigation of the Tennessee STAR Experiment and from Other Investigations of Class Size Effects," *Educational Evaluation and Policy Analysis* 21 (Summer 1999): 143–63.

11. Derek A. Neal and William R. Johnson, "The Role of Premarket Factors in Black-White Wage Differential," *Journal of Political Economy* 114(5) (1996): 869–95.

12. Andrew M. Weiss, "Human Capital versus Signaling Theories of Wages," *Journal of Economic Literature* 9, no. 4 (1995): 133–54. This study concludes that a substantial portion of the economic return to education estimated by economists really represents a "signaling" effect, or employers' perception of increased productivity, rather than a true increase in productivity caused by education.

13. Janet Currie and Duncan Thomas, "Early Test Scores, Socioeconomic Status and Future Outcomes," Working Paper 6943 (Cambridge, Mass.: National Bureau of Economic Research, February 1999).

14. The discount rate is the rate at which future benefits are downweighted to account for the fact that the benefits are delayed; that is, the value of a dollar today is lower than the value of having the same dollar tomorrow. Economists normally use short-term interest rates as the measure of the discount rate, which is why the two are used interchangeably in the text. Furthermore, the fact that the internal rates of return from the Krueger studies are higher than current short-term interest rates suggests that the net benefits are positive.

15. Douglas N. Harris, "Identifying Optimal Class Sizes and Teacher Salaries," in *Cost Effectiveness Analysis in Education*, edited by Henry Levin and Patrick McEwan (Larchmont, N.Y.: American Education Finance Association, 2002).

16. Charles Manski, "Academic Ability, Earnings, and the Decision to Become a Teacher: Evidence from the National Longitudinal Study of the High School Class of 1972," in *Public Sector Payrolls*, edited by David A. Wise (University of Chicago Press, 1987). Manski documents how teacher salaries affect both teacher quality and quantity; those estimates are the basis of my earlier analysis of salaries versus smaller class sizes. Manski's assumption that SAT scores are good indicators of quality is contradicted by recent evidence: Douglas N. Harris and Tim R. Sass, "The Effects of Teacher Training on Teacher Value-Added," paper presented at the 2006 conference of the American Education Finance Association, Denver, Colorado.

17. There are various biases in the results noted by Harris in his 2002 article; most are deliberately in favor of class-size reduction being cost-effective. First, Manski finds that hiring more teachers reduces average teacher quality, but the loss of teacher quality from class-size reduction is not incorporated into the estimated benefits of the STAR class-size experiment. Second, the costs of building additional classrooms for the purpose of class-size reduction are excluded. Third, there may be more cost-effective ways to increase teacher quality besides raising the average salary. There is also one reason to believe that the results may be biased in the other direction: the effects of salary increases are assumed to occur immediately when, in fact, they are delayed.

18. If the optimal teacher salary for this calculation turned out to be lower than the actual salary, then that might call into question the comparison of the class size and salary results. The reason

is that a lower salary will reduce the number of teachers willing to work and therefore make it unrealistic to assume that class size is "held constant" in any meaningful sense.

19. State average pupil-teacher ratios ranged from 12.1 in Maine to 20.4 in Oregon in 2002. National Center for Education Statistics, *Digest of Education Statistics*, table 65 (2005). The ranges within states are likely much larger.

20. Strictly speaking, economists discuss returns to scale in terms of what happens to output when all inputs are increased by the same percentage.

21. Kalyan Chakraborty, Basudeb Biswas, and W. Cris Lewis, "Economies of Scale in Public Education: An Econometric Analysis," *Contemporary Economic Policy* 18, no. 2 (2000): 238–47.

22. Valerie E. Lee and Julia B. Smith, "High School Size: Which Works Best for Whom?" *Educational Evaluation and Policy Analysis* 19, no. 3 (1997): 205–27.

23. Matthew Andrews, William Duncombe, and John Yinger, "Revisiting Economies of Size in American Education: Any Closer to Consensus?" *Economics of Education Review* 21 (2002): 245–62.

24. Lawrence W. Kenny, "Economies of Scale in Schooling," *Economics of Education Review* 2 (1982): 1–24.

25. A cost function in which the educational outcome is replaced with a set of factors measuring demand for those outcomes is called an expenditure function instead of a cost function. The advantage of the expenditure function approach is that it takes into account outcomes without requiring them to be measured. See Chakraborty, Biswas, and Lewis, "Economies of Scale in Public Education," for more extensive discussion.

26. Another problematic assumption is that schools are "technically efficient" and therefore choose combinations of inputs that maximize output. As a counterexample, suppose that extremely small school districts are inefficient and therefore achieve lower education outcomes at any given cost. In this case, it may appear that small schools are inefficient when in fact the lower outcomes are related to some other inefficiency in the system. For a clear and detailed discussion of these and related issues, see William F. Fox, "Reviewing Economies of Size in Education," *Journal of Education Finance* 6 (Winter 1981): 273–96.

27. Most of the research estimating educational cost functions focuses on increasing returns to scale of school districts rather than individual schools. In addition to the independent interest in school district consolidation, one reason for the district-level focus is that cost data are much more frequently available at the district level than the school level. The district studies are of little interest here, however, because the factors affecting returns to scale at the district level appear to be different from those at the school level.

28. See the studies reviewed by Fox, "Reviewing Economies of Size in Education," as well as the newer studies focusing on elementary and secondary schools in Wyoming, elementary and secondary schools in Utah, and elementary schools in New York state. The newer studies are found, respectively, in Tyler J. Bowles and Ryan Bosworth, "Scale Economies in Public Education: Evidence from School Level Data," *Journal of Education Finance* 28 (Fall 2002): 285–300; Chakraborty, Biswas, and Lewis, "Economies of Scale in Public Education"; and William Duncombe, Jerry Miner, and John Ruggiero, "Potential Cost Savings from School District Consolidation: A Case Study of New York," *Economics of Education Review* 14, no. 3 (1995): 265–84.

29. Estimating an optimal school size requires the researcher to allow for a nonlinear cost curve, such as the U-shaped curve in figure 1 of this paper. Most research restricts the cost curve to being linear, and therefore makes it impossible to identify an optimal size.

30. This is based on the discussion by Fox, "Reviewing Economies of Size in Education," of the following studies: Elchanan Cohn, "Economies of Scale in Iowa High School Operations," *Journal of Human Resources* 3, no. 4 (1968): 422–34;.Gary P. Johnson, "The Estimation of a Long-Run Cost Function for West Virginia Public High Schools," paper presented at the annual meeting

of the American Educational Research Association (1972); and John Riew, "Economies of Scale in High School Operation," *Review of Economics and Statistics* 48, no. 3 (1966): 280–87.

31. Leanna Stiefel and others, "High School Size: Effects on Budgets and Performance in New York City," *Educational Evaluation and Policy Analysis* 22, no. 1 (2000): 27–39.

32. One exception to this is that small schools appear to be highly inefficient for transfer students.

33. Ilyana Kuziemko, "Using Economic Shocks to School Enrollment to Estimate the Effect of School Size on Student Achievement," *Economics of Education Review* 25 (2006): 63–75.

34. Jim Taylor and Steve Bradley, "Resource Utilization and Economies of Size in Secondary Schools," *Bulletin of Economic Research* 52, no. 2 (2000): 123–51.

35. Note that, as in the Krueger studies, this is the present discounted value of the net benefits over more than a half-century from the time that workers start school to the time that they retire. That means that $3,000 per student, while positive, is not extremely large. At the same time, it probably is an underestimate of the true net present value for two reasons. First, Kuziemko assumes that the new schools would be built at an average cost equal to the average cost of construction in the year 2000. Because the new schools would be smaller, by definition, these average construction costs would also be lower. In addition, it is well known that building traditional school buildings is more costly than renting, due to state and federal requirements. It is likely that very small schools would have to be built under a different, and perhaps less stringent, set of rules. Finally, note that Kuziemko's approach of looking for schools in which there are enrollment "shocks" is problematic because the shock itself may be disruptive to school operations. This initial shock may reduce the apparent longer-term benefit of smaller schools.

36. National Center for Education Statistics, *Digest of Education Statistics*, table 92 (2005).

37. Lee and Smith, "High School Size: Which Works Best for Whom?"

38. Clearly, more research is necessary to resolve these remaining issues. Unlike with class size, there is no experimental evidence on the effects of smaller schools that could be used to measure the effects on human capital. Also, better information is needed regarding costs, such as transportation and building costs, which typically are excluded. As a result, the studies are actually estimating short-run average cost curves (excluding most of the fixed costs), which implies further that the resulting estimates of optimal school size will be biased downward. Put differently, the point at which long-run average cost is minimized would be lower if fixed capital costs were included.

39. Phi Delta Kappa International, *The 30th Annual Phi Delta Kappa/Gallup Poll of the Public's Attitudes toward the Public Schools: Politics and the Public Schools*. Other reforms also were considered in the survey, and the only one to receive (slightly) greater support was providing help to repair school buildings.

40. Public Agenda, *Issue Guides: Education*. The question from this poll was as follows: "I'm going to read you some education proposals. For each one, please tell me whether you strongly favor, somewhat favor, somewhat oppose, or strongly oppose the proposal." The proposals included smaller classes, higher teacher salaries, more computers, tutoring, and school construction. All four received similarly strong support. The survey, which included 1,003 adults, was administered by the Educational Testing Service (ETS). No documents were available from ETS; therefore the discussion above relies on the reports reported by Public Agenda.

41. Douglas N. Harris, "High-Flying Schools, Student Disadvantage, and the Logic of NCLB," *American Journal of Education* (forthcoming).

42. Public Agenda, *Issue Guides: Education*. The question from this poll was as follows: "Among these three reforms, which do you think would be a better way to improve the quality of teaching: (a) improve working conditions in school by reducing class size; (b) expand the pool of qualified applicants by increasing pay for all teachers; or (c) make it easier for districts to financially reward outstanding teachers?" Forty-seven percent of respondents indicated (a) and 39

percent indicated (b). The sample included 1,345 K-12 public school teachers. With regard to class size and teacher salary, a more interesting question would be to compare trade-offs between specific changes in teacher salaries (for example, $5,000 per teacher) and specific reductions in class size (for example, a reduction of two students per class). That would more clearly incorporate the costs involved with each option.

43. Douglas N. Harris and Scott J. Adams, "Understanding the Level and Causes of Teacher Turnover: A Comparison with Other Professions," *Economics of Education Review* (forthcoming). This study provides evidence that teachers and other workers respond to salaries in similar ways.

44. Terry Moe, "Political Control and the Power of the Agent," *Journal of Law, Economics, and Organization* 22, no. 1 (Spring 2006).

45. Phi Delta Kappa International, *The 30th Annual Phi Delta Kappa/Gallup Poll of the Public's Attitudes toward the Public Schools: Effectiveness of Public Schools*. The numbers were similar for public school parents and those who had no children in school.

46. Harris, "High-Flying Schools, Student Disadvantage, and the Logic of NCLB."

High School Size, Organization, and Content: What Matters for Student Success?

LINDA DARLING-HAMMOND,
PETER ROSS, AND MICHAEL MILLIKEN

In recent years, the large comprehensive high school has been a subject of growing critique by researchers and reformers. "Factory model" schools have been criticized for their impersonal structures, fragmented curricula, segregated and unequal program options, and inability to respond effectively to student needs.[1] Some studies have found that, other things equal, smaller schools appear to produce higher achievement, lower dropout rates, lower rates of violence and vandalism, more positive feelings about self and school, and more participation in school activities. These outcomes appear more pronounced for students who are traditionally lower achieving.[2] In addition, the belief that large schools are necessarily more cost-effective has been challenged by studies finding equivalent operating costs and lower costs per graduate in smaller schools.[3]

However, there are competing findings about the effects of smaller schools for different groups of students and about the effects of school size and organizational features in diverse contexts. This review examines these findings across a wide range of studies over the last thirty years. We conclude that the influences of size appear to be mediated by other features of school organizations that are sometimes, but not always, associated with size, making the relationship between school size and many desired outcomes an indirect one. These other features are associated with aspects of school design, including how adults and students are organized to work together, the nature of the cur-

---

The authors gratefully acknowledge helpful comments and suggestions from Jack Buckley, David Ferrero, and Valerie Lee.

riculum, and how access to knowledge is organized. Smaller schools may provide the opportunity for important educational conditions such as stronger relationships, greater student involvement, and greater academic press, but they do not, by themselves, guarantee that those conditions will exist.

Furthermore, the processes used to create smaller schools or units within large schools have been highly varied, including many different models (for example, schools within a school with varying degrees of autonomy, house plans, mini-schools, learning communities, clusters, magnets, and charters within larger schools or as stand-alone schools) that have been launched under widely differing conditions. We would expect—and research has confirmed—variable levels of success among school restructuring efforts launched with different designs, varying amounts of planning time and resources, and varying levels of staff experience and quality, as well as under different political conditions, collective bargaining agreements, and other factors.

Finally, there are questions about what "smaller" means and about what school size may be optimum, since comparative studies have examined different size ranges. For example, research looking at data from different systems in different eras has resulted in recommended maximum high school enrollments ranging from 500 to 1,000.[4] Some analysts suggest that optimum size varies with the socioeconomic status of the community, with 1,000 probably the upper limit for schools serving affluent students and substantially smaller sizes for schools serving low-income students.[5] Our review of the available evidence suggests that, in addition to student backgrounds, important variables influencing high school outcomes for different groups of students include organizational structures that create more coherence and "communal" orientation, reduce curriculum differentiation, increase instructional authenticity and rigor, and enhance personalization (that is, the extent to which students are well known by adults).

While we have found no research support for the large urban comprehensive schools serving several thousand students that still exist in many cities, many questions remain about what kinds of organizations should replace these gargantuan institutions. We believe that interpreting competing findings in ways that can guide productive decisionmaking requires a much more nuanced analysis of the interacting elements of relative school size, student body composition, organizational design, curriculum content, and instructional features than is typically undertaken. As Bickel and Howley note, "Seldom have policymakers or researchers asked 'Better for whom?' or 'Better for what?' or 'Better under what conditions?'"[6] In what follows, we seek to address these questions.

Research on School Size

Much of the research on school size is quantitative and correlational, using state administrative data or large national data sets such as the High School and Beyond Study and the National Education Longitudinal Study of 1988 (NELS:88).[7] These studies use more and less sophisticated statistical controls to handle concerns regarding the comparability of student populations and the many other school- and community-related variables that could influence student outcomes. In addition, a growing body of case literature on small high schools or "small learning communities" describes outcomes of specific change processes and school designs, adding texture to the findings of the larger-scale studies.[8] Some of these studies have examined how the same or similar students fare under different schooling conditions and what the influences of deliberate design decisions may be. These schools are small "by design," whereas others are small or large "by default," as a function of the size and nature of their community or historical tradition. These two types of schools offer different perspectives on the role that size may play in constructing or constraining school practices and outcomes. Examining both of these bodies of work is useful, as each provides a different lens on questions of whether and under what circumstances size may matter.

However, there are many challenges in interpreting current research on school size. Since there are no studies using randomized trials, strong causal claims are difficult to make. As Stern and Wing point out, many correlational studies may find relationships between size and various outcomes that could actually result from unmeasured variables not fully captured by controls.[9] For example, it is possible that small rural schools tend to exist in more cohesive, supportive communities and large urban schools tend to exist in settings that have more concentrated challenges to student attachment and success. Small schools in these settings may often be magnet schools or other schools of choice that introduce selectivity bias. Medium-size schools may predominate in suburban districts that are wealthier and have more resources for education. Controls for student poverty, urbanicity, spending, and prior achievement help to capture these external forces, but we do not know the extent to which they offset the many factors that may matter.

In addition to being alert to these potentially unmeasured variables, it is important to look at studies where small schools have replaced larger schools and where the characteristics of students and communities can be examined or are held constant. It is critically important in examining studies of these emerging small-school reforms to evaluate the care with which potential selection biases are taken into account and student characteristics are addressed. It is also important to attend to the mechanisms by which changes in size may be associated with changes in other mediating variables, since, presumably, if size matters, it is because it causes or enables relationships or academic opportunities to change in some fundamental ways.

This concern is related to another limitation in the literature. Many studies do not distinguish between schools that happen to be small and new schools designed to be both small and innovative in various ways, failing to acknowledge that these two kinds of schools may have different influences on student perseverance and learning, as the literature on school design suggests. Where possible, we distinguish between studies of these different kinds of schools, and we give greater weight to studies that attend to issues of school selection and design and that carefully account for student composition.

A final difficulty in drawing policy-relevant conclusions from the school-size literature is that, ironically, many studies do not provide information about the range of sizes of schools they are comparing, and few understand the relationship between size and other outcome variables as potentially curvilinear. Interpreting the effects of school size on student outcomes in cities like New York or Los Angeles—where some schools are as large as 6,000—is very different from looking at size effects across a rural state where the smallest schools may have fewer than fifty students and the largest reach only 1,000. If the relationship between school size and outcomes is not monotonic, one could find positive coefficients on student enrollment in one context and negative coefficients in another, based simply on the relative sizes of schools in the sample. Clearly these kinds of issues need to be sorted out in evaluating what we know—and do not know—about the effects of size.

School Size and Costs

Much of the early research on school size focused on the influences of both school and district size on costs, attempting to evaluate whether there are economies of scale in the education sector. Over several decades, researchers have found evidence of economies of scale for schools and school districts.[10] With one exception,[11] these studies typically do not use strong measures of student achievement, other than to include rough proxy measures like school graduation rates as an independent variable in the cost or expenditure function. Most studies use a linear term for school size, and few specify the size of schools being examined.

It is worth noting that a number of the studies finding greater cost-efficiency for larger schools were conducted in rural states with a large proportion of very small schools, such as Iowa and Utah.[12] In these contexts, the category of "large" schools could reach 500–1,000 students, a scale that would be labeled "small" in many large cities. It is likely that the comparison set is relevant to the conclusions drawn about cost-efficiencies. For example, the Public Education Association has examined the costs of small schools in New York City and found that small schools (generally about 400–500 students) are not more expensive than very large schools (generally above 3,000), which require greater nonteaching staff to coordinate all of the complex functions associated with their size; however, the small schools produce relatively more graduates.[13] Riew identified scale economies in the operation of high schools up to a size of about 1,675 students, suggesting that there are diminishing returns above a threshold.[14]

As concerns have turned to the nonfinancial implications of school size, researchers have examined relationships between enrollments and student engagement with school as well as achievement. We turn to these issues next.

Students' Participation, Attendance, and Dropout Rates

For some time, researchers have found evidence of more positive affective environments in smaller schools—such as feelings of belonging, connection, and being known by adults—and have associated these with findings of higher attendance rates and lower dropout rates.[15] Some of these studies are correlational analyses of data sets representing existing (not newly created) schools, while others have found improvements in attendance, reported engagement, and school continuation when new schools or small-school units are created to replace large urban schools.[16]

These affective attributes of small schools are also cited in a number of studies that have found lower levels of violence, vandalism, truancy, substance abuse, and disorderly behavior in smaller schools.[17] A recent study suggests that the percentage of schools reporting serious crimes is as much as five times greater in schools with more than 1,000 students than in those with fewer than 1,000.[18]

A limitation of some of this work is that, absent adequate controls, the correlation between school size and urbanicity may incorrectly attribute to school size alone the influence of many factors operating in urban neighborhoods. Also, databases in which the school is the unit of analysis may make it difficult to address selection biases that can operate in the choices that bring some students into smaller schools. To address these problems, a recent study by Leung and Ferris used an individual-level database of young men and controlled for the influences of the student's family situation, living arrangements, and parental education; the location and character of the school attended; and peer group factors, including associations with friends and gang participation. After controlling for these other factors known to affect violent behavior, the study found that school size (which ranges from 100 to more than 3,000 in the study sample) continues to be significantly related to violent behavior, with students in the largest schools (enrollments over 2,000) more than 20 percent more likely to engage in violent behavior than those in schools under 1,000.[19] Because this study is limited to urban youth with low socioeconomic status (SES), we do not know whether these results would generalize to more affluent youth in other settings.

If this relationship between school size and social behavior is real, why might it exist? Many studies have suggested that smaller schools appear to promote more attachment to school and more participation in school activities. Studies conducted as early as the 1960s indicate that, on average, students participate in fewer activities in large schools than they do in smaller schools.[20] In larger, comprehensive high schools there is greater competition for spots on the soccer team or in the school play. Students respond by specializing in the activities in which they have above-average ability, with fewer students participating in a narrower range of activities as they progress in school. By contrast, students in smaller schools report feeling a greater sense of opportunity, even responsibility, to participate in extracurricular activities, irrespective of ability, in order to field a team or put on a play. Thus in smaller schools, a greater percentage of students participate in extracurricular activities, and they join a wider variety of such activities on average.[21] This much-studied phenomenon appears to cut across class lines and types of communities.

Holland and Andre's review of research on extracurricular participation and adolescent development found that lower-achieving and lower-SES students are more likely to be involved in school life in smaller schools than in larger schools. They also found that the greater extracurricular participation of students in smaller schools has important developmental implications. In contrast to larger schools, where students report receiving satisfaction from participating vicariously in activities as part of a large crowd, smaller-school students report satisfaction from participating directly, which leads them to feel needed, challenged, and more self-confident.[22] Some analysts suggest that participation in activities may strengthen identity with the school, which, in turn, reduces the likelihood of dropping out.[23]

For example, in an analysis of 744 high schools from the High School and Beyond data set, Pittman and Haughwout found smaller school size to be strongly correlated with a composite measure of school climate including student participation, interaction with faculty, sense of cohesion, and infrequent problems with discipline. This variable is, in turn, strongly and negatively associated with dropout rates. Based on path analyses, the authors concluded that the relationship between school size and dropout rates is an indirect one: "Larger student bodies appear to produce a less positive social environment, less social integration, and less identity with the school."[24]

Lee and Burkham's study of dropouts offers additional evidence that, while smaller size matters, the organizational features of smaller schools are also critical. The researchers examined school influences on dropout rates using hierarchical linear modeling methods, controlling for students' academic and social backgrounds on many key dimensions. The data include a sample of 3,840 students from 190 urban and suburban schools taken from the High School Effectiveness Supplement of the NELS:88 study. They found that school size alone is unlikely to have a direct impact on dropout rates. However, students are less likely to drop out of schools with fewer than 1,500 students in which the curriculum is composed primarily of academic courses and in which student and teacher relationships are consistently positive. They also found that positive interpersonal relationships reduce the likelihood of students dropping out only within the structure of these smaller schools; in larger schools, such relationships are not sufficient to prevent dropping out.[25] Other research suggests that this may be because the structure of smaller schools allows teachers to have the closeness of contact and knowledge of students that permit them to use those relationships productively to keep students in school. Still, small schools must work to create and maintain these relationships.

Efforts to create new small schools or smaller units within larger campuses have also often been found to improve attendance rates, while reducing dropout rates, suspension rates, and disciplinary referral rates.[26] The strongest studies of this phenomenon have been able to account closely for key demographic characteristics of students in the new schools and in comparison schools (sometimes in the schools that were previously offered students in the same neighborhood) and to address or rule out selection effects.

For example, in their quantitative study of 143 small schools launched in Chicago during the 1990s, Wasley and colleagues found that, compared to students in larger schools and controlling for race, socioeconomic status, student mobility, and prior achievement, students in small schools (serving fewer than 400 students each) had better attendance rates, lower rates of violence, greater parent and student participation and satisfaction, much lower dropout rates (about one-third the rate of larger schools), and higher graduation rates, despite the fact that the students came from lower-income families and entered school performing below average.[27]

Another study of five new small schools launched in New York City to replace a failing comprehensive high school also found graduation rates of over 85 percent for these schools, more than double the graduation rate of the school they replaced and far exceeding that of New York City schools overall, despite the fact that the new schools served more low-income, initially low-achieving, and limited English-proficient students than the school they replaced.[28] This study tracked the assignment and recruitment process for the new schools, documenting that the new schools were "chosen" or assigned to most of the new entrants by neighborhood, they did not employ selective admissions processes, and differences in the composition of the student body were in the direction of greater educational needs, rather than fewer.

Similarly, Fine, Stoudt, and Futch's quantitative and qualitative cohort analysis of the New York–based International High Schools found that, although the schools only admit new immigrants with little or no English language proficiency, the students have significantly higher graduation rates than students in other New York City schools generally and than other limited English-proficient students. The seven-year graduation rate for the International High Schools' 1998 cohort was 89 percent compared to 31 percent for the same cohort of English language learners citywide and 69 percent for New York City students who were *not* English language learners. While students can "choose" these schools, they can only be assigned to the schools if they score in the lowest quartile on the English language proficiency test and are recent immigrants to the United States. Poverty rates for students in the schools exceed those of the city as a whole.[29]

While the new, small schools examined in these three studies are all smaller than 500 students, they also all have other unique design features relevant to their success. These are discussed in the section of this paper on school design. Among other things, all of these schools offer a college preparatory curriculum to all of their students. Whereas the diverse course selection available to students in larger schools was once commonly thought to prevent dropping out by accommodating students' interests and abilities, some studies have found the increases in course variety associated with larger schools tend to be associated with an increase, rather than a decrease, in dropout rates.[30]

Student Achievement

In addition to keeping more (typically low-achieving) students enrolled who would otherwise drop out, smaller schools have sometimes been found to produce higher levels of student achievement. The evidence is fairly consistent at the elementary school level.[31] At the high school level, some evidence also points to the benefits of smaller schools for student achievement,[32] but the results are more varied, and subtleties in the data require careful analysis and interpretation. It is important to locate the studies within specific contexts, size ranges, and pupil populations and to consider aspects of school design.

The production function literature has yielded a range of different findings about the relationship between size and achievement. Early research found positive associations between smaller school size and student achievement when controls for student socioeconomic status were introduced.[33] However, these findings were not uniform.[34] A 1976 study by Anita Summers and Barbara Wolfe suggested that, to the extent that school size matters, its influence may be greater for some students than for others. For example, they found stronger associations between school size and achievement for African American students in Philadelphia elementary schools and for low achievers in the city's high schools.[35]

In interpreting the disparate findings, it may be important to keep in mind the differences in samples, eras, and locations. Consider, for example, the different findings of two studies of school and district size, both of which control for key variables like student socioeconomic status, class size, and school expenditures. Using fairly old data, Kenny looked at the achievement scores of twelfth-grade boys from the 1960 Project Talent database, concluding that school size positively influences achievement. Since about 40 percent of students failed to graduate from high school in 1960, his sample of twelfth-grade boys excluded a large share of the population, disproportionately lower income and lower achieving, whose persistence to graduation and achievement were not measured.[36] If there are differential effects of school size by type of student, with less advantaged students benefiting from smaller schools, they are not visible in this kind of study.

The shortcomings of the sample notwithstanding, Kenny's well-controlled student-level analysis also found significant influences on achievement of a number of student factors that are often not measured, such as student health, absences, number of changes of school, number of jobs held by parents, split custody, and parental education (many of them associated with family income and urbanicity), and a number of school factors, such as instructional hours and days, class sizes, and level of teachers' education. These factors, a number of which may vary with school size, were controlled when looking at the enrollment coefficients. Clearly, if size matters, it is not the only thing that counts, and making sense of the research on this topic depends on teasing out what is (and is not) being evaluated in different studies.

Kenny also reported positive influences of district size, using a database of ninth- to twelfth-grade students from California districts in 1970, although he did not present his regression estimates for this study. By contrast, in highly urbanized New Jersey during the 1980s, Fowler and Walberg found that smaller elementary and secondary schools and smaller districts produced higher achievement and higher passing rates on several state tests. Schools in their sample ranged in size from just over 100 students to over 4,000.[37] The findings of either of these studies might be a function of size, but they could be picking up other context factors as well, including urbanicity and the relative supports for large urban schools and districts. It may be relevant that in 1970 most California cities outspent most smaller, low-wealth rural districts. In contrast, by the mid-1980s in New Jersey, most cities were heavily minority and funded at levels well below their surrounding suburbs. Thus many other factors could be associated with these disparate findings about size.

More recent research has found affective and academic benefits of small secondary schools. In a large-scale, well-controlled study using data on more than 11,000 students in 830 schools, Lee and Smith found that student engagement and achievement gains are significantly higher in smaller high schools. As we discuss later, they also found gains for schools that engage in a set of practices associated with school restructuring.[38] This study and others have found that the strength of these relationships appears particularly pronounced for students deemed to be at risk of failing or dropping out.[39]

Some evidence also suggests that school size may influence the equitable distribution of achievement, as socioeconomic status is less predictive of achievement in smaller schools than in larger schools.[40] One potential reason for this is that large schools typically stratify students in curriculum tracks that offer very different learning opportunities, and these are allocated in such a manner that students' background characteristics (socioeconomic status and race) predict their course taking, which is then associated with student achievement.[41]

Some new small schools are designed to provide a common academic curriculum, along with much stronger adult-student relationships, to low-income, minority, and recent-immigrant students who normally would not gain access to such a curriculum. Darling-Hammond, Ancess, and Ort tracked students over seven years in five such new small schools created to replace a failing comprehensive high school in New York City, finding higher performance on state reading and writing tests and comparable performance on mathematics tests when compared to students in state-designated "similar schools" (that is, schools serving similar populations of students). In addition, the new schools, serving more "at-risk" students than the previous school or the city as a whole, had much lower annual dropout rates (3.4 percent on average as compared to 6.7 percent for New York City) and much higher college-going rates, averaging 86 percent for the first cohort of graduates and 91 percent for the second cohort.[42]

Like other studies that have used college admissions tests like the SAT or ACT,[43] this one did not find strong relationships between school size and average scores on the college entrance examination. However, such scores are difficult to interpret, because the proportion and mix of students taking these tests in a given school is highly variable. For example, while Darling-Hammond, Ancess, and Ort found no advantage in average SAT scores for students in the new small schools, they did find much larger proportions of students taking the tests in these small schools—a critical variable for interpreting average student scores on such measures—as well as larger proportions of students staying in school, graduating, and going on to college.

Similarly, in their analysis of more than fifty new small Chicago high schools, which include free-standing high schools, schools within a school, and multischools (buildings completely divided into smaller schools), Wasley and colleagues found higher grade point averages, stronger reading achievement, and comparable math achievement for students in the new smaller schools and units as compared to peers in larger schools, controlling for student characteristics and prior achievement. The authors note that achieving comparable scores on average to those of schools with higher dropout rates constitutes an improvement in student performance. With annual dropout rates averaging less than 5 percent in the new small schools as compared to nearly 13 percent in comparison schools, the average performance of students in the new schools represents a wider band of students, uninflated by the loss of students with lower scores.[44]

Optimal School Size

Whereas the literature is fairly consistent in finding positive relationships between smaller elementary school size and student achievement, the questions raised for high schools are more complex. These derive, in part, from the specialized nature of the curriculum and teaching assignments and the multiple interests and trajectories of students. There has long been a tension between the desire to support more specialized curriculum offerings and the need to know students well enough to support them through their formative adolescent years. As Lee notes, economists have generally favored larger schools that may generate economies of scale, supporting more specialized programs and facilities at a lower cost per pupil, while sociologists have generally favored smaller schools that allow the construction of strong social and interpersonal bonds.[45] Framing the question of size around some notion of "optimum" enrollments is particularly important in high schools, as policymakers try to find a size that is large enough to support an adequate academic curriculum and small enough to produce the affective benefits of a more personalized environment.

A number of reformers over the years have suggested that an adequate academic curriculum in a personalized environment can be sustained at a high school size of about 400–600, and some of the research we have reviewed supports this view. It is interesting that this size range appears in the recommendations of reports by James Bryant Conant, the father of the American comprehensive high school, in 1959, by John Goodlad in his major study of high schools in 1984, and by the National Association of Secondary School Principals in its 1996 reform proposal, *Breaking Ranks*.[46] The earliest intuitive estimates were not built on empirical findings, but this size range characterizes most of the new small schools in New York, Philadelphia, and Chicago found to be successful in producing both greater attachment and achievement for low-income students of color. It is important to note, however, that the schools studied may be more effective than small schools that do not share the same design features.

For example, although not designed to test for "optimal" size, the Chicago small-schools study cited earlier found positive environmental and academic outcomes of elementary schools smaller than 350 students and high schools smaller than 400 students, controlling for student background characteristics and prior achievement. Launched as part of a citywide school reform initiative, the 150 schools studied generally emphasize development of a clear vision to guide work and measure progress; student-focused curriculum; instruction and assessment informed by data-driven decisionmaking; an emphasis on personalized relationships and rigor; ongoing communication with parents and other stakeholders; and ongoing, school-based professional development.[47] As discussed in a later section, these features are shared by other small urban schools found in other research to produce strong outcomes for low-income students of color. These features, however, are not necessarily shared by all small schools.[48]

When considering evidence that smaller schools appear to produce higher average student achievement than very large schools, some studies have suggested that the relationship between size and achievement is neither monotonic nor impervious to other aspects of school composition, design, and organization.[49]

For example, in a well-controlled study that takes into account prior student achievement and many aspects of students' backgrounds, Lee and Smith found a curvilinear relationship between size and achievement. The study reviews three waves of data from NELS:88 and examines the same 9,812 students from 789 public, Catholic, and elite private high schools in eighth, tenth, and twelfth grades. In their analysis, schools enrolling between 600 and 900 students generally have the highest average gains in reading and math compared to smaller and, especially, much larger schools. The influences of school size on learning are strongest in schools enrolling proportionately more students of color and lower-SES students.[50]

This study, and others by Lee and colleagues, is noteworthy not only because it carefully controls for student characteristics that might be related to selection bias, but also because it uses hierarchical linear modeling to address the fact that the relationship of school size to achievement or other student outcomes is multilevel. Size is a school-level variable, while achievement is a student-level variable. Most studies ignore this, either by aggregating achievement to the school level and running a school-level regression or by appending school size to student-level information. Both approaches can misestimate the influence of the school-level variable (in this case size) on the outcomes of interest by inadequately contending with the sources of between- and within-school variability in the dependent variable.

While applauding the study design, other researchers have suggested that both the nature of the data set and the methods of analysis do not fully prove that there is a single optimal size range for schools of 600–900.[51] Stern and Wing suggest that Lee and Smith's empirically sophisticated study still leaves open questions about whether the ideal size range emerges because more medium-size schools exist in suburbs and small towns that serve more affluent families and offer higher levels of resources for education.[52] A reanalysis of Lee and Smith's data by Howley and Howley found that optimal size appears to vary by student socioeconomic status and that schools in the smallest decile nationally appear to maximize the achievement of the lowest-income students. They observe that achievement equity in mathematics is maximized in high schools enrolling fewer than 300 students, and equity in reading is maximized in schools enrolling 300–600 students; inequity is greatest in schools enrolling more than 1,500 students.[53]

In her response to Howley and Howley, Lee makes the point that "research attempting to establish a direct link between school size and student outcomes may be misguided. Rather, school size influences student outcomes only indirectly, through the academic and social organization of schools."[54] She notes, "Size facilitates or constrains how people relate to one another, the offerings that schools can muster, the web of relationships that surrounds adults' efforts to facilitate the academic development of the young people they serve."[55]

Although Lee and Smith's 1997 study does not take school structure into account, an earlier study by the same authors does.[56] This study on the effects of school restructuring finds that critical aspects of school design—including continuous, long-term relationships between teachers and students, teacher-involved problem solving, parental engagement, interdisciplinary teaching teams, and a cooperative learning focus—are associated with higher levels of average achievement and with more equitable achievement than found in traditionally structured schools, whether small or large. Other researchers note that the interactions between school size and structural elements may be very different in the cases of reforms of previously large urban schools and historically small rural schools.[57]

Another group of studies conducted by Friedkin and Necochea in California and replicated by Howley and Bickel across six other states uses interaction terms in multivariate analyses to examine how socioeconomic status may interact with school size in producing student achievement.[58] These studies find that the relationships between school size and student achievement are closely related to the socioeconomic status of the community, with smaller schools appearing to be most beneficial in low-income communities. In analyses of school- and district-level achievement, small schools are found to reduce the influence of poverty on school and district performance, "disrupting the usual negative relationship between socioeconomic status and student achievement."[59]

In a study conducted in West Virginia, for example, a negative relationship between school size and achievement was found to increase markedly with each increment of students eligible for free and reduced-price lunch, with sizable associations noticeable above 30 percent low-income students and growing ever stronger as the poverty rate increased.[60] On the other hand, in communities where fewer than 25 percent of students qualify for free or reduced-price lunch, somewhat larger schools showed a modest positive relationship with student achievement at the eleventh-grade level, though not at the ninth-grade level. To get a sense of the size of these differentials, at grade nine, the effect of a standard deviation increase in size (about 260 students) in the poorest communities was a loss of just over 0.5 standard deviation in achievement, or about half a year of learning, while there was no effect in the wealthiest communities. At grade eleven, the negative effect of size in the poorest communities was about 0.6, while the positive effect of size in the wealthiest communities was about 0.25.

These findings are based on correlational research that does not control for the features of schools and students, beyond socioeconomic status, that may influence outcomes. Thus they should be considered as a provocative hypothesis to be explored further rather than as a demonstrated effect. The possibility of differential influences of school size for students of different backgrounds is, however, compatible with other evidence suggesting that more advantaged students may benefit more from the broader curriculum opportunities afforded by somewhat larger schools, while less advantaged students who have fewer academic supports at home may benefit more from the personalization, strong supports, and close attachments possible in somewhat smaller schools.

In a summary of this set of studies, Howley and Bickel argue that "a one-best, everywhere 'optimal,' school size is a figment. The appropriate size for a school, when the aim is to maximize aggregate student achievement, depends on community circumstance, operationalized here as aggregate SES."[61] They suggest a rule of thumb for determining upper limits of school size, with 500 as the upper limit for an elementary school and 1,000 (based on a maximum of 250 students per grade) as the proposed upper limit for a high school serving an affluent community. They suggest that high schools serving low-income communities should be considerably smaller.

One other variable often considered in debates about optimum school size is the affordability of a comprehensive curriculum. Long-standing arguments for large schools emphasize both the smaller per-pupil cost of facilities offering expansive fields and expensive equipment for athletics, vocational programs, science programs, and the like and the costs of a range of curriculum offerings. However, the requirement that schools be large in order to offer an adequate curriculum was questioned by empirical evidence even before contemporary notions emerged that districts might offer a portfolio of more specialized, smaller high schools.[62]

For example, David Monk found in New York State in the 1980s that larger schools do not always offer a more academically enriched curriculum and that schools with as few as 400 students can offer "a curriculum that compares quite favorably in terms of breadth and depth with curriculum offered in much larger settings."[63] In a larger study of more than 1,000 schools in the High School and

Beyond surveys, Monk and Haller found that the impact of school size on academic curricular offerings differs by setting, depending on student SES, type of community, and curriculum area. For example, large urban schools do not tend to offer a substantially enriched academic curriculum for more students as a function of size. They conclude that there is no inevitable relationship between larger schools and a stronger academic curriculum.[64]

Part of the reason for this may be that it takes a considerable increase in enrollment to generate much diversity in curricular offerings, within the usual limits of school funding. An early estimate suggested that a 100 percent increase in enrollment produced only a 17 percent increase in course variety.[65] Greater course variety may also be associated with greater tracking, which may consign many students to a less rigorous and often less engaging curriculum, as discussed later.

Finally, in a study of 2,829 students from fifty-one schools from the Longitudinal Study of American Youth, Haller, Monk, and Tien found no achievement advantages to large schools as a function of the greater number of courses they can offer. They found that, while larger schools do offer more advanced courses in math and science than smaller schools, on average, those additional offerings do not lead to stronger student achievement with respect to higher-order thinking skills in those subjects.[66]

Summary

Although there are limitations in the research base, evidence accumulated over several decades suggests that smaller high schools tend to be associated with more positive student attitudes about school, lower dropout rates, and higher levels of student participation and attendance. These findings are consistent across correlational studies using large extant data sets and comparison group studies examining new schools designed to be both small and organized for personalization.

The evidence is more mixed with respect to achievement effects of school size, raising the questions, "Smaller (or larger) than what?" and "for whom?" Studies that have found positive influences of "larger" school sizes on student achievement often have been conducted in rural states where many schools are extremely small and the largest schools are themselves fairly small by urban standards. Some studies also find benefits for "larger" schools for more academically successful students and for students in more affluent communities. Studies that have looked at specific sizes tend to record findings of positive influences, even for these students, as occurring up to a high school size of about 1,000. One study pegs the optimum size at around 600–900. Another reanalysis of the same data suggests that the optimum size may be smaller for less advantaged students.

There is strong evidence that low-SES students and students of color are generally poorly served by very large high schools. And there is a growing body of research suggesting that such students both stay in school and achieve at higher levels in smaller, sometimes very small, schools (that is, fewer than 500 students), when these schools are designed to offer a common academic curriculum with strong supports for learning. These features, however, are not shared by all small schools.[67] Whereas small size alone may create the affective conditions for greater attachment and more positive behavior, any influences of school size on student achievement are likely to depend as well on other features of the environment that shape what students have the opportunity to learn—the quality of curriculum and teaching as well as academic supports. We treat the critical intersection between school size and design in the next section.

School Design

Clearly, school size is not the only thing that influences student achievement. As we have suggested, school organization, curriculum content, and teaching quality matter too. Case studies of nonselective new small schools successfully serving high-need students tend to highlight similar features of their designs.[68] These include structures that personalize relationships—such as advisory systems, smaller pupil loads, and teams of teachers working with the same students over multiple years—and less differentiated, more academically rigorous and engaging curriculum and instruction.

In these studies, students are found to be more attached and engaged because teachers know them well, have high expectations, and offer adaptive instruction around a project-based curriculum connected to real-world problems and performances. Successful classrooms feature teaching that engages and challenges students through the use of various instructional strategies, a focus on higher-order skills such as researching, interpreting, and critiquing information, and an emphasis on student participation. Moreover, as Wasley and colleagues note, "Teachers felt more committed to and more efficacious in small schools."[69] Teachers in these redesigned small schools are more likely to collaborate with colleagues, participate in decisionmaking, and engage in professional development they find valuable.

Not all small schools or small "learning communities" are successful, however. Those that incorporate fewer personalizing features and less ambitious instruction have been found to produce fewer benefits.[70] Quite often house structures are little more than a "superficial overlay."[71] Some strategies to create schools within a school have created successful, equitable communities, while others have reinforced academic stratification, producing greater success for some students and less for others.[72] The process of change in creating small learning communities has also sometimes been divisive, introducing contentions among staff and parents that are not readily resolved.[73]

Indeed, the questions about the effects of school size may need to be considered very differently when weighing decisions about *starting* new small schools, *breaking up* existing large schools, or *maintaining versus consolidating* existing small schools. As Howley notes,

> In cities and suburbs, "small schools" has recently become a *reform movement*. Rural communities, however, struggle to *maintain* small schools in the face of states' attempts to close them on business principles based on cheap inputs. . . . Confounding *new, reformist* small schools with *extant, traditional* small schools obscures the salient structural issues that are the actual object of most research related to small schools.[74]

In addition to the differences in circumstances under which small schools or school units exist or are being created, there are differences in what goes on inside new small schools or smaller units within large schools. Some restructured schools have paid scant attention to the purposes for their restructuring and have pursued new structures without changing either relationships or academic rigor.[75] Changing school size or structure without attending to the purposes for such changes may not improve outcomes. As Newman and colleagues suggest, "The challenge is not just to adopt innovation, but to learn how to use new structures to enhance faculty and student concern for learning of high intellectual quality. Without aiming toward this end, there is little reason to implement innovative structures."[76]

A branch of recent research on school effects focuses on the degree to which various structural features of schools are associated with particular outcomes. Although this literature focuses primarily on the structural features of schools, it identifies several cultural and normative features associated with effective "restructured" schools. These include personalization, a shared school mission focusing on high-quality student learning, a strong core curriculum for all students, high-quality "authentic" instruction, and professional community. These features appear to mediate the effects of school size. While they may be more likely to be present in small, redesigned schools, they are neither inevitable in small schools nor, perhaps, impossible in somewhat larger schools if they are explicitly incorporated into organizational strategies.

Personalization

A number of studies have found that, all else equal, schools have higher levels of achievement when they create smaller, more personalized units in which teachers work together and students see a smaller number of teachers over a longer period of time, so that teachers and students are able to know one another well.[77] In addition to smaller school size, personalization is variously accomplished through smaller class sizes; longer class periods, often in conjunction with fewer courses per term and sometimes combining disciplines (for example, humanities courses that combine literature and history); advisories (classes in which teachers meet regularly with students to advise and support them regarding their work in school); teaming (in which a few teachers share the same group of students in order to discuss regularly the students' progress); and looping (in which teachers stay with the same group of students for more than one year).[78]

Researchers suggest that, in such "communitarian" schools, students are better known and faculty develop a more collective perspective about the purposes and strategies for their work.[79] Greater coherence and attachment are both thought to contribute to higher achievement. For example, a study of 820 high schools in the NELS, which controlled for both student characteristics and prior achievement as well as many school characteristics, found that schools that have restructured to personalize education and develop collaborative learning structures produce significantly higher achievement gains that are also distributed more equitably.[80] The schools' practices include creating small units within schools, keeping students together over multiple years, forming teaching teams, assuring common planning time for teachers, involving staff in schoolwide problem solving, involving parents, and fostering cooperative learning.

Bryk and colleagues also attribute the comparative success of Catholic schools in part to the increased personalization they provide, through their smaller size, attention to the whole student, and community-oriented settings.[81] Analysts suggest that smaller, personalized settings improve teachers' ability to meet the individual learning needs of students and increase their sense of responsibility for students in and out of class.[82] The personalized environments in these schools can lead to higher expectations and greater levels of accountability among parents, teachers, and students.[83] As one teacher noted, "Since you become so close to kids, it's important to them that they meet our expectations. They know very well how much we want them to succeed. The kids want to please you."[84]

From the students' perspective, these personalized settings tend to promote improved relationships with teachers and increased student engagement and attachment to school.[85] As a student in one study commented, "The teachers always give you attention. They really care about us. My teacher knows when I'm doing good or not."[86] Another small-school student noted, "School should not be mass production. It needs to be loving and close. That is what kids need."[87] Particularly in the high-poverty urban environments in which these particular schools operate, close relationships between students and adults may be especially important to supporting student success.

Shared School Mission

A common theme running throughout the school restructuring research is that school form should follow purpose.[88] As much research on school effectiveness indicates, having a clear, shared focus on student learning appears to be critically important. Such a shared purpose promotes program consistency so that the school's educative effects build upon each other from teacher to teacher and grade to grade. In addition, a clearly defined common purpose can provide organizing principles to guide decisions regarding structures, practices, and inquiry processes.[89]

In their review of the research on long-standing small schools (as opposed to the new wave of reform-generated schools), Howley and Harmon note four factors that explain why "small size works."[90] In addition to the personalization that facilitates greater participation among marginal students, they point to three other factors, all associated with developing a shared school mission:

—Faculty communication, which allows staff to develop a sense of common purpose as more of them interact routinely,

—Community ownership, in the form of genuine links to the local culture and community that allow the community to exert ownership and kinship, and

—Common purpose and curricular focus, facilitated by the necessarily narrower curriculum.

The achievement of a common purpose and focus tends to be undermined in big schools by the way they usually differentiate administrators, teachers, and students into distinctive curriculum tracks and multiple programs. The habits of fragmentation and diffuse organizational structures developed by comprehensive high schools are hard to break and are sometimes replicated in school conversions. A problem reported among less successful restructured schools is goal diffusion, where schools lose focus on teaching and learning due to both managerial and political distractions.[91]

A Strong, Core Academic Curriculum

Intellectual content also matters. The typical American high school offers a wide variety of curricular offerings, sometimes characterized more as a "shopping mall" than a coherent path to intellectual competence.[92] Although the original rationale for curriculum differentiation was to keep students interested in and attending school, greater school retention generally has not been associated with curriculum spread.[93] Furthermore, the typically broad, diffuse, and stratified curriculum can reduce average achievement and increase inequity in achievement. Whereas high-achieving students may benefit from the more advanced offerings available in some large schools, research indicates that offering such courses is not a close function of size, as previously assumed: Large schools do not always offer a greater range or quality of academic courses, and relatively small schools can successfully offer an academic curriculum to previously low-achieving students when it is coupled with strong supports.

Schools that reduce student choice and provide a more common curriculum and a narrower range of courses with an academic emphasis appear to achieve more equitable outcomes and have higher average achievement.[94] Schools that create less internal differentiation and provide a strong emphasis on academic pursuits also appear to have less absenteeism and stronger graduation rates.[95]

There is considerable evidence that when students are tracked into classes that are academically unchallenging and hold low expectations, they achieve at lower levels and exhibit more behavioral problems.[96] The usual rationale for this curriculum differentiation is the desire to match content to student "abilities." However, a number of studies have found that when students of similar backgrounds and initial achievement levels are exposed to more and less challenging curriculum material, those given the richer curriculum opportunities outperform those placed in less challenging classes.[97]

At the high school level, particular concerns arise around exclusion from gateway courses such as algebra, which can preclude further advancement for students before their high school career even gets started. Despite the obvious challenges of teaching a common curriculum to students with widely differing achievement, access to more rigorous courses appears to help even lower-achieving students. For example, one study that randomly assigned seventh-grade "at-risk" students to remedial, average, and honors mathematics classes found that, at the end of the year, the at-risk students who took the honors class offering a pre-algebra curriculum outperformed all other students of similar background.[98] In another longitudinal study of 12,500 eighth graders using NELS:88 data, Gamoran and Hannigan found that all students, even those whose prior achievement was very low, benefited from taking algebra.[99] However, when faced with a widely differentiated curriculum, many students will choose—or be placed in—less academically demanding courses, and these "losers" in the educational marketplace are disproportionately students from low-SES backgrounds and students of color.[100]

As we have noted, smaller schools offering a narrow band of academically rigorous coursework have demonstrated notable success in producing higher levels of achievement for all students, particularly with respect to course taking, graduation, and college going.[101] Developing such environments is difficult to do, however. As Gamoran and Weinstein found in their study of twenty-four restructured schools, reducing tracking is more often an unrealized goal than an achievement. The researchers found that high schools are more resistant to de-tracking than elementary schools and that secondary mathematics courses are the least likely to be de-tracked. The authors' in-depth study of one restructured high school with heterogeneous grouping reveals that several key attributes contribute to high-quality instruction, including "strong intellectual leadership, small class size, some control over who attends and who teaches at the school, and resources that permit extra tutoring for students who may be falling behind."[102]

Other studies have noted, as well, that schools which successfully bring a more common academic curriculum to students with widely varying levels of initial achievement have needed to create a variety of supports and interventions alongside this curriculum. These include after-school help with homework and tutoring, support classes alongside college preparatory courses, and very skillful planning and teaching on the part of teachers.[103] None of these features is necessarily unique to small schools, although they may be easier to achieve in schools that have been designed around a reconceptualized mission to educate more students to higher academic standards.

Adaptive, Authentic Instruction

Some studies have found positive influences on achievement of what Fred Newmann and colleagues call "authentic pedagogy"—that is, meaningful instruction, curriculum, and assessment that requires students to construct and organize knowledge, consider alternatives, apply disciplinary processes to content central to the discipline (for example, use of scientific inquiry, historical research, literary analysis, or the writing process), and communicate effectively to audiences beyond the classroom and school.[104] For example, in a large-scale study using NELS data, students in schools with high levels of what the researchers call authentic instruction—instruction focused on active learning calling for disciplined inquiry, higher-order thinking, extended writing, and an audience for student work—are found to experience larger achievement gains on standardized tests than those experiencing more traditional instruction.[105]

In addition, a study of more than 2,100 students in twenty-three restructured schools found significantly higher achievement on intellectually challenging performance tasks for students who experience "authentic pedagogy."[106] Influences on student scores on these tasks were estimated using hierarchical linear modeling, with controls for prior knowledge, as well as race, ethnicity, gender, and SES. The use of authentic pedagogy was found to predict student performance more strongly than any other variable, including student background and prior achievement. The twenty-three schools in this study, identified through a national search, demonstrated "substantial departures from typical organizational features,"[107] including shared governance models, teachers working in teams with common planning time, extended instructional periods or block scheduling, heterogeneous grouping of students, and use of cooperative learning and group work. Despite the fact that all of the schools had made substantial progress on organizational restructuring, there was a very large range in pedagogical practices and achievement both within and across the schools.

These findings reinforce the point made earlier that neither school size nor organizational design fully predicts teaching and learning activities or outcomes. At the same time, case studies of new small schools that were deliberately designed to focus on authentic instruction point out the important interactions between school organization and opportunities for challenging intellectual work. As a veteran teacher at one new small school explained,

> Small size means I can do a literature seminar with the bottom 20 percent of kids in the city. Kids who didn't read are reading books like *Jane Eyre* to write their essay. We can work with them during lunch. You find out who can't read, type, etc. These are the kids who would sit in the back of the room, be in the bathroom, and would deliberately get lost. I know dedicated teachers in big schools who teach 150 kids. They can't do this.[108]

Another key organizational feature highlighted in these cases is the use of performance-based assessments. Assessments such as portfolios and exhibitions set challenging tasks that are intended to encourage deep learning and create a sense of high expectations and mutual accountability. Typically these involve social science research papers, science experiments, literary essays, and mathematical models or projects that require in-depth study, extensive writing, and oral presentation before committees of teachers and outside jurors, rather like a dissertation defense. The tasks are evaluated according to preset standards and revised until they meet the standards. Analysts note that these tools can create higher academic expectations and a sense of shared standards across a school.[109] Students observe that they are forced to work harder and think more deeply about their work when they must present it publicly. These student comments are illustrative:

> You get to do most of the thinking when you work with your portfolio. You have to explain in detail how to do something or why something is important, so that someone who doesn't know it can understand it.
>
> The portfolio makes you develop your writing. [In addition,] it makes more sense for us to have to do an oral presentation, to answer oral questions about our work to see how we learned English [from a new English language learner].
>
> When you take a test, you don't feel like you need to know it after it is done. The portfolio sticks in your brain better.[110]

For faculty, the potential benefit of such strategies is that they set common, high expectations across the school and give teachers opportunities to calibrate their own standards and teaching strategies with those of other faculty. Conversations about how to improve student performance can create an engine for continual classroom improvement.[111]

Professional Community

Many researchers have identified the collaboration associated with a professional community of teachers as a key element of successful schools.[112] Bryk, Camburn, and Louis find that smaller school size facilitates the development of professional community, which they define as teachers' focus on student learning, collective responsibility for school improvement, deprivatized practice (for example, observing others' teaching and receiving meaningful feedback on their practice from colleagues), reflective dialogue (for example, discussing the goals of the school with colleagues), and staff collegiality and collaboration.[113]

Newmann and colleagues found in their intensive study of twenty-four restructured schools that professional community is one of three commonalities among schools achieving high levels of student learning. (The others are a shared focus on high-quality student learning and authentic pedagogy.)[114] Their research and that of others suggests that smaller schools providing more collegial professional environments for teachers generate greater collective responsibility for school improvement and student learning.[115]

As one small-school teacher noted, "The smallness has created a sense of commitment and camaraderie that you would not find in a large school."[116] Moreover, as a small-school principal and former large-school teacher commented, in a small school "teachers share what they are doing in a formal way in team meetings. They plan together and share what they have done. There is whole school sharing, and there are summer institutes where we have more time to reflect. There is more coherence than in big schools where teachers work alone."[117]

Lee and Loeb found that this sense of collective responsibility in small schools positively influences student learning. In an analysis of 23,000 students and 5,000 teachers in 264 Chicago schools with classes from kindergarten through the eighth grade, the authors found that teachers in smaller schools (that is, 400 or fewer students) have more positive attitudes about their responsibility to improve student learning and that these attitudes are, in turn, related to student achievement. The authors argue that school size indirectly influences both students and teachers.[118] Smaller size may enable the type of social interactions between teachers that are needed to create the personalization and shared knowledge that translates into stronger teaching and learning.

The School Change Process

A modest but growing body of research suggests that at least some secondary schools appear to be more effective when they offer personalized environments with a common academic curriculum, a shared mission that focuses on authentic instruction in support of high-quality student learning, and a strong professional community. While it is tempting to hold up this list of features as a recipe for success, research on school reform suggests that throwing a set of expectations together and hoping they will translate automatically into successful organizations is foolhardy. School design is a complex business of matching context, structures, resources, personnel, and purpose through collaborative processes that require intensive attention and effort.

Researchers who have studied the processes of trying to create new or redesigned schools warn against oversimplifying their findings or approaching major reform expecting ready-made solutions. School size and structural features are potential tools to help schools attain specific functions, but the results they produce depend in large part on how these elements are understood and implemented. In this section, we discuss many of the implementation issues that have been identified by researchers examining school change at the school and district levels.

Design and Implementation Issues

Despite evidence of successful new school models, a number of schools, particularly schools within schools, have sought to restructure without securing major improvements as a result.[119] The literature includes accounts of small schools that have replicated the fragmentation and stratification of large schools as well as restructuring efforts that have adopted select elements of structural change without accomplishing the primary goals of reform.[120]

PROBLEMS AND BARRIERS. One set of problems has been identified with the design of some single small schools as alternatives within large schools. These include splitting teachers' time and obligations between the school within a school (SWS) and the larger school in ways that dilute the possibilities for personalized relationships between teachers and students.[121] Such initiatives have sometimes exacerbated divisiveness among groups and ideologies within schools, as the "alternative" school is viewed with suspicion by those in the "regular" school, and clashes over resources, routines, and student recruitment often occur.[122]

Another set of problems can occur when the creation of multiple units (houses, clusters, academies, "small learning communities") within large buildings is poorly managed. One critical problem that can occur with the school-within-a-school model is segregated student grouping across SWSs or houses. In particular, students who are low achievers, are identified for special education, or have repeated a grade are less likely to be welcomed or assigned to a high-status SWS unit.[123] Student choice can also create or reinforce segregation. For example, in a study focused on five nationally representative SWS sites, Lee and Ready found that higher-achieving students tend to select subunits with reputations for rigor, while lower-achieving students choose subunits with reputations for lower standards. This segregation falls along race and class lines.[124]

In an analysis of a number of SWS models, Raywid details problems, including rivalries between subunits for resources, lack of clarity around issues of space and autonomy, unclear lines of responsibility and accountability, teacher ambivalence over loyalty to the subunit or to the whole, and a lack of cultural changes to accompany structural changes, leading to a tendency to blame students as the source of problems. In some cases, an incremental approach adds new elements onto existing structures rather than replacing them, leading to greater organizational complexity without the benefits of personalized communities the small schools are intended to achieve.[125] As one disappointed teacher put it, "A house is not necessarily a home."[126]

The SWS designs Lee and Ready studied tried to maintain elements of the comprehensive high school, including a diversified curriculum and teacher assignments outside of the small-school units.[127] In these circumstances, teachers could not concentrate on a single shared group of students and felt mixed allegiance between the subunit and the larger school. As one principal noted, "The staff had come to realize that the school-within-school process had failed, was failing. It deteriorated. You're running a small-schools concept that was bastardized [from] what it was supposed to be. Then you're running a comprehensive high school, *and you can't run both.*"[128] Based on their analysis of the operations of different subunits, Lee and Ready conclude that more autonomous SWSs are more likely to provide personalized learning communities and other benefits associated with small schools.

FACTORS INFLUENCING SUCCESS. Despite the many challenges of converting larger schools into smaller entities, there are some examples of successful reforms. Philadelphia's effort to create SWSs, called charters, found that ninth-grade charter students substantially outperformed their nonchartered peers, with higher attendance, higher rates of passing major subjects, more accumulation of credits, and lower dropout rates.[129] Like Lee and Ready's findings about the value of coherent, autonomous units, McMullan and colleagues found that these positive results are stronger in schools where students are separated into distinct subunits in which they take classes only with other students from their subunit. The most successful charters were based on a strongly personalized design in which a group of core teachers worked together with a group of 200 to 400 students through to graduation, sharing students and planning time. The authors note, "We . . . observed a persistent, net effect of charter participation on academic performance. Further, when we used a stricter definition of charter participation (taking three or more courses in the home charter) we found an even stronger net effect on student performance."[130]

A number of other researchers and practitioners who have tracked school restructuring efforts share their conclusion that small-school autonomy—or perhaps cohesiveness—is associated with stronger outcomes.[131] Dramatic changes like those documented in the Julia Richman Education Complex in New York City have typically used models that develop small, autonomous schools. As Ancess, Ort, and Darling-Hammond found:

> From an academically failing, physically unsafe, graffiti-ridden school of 2,600 that graduated only a third of its students, Julia Richman became a vibrant multi-age

complex of six schools, including four high schools that now graduate more than 90 percent of their students and send about 90 percent to college.[132]

The redesign process involved phasing out the comprehensive high school and "hot housing" a set of new autonomous schools in locations off-site, each with its own budget, staff, students, parent group, curriculum, and instructional approaches. The new complex includes a successful anchor high school that had existed for more than a decade as a free-standing small school in a different location; it also includes an elementary school, a day care center, a health clinic, and a teacher center. Collaboration is negotiated via a building council that uses a consensus model involving representatives from each school and organization housed in the complex.[133]

In tracking the development and outcomes of the new small schools created to serve the students who had previously attended Julia Richman, Darling-Hammond, Ancess, and Ort identify a set of design features associated with the higher levels of attendance, safety, achievement, graduation, and college going they produced. These include "small size; structures that allow for personalization and strong relationships; a carefully constructed curriculum aimed at specific proficiencies; teachers' pedagogical approaches, especially their explicit teaching of academic skills and their ability to adapt instruction to students' needs; a schoolwide performance assessment system; the creation of flexible supports to ensure student learning; and strong teachers supported by collaboration in planning and problem solving."[134]

A similar set of features was found to be associated with the early success of the First Things First initiative in Kansas City and with the successes of four other "conversion" initiatives across the country that transformed large, comprehensive high schools into smaller units that produced greater student success without the segregation, fragmentation, and divisiveness of many other attempts.[135] In all of these studies, the researchers argue that a key element of successful redesign is the ability to translate structural changes into improved instructional practice by coupling smaller class sizes and pupil loads with more instructional time, more long-term relationships between teams of teachers and shared groups of students, and a more purposeful and engaging curriculum.

Issues in Scaling up "Scaled-Down" Schools

The evidence on high school size and restructuring, despite the tantalizing potential benefits, is far from dispositive and raises many questions for future research. One set of questions concerns how to conceptualize school designs likely to be successful for different contexts and groups of students. Key issues concern decisions about school size, autonomy, the content and organization of curriculum, and the organization of students and teachers to do their work together. While there is some convergent evidence about the features of small schools that are often more successful than comparison large schools, especially in urban districts serving concentrations of low-income students, how to create these smaller-scale units is much less clear.

The research on new, autonomous schools appears generally stronger than the research on schools within a school, which describes many challenges for these efforts.[136] With some noteworthy exceptions,[137] there are few case studies of successful efforts to create smaller learning communities that can guide practitioners in navigating the obstacles to this strategy for improving high school design and outcomes.

Although restructuring schools typically need technical assistance, few districts have been well organized to support the innovation process for new or restructured schools.[138] However, some practitioners have organized school networks to support the transfer of knowledge. For example, a critical factor in launching the schools that eventually became the Julia Richman Education Complex was the use of a mentoring strategy by which leaders who had previously started successful small schools provided intellectual resources and mentoring to the new schools, both directly and through networks created between older schools and new start-ups. In addition, many of the new small schools were led by individuals who had previously taught in or administered one of the older, successful small schools, providing an internalized approach to knowledge transfer.[139]

Each of the studies of successful restructuring efforts mentioned earlier points out the importance of professional partners who help to stabilize reform efforts and provide support for instructional improvement. In several cases, the national Coalition of Essential Schools or its local affiliates were central partners in providing knowledge about successful design strategies, models of curriculum, professional supports for instructional improvement, and real-time coaching about the school change process. Other partners, including universities and organizations, such as the Institute for Research and Reform in Education (responsible for the First Things First approach), Talent Development, the School Redesign Network, the Small Schools Project, and the Small Schools Workshop, have provided these kinds of supports in other settings. In addition to professional development support and design advice, these kinds of organizations sometimes have provided assistance in buffering change efforts from rough political winds. While helpful in guiding some successes, none of these external support providers has been able to guarantee success under varied circumstances in diverse contexts.

Although it is possible to tease out elements that appear to have been associated with more and less successful small-school initiatives, it is not possible to articulate a set of factors that will guarantee successful reform. There are so many variables at play in the schools and districts where reforms are undertaken that an approach which appears to have been successful in one district may be less successful in another, and some apparently successful school-level reforms may not survive the winds of district and school-level discord or changes in leadership long enough to become institutionalized.[140]

Conclusion

School size is but one of many variables influencing students' opportunities and outcomes in high school. Although early economic studies sought to establish direct relationships between size, costs, and rudimentary outcomes in order to evaluate economies of scale, more recent organizational studies have illustrated that, to the extent size matters, it is because it can create conditions conducive to other relationships and opportunities more directly relevant to student attachment and learning.

The available research base has been limited by both the methods and databases used to explore these dynamics, so the findings that have accrued are offered as starting points for additional research, rather than as dispositive conclusions. In addition, many studies reporting the influences of "smaller" and "larger" schools have failed to indicate the size of schools they are examining, which impedes clarity in the discussion, as high schools range in size from under 100 to more than 6,000 students across the country, and what constitutes "larger" or "smaller" sizes varies substantially among different communities. Thus rather than offering strong conclusions, we offer the following evaluation of the evidence in the spirit of provoking further inquiry.

Many studies over forty years suggest that "smaller" high schools, whatever the metric, tend to be associated with more positive student attitudes about school, lower dropout rates, lower rates of violence, and higher levels of student participation and attendance. Controlling for student characteristics, behavioral differences along these dimensions have been especially noted in large schools (above about 1,500) in comparison to smaller schools. These affective benefits of smaller school environments appear to be true of schools that are small both by default and by design, and they may be a logical outgrowth of the necessarily close personal contact that smaller size affords and the difficulty of establishing close ties in schools that are too large.

The evidence is more mixed, however, with respect to the influences of school size on achievement, and these influences appear to be connected to other elements of school design. While there is a large body of research indicating that low-SES students and students of color are poorly served by very large urban high schools and little evidence of size-related advantages for schools above about 1,000 to 1,200 students, there are many questions about the influence of size within the group of schools below this threshold.

Various studies peg optimum sizes for high schools from about 400—roughly the size of many newly designed small schools that have been examined in comparison group studies—to a range of about 600–900, the estimate developed in one carefully controlled study of a large database composed largely of long-standing schools (that is, schools not specifically engineered to a particular design). Some research suggests that there may be an interaction between school size and student body composition, with less advantaged students benefiting most from schools that are smaller. Although this hypothesis needs further testing, it would be sensible that students who have strong family supports and academic backgrounds might have an easier time negotiating the complexities and attaining the potential benefits of large, comprehensive high schools than students who have fewer home supports and greater academic needs. Strong, routinely available interpersonal and academic supports in the context of close adult relationships might be most important for many lower-SES students.

There is unlikely, however, to be some magic number that describes a perfectly sized school, since much of the influence on student outcomes is associated with how adult-student relationships and access to knowledge are organized within the school. School size matters primarily in the ways it makes more likely certain conditions for learning. These conditions are neither inevitably present in small schools nor irrevocably absent in larger schools.

A number of design features that appear to influence student achievement in secondary schools have been identified both in correlational studies of large extant databases and in comparison studies of newly created small schools with distinctive designs. These include:

—Mechanisms that personalize student-teacher relationships, so that students can be well known and better supported,

—A shared school mission emphasizing academic success that creates cohesiveness in the norms that guide behavior and in the content of the curriculum across grades and classes,

—A strong academic core curriculum that provides access to more challenging learning opportunities for most or all students,

—Instruction that is responsive to student learning and that ensures the application of knowledge to genuine disciplinary problems and purposes, and

—A professional community that encourages teachers to take responsibility for student learning and provides them with tools to do so, through collaboration around learning problems and effective teaching practices.

These elements, too, should be treated as hypotheses for future research, rather than as principles set in stone. In the final analysis, developing a better understanding of how school size, organization, and curriculum content can influence student outcomes will provide some clues, but not a formula, for developing more successful high schools. Larger-scale and better-controlled research that can more fully address potential selection effects is needed to explore the ways in which various school features—individually and in combination—can support and constrain the possibilities for attachment, engagement, and learning for different groups of students.

Equally important, researchers, practitioners, and change agents need to pay much greater attention to understanding how the processes of school- and district-level change support or undermine the success of new school models, whether these are charters, pilot schools, alternatives within large schools, or multischool campuses. The field needs much greater understanding of how to develop and sustain new designs if the findings of organizational research are to be useful to practitioners and, ultimately, productive for the students who are least well served by the schools they currently attend.

Notes

1. See, for example, Valerie E. Lee, Anthony S. Bryk, and Julia B. Smith, "The Organization of Effective Secondary Schools," in *Review of Research in Education*, edited by Linda Darling-Hammond (Washington: American Educational Research Association, 1993); Arthur G. Powell, Eleanor Farrar, and David K. Cohen, *The Shopping Mall High School: Winners and Losers in the Educational Marketplace* (Boston: Houghton Mifflin, 1985); Theodore R. Sizer, *Horace's Compromise: The Dilemma of the American High School* (Boston: Houghton Mifflin, 1984).

2. Valerie E. Lee and Julia B. Smith, "Effects of High School Restructuring on the Achievement and Engagement of Middle-Grade Students," *Sociology of Education* 66, no. 3 (1993): 164–87; Valerie E. Lee and Julia B. Smith, "Effects of High School Restructuring and Size on Early Gains in Achievement and Engagement," *Sociology of Education* 68, no. 4 (1995): 241–70.

3. On costs in smaller schools, see Public Education Association, *Small Schools' Operating Costs: Reversing Assumptions about Economies of Scale* (New York, 1992). On costs per graduate, see Leanna Stiefel and others, "High School Size: Effects on Budgets and Performance in New York City," *Educational Evaluation and Policy Analysis* 22, no. 1 (Spring 2000): 27–39.

4. For the range of 500–600, see National Association of Secondary School Principals, *Breaking Ranks: Changing an American Institution* (Reston, Va., 1996); Richard Riley, "Schools as Center of Community," remarks prepared for presentation by U.S. Secretary of Education Richard W. Riley, Department of Education, 1999; Thomas Sergiovanni, *Building Communities in Schools* (San Francisco: Jossey-Bass, 1994); Pat Wasley and others, *Small Schools: Great Strides; A Study of New Small Schools in Chicago* (New York: Bank Street College of Education, 2000). For the range of 900–1,000, see Valerie E. Lee and Julia B. Smith, "High School Size: Which Works Best and for Whom?" *Educational Evaluation and Policy Analysis* 19, no. 3 (1997): 205–27; Diana Oxley and Joan G. McCabe, *Restructuring Neighborhood High Schools: The House Plan Solution* (New York: Public Education Association and Bank Street College of Education, 1990).

5. Craig B. Howley and Robert Bickel, *The Matthew Project: National Report* (Charleston, W.Va.: Appalachia Educational Laboratory, 1999).

6. Robert Bickel and Craig Howley, "The Influence of Scale on School Performance: A Multilevel Extension of the Matthew Principle," *Education Policy Analysis Archives* 8, no. 22 (2000) (epaa.asu.edu/epaa/v8n22/ [October 2006]); see also Lee and Smith, "High School Size: Which Works Best and for Whom?" 1997.

7. See, for example, Lee and Smith, "High School Size: Which Works Best and for Whom?" Robert B. Pittman and Perri Haughwout, "Influence of High School Size on Dropout Rate," *Educational Evaluation and Policy Analysis* 9, no. 4 (1987): 337–43.

8. Linda Darling-Hammond, Jacqueline Ancess, and Susanna Ort, "Reinventing High School: Outcomes of the Coalition Campus Schools Project," *American Educational Research Journal* 39, no. 3 (2002): 639–73; Michelle Fine, ed., *Charting Urban School Reform: Reflections on Public High Schools in the Midst of Change* (Teachers College Press, 1994); Michelle Fine, Brett Stoudt, and Valerie Futch, *The Internationals Network for Public Schools: A Quantitative and Qualitative Cohort Analysis of Graduation and Dropout Rates* (City University of New York, Graduate Center, 2005); Craig B. Howley and Hobart L. Harmon, eds., *Small High Schools That Flourish: Rural Context, Case Studies, and Resources* (Charleston, W.Va.: Appalachia Educational Laboratory, 2000); Wasley and others, *Small Schools: Great Strides*.

9. David Stern and Jean Wing, *Is There Solid Evidence of Positive Effects for High School Students?* (Berkeley, Calif.: Career Academy Support Network, 2004).

10. On economies of scale for schools, see, for example, Elchanan Cohn, "Economics of Scale in Iowa High School Operations," *Journal of Human Resources* 3, no. 4 (1968): 422–34; John Riew, "Economies of Scale in High School Operation," *Review of Economics and Statistics* 48, no. 3 (August 1966): 280–87; John Riew, "Scale Economies, Capacity Utilization, and School Costs: A Comparative Analysis of Secondary and Elementary Schools," *Journal of Education Finance* 11, no. 4 (Spring 1986): 433–46; Lawrence W. Kenny, "Economies of Scale in Schooling," *Economics of Education Review* 2, no. 1 (1982): 1–24; Ramesh C. Kumar, "Economies of Scale in School Operation: Evidence from Canada," *Applied Economics* 15, no. 3 (1983): 323–40. For economies of scale for school districts, see Richard Butler and David Monk, "The Cost of Public Schooling in New York State: The Role of Scale and Efficiency in 1978–79," *Journal of Human Resources* 20, no. 3 (1985): 361–81; Kalyan Chakraborty, Basudeb Biswas, and W. Cris Lewis, "Economies of Scale in Public Education: An Econometric Analysis," *Contemporary Economic Policy* 18, no. 2 (2000): 239–47.

11. Cohn, "Economics of Scale in Iowa High School Operations"; Kenny, "Economies of Scale in Schooling."

12. For Iowa, see Cohn, "Economics of Scale in Iowa High School Operations." For Utah, see Chakraborty and others, "Economies of Scale in Public Education."

13. Public Education Association, *Small Schools' Operating Costs*.

14. Riew, "Economies of Scale in High School Operation"; Riew, "Scale Economies, Capacity Utilization, and School Costs."

15. See, for example, Roger G. Barker and Paul V. Gump, eds., *Big School, Small School: High School Size and Student Behavior* (Stanford University Press, 1964).

16. On existing schools, see Mark Fetler, "School Dropout Rates, Academic Performance, Size, and Poverty: Correlates of Educational Reform," *Educational Evaluation and Policy Analysis* 11, no. 2 (1989): 109–16; William J. Fowler and Herbert J. Walberg, "School Size, Characteristics, and Outcomes," *Educational Evaluation and Policy Analysis* 13, no. 2 (Summer 1991): 189–202; Phil Schoggen and Maxine Schoggen, "Student Voluntary Participation and High School Size," *Journal of Educational Research* 81, no. 5 (May-June 1988): 288–93. On newly created schools, see Fine, ed., *Charting Urban School Reform*; Fine, Stoudt, and Futch, "The International Network for Public Schools"; Wasley and others, *Small Schools: Great Strides*.

17. James Garbarino, "The Human Ecology of School Crime: A Case for Small Schools," in *School Crime and Disruption: Prevention Models*, edited by Ernst Wenk and Nora Harlow (Department of Education, National Institute of Education, 1978); Denise Gottfredson, *School Size and School Disorder*, Report 360 (Baltimore, Md.: Center for the Social Organization of Schools, 1985); Emil J. Haller, "High School Size and Student Indiscipline: Another Aspect of the School Consolidation Issue?" *Educational Evaluation and Policy Analysis* 14, no. 2 (Summer 1992): 145–56; Sheila Heaviside and others, *Violence and Discipline Problems in U.S. Public Schools: 1996–97*, Publication 98-030 (Department of Education, National Center for Education Statistics, 1998); Randy Page, "Adolescent Use of Alcohol, Tobacco, and Other Psychoactive Substances: Relation to High School Size," *American Secondary Education* 19, no. 2 (1991): 16–20.

18. J. Stephen Ferris and Edwin G. West, *Economies of Scale, School Violence, and the Optimal Size of Schools*, Carleton Economic Paper 02-01 (Ottawa: Carleton University, 2002).

19. Ambrose Leung and J. Stephen Ferris, *School Size and Youth Violence*, Carleton Economic Paper 02-10 (Ottawa: Carleton University, 2002).

20. Barker and Gump, eds., *Big School, Small School*; see also Roger Barker and E. R. Hall, "Participation in Interschool Activities and Extracurricular Activities," in *Big School, Small School*, edited by Barker and Gump, pp. 64–74.

21. William J. Fowler, "What Do We Know about School Size? What Should We Know?" paper presented at the annual meeting of the American Educational Research Association, San Francisco, Calif., 1992; W. Campbell and others, "Effects of School Size upon Some Aspects of Personality," *Journal of Educational Administration* 19, no. 2 (Summer 1981): 201–30; Gary Green and Wanda Stevens, "What Research Says about Small Schools," *Rural Educator* 10, no. 1 (1998): 9–14; Craig B. Howley and Gary Huang, "Extracurricular Participation and Achievement: School Size as Possible Mediator of SES Influence among Individual Students," *Resources in Education* (July 1991): 1–36; Paul Gump, "Big Schools, Small Schools," in *Habitats, Environments, and Human Behavior*, edited by Roger Barker (San Francisco, Calif.: Jossey-Bass, 1978); Paul Lindsay, "The Effect of High School Size on Student Participation, Satisfaction, and Attendance," *Educational Evaluation and Policy Analysis* 4, no. 1 (1982): 57–65; Paul Lindsay, "High School Size, Participation in Activities, and Young Adult Social Participation: Some Enduring Effects of Schooling," *Educational Evaluation and Policy Analysis* 6, no. 1 (1984): 73–83; Neil G. Stevens and Gary L. Peltier, "A Review of Research on Small-School Student Participation in Extracurricular Activities," *Journal of Research in Rural Education* 10, no. 2 (1994): 116–20.

22. Alyce Holland and Thomas Andre, "Participation in Extracurricular Activities in Secondary School: What Is Known, What Needs to Be Known?" *Review of Educational Research* 57, no. 4 (1987): 448.

23. Vincent Tinto, "Dropout from Higher Education: A Theoretical Synthesis of Recent Research," *Review of Educational Research* 45, no. 1 (1975): 89–125.

24. Pittman and Haughwout, "Influence of High School Size on Dropout Rate," p. 343.

25. Valerie E. Lee and David T. Burkam, "Dropping out of High School: The Role of School Organization and Structure," paper presented at the conference Dropouts in America: How Severe

Is the Problem? What Do We Know about Intervention and Prevention? Harvard Graduate School of Education, 2000.

26. Pamela R. Aschbacher, "Effects of Restructuring on Disadvantaged Students: Humanitas; A Case Study," paper presented at the American Educational Research Association annual meeting, Chicago, 1991; Thomas B. Corcoran, "Restructuring Education: A New Vision at Hope Essential High School," in *Allies in Educational Reform*, edited by Jerome M. Rosow and Robert Zager (San Francisco: Jossey-Bass, 1989), pp. 243–74; Darling-Hammond, Ancess, and Ort, "Reinventing High School"; Charles Dayton, *Peninsula Academies Reputations: 1985–86 Evaluation Report* (Berkeley, Calif.: Policy Analysis for California Education, 1987); Fine, Stoudt, and Futch, *The International Network for Public Schools*; Jeffrey Fouts, *A School within a School: Evaluation Results of the First Year of a Restructuring Effort* (Seattle Pacific University, School of Education, 1994); Randy Gordon, *School within a School, Grades 7, 8, 9, 10: Focus on Program Evaluation* (Des Moines, Iowa: Des Moines Public Schools, 1992); Bernard J. McMullan, Carol L. Sipe, and Wendy C. Wolf, *Chapter and Student Achievement: Early Evidence from School Restructuring in Philadelphia* (Philadelphia: Center for Assessment and Policy Development, 1994); John Tompkins, *Dropout Prevention Programs, 1987–88: Report of Evaluation* (Des Moines, Iowa: Des Moines Public Schools, 1988); Wasley and others, *Small Schools: Great Strides*.

27. Wasley and others, *Small Schools: Great Strides*.

28. Darling-Hammond, Ancess, and Ort, "Reinventing High School."

29. Fine, Stoudt, and Futch, *The International Network for Public Schools*.

30. For the former, see Powell and others, *The Shopping Mall High School*. For the latter, see Pittman and Haughwout, "Influence of High School Size on Dropout Rate."

31. Anthony Bryk, Eric Camburn, and Karen Louis, "Professional Community in Chicago Elementary Schools: Facilitating Factors and Organizational Consequences," *Educational Administration Quarterly* 35 (supplement, December 1999): 751–81; Stephen J. Caldas, "Reexamination of Input and Process Factor Effects on Public School Achievement," *Journal of Educational Research* 86, no. 4 (March-April 1993): 206–14; Ronald F. Ferguson, "Racial Patterns in How School and Teacher Quality Affect Achievement and Earnings," *Challenge* 2, no. 1 (1991): 1–35; William J. Fowler, "School Size and Student Outcomes," in *Advances in Educational Productivity*, vol. 5, edited by Benjamin Levin, William Fowler, and H. J. Walberg (Greenwich, Conn.: JAI Press, 1995), pp. 3–26; Valerie Lee and Susanna Loeb, "School Size in Chicago Elementary Schools: Effects on Teachers' Attitudes and Students' Achievement," *American Educational Research Journal* 37, no. 1 (2000): 3–31; Wasley and others, *Small Schools: Great Strides*; Wendy Wendling and Judith Cohen, "Education Resources and Student Achievement: Good News for Schools," *Journal of Education Finance* 7, no. 1 (1981): 44–63.

32. Fowler, "School Size and Student Outcomes"; Craig Howley, "Small Schools," in *School Reform Proposal: The Research Evidence*, edited by Andrew Molnar (Arizona State University, College of Education, Education Policy Studies Laboratory, 2002), pp. 3.0–3.33; Magdalena Mok and Marcellin Flynn, "School Size and Academic Achievement in the HSC Examination: Is There a Relationship?" *Issues in Educational Research* 6, no. 1 (1996): 57–78.

33. Randall Eberts, Ellen Kehoe, and Joe Stone, *The Effect of School Size on Student Outcomes: Final Report* (University of Oregon, Center for Educational Policy and Management, 1984); Edwin Giesbrecht, *The Attainment of Selected Mathematical Competencies by High School Students in Saskatchewan*, Research Centre Report 48 (Saskatchewan School Trustees Association, 1978); Herbert J. Kiesling, "High School Size and Cost Factors: Final Report," unpublished report, 1968; Marshall S. Smith, "Equality of Educational Opportunity: The Basic Findings Reconsidered," in *On Equality of Educational Opportunity*, edited by Frederick Mosteller and Daniel P. Moynihan (New York: Random House, 1972), pp. 230–42.

34. Byron Brown and Daniel Saks, "The Production and Distribution of Cognitive Skills within Schools," *Journal of Political Economy* 83, no. 3 (June 1975): 571–93. Brown and Saks find a negative relationship between school size and achievement only in rural districts and no relationship in other districts.

35. Anita Summers and Barbara L. Wolfe, "Which School Resources Help Learning? Efficiency and Equity in Philadelphia Public Schools," *IRCD Bulletin* 11, no. 3 (1976): 1–15; Anita Summers and Barbara L. Wolfe, "Do Schools Make a Difference?" *American Economic Review* 67, no. 4 (1977): 639–52.

36. Lawrence W. Kenny, "Economies of Scale in Schooling," *Economics of Education Review* 2, no. 1 (1982): 1–24.

37. Fowler and Walberg, "School Size, Characteristics, and Outcomes."

38. Lee and Smith, "Effects of High School Restructuring and Size on Early Gains in Achievement and Engagement."

39. Lee and Smith, "Effects of High School Restructuring on the Achievement and Engagement of Middle-Grade Students"; Valerie Lee and Julia Smith, *Effects of High School Restructuring and Size on Gains in Achievement and Engagement for Early Secondary School Students* (Madison: Wisconsin Center for Education Research, 1994); Lee and Smith, "Effects of High School Restructuring and Size on Early Gains in Achievement and Engagement"; Diana Oxley, "Smaller Is Better," *American Educator* 13 (1989): 28–31, 51–52; Jean Stockard and Maralee Mayberry, *Learning Environments: A Review of the Literature on School Environments and Student Achievement: Final Report* (Oregon University, Center for Educational Policy and Management, 1985).

40. Noah Friedkin and Juan Necochea, "School System Size and Performance: A Contingency Perspective," *Educational Evaluation and Policy Analysis* 10, no. 3 (1998): 237–49; Craig Howley, "The Matthew Principle: A West Virginia Replication?" *Education Policy Analysis Archives* 3, no. 18 (1995): 18; Howley and Bickel, *The Matthew Project*; Lee and Smith, "Effects of High School Restructuring and Size on Early Gains in Achievement and Engagement"; Lee and Smith, "High School Size"; Lee and Loeb, "School Size in Chicago Elementary Schools"; Valerie Lee, Julia Smith, and Robert Croninger, "How High School Organization Influences the Equitable Distribution of Learning in Mathematics and Science," *Sociology of Education* 70, no. 2 (1997): 128–50.

41. Anthony Bryk, Valerie Lee, and Peter Holland, *Catholic Schools and the Common Good* (Harvard University Press, 1993); Lee and Smith, "High School Size."

42. Darling-Hammond, Ancess, and Ort, "Reinventing High School."

43. Leonard Baird, "A Study of the Role Relations of Graduate Students," *Journal of Educational Psychology* 60, no. 1 (1969): 15–21; Robert Jewell, "School and School District Size Relationships: Costs, Results, Minorities, and Private School Enrollments," *Education and Urban Society* 21, no. 2 (February 1989): 140–53.

44. Wasley and others, *Small Schools: Great Strides*.

45. Valerie Lee, "School Size and the Organization of Secondary Schools," in *Handbook of the Sociology of Education*, edited by Maureen T. Hallinan (New York: Kluwer Academic, Plenum Publishers, 2000).

46. James Bryant Conant, *The American High School Today: A First Report to Interested Citizens* (New York: McGraw-Hill, 1959); John Goodlad, *A Place Called School* (New York: McGraw-Hill, 1984); National Association of Secondary School Principals, *Breaking Ranks*.

47. Wasley and others, *Small Schools: Great Strides*.

48. See, for example, Valerie Lee and others, "Inside Large and Small High Schools: Curriculum and Social Relations," *Educational Evaluation and Policy Analysis* 22, no. 2 (2000): 147–71.

49. Craig Howley, Marty Strange, and Robert Bickel, *Research about School Size and School Performance in Impoverished Communities* (Charleston, W.Va.: ERIC Clearinghouse on Rural Education and Small Schools, 2000); Bickel and Howley, "The Influence of Scale on School Per-

formance"; Friedkin and Necochea, "School System Size and Performance"; Howley, "The Matthew Principle"; Lee and Smith, "High School Size."

50. Lee and Smith, "High School Size."

51. Craig Howley and Aimee Howley, "School Size and the Influence of Socioeconomic Status on Student Achievement: Confronting the Threat of Size Bias in National Data Sets," *Education Policy Analysis Archives* 12, no. 52 (September 2004): 52; David Stern and Jean Wing, "Is There Solid Evidence of Positive Effects for High School Students?" (Berkeley, Calif.: Career Academy Support Network, 2004).

52. Stern and Wing, "Is There Solid Evidence of Positive Effects for High School Students?"

53. Howley and Howley, "School Size and the Influence of Socioeconomic Status on Achievement."

54. Valerie Lee, "Effects of High School Size on Student Outcomes: Response to Howley and Howley," *Education Policy Analysis Archives* 12, no. 53 (2004): 2.

55. Ibid., p. 13.

56. Lee and Smith, "Effects of High School Restructuring and Size on Early Gains in Achievement and Engagement."

57. Howley and Howley, "School Size and the Influence of Socioeconomic Status on Achievement."

58. Friedkin and Necochea, "School System Size and Performance"; Bickel and Howley, "The Influence of Scale on School Performance"; Howley and Bickel, *The Matthew Project*; Howley, "The Matthew Principle."

59. Howley, "The Matthew Principle," p. 2.

60. Ibid.

61. Howley and Bickel, *The Matthew Project*, p. 18.

62. See, for example, Bill and Melinda Gates Foundation, "High-Performing School Districts: Challenge, Support, Alignment, and Choice" (Seattle, June 2005).

63. David Monk, "Secondary School Size and Curriculum Comprehensiveness," *Economics of Education Review* 6, no. 2 (1987): 148.

64. David Monk and Emil Haller, "Predictors of High School Academic Course Offerings: The Role of School Size," *American Educational Research Journal* 30, no. 1 (1993): 3–21.

65. Gump, "Big Schools, Small Schools."

66. Emil Haller, David Monk, and Lydia Tien, "Small Schools and Higher-Order Thinking Skills," *Journal of Research in Rural Education* 9, no. 2 (1993): 66–73.

67. See Lee and others, "Inside Large and Small High Schools."

68. See, for example, Darling-Hammond, Ancess, and Ort, "Reinventing High School"; Wasley and others, *Small Schools: Great Strides*; Fine, Stoudt, and Futch, *The Internationals Network for Public Schools*.

69. Wasley and others, *Small Schools: Great Strides*, p. 38.

70. Mary Ann Raywid, "Alternative Education: The Definition Problem," *Changing Schools* 18, no. 4-5 (1990): 4–5, 10; Mary Ann Raywid, "The Wadleigh Complex: A Dream That Soured," in *The Politics of Education and the New Institutionalism: Reinventing the American School,* edited by R. L. Crowson, W. L. Boyd, and H. B. Mawhinney (Washington: Falmer Press, 1995), pp. 101–14; Gary Wehlage, Gregory Smith, and Pauline Lipman, "Restructuring Urban Schools: The New Futures Experience," *American Educational Research Journal* 29, no. 1 (Spring 1992): 51–93; McMullan, Sipe, and Wolf, "Chapter and Student Achievement."

71. Sara Lightfoot, *The Good High School* (New York: Basic Books, 1983), p. 184.

72. Valerie E. Lee and Douglas D. Ready, *Schools-within-Schools: Possibilities and Pitfalls of High School Reform* (Teachers College Press, in press).

73. Donna Muncey and Patrick McQuillan, "School-within-a-School Restructuring and Faculty Divisiveness: Examples from a Study of the Coalition of Essential Schools," Working Paper 6 (Brown University, School Ethnography Project, 1991).

74. Howley, "Small Schools," p. 3.

75. Lee and Ready, *Schools-within-Schools.*.

76. Fred Newmann and Gary Wehlage, *Successful School Restructuring: A Report to the Public and Educators* (Madison, Wis.: Center on Organization and Restructuring of Schools, 1995), p. 29.

77. Jomills Braddock and James McPartland, "Education of Early Adolescents," in *Review of Research in Education,* edited by Linda Darling-Hammond (Washington: American Educational Research Association, 1993), pp. 135–70; Bryk and others, *Catholic Schools and the Common Good*; Gary Gottfredson and Denise Daiger, *Disruption in 600 Schools* (Baltimore: Center for Social Organization of Schools, 1979); Lee, Bryk, and Smith, "The Organization of Effective Secondary Schools"; Fred Newmann, *Authentic Achievement: Restructuring Schools for Intellectual Quality* (San Francisco: Jossey-Bass, 1996); Gary Wehlage and others, *Reducing the Risk: Schools as Communities of Support* (New York: Falmer Press, 1989); Wasley and others, *Small Schools: Great Strides.*

78. Linda Darling-Hammond, *The Right to Learn: A Blueprint for Creating Schools That Work* (San Francisco: Jossey-Bass, 1997); Michelle Fine, ed., *Charting Urban School Reform: Reflections on Public High Schools in the Midst of Change* (Teachers College Press, 1994); Michelle Gambone and others, *First Things First: Creating the Conditions and Capacity for Communitywide Reform in an Urban School District* (New York: Manpower Research Demonstration Corporation, 2002); Lee and Smith, "Effects of High School Restructuring and Size on Early Gains in Achievement and Engagement"; Newmann, *Authentic Achievement.*

79. For reviews, see Lee, Bryk, and Smith, "The Organization of Effective Secondary Schools"; Newmann and Wehlage, *Successful School Restructuring.*

80. Lee and Smith, "Effects of High School Restructuring and Size on Early Gains in Achievement and Engagement."

81. Bryk, Lee, and Holland, *Catholic Schools and the Common Good.*

82. Ibid. Newmann, *Authentic Achievement.*

83. Wasley and others, *Small Schools: Great Strides.*

84. Ibid., p. 35.

85. Bryk, Lee, and Holland, *Catholic Schools and the Common Good*; Wasley and others, *Small Schools: Great Strides.*

86. Wasley and others, *Small Schools: Great Strides,* p. 37.

87. Darling-Hammond, Ancess, and Ort, "Reinventing High School," p. 654.

88. Newmann, *Authentic Achievement*; Wasley and others, *Small Schools: Great Strides.*

89. Bryk, Lee, and Holland, *Catholic Schools and the Common Good*; Newmann, *Authentic Achievement*; Newmann and Wehlage, *Successful School Restructuring.*

90. Howley and Harmon, eds., *Small High Schools That Flourish,* pp. 15–18.

91. Newmann, *Authentic Achievement.*

92. Powell and others, *The Shopping Mall High School.*

93. Barker and Gump, eds., *Big School, Small School*; Pittman and Haughwout, "Influence of High School Size on Dropout Rate."

94. Valerie Lee, Robert Croninger, and Julia Smith, "Course-Taking, Equity, and Mathematics Learning: Testing the Constrained Curriculum Hypothesis in U.S. Secondary Schools," *Educational Evaluation and Policy Analysis* 19, no. 2 (Summer 1997): 99–121; Bryk, Lee, and Holland, *Catholic Schools and the Common Good*; Newmann and Wehlage, *Successful School Restructuring.*

95. Anthony Bryk and Yeow Meng Thum, "The Effects of High School Organization on Dropping Out: An Exploratory Investigation," *American Educational Research Journal* 26, no. 3 (1989): 353–83.

96. Jeannie Oakes, *Keeping Track: How Schools Structure Inequality,* 2nd ed. (Yale University Press, 2005).

97. Karl Alexander and Edward McDill, "Selection and Allocation within Schools: Some Causes and Consequences of Curriculum Placement," *American Sociological Review* 41, no. 6 (December 1976): 963–80; Robert Dreeben and Adam Gamoran, "Race, Instruction, and Learning," *American Sociological Review* 51, no. 5 (1986): 660–69; Robert Dreeben, "Closing the Divide: What Teachers and Administrators Can Do to Help Black Students Reach Their Reading Potential," *American Educator* 11, no. 4 (1987): 28–35; Adam Gamoran and Mark Berends, "The Effects of Stratification in Secondary Schools: Synthesis of Survey and Ethnographic Research," *Review of Educational Research* 57, no. 4 (Winter 1987): 415–36; Adam Gamoran and Robert Mare, "Secondary School Tracking and Educational Inequality: Compensation, Reinforcement, or Neutrality?" *American Journal of Sociology* 94, no. 5 (1989): 1146–83; Oakes, *Keeping Track*; Penelope Peterson, "Remediation Is No Remedy," *Educational Leadership* 46, no. 60 (1989): 24–25.

98. Peterson, "Remediation Is No Remedy."

99. Adam Gamoran and Eileen Hannigan, "Algebra for Everyone? Benefits of College-Preparatory Mathematics for Students with Diverse Abilities in Early Secondary School," *Educational Evaluation and Policy Analysis* 22, no. 3 (Fall 2000): 241–54.

100. Powell and others, *The Shopping Mall High School.*

101. Deborah Meier, *The Power of Their Ideas* (Boston: Beacon Press, 1995); Bryk, Lee, and Holland, *Catholic Schools and the Common Good*; Newmann, *Authentic Achievement*; Newmann and Wehlage, *Successful School Restructuring*; Darling-Hammond, Ancess, and Ort, "Reinventing High School"; Fine, Stoudt, and Futch, *The International Network for Public Schools.*

102. Adam Gamoran and Matthew Weinstein, "Differentiation and Opportunity in Restructured Schools," *American Journal of Education* 106, no. 3 (1998): 405.

103. Darling-Hammond, Ancess, and Ort, "Reinventing High School:"; Wasley and others, *Small Schools: Great Strides.*

104. Newmann, *Authentic Achievement.*

105. Valerie Lee, Julia Smith, and Robert Croninger, "Another Look at High School Restructuring," *Issues in Restructuring Schools* 9 (Fall 1995): 1–10; Newmann and Wehlage, *Successful School Restructuring.*

106. Fred Newmann, Helen Marks, and Adam Gamoran, "Authentic Pedagogy and Student Performance," *American Journal of Education* 104, no. 4 (1996): 280–312.

107. Ibid., p. 293.

108. Darling-Hammond, Ancess, and Ort, "Reinventing High School."

109. Newmann, Marks, and Gamoran, "Authentic Pedagogy and Student Performance."

110. Darling-Hammond, Ancess, and Ort, "Reinventing High School," p. 661.

111. Richard Murnane and Frank Levy, *Teaching the New Basic Skills: Principles for Educating Children to Thrive in a Changing Economy* (New York: Free Press, 1996); Newmann, Marks, and Gamoran, "Authentic Pedagogy and Student Performance."

112. Judith Warren Little, "Norms of Collegiality and Experimentation: Workplace Conditions of School Success," *American Educational Research Journal* 19, no. 3 (1982): 325–40; Milbrey McLaughlin and Joan Talbert, *Professional Communities and the Work of High School Teaching* (University of Chicago Press, 2001).

113. Anthony Bryk, Eric Camburn, and Karen Louis, "Professional Community in Chicago Elementary Schools: Facilitating Factors and Organizational Consequences," *Educational Administration Quarterly* 35 (supplement, December 1999): 751–81.

114. Newmann, Marks, and Gamoran, "Authentic Pedagogy and Student Performance."
115. Darling-Hammond, Ancess, and Ort, "Reinventing High School"; Lee and Loeb, "School Size in Chicago Elementary Schools"; Wasley and others, *Small Schools: Great Strides*.
116. Wasley and others, *Small Schools: Great Strides*, p. 38.
117. Darling-Hammond, Ancess, and Ort, "Reinventing High School," p. 663.
118. Lee and Loeb, "School Size in Chicago Elementary Schools."
119. Lee and Ready, *Schools-within-Schools*; Newmann and Wehlage, *Successful School Restructuring*; Newmann, *Authentic Achievement*; Raywid, "The Wadleigh Complex."
120. On the first approach, see Elle Rustique-Forrester, "Why Wasn't I Taught This Way?" in *Creating New Schools: How Small Schools Are Changing American Education*, edited by Evans Clinchy (Teachers College Press, 2000), pp. 80–100. On the second, see Valerie Lee and Douglas Ready, "The Schools-within-Schools Reform: A Viable Solution to the Problems of Large High Schools?" in *General Issues in the Education of Adolescents*, edited by Tim Urdan and Frank Pajares (Greenwich, Conn.: Information Age Publishing, 2004), pp. 179–206.
121. Mary Ann Raywid, *Taking Stock: The Movement to Create Mini-Schools, Schools-within-Schools, and Separate Small Schools* (Eric Clearinghouse on Urban Education, 1996).
122. Muncey and McQuillan, "School-within-a-School Restructuring and Faculty Divisiveness."
123. Raywid, *Taking Stock*.
124. Lee and Ready, "The Schools-within-Schools Reform."
125. Raywid, *Taking Stock*.
126. Quoted in Joan Talbert, "Boundaries of Teachers' Professional Communities in U.S. High Schools: Power and Precariousness of the Subject Department," in *The Subjects in Question: Departmental Organization and the High School*, edited by L. S. Siskin and J. W. Little (Teachers College Press, 1995), p. 35.
127. Lee and Ready, "The Schools-within-Schools Reform."
128. Ibid., p. 190.
129. McMullan, Sipe, and Wolf, "Chapter and Student Achievement."
130. Ibid., p. 49.
131. Bryk, Lee, and Holland, *Catholic Schools and the Common Good*; Ann Cook, "The Transformation of One Large Urban High School: The Julia Richman Education Complex," in *Creating New Schools*, edited by Clinchy, pp. 101–20; Meier, "The Power of Their Ideas"; Linda Nathan and Larry Myatt, "A Journey toward Autonomy," in *Creating New Schools*, edited by Clinchy, pp. 17–37; Newmann and Wehlage, *Successful School Restructuring*; Wasley and others, *Small Schools: Great Strides*; Robert Pearlman, "Smarter Charters? Creating Boston's Pilot Schools," in *Creating New Schools*, edited by Clinchy, pp. 38–48.
132. Jacqueline Ancess, Susanna Ort, and Linda Darling-Hammond, *The Julia Richman Education Complex: Creating Successful Small Schools from a Failing Urban High School* (New York: National Center for Restructuring Education, Schools, and Teaching, 2004).
133. Cook, "The Transformation of One Large Urban High School."
134. Darling-Hammond, Ancess, and Ort, "Reinventing High School," p. 653.
135. On the First Things First initiative, see Gambone and others, *First Things First*; Quint and others, *The Challenge of Scaling up Educational Reform: Findings and Lessons from First Things First* (New York: Manpower Research Demonstration Corporation, 2005). On the other initiatives, see Diane Friedlaender and Ash Vasudeva, *Windows on Conversion: A Mutlimedia Exploration of Redesign at Four Comprehensive High Schools* (Stanford, Calif.: School Redesign Network, 2006).
136. Robert Croninger and others, "Schools-within-Schools: A High School Reform for What and for Whom?" paper presented at the annual meeting of the American Educational Research Association, New Orleans, April 2000; Tom Gregory, "School Reform and the No-Man's Land of High School Size," Bloomington, Ind., 2000; Raywid, "The Wadleigh Complex."

137. McMullan, Sipe, and Wolf, "Chapter and Student Achievement"; Friedlaender and Vasudeva, *Windows on Conversion.*

138. On the need for technical assistance, see Croninger and others, "Schools-within-Schools"; Cook, "The Transformation of One Large Urban High School"; Wasley and others, *Small Schools: Great Strides.* On the inability of districts to support the innovation process, see Meier, "The Power of Their Ideas"; Nathan and Myatt, "A Journey toward Autonomy"; Newmann and Wehlage, *Successful School Restructuring*; Newmann, *Authentic Achievement*; Judith Rizzo, "School Reform: A System's Approach," in *Creating New Schools*, edited by Clinchy, pp. 133–49.

139. Darling-Hammond, Ancess, and Ort, "Reinventing High School."

140. On the difficulty of transferring success from one district to another, see Quint and others, *The Challenge of Scaling up Educational Reform.* For the successful reforms that ultimately failed to become institutionalized, see, for example, Raywid, *Taking Stock.*

What Have Researchers Learned from Project STAR?

DIANE WHITMORE SCHANZENBACH

Project STAR (Student/Teacher Achievement Ratio) was a large-scale randomized trial of reduced class sizes in kindergarten through the third grade. Because of the scope of the experiment, it has been used in many policy discussions. For example, the California statewide class-size-reduction policy was justified, in part, by the successes of Project STAR. Recent (failed) proposals in the Senate that sought federal assistance for class-size reductions were motivated by Project STAR research. Even the recent discussion of small schools often conflates the notion of small schools and smaller classrooms.

Because of the importance of Project STAR, it has been studied by many scholars looking at a wide variety of outcomes and even exploiting the randomization to understand variations in inputs and other aspects of the education production function that do not directly relate to class size. This paper provides an overview of the academic literature using the Project STAR experiment.

What Was Project STAR?

Project STAR was a randomized experiment that assigned students to a small-size class (target of thirteen to seventeen students), a regular-size class (target of twenty-two to twenty-five students), or a regular-size class with a full-time teacher's aide. Teachers were also randomly assigned to class types. Randomization was done within school, so all analysis presented here looks at within-school differences by class size. The experiment took place in seventy-

The author thanks Alan Krueger, Dan Goldhaber, and Diane Ravitch for helpful comments and Rachel Henry Currans-Sheehan for comments and research assistance.

nine Tennessee public schools for a single cohort of students in kindergarten through third grade in 1985–89. Eventually, 11,600 students and 1,330 teachers took part in the experiment. The experiment was funded by the Tennessee legislature under Governor Lamar Alexander (later the secretary of education under President George H. W. Bush and currently a U.S. senator), at a total cost of approximately $12 million.[1]

In the ideal implementation of this experiment, students were to remain with the same randomly assigned class type from kindergarten through the end of the third grade. In practice, there were several major sources of deviation from this model. Students who entered a participating school while the cohort was in first, second, or third grades were added to the experiment and randomly assigned to a class type. There was a substantial number of new entrants: 45 percent of eventual participants entered after kindergarten. An especially large group of students entered in first grade—fully one-third of first-grade participants were new in first grade—in part because, at the time, kindergarten was not required in Tennessee. A relatively large fraction of students exited Project STAR schools (45 percent of overall participants), due to school moves, grade retention, or grade skipping, which also caused deviations from the original plan.[2] Students who were male, African American, or on free or reduced-price lunch were more likely both to exit and to enter Project STAR. In addition, in response to parental concerns about fairness to students, all students in regular and regular-aide classes were randomized again in the first grade.

Finally, a smaller number of students (about 10 percent of participants) were moved from one type of class to another in a nonrandom manner. Most of these moves reportedly were due to student misbehavior and not typically the result of parental requests to move their child to a small class.[3] This weakness of the experiment can be addressed through use of an "intent-to-treat" setup—that is, use of the variation caused by initial randomly assigned class instead of the actual (possibly nonrandom) class attended.

The experiment only manipulated class size and did not provide additional teacher training, new curriculum, or any other intervention. One exception is that teachers in fifteen schools were offered a three-day training seminar between years two and three of the experiment (that is, as the students were entering second grade) and again the following year. The training was given to all teachers in the Project STAR grades in those schools and occurred prior to assigning teachers to a class type. Investigation of the impacts of the training has shown that teachers who received the additional training performed no better (or worse) than teachers who were not offered the training.[4]

Table 1. Characteristics of Students in STAR, Tennessee, and the United States

Characteristic	STAR (1)	Tennessee (2)	United States (3)
Percent minority students	33.1	23.5	31.0
Percent black students	31.7	22.6	16.1
Percent of children below poverty level	24.4	20.7	18.0
Percent of teachers with master's degree or higher	43.4	48.0	47.3
Average ACT score	19.2	19.8	21.0
Average third-grade enrollment across schools	89.1	69.5	67.1
Average current expenditures per student across schools (dollars)	3,423	3,425	4,477

Source: With the following exceptions, data are from the 1990 Common Core of Data (CCD) from the Department of Education. For comparability, the Project STAR characteristics are calculated from the CCD. (Nevertheless, the characteristics are very similar when calculated directly from Project STAR data.) Teacher education data for third-grade teachers are from Project STAR data; for 1993–94 public elementary and secondary school teachers are from the *Digest of Education Statistics*. Race and poverty statistics for the United States are from the Census Bureau. ACT scores for Tennessee and the United States are from ACT, Inc.

A few aspects of the sample may limit the validity of generalizing the study to other settings. In order to be eligible to participate in the program, schools were required to have a minimum-size cohort of fifty-seven students, enough to sustain both a regular and a regular-aide classroom of twenty-two students and one small class of fifteen students. As a result, the schools that participated were about 25 percent larger, on average, than other Tennessee schools. The implications of this requirement are discussed in more detail below. Because of requirements imposed by the legislature for geographic diversity, schools in inner cities were overrepresented, and the students included were more economically disadvantaged and more likely to be African American than those in the state overall (see table 1). Even though the percentage non-white in STAR closely mirrors the percentage in the United States overall (33 versus 31 percent), this masks the fact that there were very few Hispanic and Asian students in Tennessee at the time compared to the rest of the nation. Finally, average school spending in Tennessee was about three-fourths of the nationwide average, and teachers were less likely to have a master's degree. If additional resources have greater impacts when the baseline levels are already low, this could mean that schools with higher levels of spending might experience a smaller impact from class-size reduction.

Was Randomized Assignment Maintained?

Volumes of research have looked at the relationship between class size and student performance in nonexperimental settings, but Project STAR is the first (and only) large-scale experiment to address class size.[5] An experiment typically offers more compelling evidence than a nonexperimental study, because it allows researchers to isolate the impact of the policy they are testing. In the absence of an experiment, the effect of a policy may be confounded by other observable or unobservable factors that may be correlated with the policy. To solidify this idea, take the following model of student achievement as an example:

(1) $$Y_{ij} = aS_{ij} + bF_{ij} + \varepsilon_{ij},$$

where Y represents a measure of student achievement for student i in school j, S contains information on school-level inputs that affect achievement, F contains family inputs, and ε is an error term. Both S and F measure inputs over the child's entire lifetime and may contain inputs that are not observable to the econometrician. These omitted factors lead to biased coefficients if the omitted variables are correlated with included variables. For example, if students are assigned to small classes or better teachers in a compensatory manner— perhaps because of low baseline test scores or low levels of family inputs—but that information is not available to the researcher, the estimated impact of school resources will be biased. Similarly, bias will result if parents who are more involved in their child's education are more likely to push for a smaller class or better teachers and parental involvement is not measured in the data set.

The benefit of using a randomized experiment is that the treatment assignment is not related to any omitted characteristics. With a well-designed experimental assignment, a straightforward comparison of means by type of class will provide an unbiased estimate of the impact of class size on achievement. In the case of (an idealized version of) Project STAR, the equation to be estimated is as follows:

(2) $$Y_{ics} = \beta_0 + \beta_1 SMALL_{cs} + \beta_2 AIDE_{cs} + \mathbf{X}_{ics}\gamma + \alpha_s + \upsilon_{ics},$$

where $SMALL$ and $AIDE$ are binary variables indicating small-class and regular-aide-class assignments, respectively, and c indexes class c in school s. $\mathbf{X}$ is a vector of student-level characteristics.[6] When treatments are randomized, student-level covariates are not related to class assignment, and their inclusion should not change the estimated effect on class size, but their inclusion should contribute to the overall explanatory power of the model. A school-level fixed effect, α, is included, so that class-type effects are identified from within-school comparisons. Finally, the error term υ contains class-level and individual-level components.

In practice, the nonrandom transitions and new entrants described above complicate the approach somewhat. Because of nonrandom transitions after initial assignment, it would be inappropriate to use current-year class type; instead, initial class-type assignment (the "intent-to-treat" measure) is used throughout all estimations in this paper.[7] That is, all impacts are measured with regard to the class that students were assigned to, not the class they actually attended. The intent-to-treat measure likely understates the impact of small classes by up to 15 percent.[8] As described above, new entrants into the program were randomly assigned to class types. So even though new entrants in first, second, and third grades are, on average, more disadvantaged than kindergarten entrants, randomization allows us to compare new entrants in each grade to other new entrants in the same school across class types. In practice, then, the school-level fixed effect in equation 2 is replaced with a fixed effect that combines school with a student's grade of entry (kindergarten, first grade, second grade, or third grade) to the experiment.

Impacts of reduced class size are straightforward to measure as the within-school (and entry wave) difference between class types, provided the randomization was done correctly. A compelling check of randomization is to examine a pretest to ensure that there are no measurable differences in the dependent variable between class types before the program began. Unfortunately, no baseline test was conducted. Another way to investigate whether randomization was done properly is to compare student characteristics that are related to student achievement but cannot be manipulated in response to treatment, such as student race, gender, and age. If there are no systematic differences in observable characteristics across class types, this provides support that the randomization was done properly. Table 2 presents student characteristics by entry wave and class type. The joint p value for a test of equality across the columns is conditional on school fixed effects. The first four rows show that there are no systematic differences in background characteristics between class type along race, gender, free-lunch status, and age. It is also apparent that later entrants to Project STAR are more disadvantaged, with a substantially higher fraction of later entrants on free lunch and likely to be older (which may signal that they were retained in grade).[9]

Another drawback is that initial random assignment was not recorded; rather initial *enrollment* was measured. If parents successfully lobbied for a class change in the days between class assignments and the beginning of school, this would be masked in the data. To test whether this is a serious limitation, Krueger collected data on initial assignment from eighteen participating schools for 1,581 students.[10] He finds that only 0.3 percent of stu-

Table 2. Mean Characteristics, by Entry Wave

Entry wave and characteristic	Small (1)	Regular (2)	Regular-aide (3)	P value (4)
Students who entered STAR in kindergarten				
Free lunch	0.47	0.48	0.50	0.46
White or Asian	0.68	0.67	0.66	0.66
Age in 1985	5.44	5.43	5.42	0.38
Female	0.49	0.49	0.48	0.87
Attrition rate	0.49	0.52	0.53	0.01
Days absent	10.00	10.50	10.90	0.01
Class size in kindergarten	15.10	22.40	22.80	0.00
Standardized test score in kindergarten	0.17	0.00	0.00	0.00
Students who entered STAR in first grade				
Free lunch	0.59	0.62	0.61	0.29
White or Asian	0.62	0.56	0.64	0.28
Age in 1985	5.78	5.86	5.88	0.12
Female	0.49	0.44	0.46	0.33
Attrition rate	0.53	0.51	0.47	0.07
Days absent	8.20	7.70	7.70	0.95
Class size in first grade	15.90	22.70	23.50	0.00
Standardized test score in first grade	-0.04	-0.24	-0.09	0.00
Students who entered STAR in second grade				
Free lunch	0.66	0.63	0.66	0.58
White or Asian	0.53	0.54	0.44	0.15
Age in 1985	5.94	6.00	6.03	0.48
Female	0.43	0.45	0.46	0.56
Attrition rate	0.37	0.34	0.35	0.58
Days absent	n.a.	n.a.	n.a.	n.a.
Class size in second grade	15.50	23.70	23.60	0.00
Standardized test score in second grade	-0.11	-0.16	-0.27	0.40
Students who entered STAR in third grade				
Free lunch	0.60	0.64	0.69	0.18
White or Asian	0.66	0.57	0.55	0.21
Age in 1985	5.95	5.92	5.99	0.40
Female	0.43	0.47	0.46	0.62
Attrition rate	n.a.	n.a.	n.a.	n.a.
Days absent	6.00	7.60	7.60	0.00
Class size in third grade	16.00	24.10	24.40	0.00
Standardized test score in third grade	-0.10	-0.20	-0.30	0.01

Source: Author's calculations. See table 1 for details.
n.a. Not available.

a. The *p* value is for *F* test of equality of all three groups, conditional on school fixed effects. Sample size ranges as follows: for students who entered in kindergarten, 6,299–6,324; for students who entered in first grade, 2,240–2,314; for students who entered in second grade, 1,585–1,679; for students who entered in third grade, 1,202–1,283. Free lunch pertains to the fraction receiving free lunch when they were randomly assigned. Test scores are scaled in units of the standard deviation of non-small classes, with mean non-small class score = 0.

dents failed to attend their initially assigned class type in kindergarten, and only one of those was moved into a small class from a regular-size one. If rates were similar at the other schools, then this would not appear to be a serious limitation.

If families feel that their child is well served by attending smaller classes (or are upset that their child has been randomly assigned to a regular class), this might yield a differential attrition rate or better attendance rates by class type.[11] Table 2 provides some evidence that this is true for the cohort entering in kindergarten. Small-class students are 3 to 4 percentile points more likely to stay at a Project STAR school through third grade and, on average, miss a fraction of a day less during their kindergarten year.[12] If students who gain the most from small classes are the ones induced to stay, then the impact of small classes may be overstated during the experimental period. Long-term follow-up data, which add back in the early exits from Project STAR, alleviate this problem. The differential attrition rate subsides in the entering waves after kindergarten. Table 2 confirms that, indeed, there was a "program"—students assigned to small classes have about seven fewer students in their class than those assigned to non-small classes. There is no difference in class size between regular and regular-aide classrooms. Finally, the table previews the results described in the next section. With the exception of the second-grade entry wave, by the end of the first year in Project STAR, the students in small classes statistically significantly outperform those in non-small classes.

Finally, it is crucial that teachers were randomly assigned. If the most effective teachers were disproportionately placed with small (or regular) classes, then the class-size effect would pick up this effect as well. Only limited data are available to confirm random assignment of teachers, which are displayed in table 3. Overall, almost all of the teachers are female, and about 80 percent are white. Average years of experience range between nine and fifteen, depending on the class type and year. In most cases, there is no within-school difference across the teachers' race, gender, experience level, or highest level of education.[13] Where there is a significant difference in teachers' characteristics across class type (for total experience in first grade and master's degree in third grade), the "best" attributes (more experience and higher degrees) are not more likely to be found in small classes, so there is no evidence that assignment was done based on seniority, measured qualifications, or anything else that would violate random assignment.

Table 3. Teacher Characteristics, by Grade

Characteristic	Small (1)	Regular (2)	Regular-aide (3)	P value (4)
Kindergarten teachers				
White	0.866	0.780	0.838	0.327
Female	1.000	1.000	1.000	n.a.
Master's degree	0.323	0.364	0.374	0.653
Total experience	9.0	9.1	9.7	0.404
Sample size	127	99	99	n.a.
First-grade teachers				
White	0.813	0.835	0.820	0.462
Female	0.976	1.000	1.000	0.139
Master's degree	0.358	0.313	0.390	0.674
Total experience	12.2	10.7	12.7	0.069
Sample size	123	115	100	n.a.
Second-grade teachers				
White	0.794	0.770	0.804	0.583
Female	0.992	0.980	0.972	0.291
Master's degree	0.344	0.340	0.439	0.305
Total experience	13.0	12.7	13.9	0.542
Sample size	131	100	107	n.a.
Third-grade teachers				
White	0.775	0.798	0.776	0.650
Female	0.964	0.944	0.972	0.465
Master's degree	0.377	0.427	0.523	0.077
Total experience	13.3	13.6	14.8	0.368
Sample size	138	89	107	n.a.

Source: Author's calculations. See table 1 for details.
n.a. = Not applicable.
a. *P* values for *F* test of equality across the three class types, conditional on school fixed effects.

K–3 Test Score Results

Because of randomization, the impact of being assigned to a small class can be measured by comparing average test scores across class types. As described above, students were randomly assigned to small and regular classes within schools by entry wave, so all analysis controls for separate school effects for each entering cohort while estimating the treatment effect of being assigned to a small class. Results in this section report the estimated coefficient on small-class treatment from a regression estimated using the following equation:

(3) $\quad Y_{igs} = \beta_{0g} + \beta_{1g} SMALL_{is} + \beta_{2g} AIDE_{is} + \beta_{3g} \mathbf{X}_{is} + \alpha_{sw} + \varepsilon_{igs},$

where g indexes the grade (K–8) of the test score. Both the *SMALL* and *AIDE* variables are measured as initial assignment, not actual class attendance. The fixed effect varies by school and entry wave w. The coefficient on the control for classes with a teacher aide is not reported here. Because there is no impact of teacher aides on student performance, the small-class effect is similar whether or not aide classes are controlled.

Table 4 reports the impact of initial assignment to a small class on student test scores, and figure 1 represents the small-class impact graphically. As many researchers have found, overall students benefit about 0.15 standard deviation from assignment to a small class.[14] When the results are disaggregated by race, it appears that black students benefit about twice as much as white students (0.24 versus 0.12 standard deviation) from being assigned to a small class. Krueger and Whitmore find that this result is driven primarily by a larger treatment effect for all students in predominantly black schools, regardless of race, suggesting that benefits from additional resources are higher in such schools.[15] There is also a small, positive within-school interaction between small class and an indicator variable for black students, which means that black students gain a little more from small classes than their white classmates. Both of these findings suggest that smaller classes might be an effective strategy to narrow the black-white achievement gap.

Similar—but less stark—differences appear between free-lunch-eligible students (who must have a family income less than 185 percent of the poverty line to qualify) and non-free-lunch-eligible students. In third grade, free-lunch-eligible students gain about 0.055 standard deviation more than non-free-lunch-eligible students. Boys appear to have slightly larger small-class gains than girls, but the difference is not statistically significant.[16] There is also considerable heterogeneity in size of impact based on teacher experience. Whether or not the results are conditioned on school fixed effects, students with more experienced teachers show large, statistically significant gains. In contrast, students who have a teacher with fewer than five years of experience show smaller and often not statistically significant gains from small classes. This could help to explain the difference between the large impacts

Table 4. Small-Class Effects on Test Scores[a]

Subgroup	Kindergarten (1)	First grade (2)	Second grade (3)	Third grade (4)
Overall	0.187	0.189	0.141	0.152
	(0.039)	(0.035)	(0.034)	(0.030)
Race				
Black	0.214	0.249	0.207	0.242
	(0.074)	(0.063)	(0.054)	(0.060)
White	0.172	0.161	0.105	0.115
	(0.042)	(0.040)	(0.042)	(0.034)
Free-lunch eligibility				
Free lunch	0.188	0.195	0.174	0.174
	(0.046)	(0.042)	(0.041)	(0.039)
No free lunch	0.177	0.194	0.126	0.118
	(0.051)	(0.047)	(0.047)	(0.041)
Gender				
Male	0.209	0.192	0.144	0.172
	(0.041)	(0.040)	(0.039)	(0.400)
Female	0.157	0.180	0.132	0.122
	(0.049)	(0.040)	(0.042)	(0.040)
Teacher experience				
Less experience	0.310	0.057	0.073	0.171
(less than or equal to four years)	(0.121)	(0.081)	(0.064)	(0.100)
More experience (more than five years)	0.181	0.269	0.179	0.154
	(0.044)	(0.056)	(0.037)	(0.034)

Source: Author's calculations. See table 1 for details.

a. Standard errors clustered on classroom are in parentheses. Coefficients represent the impact of being randomly assigned to a small class on test scores, in terms of standard deviation units. Each cell represents a separate regression. Other covariates included in the model (where appropriate) are indicators for white, female, and free-lunch eligibility and school-by-entry-wave fixed effects.

found in Project STAR and the disappointing results from California's statewide class-size-reduction effort.[17] In California, many districts were forced to hire new, inexperienced teachers in order to reduce class size, and there is evidence in Project STAR that these inexperienced teachers are not particularly more effective when given small classes.

One concern about the results is that they may be driven by Hawthorne effects, meaning that students and teachers behave differently simply because they are given special treatment. If this were the case, then benefits from small classes would dissipate if the class-size reduction were made permanent and the students and teachers were no longer being studied and made to feel special. Krueger addresses this by investigating differences in achievement using the variation in regular-size classes.[18] There is little reason to think that

Figure 1. Small-Class Impacts on Test Scores

Effect size (standard deviation units)

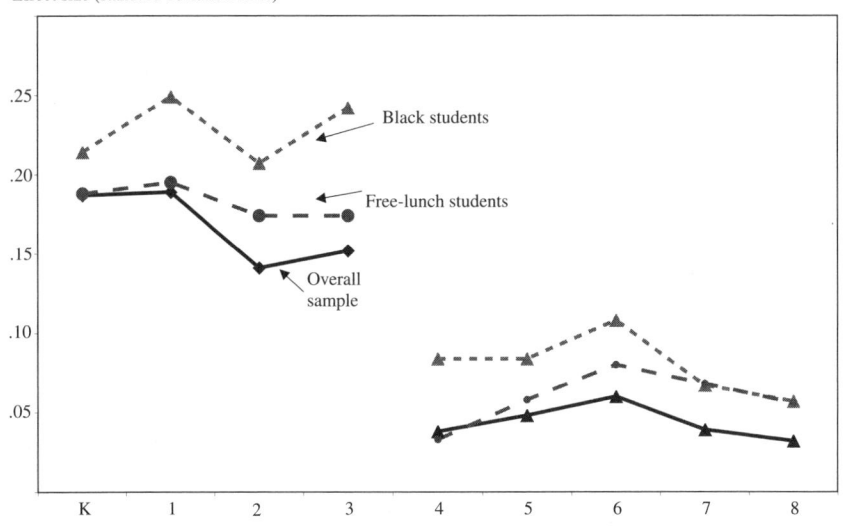

[Figure: Line chart showing effect sizes from Kindergarten through 8th grade for Black students, Free-lunch students, and Overall sample. Values range from about .14 to .25 for grades K–3, with a gap, then from about .03 to .10 for grades 4–8.]

Source: Author's calculations.

Hawthorne effects would cause some classes to behave differently than other classes in the treatment group. Regular-size classes range from sixteen to thirty students, but the bulk of the distribution is between twenty and twenty-six students. Whether or not school effects are controlled, students in a regular class with slightly fewer members outscore students in larger regular classes. The estimated magnitude of a one-student reduction in class size is consistent with the magnitude of the experimental results (which estimate the impact of a seven-student reduction).

Another concern might arise regarding generalizability of the findings to a larger population, because of the size restrictions in place for participation in the experiment. Schools were required to be large enough to support three classrooms per grade, and on average Project STAR schools were about 30 percent larger than schools across Tennessee or the United States. If larger schools are somehow more or less effective if given additional resources, then the findings in Project STAR may not be generalizable to smaller school settings.[19] One way to address this using the available data is to compare the small-class advantage across the wide range of school sizes in Project STAR. In third grade, the largest school had more than 200 students, while the smallest participating school had only fifty-six students. To test whether school size is related to the magnitude of the class-size effect, I separate schools into enrollment quartiles. The lowest quartile had an average of about sixty students, while the highest had more than twice that number, at 130 students. There is no statistically significant relationship between school size and test performance or between school size and small-class impact. This suggests that limiting Project STAR to relatively large school sizes is not a major drawback in terms of generalizability to other samples.

Follow-up Studies on Test Performance

In fourth grade, the class-size-reduction experiment concluded, and all students returned to regular-size classes. At the same time, the assessment test was changed from the SAT-9 to the Comprehensive Test of Basic Skills (CTBS). Both tests are multiple-choice standardized tests that measure reading and math achievement and are taken by students at the end of the school year. The CTBS results are scaled in the same manner as the SAT-9, in terms of standard deviation units. One important difference in the data is that all students in public schools statewide who participated in Project STAR were included in the follow-up study, even if they were retained a grade.[20] As a result, some students took the fourth-grade test in 1990, while others took it in later years or even took it more than once. In the analysis reported here, all scores for a given grade—no matter what year a student was in that grade—are compared. In the event that a student was retained in a particular grade and took that grade's test more than once, the first available score is used.[21] As before, all estimates are conditional on school-by-entry-wave fixed effects.

Results for grades four to eight are reported in table 5 and illustrated in figure 1. Overall, there is a persistent positive impact of small-class assignment that is statistically significant (or borderline significant) through eighth grade, as found in previous studies.[22] The magnitude of the gain is one-third to half the size observed while the students were in the experimental classes. When the results are disaggregated, though, the impact appears to remain stronger with black and free-lunch-eligible students than with more advantaged students.

Another potential measure of achievement is whether students take either the SAT or the ACT college entrance exam, which can be used as an early proxy for college attendance.[23] In order to measure this, the Educational Testing Service and ACT matched Project STAR student data to their national databases of test records, as described by Krueger and Whitmore.[24] To examine whether assignment to a small class influences the rate of taking a college

Table 5. Small-Class Effects on Long-Term Test Scores[a]

Subgroup	Fourth grade[b] (1)	Fifth grade[b] (2)	Sixth grade[b] (3)	Seventh grade[b] (4)	Eighth grade[b] (5)	Took college entrance test[c] (6)
Overall	0.035 (0.025)	0.048 (0.024)	0.060 (0.025)	0.040 (0.025)	0.036 (0.025)	0.024 (0.010)
Race						
Black	0.078 (0.048)	0.080 (0.043)	0.105 (0.045)	0.066 (0.042)	0.063 (0.046)	0.050 (0.018)
White	0.026 (0.027)	0.028 (0.029)	0.043 (0.029)	0.031 (0.031)	0.027 (0.030)	0.011 (0.013)
Free-lunch eligibility						
Free lunch	0.029 (0.036)	0.058 (0.031)	0.080 (0.034)	0.067 (0.031)	0.064 (0.034)	0.031 (0.014)
No free lunch	0.048 (0.035)	0.036 (0.034)	0.027 (0.036)	0.003 (0.038)	-0.012 (0.038)	0.018 (0.017)
Gender						
Male	0.046 (0.032)	0.063 (0.034)	0.065 (0.036)	0.086 (0.032)	0.061 (0.035)	0.029 (0.014)
Female	0.011 (0.037)	0.026 (0.033)	0.039 (0.031)	-0.017 (0.035)	0.002 (0.034)	0.015 (0.016)

Source: Author's calculations. See table 1 for details.
a. Standard errors clustered on initial school are in parentheses. Coefficients represent the impact on test scores of being randomly assigned to a small class, in terms of standard deviation units. Each cell represents a separate regression. Other covariates included in the model (where appropriate) are indicators for white, female, and free-lunch eligibility and school-by-entry-wave fixed effects.
b. z score.
c. 1 = yes.

entrance exam, a binary variable indicating that a college entrance exam is taken is the dependent variable in equation 3. The impact of small-class assignment on college test taking is included as the final column in table 5. Overall, test-taking rates are about 2 percentage points higher for small-class students. For white students, the impact is small and not statistically significant. However, black students are 5 points more likely to take the SAT or ACT if they were assigned to a small rather than regular-size class.[25] This corresponds to a rate of 38 percent of black students assigned to small classes who take at least one of the college entrance exams, compared with 33 percent in regular classes. The chance of such a large difference in test-taking rates between the small- and regular-class students occurring by chance is less than 1 in 10,000. Krueger and Whitmore interpret the magnitude of these effects as a reduction in the black-white test-taking gap.[26] For students in regular classes, the black-white gap in taking a college entrance exam is 12.9 percentage points, compared to 5.1 percentage points for students in small classes. Thus assigning all students to a small class is estimated to reduce the black-white gap in the test-taking rate by an impressive 60 percent. After controlling for increased selection into the test among small-class students, the impact on test scores for blacks is 0.15 standard deviation, about the same as the test-score impact in third grade.

Follow-up Studies on Non-Test Outcomes

Increased investments in school quality may also affect the frequency of negative social outcomes such as crime, welfare receipt, and teen pregnancy. For example, the Perry Preschool Project was an intervention that increased preschool quality and yielded large, persistent effects on outcomes of participants through age forty, despite disappointing impacts on standardized test scores when participants were younger.[27] To date, only limited outcomes have been studied in the Project STAR data, but as the sample ages, more research should be done on outcomes such as earnings, criminal behavior, and welfare utilization. To the extent that reductions are measured along these lines, the social cost-benefit analysis of reducing class size in the early grades would increase.

One measure of outcome is criminal arrest data, which come from Tennessee Department of Corrections records.[28] The data match was only available for Shelby County, Tennessee, which contains the city of Memphis. All criminal arrests through April 2001 were included. Data on arrests for criminal offenses were collected and analyzed for 3,300 students who originally attended one of the 20 Memphis elementary schools included in Project STAR. Criminal arrests in this sample are rare (but much more likely for males than for females): only 6.3 percent of male Project STAR students are reported as having been arrested compared with 4.3 percent for females. Because the outcome is so rare, results are estimated using a probit model, where the dependent variable equals 1 if a student has been arrested or, in some cases, arrested for a particular type of crime. Using this approach, it is found that males assigned to small classes are 2.2 percentage points less likely to be arrested for any crime than those in regular-size classes (p value = 0.12). Reductions were particularly strong for violent and property crimes, in which small-class attendance decreased criminal arrest rates by 55 (p value = 0.09) and 57 percent (p value = 0.02), respectively. No statistically meaningful decreases were apparent for drug or traffic crime arrests. Results are similar when both males and females are included. Another outcome that has been measured is the teen birth rate. Birth records, like crime records, are matched in Tennessee only. Birth records are only available by calendar year. The analysis is restricted to births during 1997 and 1998 because most students graduated from high school in 1998. Unlike all other outcomes discussed so far, birth records are not available for individuals and are aggregated up to a school-by-class-type level. Small-class assignment is associated with a statistically significant 1.6 percentage point (or 33 percent impact; t ratio = 2.29) lower teen birth rate for white females but has no measured impact on black females.

In addition to investigating straightforward impacts of the program, several researchers have exploited aspects of the randomization to answer other important questions about the education production function that are not directly related to class size. Dee uses the random assignment of teachers and students to investigate the impact on achievement of having a teacher who is the same race as the student.[29] He finds that having an own-race teacher increases students' performance by a statistically significant amount (3–5 percentile rank points) for both black and white students. Dee and Keys find that students perform better in math when they are randomly assigned to a teacher who is receiving merit pay.[30] Several other recent papers use randomization into class types to identify the impact of peer composition on student achievement. Graham finds that being randomly assigned to a classroom with average peer test scores in the seventy-fifth percentile leads to a 1.1 standard deviation increase in student performance, while peers with average scores in the twenty-fifth percentile decrease their own performance by 0.9 standard deviation.[31] Schanzenbach finds that if a child's peers are made up of a higher-than-average fraction of girls, there is about a 2 percentile point positive impact on the student's own test score.[32] The effect seems to work through two channels: girls, on average, have higher test scores, but even after factoring that part out, there is a positive effect of having more girls in the classroom. This suggests that girls may change the culture of a classroom—at least in the early grades—to facilitate more learning for both boys and girls. Cascio and Schanzenbach find that conditional on a student's own age, being older than average relative to one's classmates is associated with higher test scores.[33]

Why Might Small Classes Matter?

As described previously, the Project STAR experiment only manipulated class size. There were no changes in curriculum, there was no additional teacher training at most schools, and few, if any, new teachers needed to be hired given the limited scope of the project. What, then, caused the impact on student performance?

Lazear puts forth a useful theory of educational production.[34] In it, gains from class-size reduction are driven by a decrease in the amount of time that the classroom is being disrupted. A simple summary of the model is as follows: a child is behaving in class at a given moment with probability p and misbehaving with probability $(1 - p)$. In the model, misbehaving might mean disrupting class by talking or fighting or be as benign as asking questions that slow down the class or monopolizing the teacher's time. When there are n children in the classroom, p^n is the probability that the entire class is behaving and learning is taking place (assuming that p is independent across children). Assuming a constant disruption rate, having fewer students in the class means that learning is taking place a larger fraction of the time.

In the model, the impact of reducing class size depends not only on the size of the class but also on the behavior of the students in it. As a result, Lazear's theory predicts that class-size effects should be larger for classes with more poorly behaved students. There is some evidence that teachers report higher rates of misbehavior in predominantly black schools compared to predominantly white schools, so the theory fits well with the observation that class size has a larger impact in black schools.

Another potential mechanism is that early interventions improve noncognitive skills in addition to the cognitive skills measured by standardized test scores.[35] During kindergarten (at least during the period studied here), a primary focus in the classroom is to build noncognitive skills such as listening, sitting still, and cooperating. To the extent that kindergarten teachers could be more effective in teaching these skills in small classes, an improvement in noncognitive skills might spill over to later outcomes even if cognitive gains are modest. I test two approaches to isolating the impact of small classes on noncognitive skills. An indirect test is to compare the observed increase in a non-test outcome to the increase that would be predicted by the improvement in test scores. For example, there is a large increase in college test taking for black students assigned to a small class, which is a signal that more small-class students are going on to college. Is that increase larger than what would be predicted by the test-score increase observed in third grade (or kindergarten)? To test this, the observed relationship between test-taking rates is compared with standardized test scores in the early grades. Within regular-size classes only, the probability that a black student takes a college entrance exam increases by 0.6 percentage point for each additional percentile rank attained on the third-grade test ($R^2 = 0.17$). As reported in Krueger and Whitmore, the percentile rank increase for black students in third grade is 7.6 points for small classes.[36] The point estimate implies that 4.5 points of the observed 8-point increase in college test taking for small-class students can be attributed to improved test scores in third grade alone.[37] Taking account of sampling variability, it is possible that most of the increase in college test taking is explained by higher cognitive test scores in third grade. On the other hand, part of the increase in college test taking could be explained by improvements in (unmeasured) noncognitive skills that might have been associated with small-class attendance in the early grades.

A more direct way to isolate the impact of small-class size is to investigate a few measures of noncognitive skills collected in the data (such as listening, self-concept, and motivation). Measures of self-concept and motivation are from the Self-Concept and Motivational Inventory (SCAMIN), which was given at the end of the school year in all grades. The measure has been found to be only moderately reliable and is thought to be most reliable for middle-income, suburban students.[38]

Results are presented in table 6. Columns 1–4 present self-concept and motivation scores in standard deviation units. As with other results, this table shows the coefficient on an indicator for initial small-class assignment in a regression framework that controls for school-by-entry-wave fixed effects. By the end of kindergarten, there are some apparent increases in self-concept overall and for females, blacks, and students with free-lunch status and an increase in motivation for females. This impact dissipates entirely by the end of third grade, which could be due to lack of validity in the test for older students or could reflect a catching up of students in regular classes.

Columns 5 and 6 present scores for the listening subsection of the Basic Skills First test, a curriculum-based test given to all children in Project STAR. Like the self-concept and motivation measures, listening is measured imperfectly and may reflect a combination of cognitive and noncognitive skills. Here there are strong positive impacts of small classes on listening skills for most subgroups of students in kindergarten. By third grade, the impacts are smaller and only marginally significant (in contrast to the robust findings over time for the cognitive tests of math and reading), but this may suggest that one important mechanism for improved outcomes later on is that small classes increase a student's noncognitive skills. Overall, these approaches seem to indicate that the improvement in noncognitive skills that is due to small classes may play a role in the positive outcomes, but that the results are also consistent with the outcomes' being driven by cognitive skills alone.

Table 6. Small-Class Impacts on Potential Measures of Noncognitive Skills[a]

	Self-concept		Motivation		Listening	
Subgroup	Kindergarten (1)	Third grade (2)	Kindergarten (3)	Third grade (4)	Kindergarten (5)	Third grade (6)
Overall	0.135 (0.055)	0.024 (0.035)	0.031 (0.030)	-0.084 (0.046)	0.172 (0.075)	0.104 (0.055)
Race						
Black	0.251 (0.093)	-0.032 (0.071)	0.080 (0.063)	-0.141 (0.085)	0.274 (0.132)	0.141 (0.106)
White	0.083 (0.061)	0.052 (0.036)	0.008 (0.031)	-0.058 (0.055)	0.112 (0.086)	0.089 (0.063)
Free-lunch eligibility						
Free lunch	0.218 (0.076)	0.003 (0.053)	0.051 (0.048)	-0.111 (0.073)	0.253 (0.098)	0.125 (0.078)
No free lunch	0.063 (0.062)	0.034 (0.045)	0.006 (0.034)	-0.002 (0.068)	0.090 (0.087)	0.064 (0.062)
Gender						
Male	0.088 (0.063)	0.061 (0.042)	-0.024 (0.035)	0.005 (0.055)	0.146 (0.085)	0.145 (0.072)
Female	0.178 (0.064)	0.000 (0.050)	0.086 (0.038)	-0.153 (0.066)	0.204 (0.083)	0.067 (0.068)

Source: Author's calculations. See table 1 for details.
a. Standard errors clustered on classroom are in parentheses. All tests are scaled in standard deviation units. Self-concept and motivation scores are from the SCAMIN test, and listening scores are from the Basic Skills First assessment test.

How Do Small-Class Impacts Compare to Other Interventions?

As a policy intervention, is reducing class size an economically worthwhile investment? One way to measure this is to compare the long-term benefits of higher test scores to the costs of reducing class size. To do this, I update Krueger and Whitmore's cost-benefit analysis and solve for r, the internal rate of return, in the following equation:

$$(4) \quad \sum_{t=1}^{4} C_t / (1+r)^t = \sum_{t=14}^{61} (E_t \beta \delta) / (1+r)^t,$$

where C_t is the cost of reducing class size in year t and E_t is annual earnings in year t.[39] Additionally, I calculate net present value for various assumptions about the rate of return. For this calculation, it is assumed that students begin kindergarten at age five, begin working at age eighteen, and retire at age sixty-five. The β term relates a 1 standard deviation gain in test scores during high

Diane Whitmore Schanzenbach 223

school to an increase in future earnings. It would be preferable to have a parameter that relates increases in elementary school test scores to later earnings, but I have found no such estimate in the literature. The δ term is the increase in test scores for students assigned to small classes.

The left-hand side of the equation represents the present discounted value of the costs of reduced class size. C_t is the additional cost of reducing class size by seven students, which requires a 47 percent increase in the number of classes. Assuming that the additional cost is proportional to current average spending per pupil, the additional cost each year is 47 percent of $10,551, which is the average national spending based on 2001–02 figures, inflated by the consumer price index to 2005 prices. Since students, on average, receive 2.3 years of class-size reduction, those costs are reflected as full years of class-size reduction in kindergarten and first grade and 0.3 times the additional cost in second grade. In this calculation, no costs are borne in third grade.

The right-hand side of the equation measures benefits of reduced class size over a student's working life. The test score increase (δ) is 0.152 standard deviation, from column 4 of table 4, and the estimate of β is a 0.20 increase in wages from a 1 standard deviation increase in test scores.[40] To forecast future earnings, average earnings for each age between eighteen and sixty-five are calculated for 2005 from the 2006 March *Current Population Survey*, and future real earnings growth is assumed to be 0, 1, or 2 percent a year.[41] Results are presented in table 7.

Using these assumptions, the estimated internal rate of return from the class-size effect in Project STAR ranges from 5 to 10 percent. The net present value of the investment ranges from $3,000 to $50,000.[42] Of course, exact numbers should be viewed with caution, as the calculation is based on many assumptions that may or may not prove to be reasonable. The benefits only include future increased earnings and ignore potential impacts on crime and other behavior since those results are on the margin of statistical significance. If future follow-ups of Project STAR find lasting impacts on other outcomes such as crime or welfare use, then those benefits should be added to the equation and the internal rate of return would increase.

Another way to think about whether the investment in smaller classes is worthwhile is to compare it to other proposed interventions. Some reforms such as improved teacher training have been shown to be ineffective and therefore do not make an appropriate comparison.[43] The most promising interventions aside from smaller class size come from the new literature on school choice through either vouchers or charter schools. When the Project STAR results are compared to the largest positive effects found in voucher

Table 7. Cost-Benefit Analysis of Small Classes[a]

	Net present value, assuming annual real wage growth of		
Discount rate assumption	0 percent	1 percent	2 percent
Discount rate (r)			
0.02	16,617	29,267	48,335
0.03	8,421	16,892	29,492
0.04	2,924	13,654	17,162
0.05	-821	3,178	8,965
Internal rate of return (IRR), percent	4.75	5.82	9.95

Source: Author's calculations based on data in Census Bureau and Bureau of Labor Statistics, Current Population Survey.
a. All figures in 2005 dollars. Assumes 2.3 years of exposure to small classes and a test score increase of 0.152 standard deviation. A 1 standard deviation increase in average test scores is associated with a 0.2 standard deviation increase in earnings.

experiments—the New York City results found by Howell and others—small classes yield 30 percent higher test scores but also cost 50 percent more.[44] Compared to recent work by Hoxby and Rockoff on three charter schools in Chicago that employed random assignment, small classes yield about a 35 percent improvement in test scores.[45] It is difficult to compare the costs associated with charter schools, which are allotted approximately the same in per-pupil revenues from the school district but generally raise substantial external funding. In order to determine which would be a better investment—school choice or reduced class size—we need to have some measure of willingness to pay for improved test scores and compare the smaller improvements associated (so far) with choice to the larger cost associated with class-size reduction.

Conclusion

Mosteller describes Project STAR as "one of the most important educational investigations ever carried out and illustrates the kind and magnitude of research needed in the field of education to strengthen schools."[46] Given the scarcity of large-scale educational experiments like Project STAR, it is important to learn as much as possible from the experiment. Researchers have combed through the experiment to learn not only about the effects of reduced class size on test scores but also to gain insight into classroom dynamics. Overall, Project STAR indicates that reducing class size is a reasonable economic investment: the benefits are sizable and long lasting, especially for black students, and the overall benefits outweigh the costs.

Notes

1. Elizabeth J. Word and others, *Student/Teacher Achievement Ratio (STAR): Tennessee's K–3 Class Size Study* (Nashville: Tennessee State Department of Education, 1990); Frederick Mosteller, "The Tennessee Study of Class Size in the Early School Grades," *Future of Children* 5, no. 2 (Summer-Fall 1995): 113–27.

2. Eric A. Hanushek, "Some Findings from an Independent Investigation of the Tennessee STAR Experiment and from Other Investigations of Class Size Effects," *Educational Evaluation and Policy Analysis* 21, no. 2 (1999): 154–64.

3. Of all transitions, 25 percent were into small (more desirable) classes. See Alan B. Krueger, "Experimental Estimates of Education Production Functions," *Quarterly Journal of Economics* 114, no. 2 (1999): 497–532.

4. Elizabeth Word and others, *The State of Tennessee's Student/Teacher Achievement Ratio (STAR) Project: Final Summary Report 1985–1990* (Nashville: Tennessee State Department of Education, 1990).

5. Eric A. Hanushek, "The Economics of Schooling: Production and Efficiency in Public Schools," *Journal of Economic Literature* 24, no. 3 (1986): 1141–77; Eric A. Hanushek, "Assessing the Effects of School Resources on Student Performance: An Update," *Educational Evaluation and Policy Analysis* 19, no. 2 (Summer 1997): 141–64.

6. Krueger, "Experimental Estimates of Education Production Functions."

7. Some early work uses current class size instead of initial assignment. See Jeremy D. Finn and Charles M. Achilles, "Answers and Questions about Class Size: A Statewide Experiment," *American Educational Research Journal* 27 (Fall 1990): 557–77; Word and others, *Student/Teacher Achievement Ratio*.

8. This conservative "intent-to-treat" measure based on random assignment is typically considered preferable to models that measure the impact of actual class type attended in cases in which there is nonrandom movement between classes. A simple example may help to illustrate this: if a child were moved from a regular class to a small class because his parents insisted on the move, it is reasonable to assume that the parents are especially active in other aspects of the student's education, say, by monitoring homework especially closely or providing other education-enhancing opportunities. The problem arises because we do not have perfect measures of the home environment. In the ideal case in which class type is randomly assigned, these home environment measures are not correlated with class type, and their impacts are absorbed in the error term in equation 2. When the effect of actual (nonrandom) class attended is measured instead, some of the impacts of the active home environment also may be picked up because attendance may be correlated with this "home environment" component of the error term. Using the experimentally induced variation—even though not all students attended their assigned class type, and some students' test scores "count" toward the regular class they were assigned to, even though they actually attended small classes—circumvents this problem but understates the true impact. Krueger provides a more detailed discussion of this matter; see Krueger, "Experimental Estimates of Education Production Functions."

9. In addition, tests of the interaction between race, gender, and free-lunch status and small-class assignment and a model saturated with all the interaction terms between race, gender, and free-lunch status show no statistically significant relationship between baseline characteristics and small-class assignment (p values of 0.94 and 0.15, respectively.)

10. Krueger, "Experimental Estimates of Education Production Functions."

11. Better attendance rates in small classes might also be caused by fewer classmates from whom to pick up germs and illnesses.

12. Another potential source of bias is selective withdrawal prior to entering kindergarten. Krueger reports that, of initially assigned students, 10.4 percent assigned to small kindergarten

classes failed to enroll in kindergarten in the fall. Comparable figures for regular classes are 14.3 percent (difference with regard to small classes has $t = 1.86$), and for regular-with-aide classes are 12.2 percent (difference between small classes $t = 0.86$). See Krueger, "Experimental Estimates of Education Production Functions."

13. As Hanushek points out, though, these characteristics—and most other observable characteristics—are poor predictors of teacher effectiveness. Recent work by Jacob and Lefgren indicates that principals generally can identify which teachers are at the extremes of effectiveness across the entire school but are not able to distinguish between the middle 60–80 percent of teachers in terms of effectiveness. It may be reasonable to conclude that teachers are not allocated to classes based on their potential impact if principals are not able to distinguish easily between most teachers. See Hanushek, "Some Findings from an Independent Investigation of the Tennessee STAR Experiment and from Other Investigations of Class Size Effects"; Brian A. Jacob and Lars Lefgren, "Principals as Agents: Subjective Performance Measures in Education," Working Paper 11463 (Cambridge, Mass.: National Bureau of Economic Research, 2005).

14. Finn and Achilles, "Answers and Questions about Class Size"; Word and others, *Student/Teacher Achievement Ratio*; Elizabeth R. Word and others, *The State of Tennessee's Student/Teacher Achievement Ratio (STAR) Project: Technical Report 1985–1990* (Nashville: Tennessee State Department of Education, 1994); Krueger, "Experimental Estimates of Education Production Functions"; Alan B. Krueger and Diane M. Whitmore, "The Effect of Attending a Small Class in the Early Grades on College-Test Taking and Middle School Test Results: Evidence from Project STAR," *Economic Journal* 111, no. 468 (2001): 1–28; Barbara Nye, Larry V. Hedges, and Spyros Konstantopoulos, "Do Low-Achieving Students Benefit More from Small Classes? Evidence from the Tennessee Class Size Experiment," *Educational Evaluation and Policy Analysis* 24, no. 3 (2002): 201–17.

15. Alan B. Krueger and Diane M. Whitmore, "Would Smaller Classes Help Close the Black-White Achievement Gap?" in *Bridging the Achievement Gap*, edited by John E. Chubb and Tom Loveless (Brookings, 2002).

16. Diane Whitmore, "Resource and Peer Impacts on Girls' Academic Achievement: Evidence from a Randomized Experiment," *American Economic Review* 95, no. 22 (2005): 199–203.

17. G. W. Bohrnstedt and B. M. Stecher, *What We Have Learned about Class Size Reduction in California* (Sacramento: California Department of Education, 2002).

18. Krueger, "Experimental Estimates of Education Production Functions."

19. Thanks to Dan Goldhaber for pointing this out.

20. An estimated 20 percent of students had been retained a grade by eighth grade, but this probability did not vary with initial class assignment.

21. Krueger and Whitmore use a different approach and deduct a small number of points from the test scores of students who were retained. Since class type is not correlated with the probability of grade retention, the results are robust to either approach. See Krueger and Whitmore, "The Effect of Attending a Small Class in the Early Grades on College-Test Taking and Middle School Test Results."

22. Charles M. Achilles and others, *The Lasting Benefits Study (LBS) in Grades 4 and 5 (1990–1991): A Legacy from Tennessee's Four-Year (K–3) Class-Size Study (1985–1989), Project STAR* (Nashville: HEROS, 1993); Barbara Nye and others, *The Lasting Benefits Study: Eighth Grade Technical Report* (Tennessee State University, Center of Excellence for Research in Basic Skills, 1995); Krueger and Whitmore, "The Effect of Attending a Small Class in the Early Grades on College-Test Taking and Middle School Test Results."

23. Susan Dynarski and I have been collecting college performance data, so a more direct measure of college behavior will be available soon.

24. Krueger and Whitmore, "The Effect of Attending a Small Class in the Early Grades on College-Test Taking and Middle School Test Results"; Krueger and Whitmore, "Would Smaller Classes Help Close the Black-White Achievement Gap?"

25. The numbers reported here are slightly different from those reported in Krueger and Whitmore, "The Effect of Attending a Small Class in the Early Grades on College-Test Taking and Middle School Test Results," because at that time data were only available for students who graduated on track with their kindergarten class. Updated data allow a study of the impact of class size on students who were retained.

26. Krueger and Whitmore, "Would Smaller Classes Help Close the Black-White Achievement Gap?"

27. Lawrence J. Schweinhart and others, *Lifetime Effects: The High/Scope Perry Preschool Study through Age 40* (Ypsilanti, Mich.: High/Scope Press, 2005).

28. Krueger and Whitmore, "Would Smaller Classes Help Close the Black-White Achievement Gap?" Diane W. Schanzenbach, "The Impact of Early School Intervention on Crime" (University of Chicago, 2007).

29. Thomas S. Dee, "Teachers, Race, and Student Achievement in a Randomized Experiment," *Review of Economics and Statistics* 86, no. 1 (2004): 195–210.

30. Thomas S. Dee and Benjamin J. Keys, "Does Merit Pay Reward Good Teachers? Evidence from a Randomized Experiment," *Journal of Policy Analysis and Management* 23, no. 3 (2005): 471–88.

31. Bryan S. Graham, "Identifying Social Interactions through Excess Variance Contrasts," University of California, Berkeley, 2005.

32. Diane Whitmore Schanzenbach, "Classroom Gender Composition and Student Achievement: Evidence from a Randomized Experiment," Working Paper (Harris School at the University of Chicago, 2006).

33. Elizabeth U. Cascio and Diane Whitmore Schanzenbach, "First in the Class? Academic Redshirting and Education Production," Dartmouth College, 2006.

34. Edward P. Lazear, "Educational Production," *Quarterly Journal of Economics* 116, no. 3 (2001): 777–803.

35. James J. Heckman, "Skill Formation and the Economics of Investing in Disadvantaged Children," *Science* 312, no. 5782 (2006): 1900–02; James J. Heckman and Alan B. Krueger, *Inequality in America: What Role for Human Capital Policies?* (MIT Press, 2005).

36. Krueger and Whitmore, "The Effect of Attending a Small Class in the Early Grades on College-Test Taking and Middle School Test Results."

37. Another approach is to predict college test taking based on third-grade test scores and a small-class indicator. Using this approach, the small-class indicator does not predict college test taking in a statistically significant manner (coefficient = 0.028, standard error = 0.027), which is consistent with the entire test-taking effect's being driven by higher test scores. The approach similarly yields not significant findings predicting test-taking behavior on eighth-grade scores and a small-class indicator (coefficient = 0.030, standard error 0.020).

38. Finn and Achilles, "Answers and Questions about Class Size"; Kimberly A. Gordon Rouse and Susan E. Cashin, "Children's Self-Concept and Motivation Assessment: Initial Reliability and Validity," paper presented at the annual conference of the American Psychological Association, New Orleans, 2001.

39. Krueger and Whitmore, "The Effect of Attending a Small Class in the Early Grades on College-Test Taking and Middle School Test Results."

40. From Derek Neal and William R. Johnson, "The Role of Pre-Market Factors in Black-White Wage Differences," *Journal of Political Economy* 104, no. 5 (October 1996): 869–95.

41. Census Bureau and Bureau of Labor Statistics, *Current Population Survey,* March 2006 (www.census.gov/cps/ [October 2006]).

42. Another approach to estimating a cost-benefit analysis would be to multiply the increased earnings associated with postsecondary education by the increased likelihood that a student takes the SAT or ACT. This assumes that the 0.024 increased test-taking rate translates to the same size increase in postsecondary attendance. Using a similar approach to that described above and measuring wages for high school only versus at least some postsecondary schooling, the internal rate of return ranges from 4.5 percent (in the no-growth scenario) to 6.7 percent (if real growth is assumed to be 2 percent). Further information is available from the author upon request.

43. Brian A. Jacob and Lars Lefgren, "The Impact of Teacher Training on Student Achievement: Quasi-Experimental Evidence from School Reform Efforts in Chicago," *Journal of Human Resources* 39, no. 1 (2004): 50–79.

44. William Howell and others, "School Vouchers and Academic Performance: Results from Three Randomized Field Trials," *Journal of Policy Analysis and Management* 21, no. 2 (2002): 191–218; Krueger and Whitmore, "Would Smaller Classes Help Close the Black-White Achievement Gap?"

45. Caroline M. Hoxby and Jonah E. Rockoff, "The Impact of Charter Schools on Student Achievement," Columbia Business School, 2004.

46. Mosteller, "The Tennessee Study of Class Size in the Early School Grades."

Policy from the Hip: Class-Size Reduction in California

PETER SCHRAG

California was, and remains, the largest "experiment" in class-size reduction (CSR) in the country's history. Its sweeping program to reduce the state's classes in kindergarten through the third grade covered nearly 2 million students and dropped the average class size from almost twenty-nine students per class, and often a great many more, to twenty or fewer, and it sought to do so virtually overnight. It is a fascinating and instructive story: Did CSR improve student achievement or realize other gains commensurate with the sizable investment it required? Could far more impressive gains have been made if the program had been concentrated on disadvantaged and other at-risk students? But the California story—much of it a political story—also raises deeper questions about the relationship of research to public policy. If the profession, parents, and the public—and thus politicians—embrace a policy, as they have in California, despite the lack of persuasive research support, what is the role of formal research? Is there a reliable way to calculate opportunity costs, as in higher pay for teachers? Conversely, can certain policies generate gains—in teacher morale, for example, or in greater voter support for public education—that may be equally important, despite the near-impossibility of calculating the effects of many of them?

In 1990, when he first ran for governor, Pete Wilson, a moderate Republican, made it known that reducing class sizes in California, which then had the largest classes in the country, was something the state could not afford. More important, in the five succeeding years, Governor Wilson and his administration estimated that reducing all classes by an average of even one student (in 1995) would cost somewhere around $1 billion a year. "We've got to be a little honest about these things," Wilson said during the campaign, "and not simply generalize and say we're going to cure the problem and increase the quality of education by throwing money at it that we don't have." He felt that it was a foolish way to spend taxpayer money.[1]

In fact, California's schools had not been getting all that much taxpayer money or much public attention. In the early 1970s, two state supreme court decisions, *Serrano* v. *Priest,* seeking to equalize per-pupil spending between rich and poor districts, led the state to cap additional local spending in high-wealth districts, effectively decoupling local property tax rates from local school budgets and thus reducing the incentive for affluent districts to raise their own taxes to support schools. With the passage of Proposition 13 in 1978, which rolled back local property taxes and enacted subsequent tax limitations, funding for schools was reduced further.[2] Thus per-pupil spending in California, once among the high spenders (California's per-pupil spending was fifth among the states in the late 1960s), declined to well below the U.S. average when Wilson took office in 1991 and sank even lower—to forty-first or forty-second, depending on the year and method of computation—during the recession immediately following; it has been stuck below the national average ever since. Nonetheless, because California is a high-cost state and because the California Teachers Association (CTA) has immense bargaining power, teacher salaries have remained among the highest in the country. This has raised class size even further, exacerbated California's already serious shortage of school counselors, librarians, and nurses, and led to additional cuts in programs.[3]

Equally important, much of California's education policy had been in turmoil for a decade before Wilson's tenure. The state had no testing program; the California Assessment Program (CAP)—the prior system—was itself of questionable reliability and had been defunded by Wilson's predecessor, George Deukmejian, in a battle over money with the independently elected state superintendent of public instruction, Bill Honig. Subsequently, Honig, who had worked hard to upgrade the state's academic standards, was convicted on conflict-of-interest charges and forced to resign. He was replaced by a temporary appointee who had been his deputy—two Wilson nominees were blocked by the legislature—and served until Delaine Eastin was elected in 1994. Meanwhile, a state court decision shifted the balance of influence in state education policy from the elected superintendent to the state Board of Education, which is appointed by the governor. The California Learning Assessment System (CLAS), an ambitious but flawed academic assessment program created by the state

Department of Education, was instituted. However, Wilson quickly killed it after conservatives complained that its questions invaded family privacy and after otherwise questionable items were reported in the media.[4] Thus for nearly a decade between 1989 and 1998, California had no measure of its own on how well its students were doing. Its only testing program was the basic skills test required of all students before graduation. But since each district created its own standards and its own test, it was meaningless as an indicator of statewide achievement.

In 1992, the first year that state breakdowns were available, the stunning disclosure that California students were near the bottom in both reading and math on the National Assessment of Educational Progress (NAEP) again drew the serious public and political attention that, with the exception of Honig's efforts, schools had been denied for many years. In the 1980s and early 1990s it was an issue that dominated the agenda. In 1994 California fourth graders were tied at dead last with Louisiana in reading. In 1996 California was at the bottom in eighth-grade math, tied with Tennessee, among the forty states that then participated in NAEP; 54 percent of California fourth graders, according to NAEP, were failing in basic math skills.[5]

Those numbers, reinforced by growing national attention to schools, produced a great wave of state-mandated curricular reforms—first in reading and math, then in other fields—that sought to change instruction from an essentially progressive focus on whole language, constructivist math, and discovery learning to an emphasis on phonics-based reading and direct instruction. (Maureen DiMarco, Wilson's feisty secretary of education and child development, got a lot of notice with her campaign demanding an end to "fuzzy crap.") It also led Wilson to push State Testing and Reporting (STAR), a mandatory assessment program based originally on the Stanford Achievement Test (SAT-9), a standardized, nationally normed reference test that would generate individualized scores for all students. STAR was first given in 1998, Wilson's last year in office, and later broadened to put primary emphasis on tests based on the new state standards. In 1998 California voters also passed an initiative designed to sharply restrict bilingual education in the state's schools. A new school accountability and ranking system, with rewards for staff in successful schools and sanctions for schools failing to make progress, was instituted in 1999–2000, shortly after Gray Davis, Wilson's successor, took office.

In the spring of 1996, in the midst of that great rush of school reform, Wilson, who had again ruled out class-size reduction only a few months before, had what seemed like an overnight conversion. After the recession of the early 1990s, a recovering economy generated a sizable chunk of new tax revenue for the state treasury. Under the provisions of Proposition 98, a constitutional initiative narrowly passed by California voters in 1988, a large part of that new money had to go to schools. But in the face of a television campaign sponsored by the California Teachers Association attacking Wilson for the state's crowded classrooms, the governor was determined not to hand unrestricted money to local districts, many of whose boards were dominated by local unions. Wilson often complained—mostly with good reason—that the union, despite its class-size campaign, had always preferred to allocate as much money as possible for discretionary spending and thus for additional pay. But the union had asked for smaller classes, and Wilson was determined to make them swallow what they'd asked for.[6]

Wilson initially asked the legislature to reduce classes from an average of 28.5 students to a maximum of 20.0 students per teacher (the 20-1 formula) in grades one and two. But when the state Senate, dominated by Democrats, refused to accept many of the tax cuts that the governor proposed at the same time, he expanded the CSR proposal to grade three and, ultimately, to kindergarten. Now the Democrats and the union balked, saying it was too much, too fast: "The reality is it's only physically possible to do so much at any one time," Senate President Pro Tem Bill Lockyer said as the negotiations were coming to a head. "There are only so many buildings to use and so many teachers to hire. You can throw too much money at it and just throw money away." The state had neither the teachers nor the classroom space to staff and house the estimated 21,000 additional classes that Wilson's proposal would require.[7] That was particularly true for urban schools, which had even larger classes than the state average, little space, and a tougher time attracting and keeping good teachers. Democrats and some education groups also insisted that the program should not be expanded until the extra $650 per student that the administration had budgeted for every student in a class of twenty or fewer in the first two grades in the CSR program was increased to cover the full costs to local schools, which in many cases it did not. "Why the sudden change of heart," asked Wilson, "from the union and its legislative allies? That is easier to understand when you recognize that money spent on smaller classes cannot be spent on higher salaries by union members."[8]

But there was another element as well. Since many suburban schools had smaller classes to begin with, and more space, and since they could attract good teachers more easily than crowded city schools, they found CSR much easier to adopt. In some cases, the extra money was a windfall. It was thus no great surprise that Republicans, who controlled the Assembly in 1996, moderated their insistence on tax cuts and embraced CSR. "Wilson's actions," wrote John Jacobs, the *Sacramento Bee's* political columnist, "reflect a new bipartisan political consensus in California: Once again, public schools matter. Now that former Assembly Speaker Willie Brown is gone and the powerful California Teachers Association is no longer seen as a wholly owned subsidiary of the Assembly Democratic Caucus, many Republicans appear less reluctant to support public education. More conservative Assembly Republicans, who want to emphasize school voucher programs or religious-based home schooling, have been overtaken by events."[9] And since those Republicans tended disproportionately to represent suburbs that seemed in a position to gain from CSR funding, they had at least a marginal incentive to support it. In this dance, the partners had changed sides.

The CSR proposal was loosely coupled with DiMarco's plan to get better materials into the schools and institute more intensive teacher training and a variety of other measures to back up the state's new reading standards. In DiMarco's mind at that time, there was no research support for class-size reduction unless the state could change its reading strategies to take advantage of smaller classes. Conversely, she believed, the chances of improving reading instruction would probably increase with smaller classes. But there was no magic in the 20-1 formula, nor was there any mandate to couple better teaching with CSR. The number, said a Wilson staffer who still declines to be identified, "was what we could afford."[10]

The research was inconclusive at best. The most widely respected study was Project STAR (Student/Teacher Achievement Ratio), the major longitudinal project in Tennessee showing a strong and apparently long-lasting effect of smaller classes, particularly for minority students, which the distinguished Harvard statistician Fred Mosteller called "one of the great experiments in education in U.S. history." This was the kind of study that most researchers can only dream about: "a large-scale experiment in which both teachers and students were randomized into classrooms within a broad range of participating schools," giving it (in the jargon of the trade) "both high internal validity and considerable external validity."[11]

In reviewing that study, conducted in 1985–89, but with follow-ups by others over a period of another decade and involving nearly 12,000 students, researchers Barbara Nye of Tennessee State University and Larry Hedges and Spyros Konstantopoulos of the University of Chicago found that students in primary-grade classes with thirteen to seventeen students quickly outperformed their peers in larger classes of twenty-two to twenty-six students in reading and math. More important, when those students returned to regular-size classes after grade three, they appeared to maintain those differences; they took more challenging courses, and their dropout rates were lower (conclusions that were subsequently challenged by Eric Hanushek and others).[12] But what Nye and her colleagues found most interesting was that the gains were larger for minority students: "Thus, small classes may be a way to benefit all students while reducing the gap in achievement between white and minority students."[13]

In a more recent analysis of the Tennessee STAR results, Alan B. Krueger and Diane Whitmore of Princeton also found that small classes substantially raised the percentage of black students who would take college entrance exams. "If all students were assigned to a small class," they said, "the black-white gap in taking a college entrance exam would fall by an estimated 60 percent" and would significantly raise black students' scores on those tests. Other follow-ups also suggested that the STAR students finished school at a higher rate and were more likely to continue to higher education.[14]

However valid, the Tennessee study, which compared classes of twenty-two to twenty-six students with classes of thirteen to seventeen, provided little assurance that California, with its 20-1 ratio, would reap any significant gains, much less gains commensurate with the investment called for in Wilson's proposals. Those doubts have since been reinforced by Erik Hanushek, now at the Hoover Institution at Stanford, who found both from his analysis of the STAR results and from other research that "any effects of overall class-size reduction policies will be small and very expensive. . . . The evidence does not say that class size reductions are never worthwhile and that they should never be taken. It does say that uniform, across-the-board policies . . . are unlikely to be effective."[15] Additionally, and notwithstanding the positive findings about higher graduation rates, there were questions, raised by both Hanushek and Chester Finn of the Thomas B. Fordham Foundation, about the "washout" effect of the gains made in STAR. Did the achievement gains really persist into later grades, after the STAR students returned to larger classes?

But there was no way that the legislature could resist the allure of class-size reduction. Other things not considered, it made perfect sense: smaller classes seemed to mean more individual attention. Every survey indicated that parents and teachers loved it, and, as Wilson said, the big teacher union, knowing what would appeal to voters, had run a well-financed television campaign hammering him for his failure to address the issue. A bill, sponsored by Gary Hart, who then chaired the Senate Education Committee, was enacted, reducing one ninth-grade course in every school to twenty students or fewer (in many cases from forty-two students), primarily to allow teachers to assign and read more student writing. Subsequently, Democrat Leroy Greene, then chairman of the Senate Education Committee, sponsored a class-size-reduction bill. The state's elected superintendent of public instruction, Delaine Eastin, also a Democrat, had been campaigning for it since she was elected in 1994.

The Wilson CSR bill that passed—without a dissenting vote in either house—did not mandate smaller classes, but it offered local districts an additional $650 a year, about 12 percent more than the statewide average daily attendance spending at that time, for every student who was in a class of twenty or fewer; Wilson later increased it to $800. It quickly became so popular that Wilson justifiably called it "almost a mandate" for local districts.[16]

The program, enacted in July 1996, went into effect in September, beginning in grades one and two and in grade three and kindergarten soon thereafter. But because the state provided no particular incentives for schools serving at-risk students, who, according to STAR and other studies, were likely to benefit most, and because space was especially tight in urban schools, the uneven pace of implementation was "inversely related to percent minority and percent poverty in schools."[17] The first year's cost was $771 million, which increased rapidly thereafter, rising to $1.7 billion in 2005–06 out of total state general fund school spending of roughly $36 billion.

In some districts, the transition went smoothly, although it created some resentment among fourth-, fifth-, and sixth-grade teachers who still had classes of thirty-five students. In others, the transition was slower and more difficult, in part because buildings were already overcrowded, especially in urban districts like Los Angeles that, because of budget constraints, high land prices, and bureaucratic inertia, had built few schools in the prior twenty years and, more important, because finding an additional 21,000 qualified teachers overnight was nearly impossible. In essence, the whole state was going from an average of twenty-nine students in the primary grades to twenty.[18]

The predictable result was that, in many schools, the great majority of them serving poor and minority students, the percentage of inexperienced teachers shot up, many of whom, such as interns and individuals with emergency credentials, had no formal qualifications. In the year before CSR was implemented, barely 2 percent of primary teachers lacked full credentials. By 1999–2000, that number had risen to nearly 14 percent statewide and to roughly 22 percent in schools in which 30 percent or more of the students came from low-income families. If credentials and experience mean anything—an issue itself subject to debate—the quality of the teaching force, especially in low-performing schools, was driven down. Helping to drive that decline was a bill enacted by the legislature in July 1996 making it easier for districts to hire uncredentialed teachers.[19]

Some of those new teachers were "switchers," second-career individuals from other occupations who passed subject matter tests, completed the necessary paperwork, and were assigned to a class, in theory under the supervision of a mentor, while they studied in a teacher preparation program at night. Others were green education students or recent college graduates, working on emergency credentials. Still others were hastily recruited from out of state and sometimes from out of the country. Los Angeles sent recruiters to Portland (Oregon), Cleveland, and Miami. In July 1996 the district, which already had an agreement with Mexico to bring in a few Mexican teachers, requested a formal waiver from the state to hire Spanish-speaking teachers who had not yet passed California's basic skills test. In Oakland, meanwhile, of 424 new teachers hired the first year of CSR, 40 percent were either interns or people teaching with emergency credentials. It was, said Margaret Gaston, director of the private Center on the Future of Teaching and Learning, "an interesting stew." Five years later, in 2005, as the underqualified got their credentials or were replaced, the number of underprepared teachers had declined to about 7 percent. But students in the lowest quartile in achievement still had a 40 percent chance of having had at least one underprepared teacher and a 30 percent chance of having had more than one.[20]

Because CSR required additional classrooms that many schools, especially inner-city schools, did not have, a number of large urban districts, Sacramento among them, moved very slowly on implementation, until parental pressure overwhelmed them. In many schools, classes were held in gyms, cafeterias, special education classrooms, and other spaces; playgrounds were so crammed with portables that they looked like migrant camps. They still do. And because the state subsidy did not fully cover the costs and thus encroached on other funds, many districts reallocated funds from facility maintenance, administrative services, professional development, libraries, and music, arts, and other programs to CSR. Because of that encroachment and tightening budgets, some districts subsequently either dropped one or more grades from their CSR program, beginning with grade three, or dropped CSR altogether.[21]

There were other unintended consequences as well. As expected, parents loved it, rating "selected features of their child's education higher than did parents of children in non-reduced-size classes."[22] Teachers in the smaller classes had more opportunities to work with small groups or individual students, and they reported fewer behavioral problems and fewer students "off task." But there appeared to be little change in teaching strategies or learning activities.

Wilson, who saw CSR as a "serves 'em right" response to the CTA's class-size campaign, had to watch another perverse, but hardly unexpected, outcome: class-size reduction produced some 20,000 new members for the teacher union, which quickly came to love the program and vehemently resisted subsequent attempts to make it more flexible.[23] Those 20,000 members represented an additional $3 million in dues and political action funds. That money was not decisive in helping the CTA defeat a Wilson-backed ballot measure in 1998 that would have severely curbed the ability of unions to collect dues or in beating a voucher initiative in 2000. But it was still a "major factor" in union campaigns, according to John Hein, who was then the CTA's chief political strategist.[24]

For Wilson, the political gains were inconsequential. His earlier hopes to become the GOP presidential candidate in 1996, as what might later have been called a "compassionate conservative," had long been dashed, in part by his agreement to raise taxes during the fiscal crisis of 1991, in part by his support for abortion rights, in part by the Latino backlash to his attacks on illegal immigration in 1994, and in part by a throat affliction that left him with a croak in his voice for much of the crucial preprimary period. By the time of the Republican convention in Philadelphia in 2000, the former governor of the nation's largest state had become a non-person in his own party.

On the substantive question of educational achievement, there was no demonstrable outcome. After more than five years of CSR, the only major study, conducted pursuant to state law by a consortium headed by the American Institutes of Research (AIR) and the Rand Corporation, found that "the relationship of CSR to student achievement was inconclusive." In a *Capstone Report* published in September 2002, the consortium found that student achievement had been increasing, but "only limited evidence link[ed] these gains to CSR." Where there appeared to be some link with test scores (in third grade, after controlling for differences in student and school characteristics), "the size of this CSR effect was small." In particular,

> Although both overall exposure to CSR and statewide average test scores increased across cohorts, the magnitude of the changes in test scores did not track with the incremental changes in CSR. Thus, attribution of gains in scores to CSR is not warranted. More refined school-level analysis also failed to find meaningful differences in second- or third-grade scores of students with an additional year of CSR exposure in first grade compared to students who participated only in grades two and three.[25]

By inference, the AIR-Rand study also indicated that the CSR program was not well enough integrated or aligned with California's standards-based curricular and accountability reforms. The study called for more flexibility in varying class sizes and pointed to indications from Tennessee's STAR program:

> Class-size reduction can be an especially effective policy strategy for raising the achievement of the most at-risk students if class sizes are reduced even further for that group and if those classes are staffed by skilled and qualified teachers. It is possible

to conduct carefully controlled experiments to examine the differences moving to a class size of fifteen or fewer would make, beginning with those schools that serve the largest number of low-income and minority children.[26]

The researchers also cited the fact that state funding had not kept pace with the costs of the program to local districts and that, in any case, the state should provide "solid cost data" to "assist state and local policymakers in determining the cost-effectiveness of CSR compared with other possible reform expenditures." Wisconsin's Student Achievement Guarantee in Education (SAGE) project, which focused on high-poverty schools, seemed to show that students in classes of twelve to fifteen with rigorous curricula, before- and after-school programs, and teachers trained to take advantage of those small numbers did much better than students in classes of twenty-one to twenty-five.[27] But neither those recommendations nor the SAGE findings—allowing more flexibility, creating even smaller classes in the neediest schools, bringing highly skilled and qualified teachers to those schools, trying to assess cost-effectiveness—was ever seriously addressed in California, much less translated into policy.

The consideration of cost-effectiveness may be the thorniest question of all and may well enter a realm so fuzzy that no one can calibrate it. What is the trade-off between larger classes with highly compensated, excellent teachers and smaller classes with marginal teachers?[28] And what are the attributes of good teachers? What is the value of improved morale among teachers with smaller classes or, as Gary Hart suggests, the value of high school teachers who are able to assign a respectable amount of writing in English or history classes and have time to read and react to it? What worth is parental satisfaction, even if no positive academic achievement can be attributed to it? Is there a payoff in increased public willingness to support schools and even, as California State Superintendent of Public Instruction Jack O'Connell and other CSR advocates have said, to transfer their private school children back into public schools? (In some California districts, at least, that seems to be the case.)[29] Nevertheless, what is the opportunity cost—say, in delivering enriched resources (counselors, reading specialists, librarians) to the neediest schools, perhaps reducing class sizes even further, and staffing them with well-paid, highly trained teachers who can take advantage of those classes?

After the publication of the AIR-Rand study in 2002, there appeared to be only one other study focused on the California CSR program. It was conducted by Fatih Unlu, a graduate student working under Alan Krueger at Princeton, whose unpublished paper concluded, "The CSR program has had a positive and significant influence on California students' [NAEP math] achievement scores."

The difference, Unlu said, was between 0.2 and 0.3 of a standard deviation compared to the increase "for closely matched students who were not exposed to the CSR initiative."[30]

But here, too, there are imponderables. One of his two analyses compares gains by eighth graders who were not exposed to CSR with gains by fourth graders who were. But given the familiar middle school slump and the fact that fourth graders were exposed to a great many other primary school reforms between 1996 and 2000 that eighth graders missed, the comparison leaves many questions. Similarly, his comparison of math gains between fourth graders in California and those in other states does not (and cannot) control for educational reforms in other states. As Bohrnstedt said, "California was really active on the reform front during this period, which is something that makes any analysis of CSR in California a problem—as it was for us." Asked to comment on the Unlu study, Bohrnstedt concluded that Unlu's findings were "consistent in showing positive effects for CSR in spite of varying assumptions." But he also had trouble with the fourth- and eighth-grade comparisons and the cross-state comparisons:

> There probably were some positive effects of CSR in California, but the issue of cost-effectiveness has to weigh huge in a debate about its merits. That remains true today. Any reform that is going to have significant effects has to begin with instruction. This is not to downplay leadership (both administrative and instructional), nor class size, nor professional development, nor the role of unions, etc., etc. But somehow if it is not linked to instruction, how can it have a really large impact?[31]

Given the great level of uncertainty about the academic payoff of California's investment in class-size reduction and the unexamined potential of giving local districts more flexibility—even inducements—to organize much smaller classes in schools with large numbers of disadvantaged students, what seems most troubling about the California program is that the state has commissioned no research since the AIR-Rand study was completed in 2002: none.[32] Yet in light of the popularity of the program with teachers and parents and the strong backing of the California Teachers Association, which characterizes any call for flexibility or differentiation as an attempt to abolish it, it is not surprising that the political establishment is not eager to raise questions.

For most people, it is just common sense that small classes are better: every parent knows it is easier to handle four kids than ten, and most regard decorum and good behavior as just as important as academic achievement. In that environment, questions like the possible trade-off between smaller classes and better (and higher-paid) teachers tend to become abstractions for both voters and politicians.[33] And that, in turn, raises a broader question about the belief that all good education policy must be research based. (A lot of Americans would also say that education should be based on what parents and the community want.) There is an understandable wish that research be used more effectively to drive public policy, but, as Hart and others have acknowledged, legislators tend to seize on whatever research is available to support their own preferences, no matter how inconclusive or marginal, and ignore most contrary evidence.

Over long periods of time, an accumulation of evidence may shape the conventional wisdom, as it did, for example, in persuading the public about the hazards of smoking, but where common sense indicates otherwise, it may never happen. A lot of the things we once knew for sure—about education, about health and medicine, about urban design—have turned out to be dubious, if not flat-out wrong. As John Bishop of Cornell so wisely said, maybe "we [the research community] don't have all the answers." Maybe the belief that if the practitioners "only listened to us, everything would be fixed" needs some tempering.[34] It is clear, as Stecher and Bohrnstedt concluded, "that local educators and parents may value reduced class sizes for many reasons other than improved achievement as measured by statewide test scores."[35] In a democracy, if the voters embrace a program, even a costly one, who or what is going to convince them they are wasting their money? It is apparent that CSR funds would be concentrated more profitably—and combined with instruction that is tailored to it—in schools with large numbers of at-risk students. Yet if we look at schooling as more than an enterprise in raising test scores but instead as an essential community institution depending on public support that is not only supposed to "sivilize" kids, as Huck says, but perform myriad other functions that no test measures, can we say with certainty that the money is really being wasted?

Notes

1. Author interviews with Maureen DiMarco, Wilson's secretary of education and child development, 1992–96 and February 2006. Peter Schrag, "The Class-Size Stampede," *Sacramento Bee*, January 1, 1997, p. B6; Dan Smith, "New School Proposals Drawing Mixed Reaction," *Sacramento Bee*, February 22, 1998, p. A1.

2. The full story is in Peter Schrag, *Paradise Lost: California's Experience, America's Future* (New York: New Press, 1998).

3. National Center for Education Statistics, *Education in States and Nations* (Department of Education, 1996), p. 196, table 32b. The U.S. average in 1991 was $4,600; California spent roughly $4,200. For a more comprehensive account of what happened to school spending and programs during that period, see Peter Schrag, *Paradise Lost,* pp. 66–87.

4. *Aligning California's Educational Reforms: Progress Made and the Work That Remains* (Palo Alto, Calif.: EdSource, 2001), pp. 2–3. This publication provides a tidy digest, complete with time line, of the great changes in California policy through 2001. Also see Schrag, *Paradise Lost*, pp. 80–81.

5. National Center for Education Statistics, *Digest of Education Statistics, 1995* (Department of Education, 1995), table 109. National Assessment of Educational Progress, *The Reading Report Card, 1992 and 1994* (Department of Education, 1996).

6. "'I think the governor took some delight using that money for class-size reduction and essentially calling the teachers' bluff,' said former state Sen. Gary Hart, now director of the Institute for Education Reform at California State University, Sacramento. 'Certainly a fringe benefit was keeping that money off the collective bargaining table.'" Smith, "New School Proposals Drawing Mixed Reaction." State Superintendent of Public Instruction Jack O'Connell, a strong supporter of CSR and author of one of the CSR bills, put it more briefly: "Wilson's motives," he said, "may not have been pure." Interview with O'Connell, February 9, 2006.

7. Brad Hayward, "Class Size Clash May Stall Budget," *Sacramento Bee*, June 30, 1996, p. A1.

8. Pete Wilson, "Why the Stalling on Class Size Cut?" *Sacramento Bee*, July 3, 1996, p. B9. It was relatively easy for suburban districts, which had more space and smaller classes to begin with. For them, the extra $650 could be a windfall; for the crowded urban schools, it was a burden.

9. John Jacobs, "The Education Dividend," *Sacramento Bee*, May 23, 1996, p. B8.

10. Interviews with DiMarco and other former Wilson staff people, February 2006.

11. Frederick Mosteller, "The Tennessee Study of Class Size in the Early School Grades," *Future of Children* 5, no. 2 (Summer-Fall 1995): 113–27. The Tennessee STAR program, of course, had no connection with California's STAR tests.

12. For example, Erik A. Hanushek, "Some Findings from an Independent Investigation of the Tennessee STAR Class Size Experiment and from Other Investigations of Class Size Effects," *Educational Evaluation and Policy Analysis* 21, no. 2 (Summer 1999): 143–63.

13. Barbara Nye, Larry V. Hedges, and Spyros Konstantopoulos, "The Long-Term Effects of Small Classes in Early Grades; Lasting Benefits in Mathematics Achievement at Grade 9," *Journal of Experimental Education* 69, no. 3 (Spring 2001): 245. Debra Viadero, "Tennessee Class-Size Study Finds Long-Term Benefits," *Education Week*, May 5, 1999. Also Jeremy D. Finn, B. DeWayne Fulton, Jayne B. Zaharias, and Barbara A. Nye, "Carry-over Effects of Small Classes," *Peabody Journal* 67, no. 1 (Fall 1989): 71–84; Charles M. Achilles, Barbara A. Nye, Jayne B. Zaharias, B. DeWayne Fulton, and C. Cain, "Education's Equivalent of Medicine's Framingham Heart Study," ED 402677 (Washington: ERIC Clearinghouse, 1996).

14. Alan B. Krueger and Diane M. Whitmore, "Would Smaller Classes Help Close the Black-White Achievement Gap?" Industrial Relations Working Paper 451 (Princeton University, March 2001) (www.irs.princeton.edu/pubs/working_papers.html [October 2006]). The article was reprinted in John Chubb and Tom Loveless, eds., *Bridging the Achievement Gap* (Brookings, 2002). On graduation rates and other positive effects, the most comprehensive summary is found at www.heros-inc.org/star.htm [October 2006].

15. See, for example, Eric Hanushek, "Evidence, Politics, and the Class Size Debate," in *The Class Size Debate*, edited by Lawrence Mishel and Richard Rothstein (Washington: Economic Policy Institute, 2002), p. 61. Eric Hanushek, *Some Findings from an Independent Investigation of the Tennessee STAR Experiment and from Other Investigations of Class Size Effects* (Cambridge, Mass.: National Bureau of Economic Research, March 1999), pp. 40–41.

16. Brad Hayward and Jon Matthews, "$63 Billion Budget Set for Wilson Signature," *Sacramento Bee*, July 9, 1996, p. A1. Brad Hayward, "Wilson, Lawmakers Reach Budget Deal," *Sacramento Bee*, July 4, 1996, p. A1. Brad Hayward, "Budget Wars on Smaller Classes," *Sacramento Bee*, March 3, 1997, p. A1.

17. E-mail from George W. Bohrnstedt, one of the authors of the only major study of the California program (cited in note 19), April 17, 2006.

18. In fact, schools had to begin the year with eighteen or nineteen so that they could accommodate the extra student or two who might transfer in before the year was over. Beginning with twenty and ending with twenty-two in any particular class would cost the school the extra funding.

19. Brian M. Stecher and George W. Bohrnstedt, *Class Size Reduction in California: Findings from 1999–2000 and 2000–01* (CSR Research Consortium, 2001), summary of findings, p. 1. This was one of the early phases of the study discussed at greater length below (www.classize.org/summary/99-01/index.htm [October 2006]). Pamela Burdman, "Hiring of Teachers to Get Less Strict: New Law Will Fill Job Market Created by Smaller Class Sizes," *San Francisco Chronicle*, July 20, 1997.

20. On the Los Angeles request, see "Waiver of California Basic Skills Test Requirement," motions/resolutions presented to the Los Angeles City Board of Education, July 8, 1996 (www.lausd.k12.ca.us/lausd/board/secretary/entire-year1996.pdf [October 2006]). Los Angeles is not unique in recruiting abroad. New York City has brought teachers from overseas as well. On other problems of staffing, see Venise Wagner, "Scrambling to Shrink Classes," *San Francisco Examiner*, August 20, 1996. Phone interview with Gaston, May 10, 2006. Center for the Future of Teaching and Learning, *The Status of the Teaching Profession, 2001* (Santa Cruz, Calif., 2001), pp. 5–9. Center for the Future of Teaching and Learning, *The Status of the Teaching Profession, 2005* (Santa Cruz, Calif., 2005). Fact Sheet 3 (www.cftl.org).

21. Among them, Claremont, Irvine, Livermore, Riverside, and Capistrano. In some cases, it may have been a "Washington Monument" strategy, sometimes successful, to get community support and funds to retain CSR. Marcie Grover, "Budget Blues: We Are Not Alone," *Vacaville Reporter*, March 17, 2002. "District Cuts," *Protect Proposition 98* (California Education Coalition, 2005) (www.protectstudents.org/district_cuts.html [October 2006]). According to state Department of Education officials, only four districts dropped the program completely. E-mail from Hilary McLean, a state department communications official, February 9, 2006. See also Stecher and Bohrnstedt, *Class Size Reduction in California*, p. 5.

22. George W. Bohrnstedt and Brian M. Stecher, eds., *The Capstone Report: What We Have Learned about Class Size Reduction in California*, CSR Research Consortium (Sacramento: California Department of Education, September 2002), p. 7. Much of this final report restated the conclusions of the findings in the earlier reports.

23. Bohrnstedt and Stecher, eds., *The Capstone Report*; "Coalition Battles to Preserve Class Size Reduction," *California Educator* 7, no. 8 (May 2003) (www.cta.org/media/publications/educator/archives/2003/200305_index [November 2006]).

24. Interview with Hein, May 10, 2006.

25. Bohrnstedt and Stecher, *Capstone Report*, p. 6.

26. Ibid., p. 10.

27. Alex Molnar and others, "2000–01 Evaluation Results of the Student Achievement Guarantee in Education (SAGE) Program" (Madison: Wisconsin Department of Education, January 2002) (www.asu.edu/educ/epsl/sage.htm [October 2006]). "Elizabeth Burmaster: SAGE Bridges Achievement Gap," press release (Madison: Wisconsin Department of Education, January 21, 2002).

28. The question was raised again recently by Saul Cooperman, the former education commissioner in New Jersey, and by others. Cooperman would let class sizes increase in all classes above grade three in order to get better teachers. Saul Cooperman, "Increase Class Size—And Pay Teachers More," *Education Week*, November 2, 2005, p. 40. Jay Mathews, "The New Reverse Class Struggle," *Washington Post*, February 14, 2006, p. A-8. But why not discriminate among classes even in the primary grades in order to concentrate resources—and attract the best teachers—where they are most needed?

29. Tina Nguyen, "Many Private School Students Switch to Public System," *Los Angeles Times*, October 28, 1996, p. A3. Interview with O'Connell, February 16, 2006, reconfirmed by O'Connell, April 12, 2006.

30. Fatih Unlu, "California Class Size Reduction Reform: New Findings from the NAEP," Princeton University, Department of Economics, November 2005 (www.princeton.edu/~funlu/California_CSR_Fatih_Unlu.pdf [October 2006]).

31. E-mail from Bohrnstedt, February 7, 2006, and April 17, 2006. Bohrnstedt also drew a sharp distinction between the Tennessee study—"the best we have as far as the potential effects of class size"—and California's program: "First, they had a surplus of teachers, we had a shortage; second, the race/ethnic distributions are very different; third, teachers were randomly assigned—that's huge compared to teachers self-selecting themselves in schools."

32. A $2.6 million study funded by the Gates, Hewlett, Irvine, and Stuart foundations to determine what it would cost to provide adequate resources for California's schools is now getting under way. But in response to questions at a press conference formally announcing the research, which is designed to consider efficiency in funding as well, leaders of the study indicated that they would not examine the cost-effectiveness of existing programs, even major ones like CSR. Interviews with various members of the research group and some of its foundation sponsors, March and April 2006. See also "Getting Down to Facts: A Research Project to Inform Solutions to California's Educational Problems," Stanford University, n.d. (www.mikemcmahon.info/factssummary.pdf [October 2006]); Mitchell Landsberg, "Study to Examine Public Schools," *Los Angeles Times*, March 31, 2006.

33. That is hardly unique to education. Criminologists have long argued that there may be more effective ways to use criminal justice funds than simply to impose longer sentences on felons. But in times of intense anxiety about crime, those arguments are swamped by demands for tougher punishment.

34. Hart's and Bishop's remarks were made at the conference The Effects of School Size and Class Size, Brown Center on Education Policy, May 22–23, 2006.

35. Stecher and Bohrnstedt, *Class Size Reduction in California*, p. 8.

International Evidence on Expenditures and Class Size: A Review

LUDGER WÖßMANN

In the United States, evidence abounds on the effects of expenditures and class size on student achievement, but often it is controversial.[1] In other parts of the world, hard evidence is not as easy to come by, mostly because of data limitations. But over the years, testing agencies have started to collect data on student performance and family background and on school resources in countries around the world, allowing a look at the association between school resources and student achievement in different international settings. This paper reviews what can be learned from international student achievement tests such as the Third International Mathematics and Science Study (TIMSS) and Programme for International Student Assessment (PISA) exams in terms of the effects of expenditures and class size on student achievement.

Such evidence obviously is of great interest to countries that lack a national data set that allows for empirical analysis, and for many developed countries, evidence comparable to that in the U.S. literature is largely absent. That is true particularly for countries in western Europe; Psacharopoulos claims that "more research has been done on the economics of education in developing countries than in Europe."[2] The poor state of European research on educational production is especially disappointing because European evidence would seem to be much more directly comparable to U.S. evidence than would evidence from developing countries, given the relative levels of economic development and educational attainment of the countries involved.[3]

The international evidence is also of interest in discussions of the U.S. education system. Because the education systems and levels of educational expenditures in other countries differ from those in the United States, U.S. observers can learn whether resource effects would differ in a differently structured system. Observing resource effects in countries with different levels and distributions of expenditures may also help to distinguish between varying explanations for the U.S. evidence: for example, between technical explanations based on diminishing returns to resource inputs and economic explanations based on the lack of incentives to use resources to enhance student learning effectively.[4] Also, as discussed toward the end of this paper, the controversial results from different U.S. studies may in part reflect true heterogeneity in the effect of resources, in that resources may matter in some circumstances but less so in others. Again, the international evidence may prove useful in testing for such heterogeneity, estimating resource effects on comparable data in different countries.

A final motivation to look at the international evidence stems from the fact that test scores on previous international cognitive achievement tests conducted between the mid-1960s and early 1990s have been found to be strongly associated with a country's subsequent economic growth and level of economic development.[5] That empirical evidence supports recent theories of economic growth that stress the importance of human capital.[6]

It should be emphasized at the outset that this paper is a review of results from several previous studies on the international evidence on expenditures and class size and that it aims to be both brief and nontechnical. Therefore I present only the main results of leading studies on the topic, discussing technicalities only insofar as it is absolutely necessary to understand the results. In the trade-off between brevity and detail, the review leans strongly toward brevity. For technical details and additional robustness checks, the interested reader is referred to the original sources.

The paper first reviews aggregate international evidence on the association between educational expenditures and student performance and then international student-level evidence on the effects of class size. The aggregate evidence considers variation in expenditures and performance both across countries and over time. The micro-evidence presents results of conventional estimates and two quasi-experimental strategies to identify class-size effects—one based on natural cohort fluctuations, the other on rule-induced discontinuities—implemented by using the international data in many countries. The paper closes with a brief analysis of the association between teacher quality and class-size effects, as well as brief conclusions.

The Aggregate Picture

This section presents the aggregate picture of the association between educational expenditures and student performance. It starts with a cross-country comparison and continues with a look at country-level variation over time.

Expenditures and Performance across Countries

Do the top-performing countries on international student achievement tests systematically spend more on their school systems than countries that perform at the bottom? Figure 1 presents the association between spending level and math performance on the latest international test, the 2003 PISA exam, which is conducted by the Organization for Economic Cooperation and Development (OECD). The result is well known from several previous international comparative tests: countries with higher educational expenditures do *not* systematically perform better in cross-country comparisons.

The OECD uses figure 1 to conclude that there is a positive relationship between expenditures and student performance, because there is a weak statistical significance when all countries are considered and other effects are ignored (corresponding to the weakly upward sloping regression line in figure 1).[7] However, a simple look at the figure reveals that that conclusion is hard to maintain. Obviously, this very weak positive relationship depends solely on the fact that Mexico—and to a lesser extent Greece—has low levels of both expenditures and performance, and there certainly are other reasons for the weak performance of these countries. Therefore, once we control for a country's per capita GDP (which might be seen as a proxy for average socioeconomic status), the cross-country association between student performance and expenditures loses any statistical significance (t statistic = 0.18) and even turns negative. To depict that in a very simple manner: there is no relationship whatsoever between expenditures and performance when we simply omit Mexico and Greece from the picture (see the horizontal regression line in figure 1). Statistically, differences in expenditures can explain nothing of the international variance in student performance (the R^2 of the regression line is 0.01). On average, countries with high educational expenditures perform at the same level as countries with low expenditures.

This picture, disillusioning for advocates of education policies focused on expenditure increases, was also evident in previous international student tests like the TIMSS.[8] In addition, taking into account other determining factors does not change the general conclusion, even when numerous family back-

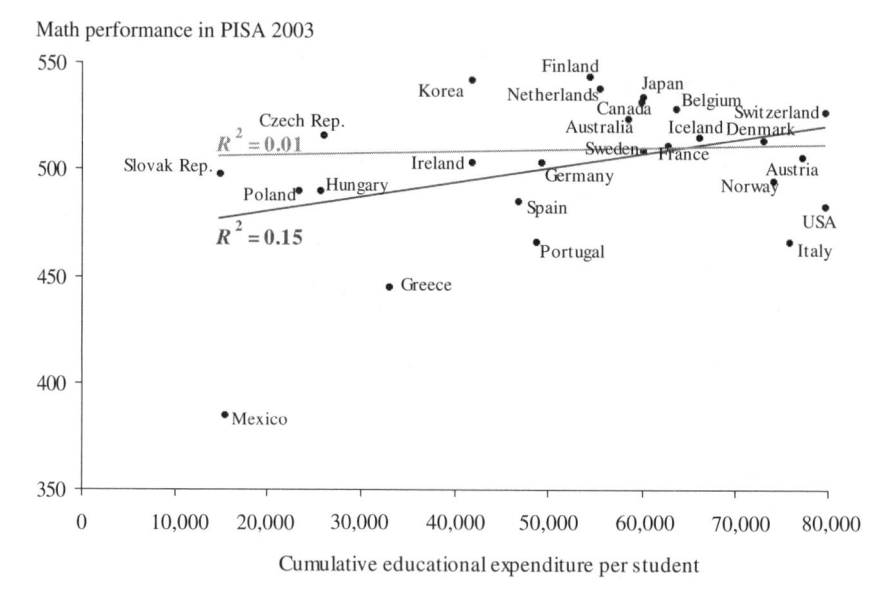

Figure 1. Expenditure per Student and Student Performance across Countries[a]

Math performance in PISA 2003

[Scatter plot showing math performance vs. cumulative educational expenditure per student for various countries. Two regression lines shown with $R^2 = 0.01$ and $R^2 = 0.15$. Countries plotted include: Finland, Korea, Netherlands, Japan, Canada, Belgium, Switzerland, Czech Rep., Australia, Iceland, Denmark, Slovak Rep., Sweden, France, Ireland, Germany, Austria, Poland, Hungary, Norway, Spain, USA, Portugal, Italy, Greece, Mexico. X-axis: Cumulative educational expenditure per student, ranging 0 to 80,000.]

Source: Organization for Economic Cooperation and Development, *Learning for Tomorrow's World: First Results from PISA 2003* (Paris: 2004), pp. 102 and 358, as well as author's calculations.

a. Association between average math performance in PISA 2003 and cumulative expenditure on educational institutions per student between ages six and fifteen, in U.S. dollars, converted by purchasing power parities.

ground and school features (including instruction time) are considered in cross-country student-level microeconometric regressions.[9]

Expenditure per student is an encompassing measure of inputs that considers not only the personnel costs but also the material costs of education. However, international comparisons of expenditures are hampered by the problem of choosing an appropriate exchange rate (conversion by purchasing power parity was chosen for figure 1). Because personnel costs make up more than three-quarters of total expenditures in nearly all countries, class size lends itself especially well to being used in international comparisons as a nonmonetary input measure that determines a large part of total expenditures. However, using class size instead of expenditure per student results in the same general picture shown in figure 1.

Expenditures and Performance over Time

Does the picture change when one looks at changes in expenditures over time within individual countries? As depicted in figure 2, an in-depth study of

Figure 2. Expenditure per Student and Student Performance over Time[a]

Change in student performance (1970 = 100)

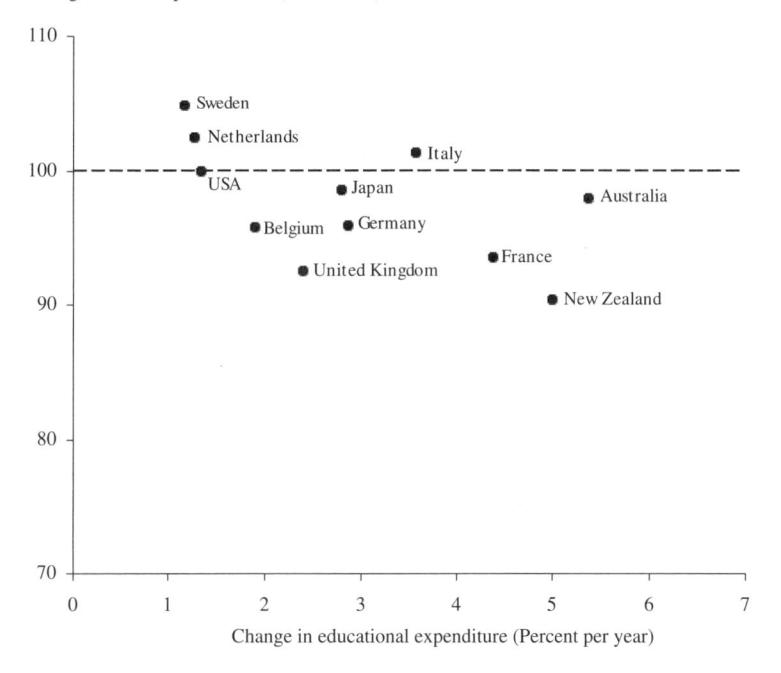

```
110 ┐
        ● Sweden
          ● Netherlands
                              ● Italy
100 ┼──●─────────────────────────────────────
       USA       ● Japan
              ● Belgium  ● Germany                    ● Australia
                              ● France
                ● United Kingdom
 90 ┤                              ● New Zealand




 80 ┤



 70 ┼────┬────┬────┬────┬────┬────┬────┬────
     0    1    2    3    4    5    6    7
         Change in educational expenditure (Percent per year)
```

Source: Ludger Wößmann, *Schooling and the Quality of Human Capital* (Berlin: Springer, 2002), p. 106.
a. Association between change in student performance (1994–95 relative to 1970) and change in educational expenditure (average annual rate of change of real educational expenditure per student between 1970 and 1994–95, in percent).

changes over time in educational expenditures and student performance has shown that educational expenditure per student has increased substantially in real terms in all OECD countries considered between the early 1970s and the mid-1990s.[10] The figures on expenditure increases already take into account the so-called "cost disease" effect of the service sector by using appropriate price deflators for schooling based on price changes in other service sectors. With an average annual increase of 1.3 percent over the twenty-five-year span, the increase in real expenditure per student in the United States is at the lower end. However, over twenty-five years, that still amounts to an increase of 40 percent. In Germany, which ranks in the middle of the countries, an average annual increase of 2.8 percent means that the real financial resources available per student have more than doubled over the same time span. In many of the countries, the expenditure increases are founded to a large extent on a decline in average student-teacher ratios over time.

How did that burst in expenditures affect students' cognitive skills? While comparing student performance levels over such a long time span is not easy, analyses of international performance comparisons have been performed in 1970 and 1994–95, and the comparisons can be linked over time using U.S. national data because the U.S. has participated in both comparisons and because the U.S. has an intertemporally comparable national test. The results suggest that nothing substantial happened to average student performance in the countries considered. If anything, student performance in math and science slightly decreased in most countries, particularly in those countries that had the largest increases in expenditures. As Gundlach, Gmelin, and Wößmann put it, constant output with increasing input implies a "decline of schooling productivity in OECD countries,"[11] and the pattern is even more severe in most other countries than in the United States, whose pattern Hanushek described as "the productivity collapse in schools."[12] In any case, the immense increases in expenditures over time did not go hand in hand with an increase in average student performance. A similar pattern of fading productivity has been found for several East Asian countries from the early 1980s to the mid-1990s.[13]

One potential explanation for this bivariate pattern might be that, on average, students' family backgrounds have deteriorated. Today's students may lack many of the basic capabilities required for successful education and thus may be increasingly expensive to educate. Such effects may play a significant role in countries that have had a large inflow of immigrant students or rising levels of poverty. But there also are counterbalancing effects. On average, parents in the countries considered enjoy higher incomes and are better educated than parents of twenty-five years ago; the average number of children per family also has declined. Hence children may actually begin their schooling with better basic capabilities than before. Indeed, a study by Grissmer and colleagues showed that in the United States, the net effect of trends in different family background features meant that students were better prepared for learning than before.[14] That makes the long-run trend of increased expenditures with constant performance more severe.

Microeconometric Evidence

The evidence reviewed in this section goes beyond the aggregate picture to analyze the microdata of one of the international achievement tests, the Third International Mathematics and Science Study, at the student level. It starts with conventional estimations of the association between class size and student performance within many countries and a discussion of possible biases in those estimates. It then goes on to two quasi-experimental identification strategies that try to extract the causal effect of class size on student performance in each of the countries.

Conventional Estimates and Endogeneity Bias

Better-performing countries did not spend more on education, and increases in spending did not go hand in hand with increases in performance. But despite the aggregate picture, is it not true that students who are taught in smaller classes learn more? Strangely, this important question has hardly been analyzed empirically in many countries. In the United States, hundreds of empirical estimations of the association between students' test performance and several measures of their class and school resource endowments, in particular class size, have been performed since the 1960s.[15] In the vast majority, the estimations reach the same conclusion as seen in the aggregate international picture: they find hardly any evidence of significant effects of better resource endowments—particularly smaller class sizes—on student performance.

CONVENTIONAL ESTIMATES OF CLASS-SIZE EFFECTS. To obtain comparable evidence for other countries, we used data from the TIMSS test conducted in 1995 by the International Association for the Evaluation of Educational Achievement (IEA), which lends itself particularly well to such an analysis. While PISA tested only a few students in each classroom of a school, TIMSS has the advantage of testing a complete seventh-grade class and a complete eighth-grade class in each school. Having test data for two grades also allows for implementation of a specific quasi-experimental estimation method, as discussed below. For each country, the data sets constitute representative samples of the country's seventh- and eighth-graders.

While similar evidence is available for other countries, in particular in East Asia and eastern Europe, the following presentation focuses on evidence from countries in western Europe, which seems most readily comparable to evidence from the United States.[16] The data sets used here encompass between 3,730 and 11,722 students in each country, from 187 to 613 classes in 95 to 327 schools in each country.[17] Average class sizes range between 19.6 and 28.4 in the countries considered. TIMSS test scores were scaled so as to have an international mean of 500 and an international standard deviation of 100 across all the participating countries. The analyses presented here focus on performance in math, which is generally viewed as being most easily compared across countries; math performance also has been found to be most strongly related to economic productivity.[18] TIMSS data for science are of lower quality because different science subjects are taught by different teachers and sometimes in different classes in many countries. On average across the European countries, the test performance difference between students in seventh grade and students in eighth grade is 32.2 points in math. Because this grade-level equivalent shows how much students learn on average during one year, it can serve as a useful benchmark to assess the size of different estimated effects.

Conventional models that estimate the association between student performance and class size do so in least squares regressions that control for family background effects.[19] The family background controls ensure that the estimated association is not driven by observable background differences; for example, children of highly educated parents may tend to attend schools with lower class sizes and may at the same time perform better for reasons linked to their family background. Because of the rich data contained in the TIMSS background questionnaires, we can control for family background in a particularly encompassing way at the individual student level.[20] The student-level microeconometric regressions produce statistically significant *positive* coefficients on class size in twelve of seventeen western European countries, and the point estimate is also positive in all but one of the other countries.[21] That is, in this conventional analysis, student performance in bigger classes is not worse, it is even *better* than in smaller classes.

While data limitations have precluded extensive international comparative work on class-size effects, a few other studies exist that report similar conventional estimates on international data. An early influential study by Heyneman and Loxley used a TIMSS predecessor study, the second International Science Study, in addition to several national studies to conclude that there was somewhat more evidence for resource effects in developing countries than in the United States.[22] That result could not be corroborated by Hanushek and Luque, who also used the TIMSS data.[23]

ENDOGENEITY BIAS. The problem with conventional estimates is that class size is not only a cause but also a consequence of student performance or of factors related to student performance (figure 3). A whole host of features may lead to the joint and simultaneous determination of class size and student performance, making class size endogenous to student performance; therefore there may be a significant association between the two without there being a causal class-size effect.

For example, schools may reduce class sizes for poorly performing students and policymakers may design compensatory funding schemes for schools with a large share of students from poor backgrounds.[24] In both cases, class

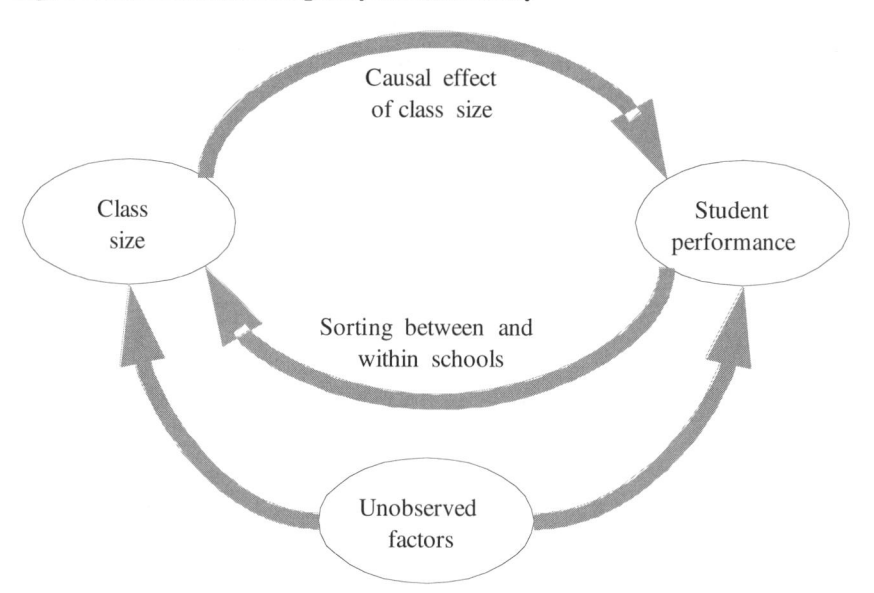

Figure 3. The Problem of Endogeneity and Simultaneity

sizes are allocated in a compensatory manner, which leads to a positive bias in the least squares coefficient on class size. In contrast, policymakers may also have high-performing students taught in special small classes, to support elite performance. Likewise, parents who are especially concerned about the education of their children may both make residential choices to ensure that their children are taught in schools with relatively small classes and support their children in many other ways, leading them to be extraordinarily high performers. In these cases, class sizes are allocated in a reinforcing manner, leading to a negative bias in least squares estimates of class-size effects.

In short, parents, teachers, schools and administrators all make choices that might give rise to a noncausal association between class size and student performance even after controlling for family background. Therefore, observed class sizes may not be exogenous to student performance. Conventional estimates of class-size effects may suffer from endogeneity bias, the direction of which is ambiguous a priori.[25]

Identifying Class-Size Effects by Natural Cohort Fluctuations

To be able to draw causal conclusions, we have to distill the causal class-size effect from the total association between class size and student performance, which is at least partly driven by student sorting. To do so requires an empirical identification strategy that identifies variation in class size that is not driven by endogeneity or simultaneity but is exogenous to student performance.

THE IDENTIFICATION OF CAUSAL CLASS-SIZE EFFECTS. The literature proposes three basic possibilities to identify random or exogenous variation in class size. The first is to perform an explicit class-size experiment, in which random assignment of students to classes of different sizes guarantees exogeneity of the class-size variation. Unfortunately, such experimental data do not seem to be available on a large scale in Europe. Actually, Project STAR, performed in the 1980s in the U.S. state of Tennessee, seems to be the only available larger-scale class-size experiment.[26]

Therefore, only the other two identification strategies, which both pursue a quasi-experimental approach, remain for international evidence. Quasi-experimental strategies identify exogenous variation in class size evoked by so-called "natural" experiments. In such cases, econometric methods restrict the estimation of class-size effects to whatever part of the total class-size variation is exogenous to student performance. In principle, such estimations compare student performance in classes whose size differs for exogenous reasons, which then allows for causal conclusions on the size of the class-size effect. Two basic varieties of quasi-experiments on class size have been proposed in the literature, and both have been implemented by using the international data.

The first quasi-experimental approach identifies causal class-size effects by using class-size variations caused by natural fluctuations in the size of subsequent student cohorts of a school.[27] In this case, the quasi-experiment consists of the idea that natural fluctuations in student enrollment lead to variations in average class size in two adjacent grades in the same school. These natural birth fluctuations around the cutoff date that splits students into different grade levels occur randomly, just as the assignments in an experiment into control and treatment groups occur randomly. Therefore, they lead to variation in class size that is driven neither by students' educational performance nor by other features that might jointly affect class size and student performance. That is, they lead to variation that is exogenous to student performance. If student performance is found to differ in classes that differ in size because of this "experimental" treatment, the difference can be attributed to a causal effect of class size.

Wößmann and West have developed a variant of this identification strategy that exploits specific features of the TIMSS database.[28] Due to the design of the TIMSS database, which tested two adjacent grades in each school, they were able to use only the variation between two adjacent grades in individual schools. That strategy aimed to exclude biases from nonrandom between-school and within-school sorting through a combination of school fixed effects and instrumental variables using grade-average class sizes as instruments.

The rationale of this approach is as follows. Any *between*-school sorting is eliminated in the first step by controlling for school fixed effects, which excludes any systematic between-school variation from the analysis. In effect, the estimate is based solely on class-size variation that exists within individual schools. Because the allocation of students to different classes in a grade also may take place nonrandomly within schools, *within*-school sorting is filtered out in the second step by instrumenting actual class size by the average class size in the relevant grade at each respective school. Through this method of instrumental-variable estimation, within-school variation in class size is used only insofar as it is caused by variation in average class size between the seventh and eighth grade of a school. Such variation is not affected by student sorting; it mainly reflects random fluctuations in birth-cohort size between the two grades in the catchment area of each school, which lead to fluctuations in average class size between the grades.[29]

Being exogenous to student performance, this random variation in class size can be used to identify the causal effect of class size on student performance. In a nutshell, causal class-size effects are identified by relating differences in the relative performance of students in seventh and eighth grade within individual schools to that part of the between-grade difference in class size in the school that reflects between-grade differences in average class size. This identification strategy is designed to take advantage of certain unique features of the TIMSS database. The use of school-level fixed effects is made possible by the fact that the study sample includes more than one class from each school. Using each school's average class size in each grade as an instrument imposes the additional requirement of obtaining data on achievement, actual class size, and grade-average class size for different grades taking part in the same achievement test. Among large-scale international studies of student achievement, the specific TIMSS test used here is the only database with this particular set of characteristics.

TWO EXAMPLES. Two graphics, for Singapore and Iceland, can illustrate the basic intuition behind this identification strategy even further.[30] As these examples are drawn for illustrative purposes only, they use data only at the classroom, not the student, level and they do not yet control for family background features. The scatter plot of class-average test scores against class size in the 268 classes tested in Singapore, depicted in the top panel of figure 4, indicates that students in larger classes performed better than students in smaller classes, as was the case in most European countries as well. Note that this positive correlation is not driven by outliers or nonlinearities; the association between class size and student performance appears to be quite linear. Interpreting this correlation as causation would lead to the counterintuitive conclusion that larger classes facilitate student learning. As argued above, however, this association between performance and class size is likely to be spurious, reflecting ability sorting of students between and within schools.

Next, for each school, we measured both the difference in average student performance between seventh and eighth grade and the difference in class size between seventh and eighth grade. This procedure, equivalent to including school fixed effects in a regression of student performance on class size, controls for the effects of between-school sorting, effectively removing any difference in the overall performance levels between schools. The remaining within-school variation in both test scores and class sizes is depicted in the middle panel of figure 4.[31] Although we once again observe a statistically significant positive correlation between performance differences and class size, the size of the positive correlation is substantially reduced. That reduction suggests that poorly performing students tend to be sorted into schools with smaller classes in Singapore.

However, this picture might still be distorted by various types of student sorting that occur within schools. The final step in the identification strategy, illustrated on the bottom panel of figure 4, eliminates any effects of within-school sorting by using only that part of the between-grade variation in actual class sizes that reflects variation in grade-average class sizes. We first regressed the between-grade difference in actual class size on the between-grade difference in grade-average class size (that is, we instrument actual class size by grade-average class size) and then used the predicted between-grade difference in class size for each school as the measure of the between-grade difference in class size on the horizontal axis. This scatter plot reflects the basic idea behind this quasi-experimental identification strategy: it relates that part of the between-grade difference in class size within each school that reflects the difference in the average class size of the two grades in the school to the between-grade difference in student performance. Having eliminated the effects of student sorting both between and within schools, we interpret the bottom panel of figure 4 to be a picture of the causal effect of class size on student performance. The picture suggests that class size has no causal effect on student performance in math in Singapore. Rather, weaker students seem to be consistently placed in smaller classes, both between and

Ludger Wößmann

Figure 4. Class Size and Math Performance in Singapore

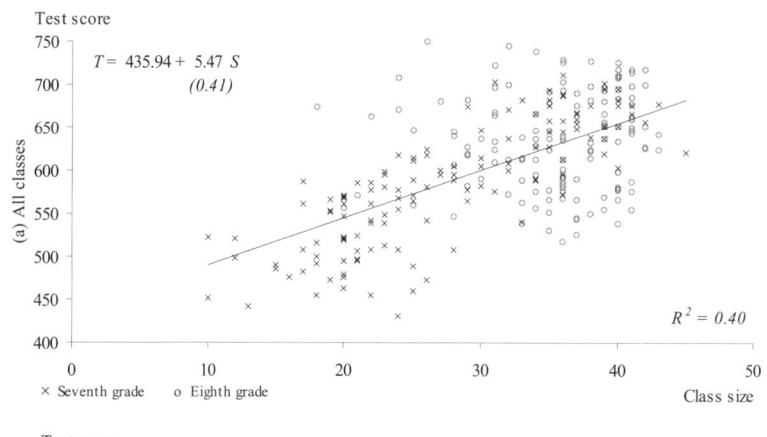

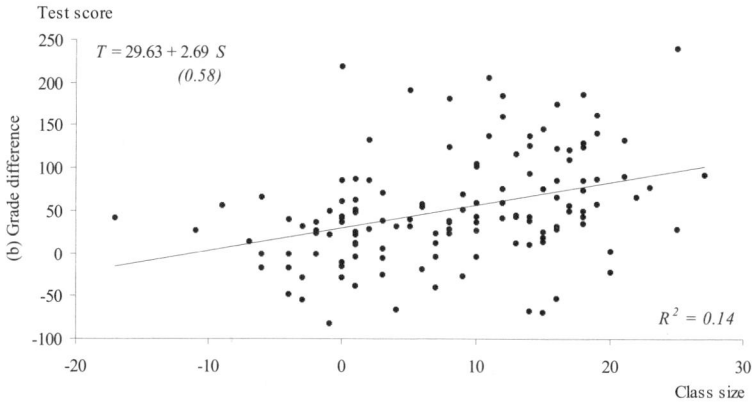

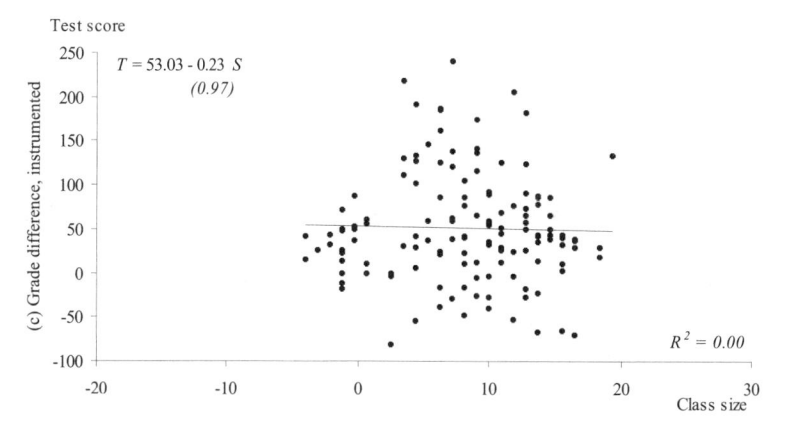

(a) All classes: $T = 435.94 + 5.47\ S$, (0.41), $R^2 = 0.40$
× Seventh grade   o Eighth grade

(b) Grade difference: $T = 29.63 + 2.69\ S$, (0.58), $R^2 = 0.14$

(c) Grade difference, instrumented: $T = 53.03 - 0.23\ S$, (0.97), $R^2 = 0.00$

Source: Ludger Wößmann and Martin R. West, "Class-Size Effects in School Systems around the World: Evidence from Between-Grade Variation in TIMSS," Kiel Working Paper No. 1099 (Kiel: Kiel Institute for World Economics, 2002).

within schools.

Figure 5 depicts the same three scatter plots for Iceland. The top panel of figure 5 shows that class size and math performance in Iceland are uncorrelated. Excluding between-school differences in the middle panel again reveals no obvious association between class size and performance. The lack of a substantial change in the slope of the trend lines in the first two panels suggests that in Iceland, unlike in Singapore, students of lower ability are not systematically sorted into schools with smaller classes. The bottom panel of figure 5 again provides the closest approximation of the quasi-experimental identification strategy, which excludes any sorting effects. This final picture reveals a statistically significant inverse association between class size and student performance: smaller classes seem to cause better math performance in Iceland.[32] Although the simple correlation between class size and student performance in Iceland suggests that they are unrelated, this observation cannot be taken at face value. The quasi-experimental identification strategy reveals that smaller classes do in fact enhance students' learning in math in Iceland. The two examples confirm that it can be highly misleading to take conventional estimates of class-size effects for causal effects. However, by applying an identification strategy that accounts for endogeneity, causal class-size effects can be distilled.

MICROECONOMETRIC RESULTS. The quasi-experimental identification strategy illustrated by these examples has been implemented by running student-level regressions. The main results of this and of the second quasi-experimental identification strategies are depicted in figure 6.[33] Both implementations control for the host of family background characteristics mentioned above as well as for peer effects, in terms of the mean performance of each student's classmates, to exclude bias from peer sorting.[34] Results based on the first quasi-experimental strategy are indicated by natural cohort fluctuations (NCF). Figure 6 presents results only for countries for which the estimates of the rather demanding estimations—which both include school fixed effects and instrument the class-size variable—are precise enough to warrant a reasonable assessment and for which additional test statistics exclude weak-instrument problems.

As is evident from figure 6, the statistically significant positive association between class size and student performance of the conventional estimation method vanishes in every country when only class-size variation induced by natural cohort fluctuations is considered. At the same time, there is only one country, Iceland, for which the NCF estimation yields a negative estimate that is statistically significantly different from zero. That is, in Iceland, students per-

Figure 5. Class Size and Math Performance in Iceland

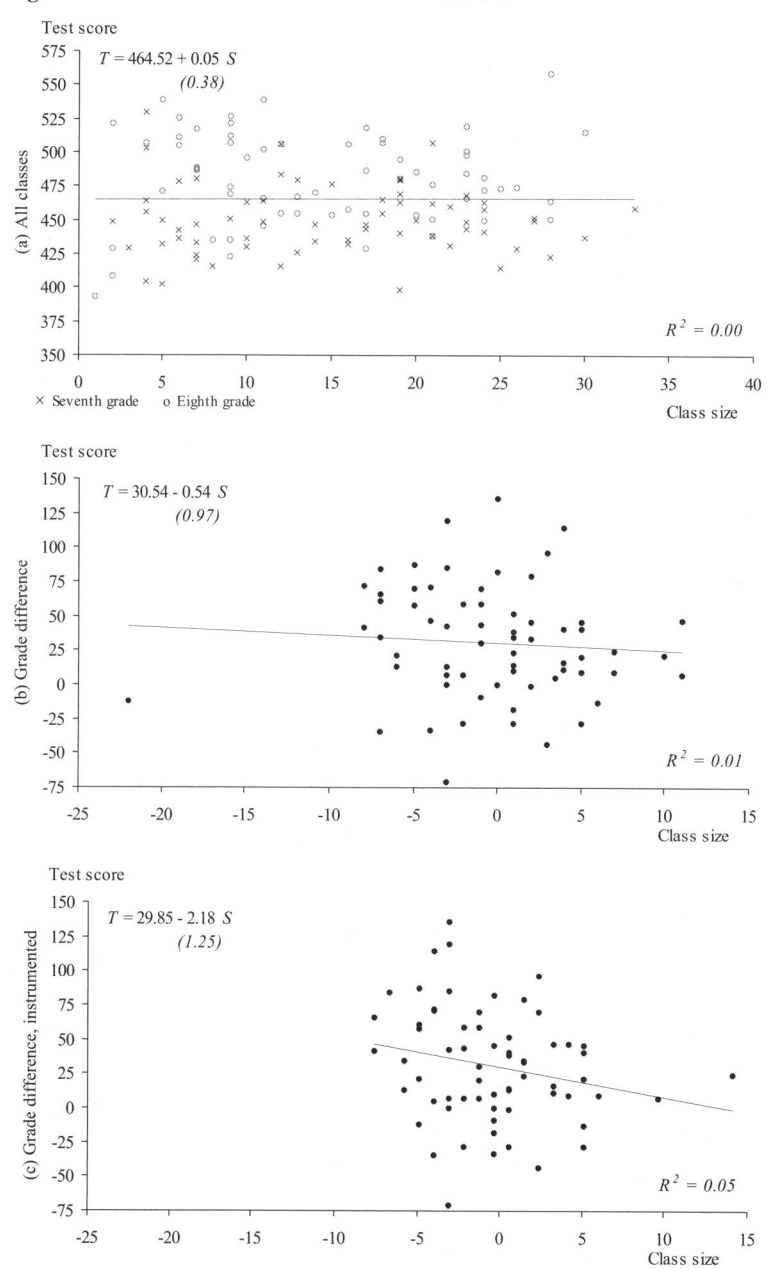

(a) All classes: $T = 464.52 + 0.05\ S$ (0.38), $R^2 = 0.00$

× Seventh grade   o Eighth grade

(b) Grade difference: $T = 30.54 - 0.54\ S$ (0.97), $R^2 = 0.01$

(c) Grade difference, instrumented: $T = 29.85 - 2.18\ S$ (1.25), $R^2 = 0.05$

Source: Ludger Wößmann and Martin R. West, "Class-Size Effects in School Systems around the World: Evidence from Between-Grade Variation in TIMSS," Kiel Working Paper No. 1099 (Kiel: Kiel Institute for World Economics, 2002).

form better when they are taught in smaller classes. In most countries, the point estimate is rather close to zero.

To assess the size and precision of the estimates, we can use the estimate of the class-size effect that Krueger obtained for the Project STAR experiment in Tennessee as a benchmark.[35] Krueger found that a 10 percent reduction in class size for one year led to an improvement in test scores of about 10 percent of a standard deviation in grades K-3. In our case, 10 percent of an international standard deviation in TIMSS test scores equals 10 test-score points, so that a coefficient on log class size comparable in size to Krueger's estimate would equal roughly −100. Krueger also presented a rough cost-benefit analysis suggesting that this effect size would approximately equalize the economic costs and benefits of the class-size reduction in the U.S. setting, although others have called the soundness of this cost-benefit analysis into question.[36] Furthermore, comparative estimates of the returns to education in the labor market suggest that the benefits of education seem to be lower in nearly all western European countries than in the United States, so that the class-size effect might have to be even higher in Europe to warrant the costs (although the costs might also be somewhat lower in most of Europe).[37]

If we still use the effect size of −100 as a benchmark for possible cost efficiency, the bands of 95 percent statistical confidence presented in figure 6 reveal that in the majority of cases, effects of the size found in Project STAR can be rejected for representative samples of students in lower secondary education in western European countries. In six western European education systems—in Flemish Belgium, French Belgium, Germany, Iceland, the Netherlands, and Scotland—the NCF estimates are precise enough to reject a causal class-size effect of the size found in Project STAR with 95 percent statistical confidence. In two additional countries—Greece and Ireland—such an effect can be rejected with 90 percent statistical confidence, and in Denmark, such an effect is rejected in a specification without peer controls. So even in Iceland, the only country with a statistically significant class-size effect, the estimate is relatively small and precise enough to reject a magnitude that would be cost-effective. The effect size in Iceland of −53 means that for every 10 percent reduction in class size, students perform 5 test-score points (or 5 percent of an international standard deviation, or less than one-sixth of an international grade-level equivalent) higher.

Additional specification tests support the finding that the NCF estimates can be interpreted as causal class-size effects. While the variation exploited by the NCF strategy is immune from the effects of the most obvious between-school and within-grade forms of sorting, in principle there may be other

Figure 6. Quasi-Experimental Estimates of Class-Size Effects[a]

Estimated class-size effect

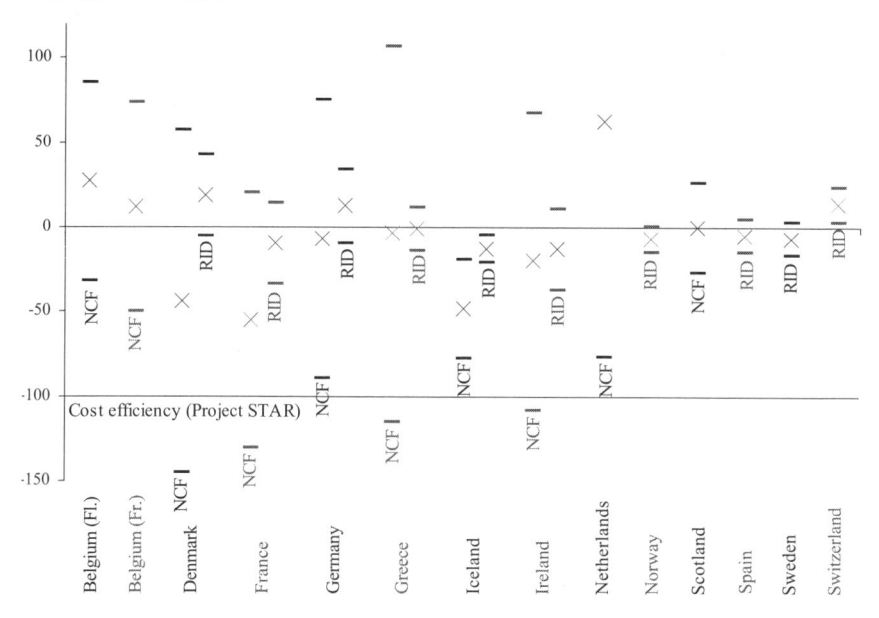

[Figure displaying point estimates (crosses) and confidence intervals for class-size effects across countries: Belgium (Fl.), Belgium (Fr.), Denmark, France, Germany, Greece, Iceland, Ireland, Netherlands, Norway, Scotland, Spain, Sweden, Switzerland. Estimates are labeled NCF or RID. A horizontal line indicates "Cost efficiency (Project STAR)".]

Source: Based on results presented in Ludger Wößmann, "Educational Production in Europe," *Economic Policy* 20, no. 43 (2005): 445–504.

a. The crosses indicate the point estimate of the effect of log class size on TIMSS math performance. The lines above and below the crosses indicate the interval of plus or minus two standard errors, which corresponds roughly to a statistical significance band of 95 percent confidence. The straight line replicates the class-size effect found in Project STAR, which might be taken as a rough indicator of cost efficiency. Quasi-experimental identification strategies: NCF = natural cohort fluctuation; RID = rule-induced discontinuities.

sources of endogeneity that are not perfectly captured. In essence, anything that sorts students or teachers between grades within individual schools in a systematic way may still bias the NCF estimates. However, Wößmann and West provide several specification tests of the NCF identification strategy that suggest that any remaining endogeneity biases are likely to be of second-order magnitude.[38] For example, they show that there are no systematic differences at all in the observable characteristics of students or teachers between the two grades in schools in which one of the two adjacent grades had substantially larger average class sizes than the other; that there are no systematic differences in the estimated class-size effects between expanding, stable, and contracting schools; and that there are no systematic differences in the estimated class-size effects between countries where seventh grade is the first grade of a particular school and countries where it is not so that grade-average class sizes might have been adjusted based on schools' experience with the particular students.

Thus, in addition to the peer controls already contained in the estimations reported here, the additional specification tests suggest that the variation exploited by the NCF specification is not affected by biases from between-grade sorting. Therefore, the NCF results suggest that class sizes are not a leading causal effect of student performance in the western European countries considered. Not a single point estimate comes close to the Project STAR estimate, and in most cases, such an effect size can be significantly rejected. Using the same identification strategy, Wößmann and West find that sizable class-size effects can also be rejected in other countries around the world, namely Canada, the Czech Republic, Romania, Singapore, and Slovenia.[39]

Identifying Class-Size Effects by Rule-Induced Discontinuities

The robustness of these results can be checked by a second quasi-experimental identification strategy to estimate class-size effects based on exogenous class-size variations.

THE SECOND IDENTIFICATION STRATEGY. This strategy, proposed (and implemented by using Israeli data) by Angrist and Lavy, builds on the idea that many countries have maximum class-size rules.[40] These rules prescribe that class sizes may not be larger than X. As long as enrollment in a grade is less than or equal to X, the class size equals X. But as soon as grade enrollment grows to $X + 1$, the school will open a second class, so that the average class size in the grade drops from X to $(X + 1) \div 2$. For example, if the maximum class size is 28, then the class size in a grade with an enrollment of 28 will be 28, while the average class size in a grade with an enrollment of 29 will be only $29 \div 2 = 14.5$. Similarly, the average class size at a grade enrollment of 56 will be $56 \div 2 = 28$, but at an enrollment of 57, it will be $57 \div 3 = 19$.

Thus maximum class-size rules induce a nonlinear association between the number of students in a grade of a school and average class size. As an example, figure 7 depicts the ensuing jigsaw-like pattern between grade enrollment and average class size for two countries with effective maximum class-size rules, Iceland and Norway. The dots in figure 7 plot the actual average class size in a grade against the total enrollment in the grade (averaging for all grades with the same enrollment), both observed in the TIMSS data. The straight lines in the figure depict the average class size that would be predicted by an uncompromising implementation of the maximum class-size rule—in these two countries, a rule of 28 students. The jigsaw-like shape that the maximum class-size rule evokes is neatly reproduced by the actual average class sizes in the two countries.

Figure 7. Grade Enrollment and Class Size[a]

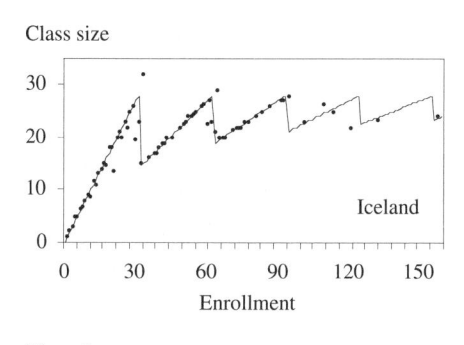

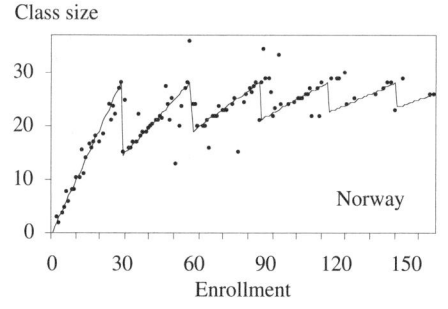

[Figure: Two scatter plots showing class size vs enrollment, one for Iceland and one for Norway, both with enrollment ranging 0-150 and class size 0-30, showing sawtooth patterns.]

Source: Ludger Wößmann, "Educational Production in Europe," *Economic Policy* 20, no. 43 (2005): 445–504.
a. Association between number of students at a grade level of a school and average class size in the grade, TIMSS data. Dots: actual association; lines: association predicted by a maximum class-size rule of twenty-eight students.

The apparent discontinuities in class size induced by maximum class-size rules can be exploited to identify causal class-size effects. Because the jumps in average class size are evoked solely by the rule, the induced class-size variation can be viewed as exogenous to students' educational performance. Again, the rule leads to what might be viewed as a "natural" experiment, so that the rule-prescribed class size based on grade enrollment may be a valid instrument for identifying exogenous variation in class size. Thus the empirical estimations use only the nonlinear fluctuations in average class size, shown in figure 7, which are induced by the rule. While there are always deviations from the rules, the TIMSS data reveal that ten western European education systems seem to implement national maximum class-size rules reasonably strictly and with enough sharpness to enable an empirical implementation of this identification strategy.[41]

MICROECONOMETRIC RESULTS. Results of this second quasi-experimental strategy, implemented in the ten countries that apparently follow class-size rules, are again depicted in figure 6, indicated by RID (rule-induced discontinuities). As is apparent, the RID estimates are very precisely estimated, so that the confidence bands are considerably narrower than for the other specification. In fact, they are of the same order of magnitude that Hoxby called "rather precisely estimated zeros."[42] In all ten countries, the possibility that the estimated class-size effects are as large as Krueger's estimate for Project STAR can be rejected with more than 99 percent statistical confidence. The RID specification yields two estimates of class-size effects that are statistically significantly negative: a marginally significant one in Norway and a highly significant one in Iceland—the same country for which the NCF specifications above also led to statistically significant estimates. The Swiss estimate is counterintuitive, being statistically significantly positive, but the statistical significance vanishes in an extensive specification with additional peer family background controls. All other countries yield estimates that are not statistically significantly different from zero.

Wößmann shows that these results are robust to several specification tests.[43] For example, the discontinuity evoked by the maximum class-size rule allows for controlling for any continuous association between grade enrollment and student performance. Adding the enrollment in the specific grade and its squared term as additional controls does not lead to substantive changes in the results (the Norwegian estimate now drops below standard levels of statistical significance, while the Spanish estimate slightly surpasses them). A general problem of implementing the rule discontinuity approach by using the whole sample of students is that some of the identification comes from observations that are far off the discontinuities. When applying the specification to a "discontinuity sample" of students whose grade enrollment is within a margin of plus or minus 5 or 6 students of the rule-based discontinuities, the instrument gets weak in about half the countries, while results remain robust in the remainder. Also, excluding especially large schools in each country (of a size three or four times the maximum class size) because the size of the induced discontinuity in class size is smaller when the grade enrollment is larger does not lead to a substantive change in results.

However, as discussed by Wößmann, some reservations remain with this second quasi-experimental identification strategy.[44] In particular, intentional exploitations of the rule by systematic between- and within-school choices might lead to remaining endogeneity in the rule discontinuity approach. Thus, there is the possibility that parents and schools can "play the system": parents who are particularly keen to ensure low class sizes for their children may make their enrollment decisions—and heads of school their acceptance decisions—on the basis of expected class size, and those decisions may be related to student performance. Furthermore, in the particular implementation that uses the TIMSS data, the enrollment observation comes from the end of the school year, so enrollment changes occurring during the school year might lead to biases. Also, the rules that determine class size are not taken from explicitly written laws, but from observation of the actual pattern of class size and enrollment. The extent to which these remaining issues may affect the reported estimates remains an open issue.

Still, in the end both quasi-experimental identification strategies come to a very similar pattern of results. That the potentially remaining biases are of a different nature in the two cases adds confidence that any remaining bias in both strategies is actually of second-order magnitude; the provided estimates therefore can be viewed as reasonable estimates of the causal effect of class size in lower secondary education in the different countries considered. Whenever both the specification based on natural cohort fluctuations and the specification based on rule-induced discontinuities can identify effects in a country, the substantive result is the same for both strategies, stressing the consistency of results.

All in all, the two identification strategies come to the conclusion that class size does not seem to be a major force in shaping performance in lower secondary school in the countries considered. There is no single country for which any of the specifications detects a statistically significant and large class-size effect. Furthermore, in every case where a method leads to a reasonably precise estimate, an effect size as large as the one that Krueger found for the Project STAR experiment can be statistically significantly rejected. There is only one country, Iceland, where we can be confident that there are causal class-size effects. However, in both specifications the estimates are relatively small and estimated precisely enough to reject the possibility of a large effect. Therefore, even in Iceland, the significant but relatively small class-size effects may or may not warrant the large costs of class-size reductions.

Teacher Quality and Class-Size Effects

Although causal class-size effects seem to be very small at best in all the countries considered, there are still differences across countries. The international data allow exploiting this international heterogeneity in class-size effects in order to investigate why class-size effects may exist in some circumstances but not in others.[45] The international evidence shows that the estimated effect size does not vary systematically for children from differing family backgrounds or for countries with different levels of average performance, economic development, average class size, or educational spending.

By contrast, the existence of class-size effects does seem to be systematically associated with the salary and education level of the teaching force. In the different studies, class-size effects were detected only in countries with relatively low teacher salaries and education. The pattern is similar within countries in which the education level of teachers varies. In these countries, the estimated class-size effect tends to be larger in classes that are taught by teachers with lower education.

If higher wages attract more capable employees, paying teachers more on average should attract higher-quality teachers; if so, average teacher salary—as well as better teacher education—may serve as a proxy for average teacher capability. Thus, the results may be interpreted as showing that relatively capable teachers do as well when teaching large classes as when teaching small classes. Therefore, no effect of class size on student performance shows up for those teachers. By contrast, less capable teachers do not seem to be up to the job of teaching large classes, while they do reasonably well in small classes. Therefore, a class-size effect does show up for them. Consequently, the evidence suggests that class-size effects occur only when the quality of the teaching force is relatively low.

Intriguingly, heterogeneity of class-size effects by teacher quality may also help to reconcile previous results on class-size effects in the United States. In two influential U.S. studies, Hoxby rejects sizable class-size effects in a quasi-experimental study for the state of Connecticut, while Krueger finds substantial class-size effects in the Project STAR experiment performed in the state of Tennessee.[46]

Now, a rough look at teacher salary levels in the United States indicates that average teacher salaries in public schools in Connecticut are the second-highest among all states, while in Tennessee, salaries are well below the U.S. average.[47] That suggests that heterogeneity of class-size effects by teacher salary may also be able to account for at least part of the differing findings of Hoxby and Krueger: there are class-size effects in Tennessee because teacher pay is relatively low, while there are no class-size effects in Connecticut because teacher pay is relatively high. Again, smaller classes seem to have an observable beneficial effect on student achievement only when the average quality of the teaching force, using average teacher salary as a proxy, is low. The pattern of teacher salaries being relatively high in Connecticut and relatively low in Tennessee is robust to measuring teacher salaries relative to average salaries in the state or relative to state average salaries of specific occupation groups whose skill levels might be viewed as being relatively similar to those of teachers.[48]

Summary and Conclusion

The aggregate international picture suggests that higher educational expenditures are not associated with superior student performance across countries or over time. Likewise, microeconometric evidence based on two alternative quasi-experimental strategies to identify causal class-size effects using the international data at the student level suggests that around the world, class size is not a major determinant of student performance in lower secondary education. In fact, in all countries where the identification strategies can be implemented with reasonable precision, substantial class-size effects can be ruled out.

The microeconometric evidence shows the importance of using convincing empirical strategies to identify causal class-size effects. The evidence reviewed here suggests that conventional least squares estimates of class-size effects are severely biased by the nonrandom placement of students between and within schools. The first reported quasi-experimental identification strategy to address these endogeneity problems, exploiting the two-grade design of the international TIMSS test, identifies class-size effects by relating differences in the relative performance of students in two adjacent grades within individual schools to that part of the between-grade difference in class size in the school that reflects between-grade differences in average class size. Between-school endogeneity is eliminated by controlling for school fixed effects, and within-school endogeneity is addressed by using the average class size in the relevant grade of each school as an instrument for actual class size. Identifying class-size variation induced by natural cohort fluctuations that occur randomly between two adjacent grades within individual schools, the results of this identification strategy rule out substantial class-size effects in secondary education in a large majority of countries. Similar results are found with the second quasi-experimental identification technique, which uses discontinuities in class size induced by maximum class-size rules in many western European countries to identify causal class-size effects.

In terms of effect heterogeneity, the international evidence suggests that noteworthy class-size effects are observed only in countries with relatively low teacher salaries and education levels. That suggests that highly capable teachers may be able to promote student learning equally well regardless of class size—they are capable enough to teach well in large classes. By contrast, less capable teachers may do reasonably well when faced with small classes, but they may not be up to the job of teaching large classes. That could explain why there are class-size effects with teachers of relatively low quality but not with high-quality teachers. This hypothesis is confirmed when using microdata on teacher education. Intriguingly, the hypothesis can also serve to reconcile some of the leading contradictory findings in the United States. In line with the hypothesis, Krueger's finding of substantial class-size effects stems from an experiment in the state of Tennessee, which has below-average teacher salaries, while Hoxby's quasi-experimental evidence rejects even small class-size effects in the state of Connecticut, whose teacher salaries are the second-highest in the nation.

Of course, when considering the effects of class size on student achievement, any benefit in terms of learning gains has to be set against the substantial costs of class-size reductions. Simple cost-benefit considerations suggest that even in Iceland, where class-size effects are statistically significant, the future income gains induced by increases in educational performance are unlikely to offset the costs induced by reductions in class size.

In many regards, international evidence on the effects of expenditures and class size on student achievement is still in its infancy. In his review of mainly U.S. evidence on the topic, Hanushek observed that "as student outcome data become more plentiful [for different countries in the future], allowing investigation of value added by teachers in schools in different environments, international evidence can be expected to grow in importance."[49] It is hoped that this review of a few first steps in using international data has shown the huge potential of the rich data collected by international student achievement tests in advancing our knowledge in this field.

Notes

1. For examples of reviews of the U.S. literature, see Gary Burtless, ed., *Does Money Matter? The Effect of School Resources on Student Achievement and Adult Success* (Brookings, 1996); David Card and Alan B. Krueger, "School Resources and Student Outcomes: An Overview of the Literature and New Evidence from North and South Carolina," *Journal of Economic Perspectives* 10, no. 4 (1996): 31–50; Eric A. Hanushek, "Publicly Provided Education," in *Handbook of Public Economics*, vol. 4, edited by Alan J. Auerbach and Martin Feldstein (Amsterdam: North Holland, 2002), pp. 2045–141; Alan B. Krueger, "Economic Considerations and Class Size," *Economic Journal* 113, no. 485 (2003): F34–F63; Eric A. Hanushek, "The Failure of Input-Based Schooling Policies," *Economic Journal* 113, no. 485 (2003): F64–F98.

2. George Psacharopoulos, "Economics of Education à la Euro," *European Journal of Education* 35, no. 1 (2000): 81–95 (quote on p. 92); compare also Hanushek, "Publicly Provided Education," pp. 2086–088.

3. For a brief survey of existing national studies from Europe, see Ludger Wößmann, "Educational Production in Europe," *Economic Policy* 20, no. 43 (2005): 445–504.

4. See Hanushek, "Publicly Provided Education," pp. 2086–087.

5. See Eric A. Hanushek and Dennis D. Kimko, "Schooling, Labor-Force Quality, and the Growth of Nations," *American Economic Review* 90, no. 5 (2000):1184–208; Robert J. Barro, "Human Capital and Growth," *American Economic Review* 91, no. 2 (2001): 12–17; Ludger Wößmann, "Specifying Human Capital," *Journal of Economic Surveys* 17, no. 3 (2003): 239–70.

6. For a simple introduction, see Charles I. Jones, *Introduction to Economic Growth*, 2nd ed. (New York: W. W. Norton, 2002).

7. Organization for Economic Cooperation and Development, *Learning for Tomorrow's World: First Results from PISA 2003* (Paris: OECD, 2004), p. 101.

8. See, for example, Ludger Wößmann, *Schooling and the Quality of Human Capital* (Berlin: Springer, 2002), section 3.2.

9. See Ludger Wößmann, "Why Students in Some Countries Do Better: International Evidence on the Importance of Education Policy," *Education Matters* 1, no. 2 (2001): 67–74; Ludger Wößmann, "Schooling Resources, Educational Institutions, and Student Performance: The International Evidence," *Oxford Bulletin of Economics and Statistics* 65, no. 2 (2003): 117–70; Thomas Fuchs and Ludger Wößmann, "What Accounts for International Differences in Student Performance? A Reexamination using PISA Data," *Empirical Economics* (forthcoming) (the working paper is available as CESifo Working Paper 1235 at www.cesifo.de).

10. For details of the analysis, see Erich Gundlach, Ludger Wößmann, and Jens Gmelin, "The Decline of Schooling Productivity in OECD Countries," *Economic Journal* 111, no. 471 (2001): C135–C147; Erich Gundlach and Ludger Wößmann, "Better Schools for Europe," *EIB Papers* 6, no. 2 (2001): 8–22; and Wößmann, *Schooling and the Quality of Human Capital*, section 3.3.

11. Gundlach, Wößmann, and Gmelin, "The Decline of Schooling Productivity in OECD Countries."

12. Eric A. Hanushek, "The Productivity Collapse in Schools," in *Developments in School Finance 1996*, edited by W. Fowler Jr. (U.S. Department of Education, National Center for Education Statistics, 1997), pp. 183–95.

13. Erich Gundlach and Ludger Wößmann, "The Fading Productivity of Schooling in East Asia," *Journal of Asian Economics* 12, no. 3 (2001): 401–17.

14. David W. Grissmer and others, *Student Achievement and the Changing American Family* (Santa Monica, Calif.: Rand, 1994). See also the discussion on aggregate U.S. time-series evidence in Eric A. Hanushek, "The Evidence on Class Size," in *Earning and Learning: How Schools Matter*, edited by Susan E. Mayer and Paul E. Peterson (Brookings, 1999), pp. 131–68.

15. For a review, see Hanushek, "Publicly Provided Education," and the other reviews referred to in note 1 above.

16. See in particular Ludger Wößmann, "Educational Production in East Asia: The Impact of Family Background and Schooling Policies on Student Performance," *German Economic Review* 6, no. 3 (2005): 331–53; and Andreas Ammermüller, Hans Heijke, and Ludger Wößmann, "Schooling Quality in Eastern Europe: Educational Production during Transition," *Economics of Education Review* 24, no. 5 (2005): 579–99. Canadian evidence is contained in Ludger Wößmann and Martin R. West, "Class-Size Effects in School Systems around the World: Evidence from Between-Grade Variation in TIMSS," *European Economic Review* 50, no. 3 (2006): 695–736. Comparative evidence on conventional estimates of education production functions for five francophone sub-Saharan African countries are reported in Katharina Michaelowa, "Primary Education Quality in Francophone Sub-Saharan Africa: Determinants of Learning Achievement and Effi-

ciency Considerations," *World Development* 29, no. 10 (2001): 1699–716. See also Eric A. Hanushek and Javier A. Luque, "Efficiency and Equity in Schools around the World," *Economics of Education Review* 22, no. 5 (2003): 481–502.

17. For details on the particular data sets used in these analyses, see Wößmann, "Educational Production in Europe." For general information on the TIMSS database, see Albert E. Beaton and others, *Mathematics Achievement in the Middle School Years: IEA's Third International Mathematics and Science Study (TIMSS)* (Chestnut Hill, Mass.: TIMSS International Study Center, Boston College, 1996); Michael O. Martin and Dana L. Kelly, eds., *Third International Mathematics and Science Study Technical Report,* vol. 2, *Implementation and Analysis: Primary and Middle School Years* (Chestnut Hill, Mass.: Boston College, 1997); and Eugenio J. Gonzalez and Teresa A. Smith (eds.), *User Guide for the TIMSS International Database: Primary and Middle School Years* (Chestnut Hill, Mass.: Boston College, 1997).

18. See, for example, John H. Bishop, "The Impact of Academic Competencies on Wages, Unemployment, and Job Performance," *Carnegie-Rochester Conference Series on Public Policy* 37 (1992): 127–94.

19. See Hanushek, "Publicly Provided Education."

20. The family background variables entered in these and all following models, obtained from background questionnaires of the students tested in TIMSS, are four dummy variables for parental education; four dummies for books at home; dummies for whether the student lives with both parents and was born in the country, student sex and age, and grade level; and two dummies for location of the school (geographically isolated or close to the center of a town). Furthermore, the estimations control for two dummies on the material endowment of the school, for instruction time, and for teacher sex, experience, and education, as well as imputation dummies. See Wößmann, "Educational Production in Europe," for details.

21. For details of the results, see Wößmann, "Educational Production in Europe."

22. Stephen P. Heyneman and William A. Loxley, "The Effect of Primary-School Quality on Academic Achievement across Twenty-Nine High- and Low-Income Countries," *American Journal of Sociology* 88, no. 6 (1983): 1162–194.

23. Hanushek and Luque, "Efficiency and Equity in Schools around the World."

24. See Martin R. West and Ludger Wößmann, "Which School Systems Sort Weaker Students into Smaller Classes? International Evidence," *European Journal of Political Economy* 22, no. 4 (2006): 944–68.

25. See Caroline M. Hoxby, "The Effects of Class Size on Student Achievement: New Evidence from Population Variation," *Quarterly Journal of Economics* 115, no. 4 (2000): 1239–85.

26. See Alan B. Krueger, "Experimental Estimates of Education Production Functions," *Quarterly Journal of Economics* 114, no. 2 (1999): 497–532.

27. See Hoxby, "The Effects of Class Size on Student Achievement."

28. Wößmann and West, "Class-Size Effects in School Systems around the World." For less technical summaries, see also Martin R. West and Ludger Wößmann, "Crowd Control: An International Look at the Relationship between Class Size and Student Achievement," *Education Next* 3, no. 3 (2003): 56–62; and Ludger Wößmann, "Where to Look for Student Sorting and Class-Size Effects: Identification and Quest for Causes," in *Contexts of Learning Mathematics and Science: Lessons Learned from TIMSS,* edited by Sarah J. Howie and Tjeerd Plomp (London: Routledge, 2006).

29. For a more detailed discussion of the validity of the identification strategy, see Wößmann and West, "Class-Size Effects in School Systems around the World."

30. The examples were first presented in Ludger Wößmann and Martin R. West, "Class-Size Effects in School Systems around the World: Evidence from Between-Grade Variation in TIMSS," Kiel Working Paper 1099 (Kiel, Germany: Kiel Institute for World Economics, 2002).

31. As seen in the figure, Singapore is the only exception among all the countries considered that has a significant difference in average class size between seventh and eighth grade, with the latter being 6.9 students larger on average. However, any effect of this apparent cross-grade difference in the rule governing class sizes on our estimates of class-size effects should be controlled for by our ignoring any average cross-grade differences in the lower panels of figure 4, as long as the existence of the rule itself is unrelated to the average performance of students in a particular grade.

32. The result stays virtually unchanged when the two outlying observations at the right-hand side of the graph are dropped. When the outlying observation at the bottom of the graph also is dropped, the coefficient on class size grows in absolute terms and its level of statistical significance increases.

33. For many additional details on the microeconometric results, see Wößmann, "Educational Production in Europe."

34. Results are very similar without the peer controls; for details on this and further aspects of the econometric specification, see Wößmann, "Educational Production in Europe."

35. Krueger, "Experimental Estimates of Education Production Functions."

36. Pedro Carneiro and James J. Heckman, "Rejoinder," in *Inequality in America: What Role for Human Capital Policies?* edited by James J. Heckman and Alan B. Krueger (MIT Press, 2003), pp. 333–54.

37. See Philip Trostel, Ian Walker, and Paul Woolley, "Estimates of the Economic Return to Schooling for Twenty-Eight Countries," *Labour Economics* 9, no. 1 (2002): 1–16; Ludger Wößmann, "Returns to Education in Europe" (book review essay), *Review of World Economics* 139, no. 2 (2003): 348–76.

38. See Wößmann and West, "Class-Size Effects in School Systems around the World," for details.

39. Ibid.

40. Joshua D. Angrist and Victor Lavy, "Using Maimonides' Rule to Estimate the Effect of Class Size on Scholastic Achievement," *Quarterly Journal of Economics* 114, no. 2 (1999): 533–75.

41. For additional details, see Wößmann, "Educational Production in Europe"; and Angrist and Lavy, "Using Maimonides' Rule to Estimate the Effect of Class Size on Scholastic Achievement."

42. See Hoxby, "The Effects of Class Size on Student Achievement," p. 1280.

43. See Wößmann, "Educational Production in Europe," for many additional details.

44. Ibid., pp. 480–82.

45. For details of the evidence on international heterogeneity of class-size effects, see Wößmann, "Educational Production in Europe"; Wößmann and West, "Class-Size Effects in School Systems around the World"; and Wößmann, "Where to Look for Student Sorting and Class-Size Effects."

46. See Hoxby, "The Effects of Class Size on Student Achievement," and Krueger, "Experimental Estimates of Education Production Functions."

47. See *Digest of Education Statistics 2002* (U.S. Department of Education, National Center for Education Statistics, 2003).

48. According to the NCES data, average annual salaries of teachers in public elementary and secondary schools in 2001–02 were $54,300 in Connecticut and $38,554 in Tennessee; the U.S. average was $44,604. Measured relative to the annual median wage in all occupations in the respective state, teacher salaries stand at 1.61 in Connecticut, 1.56 in Tennessee, and 1.61 in the United States. When we use occupation groups that might be viewed as requiring skill levels that are relatively similar to those for teaching, teacher salaries relative to wages in "life, physical, and social science occupations" stand at 0.99 in Connecticut, 0.90 in Tennessee, and 0.96 in the United States; relative to wages in "healthcare practitioner and technical occupations," they stand at 1.05

in Connecticut, 1.01 in Tennessee, and 1.02 in the United States. Data on wages in other occupations are for 2002 from the U.S. Department of Labor, Bureau of Labor Statistics, *Occupational Employment and Wages Estimates* (www.bls.gov/oes/oes_dl.htm [July 2006]).

49. Hanushek, "Publicly Provided Education," p. 2088.

The Relative Influence of Research on Class-Size Policy

JAMES S. KIM

Social science research suggests that reducing class size has its largest effects on the achievement of minority and inner-city children during the first year of formal schooling.[1] Despite scholarly disagreements about the implications of specific studies on class size, economists generally agree that targeted class-size policies rest on stronger evidence than untargeted policies. For example, economist Eric Hanushek contends that "surely class-size reductions are beneficial in specific circumstances—for specific groups of students, subject matters, and teachers."[2] Similarly, economist Alan Krueger notes that the "effect sizes found in the STAR experiment and much of the literature are greater for minority and disadvantaged students than for other students [and] economic considerations suggest that resources would be optimally allocated if they were targeted toward those who benefit the most from smaller classes."[3] However, a number of state legislatures have enacted untargeted and expensive policies to reduce class sizes in all schools, among all subgroups of students, and beyond the early elementary grades. Therefore, the central tension between research and policy in the class-size debate is this: research seems to support targeted class-size policies most strongly, but targeted policies are the exception rather than the norm in the policy arena. As a result, some social scientists have criticized across-the-board class-size reductions as prohibitively expensive and scientifically indefensible.[4]

The Politics of Class Size

In this paper, I argue that the influence of social science research on class-size policy depends partly on political context. Instead of simply asking

Table 1. Classifying and Explaining the Politics of Class-Size Reduction Policies

Benefits	Distributed costs	Concentrated costs
Distributed benefits	Majoritarian politics (Untargeted class-size reduction)	Entrepreneurial politics
Concentrated benefits	Client politics (Targeted class-size reduction)	Interest group politics

whether research affects policy, it is equally important to examine how the politics of the class-size debate shape the many uses of research in the policy arena. Social scientists cannot control the uses of research, but they can encourage evaluation of policies in terms of their effects on educational outcomes. Social scientists possess methodological tools rather than policy prescriptions, and research is a valuable resource because it helps clarify the goals of public policies without dictating the outcome of democratic debate.

Political scientist James Q. Wilson provides a way of classifying the politics surrounding policy issues such as class-size reduction. Wilson's framework can help identify some conditions under which research may influence public policy. As shown in table 1, untargeted class-size reduction represents a popular education policy that distributes benefits and costs among a large number of people. Public opinion polls suggest that a majority of voters—including teachers, superintendents, parents, and taxpayers—support reducing class sizes in order to improve their local schools.[5] When legislators cast class-size reduction as "majoritarian issue," the proposal appeals to large blocs of voters and it is generally easy to form a majority coalition supporting it. A recent example of an untargeted class-size policy is the 2002 Florida class-size amendment, which was supported by a motley collection of voters—senior citizens, union leaders, parents, and educators—who approved a multibillion-dollar policy that mandates a cap on class size in elementary, middle, and secondary schools by 2010. The Florida policy, as well as similar untargeted class-size policies in California and Nevada, follows the prediction advanced by Wilson's framework: "If a new policy is adopted and people become convinced that the promised benefits are real and worth the cost, debate ends and the program will not only continue but will also grow rapidly in size."[6] Widespread political support is sufficient to legitimize an untargeted class-size reduction policy. Therefore there is little incentive for legislators to plan for evaluation of a popular policy whose central goal is to advance political interests rather than to achieve preset educational goals.

Table 1 also shows that targeted class-size reduction policies distribute costs and concentrate benefits among "clients" of government. According to Wilson, when "benefits are concentrated, the group that is to receive those benefits has an incentive to organize and work to get them."[7] Evidence plays a more vital role in helping a policy survive and grow when it concentrates benefits on a subgroup of clients—in this case, young children who neither vote nor pay taxes. Because perceived benefits (both monetary and nonmonetary) are not distributed among a large number of individuals and interest groups, such policies do not automatically command a wide base of political support. Instead, targeted policies must rely on alternative forms of support, such as empirical evidence that demonstrates the efficacy of an intervention or normative claims about the value of improving the achievement of minority and low-income children. When class-size policy is cast as a client-based issue, there is usually a stronger incentive for state legislatures to commission research, to apply findings to class-size policy, and to draw on empirical evidence to defend and maintain the policy. In addition, there is an incentive to appeal to values and to argue that young children from minority and low-income families are legitimate and deserving clients of government. The values underpinning compensatory education programs remain strong in American society and may deepen support for targeted class-size reductions in schools and classrooms with large numbers of disadvantaged children.[8] Targeted class-size policies illustrate cases in which research can play a direct and meaningful role in the political arena by informing debate and guiding policy decisions.

This chapter examines the influence of research on class-size policy in three sections, organized chronologically. First, it reviews empirical research on the relationship between class size and student achievement. Second, it describes the role that research played in shaping class-size policies in Tennessee and Indiana in 1989 and in Wisconsin and California in 1996. Each pair of case studies illustrates substantial differences in the way state legislators framed the class-size debate and used research in determining the scope and size of their respective policies. Third, it discusses several lessons bearing on the relationship between research and policy as applied to class size in particular and education reform in general.

Research on Class Size: Evidence from the 1960s and 1970s

Research on class size evolved over the twentieth century from complex statistical analyses of national surveys to innovative meta-analyses of primary studies and ultimately, in Tennessee, to the gold standard in social science—the randomized field trial. The largest national survey to shed light on the relationship between educational inputs, such as class size, and student achievement was the 1966 Equality of Educational Opportunity survey, more famously known as the Coleman Report. Surprisingly, sociologist James Coleman and his colleagues found that "some facilities measures, such as the pupil/teacher ratio in instruction . . . showed a consistent lack of relation to achievement among all groups under all conditions."[9] Similarly, in one reanalysis of the Coleman data, sociologist Christopher Jencks concluded that "while reductions in class size can often be justified in terms of teachers' sanity, pleasant classroom atmosphere, and other advantages, they are hard to justify in terms of test scores."[10] However, since those findings were based on analyses of observational data, they were merely suggestive and tentative. The dearth of large experiments further impeded understanding of whether reduced class sizes *caused* improvements in student achievement. Summarizing the state of knowledge on class size in the early 1970s, John Gilbert and Frederick Mosteller noted that "after a half a century of tightly controlled studies of optimum class size, we have made practically no progress. . . . the studies have been too small and specialized for their implications to have much chance of holding in new situations."[11]

Glass and Smith's Meta-Analysis of Class Size

By the late 1970s, research findings on the effects of class size had been accumulating for nearly a century and the time was ripe for a "summing up" of the empirical evidence. In 1978, Gene Glass and Mary Lee Smith conducted a summary of class-size research, using an innovative but controversial technique called meta-analysis—a study of studies.[12] In their review, Glass and Smith found seventy-seven studies on the relationship between class size and student achievement, conducted between 1900 and 1978. Using meta-analysis to combine results across studies, Glass and Smith found that achievement increased "when class size is reduced below 20."[13] However, since the relationship between achievement and class size was not linear, achievement improved more dramatically when class size was reduced from twenty to ten students than from thirty to twenty students.[14]

The meta-analytic findings prompted debate among scholars. In one of the first criticisms of Glass and Smith's meta-analysis, the Educational Research Services (ERS) faulted the meta-analysis for drawing unwarranted recommendations from poorly controlled studies because only fourteen of them were true experiments.[15] The ERS study also showed that substantial achievement gains resulted only when class size was reduced to one to five students in small tutorial sessions, a prohibitively costly and infeasible policy option for most public school districts. Similarly, Robert Slavin noted that one of the studies with the largest effect sizes in the Glass and Smith meta-analysis was on tennis instruction, in which the achievement outcome involved "rallying a tennis ball against the wall . . . as many times as possible in 30 sec."[16] Another social scientist, Hans Eysenk, argued that meta-analysis was "an exercise in megasilliness," and he suggested that the adage "Garbage in equals garbage out" applied to the Glass and Smith synthesis of class size.[17] Glass retorted that the ERS report was "a dog's breakfast of pleonasms, confusion, and obfuscation."[18] Regardless of one's perspective, the debate between Glass and his critics represented what Harry Aaron called "self-cancelling" research—conflicting evidence from poorly designed research that paralyzed action.[19] Given the lack of scientific consensus on the effects of class size, few states relied on the Glass and Smith meta-analysis to enact class-size reduction initiatives in the early 1980s.[20]

Tennessee's Project STAR

During the mid-1980s, social scientists played a key role in encouraging the Tennessee state legislature to evaluate the effects of small classes on student achievement rather than implement a statewide reduction in class sizes. In 1984, as part of the broader political debate over education reforms initiated by Governor Lamar Alexander, educators and teacher unions began to push for legislation that would reduce the pupil-teacher ratio to 20:1. However, several policymakers "were not convinced that the state of research warranted the high-cost of reducing class sizes statewide."[21] The uncertainty about the effects of small class size on achievement encouraged two policy entrepreneurs to call for a more targeted and limited policy. In particular, Steve Cobb, a state legislator trained as a social scientist, and Helen Bain, an educator with deep political connections, helped lawmakers focus the scope and size of the class-size policy. The class-size debate prompted Cobb to review the Glass and Smith meta-analysis, which suggested that class sizes had to be reduced to nearly fifteen students in order to improve student achievement. Therefore Cobb concluded that an across-the-board reduction would be expensive and ineffective and began to encourage his colleagues to support a controlled evaluation of a class-size reduction initiative. Bain, a former president of the National Education Association and a college professor, also argued that class size should target the early grades, when children first start school. Eventually, Cobb and Bain worked together to forge legislation, unanimously approved by the Tennessee legislature, that authorized a demonstration project called Project STAR (Student/Teacher Achievement Ratio).[22]

The STAR legislation is notable because it focused on specific educational goals, carefully defined the treatment under study, authorized a controlled investigation, and carved out prominent roles for social scientists. Project STAR was enacted in order "to study the effects of a reduced pupil-teacher ratio on the achievement of students in public school." In addition, each class in the demonstration project was "to have a maximum enrollment of seventeen." And the legislation called for "the identification of a control group of pupils in the same school system for the purposes of measuring differences in achievement."[23] The law also authorized the state department of education to invite researchers from four Tennessee universities to carry out the evaluation. Although the original STAR legislation did not require a randomized controlled trial, it gave researchers considerable freedom in designing the evaluation. To implement an experimental design, the researchers developed a protocol for the random assignment of students to small classes with thirteen to seventeen students, regular classes with twenty-two to twenty-five students, or regular classes with teacher aides.

During its first year, the Project STAR study, which has been celebrated as one of the greatest experiments in education, involved more than 6,000 students in seventy-nine elementary schools.[24] The STAR findings have been amply documented by researchers, but the most noteworthy findings were as follows: small class sizes of thirteen to seventeen students improved student achievement by approximately .20 of a standard deviation, or 4 percentile points; effect sizes were nearly twice as large for minority students as white students; test score gains were largest in kindergarten and first grade; and long-term effects persisted in a variety of academic outcomes measured in middle and high school.[25] Social scientists have conducted numerous secondary analyses using the STAR data, and policymakers have relied on the findings to justify class-size reduction policies.[26] In short, the study has been influential among scholars and politicians.

Tennessee's Project Challenge and Indiana's Prime Time Policy

When Project STAR ended in 1989, its findings were available to state policymakers interested in using research to develop class-size policy. How, then, did the research on class size influence state policy? Case studies of Tennessee and Indiana suggest that research played a very different role in shaping each state's policy.

From Tennessee's Project STAR to Project Challenge

In 1989, a newly elected Democratic governor, Ned McWherter, used the STAR results to craft a targeted class-size policy.[27] According to professor Charles Achilles, a principal investigator of the Tennessee study, "Ned looked at STAR and was most impressed with the results for poor and minority youngsters."[28] As a result, the governor "challenged" the poorest districts in Tennessee to cobble together federal Title I dollars and any other local revenue source to reduce class sizes from kindergarten through third grade, and he promised to match local efforts with discretionary funds from the state budget. Thus, Project Challenge distributed costs and burdens on taxpayers by using federal, state, and local money to reduce class sizes to an average of fifteen students from kindergarten through third grade in seventeen districts (ultimately sixteen districts by 1992–93) with the lowest per capita income.[29] In sum, Project Challenge cost nearly $4.1 million to reduce class sizes in the poorest public school districts.

Research played a decisive role in legitimizing the Project Challenge policy, which was designed to concentrate educational benefits on minority and low-income children at risk of falling behind academically in the early grades. Ultimately, the sixteen Project Challenge districts involved a small proportion of Tennessee's 139 school districts and covered only 4 percent of classrooms in the state.[30] Although Project Challenge was not an experiment, the intervention seemed to raise the performance of the targeted districts on a standardized test of reading and mathematics from near the bottom to the median rank for all Tennessee districts.[31] In the words of statistician Frederick Mosteller, Project Challenge shows how policymakers "can make use of a valuable intervention very selectively . . . by applying it to those who need it most."[32]

Indiana's Prime Time Policy

In 1981, the Indiana legislature and then Governor Robert Orr enacted a state policy, dubbed Prime Time, to reduce pupil-teacher ratios in order to "improve basic skills in reading, writing, and arithmetic among Kindergarten, first, and second grades by reducing class size."[33] The Prime Time program—which began in 1981–82 as a small-scale pilot that provided $300,000 to nine schools to reduce the student-teacher ratio to 14:1 in grades K-2—rapidly expanded into a statewide effort to reduce the pupil-teacher ratio in all districts by the end of the decade. The performance of Prime Time classes of 14 or fewer students was compared to regular class sizes that averaged nearly 23 students. The results of the first evaluation revealed that positive effects were observed only in reading and only in first grade. Although these findings supported implementation of only a limited and targeted class-size reduction policy, they were used to support a major expansion of Prime Time.[34] By 1989–90, the Indiana legislature had committed more than $65 million to fund class-size reductions in all 302 public school districts.[35]

During the expansion of the Prime Time program in the 1980s, the state undertook a series of small studies that examined teaching and learning inside smaller classrooms. Early evaluations were based on nonexperimental studies, including ethnographies, classroom observations, and surveys of principals, teachers, and parents.[36] For example, the director of Prime Time noted that "evaluations of the first three years of the Prime Time program show happier, more productive teachers, more responsive students, and very satisfied parents" and that teachers had "more time for creative experiences, hands-on activities, drama, science exploration, and the use of learning centers."[37] In a 1990 review of studies on Prime Time, however, one analyst noted that class-size reductions were "hastily implemented" and that "little has been done to objectively determine what effect Prime Time has had on educational achievement or to train teachers to take advantage of smaller classes."[38]

The most comprehensive evaluation of Prime Time is notable because it occurred nearly ten years after statewide implementation of the policy and ultimately supported a targeted reduction in class sizes. In 1999, the state superintendent of public instruction requested an independent evaluation of the Prime Time policy by researchers at Ball State University. According to the lead researcher, Daniel Lapsley, Prime Time was a popular policy and there was little pressure from politicians to evaluate it. Instead, it was the superintendent who wanted to obtain evidence of program effectiveness based on "an elaborate quasi-experimental study that longitudinally track[ed] students in Prime Time programs and compared them with students not in Prime Time programs."[39] However, the evaluation followed a statewide class-size reduction program that had been in existence for nearly a decade, and the Ball State researchers highlighted the serious challenges and obstacles to performing an evaluation under such circumstances. The evaluation lacked sufficient controls to estimate the treatment effects, and the use of different versions of standardized tests in different schools precluded comparison based on a common metric.

Nonetheless, the evaluation reported findings consistent with those of previous research. The report's central finding was that "small class size was not associated with better achievement, except for reading and composite achievement of minority pupils."[40] This finding, the authors concluded, seemed to indicate that "a differentiated Prime Time strategy might be most appropriate, one that seeks to reduce class size in lower SES (socio-economic status) schools."[41] More precisely, these results supported a targeted class-size reduction policy for some students in some schools. Although some lawmakers have recently sought to target Prime Time funding as part of a categorical grant for at-risk students, it has been difficult to restrain a policy that provides additional money to virtually every district in the state. As one program administrator observed, the Prime Time program "is so much a part of the Indiana system [that] it would have been very difficult to completely take it away."[42]

Wisconsin SAGE Program and the California Class-Size Reduction Policy

By 1996, the existing research on the effect of small class sizes on student outcomes was strengthened by the Project STAR experiment in Tennessee, which inspired both federal and state efforts to reduce class sizes. According to Marshall Smith, "nearly all of these initiatives are motivated, at least in part, by the findings of the Tennessee experiments."[43] In 1996, Wisconsin and California enacted class-size policies that represented two very different policy strategies. The centerpiece of the Wisconsin SAGE policy was a targeted reduction of class sizes to 15 or fewer students in kindergarten and first grade in twenty-one high-poverty districts. Given the small scale of the program, the legislature spent only $4.2 million to fund SAGE schools in the 1996–97 school year. The California policy was an untargeted class-size reduction policy involving all California school districts that cost approximately $1 billion in 1996–97, the first year of implementation. Although both policies have grown in size to include more students in more grades, the Wisconsin and California legislature used research in different ways to develop their policies.

Wisconsin SAGE Program

The Wisconsin SAGE program was conceived as a targeted class-size reduction program reserved primarily for lower-performing students in the early elementary grades who lived in high-poverty districts. In 1994, the state department of public instruction created the Urban Initiative Task Force, which included thirty-four members representing diverse political constituencies in Wisconsin. The primary goal of the task force was to discuss strategies for addressing the achievement gap and improving performance among low-income children. Wisconsin policymakers therefore framed the problem as one of low achievement among a subgroup of students and recommended a targeted policy to address the issue. In 1996–97, the Wisconsin legislature funded a limited five-year pilot program that provided money to high-poverty schools to reduce class sizes to an average of 15 students in kindergarten and first grade, with additional grades to be added in 1997–98 (second grade) and 1998–99 (third grade).[44]

Since the purpose of SAGE was to examine the effects of class-size reduction on children's academic outcomes, the Wisconsin legislature required an evaluation to determine whether the intervention accomplished its educational objective. The legislature authorized researchers at the University of Wisconsin–Milwaukee to conduct an evaluation comparing the academic performance of thirty SAGE schools and fourteen to seventeen comparison schools matched on student achievement and demographic characteristics.[45] The SAGE program was accompanied by a mandatory evaluation, and the quasi-experimental design was the next best alternative to a true experiment. It also was capable of addressing the relevant policy question—does class-size reduction in the early grades improve the cognitive skills of children in high-poverty elementary schools?

The year 1 (1996–97) and year 2 (1997–98) evaluation of the Wisconsin SAGE program produced findings that replicated the key findings from Tennessee's Project STAR. Similar to the schools in the Tennessee study, SAGE schools were required to reduce class sizes by having 1 teacher per 15 students or 30 students with 2 teachers in a single classroom. The sizable reduction in class size meant that pupil-teacher ratios were, on average, between 12:1 and 15:1 in SAGE classrooms and between 21:1 and 25:1 in comparison classrooms. Given the substantial contrast in the number of students in SAGE and control classrooms, Alex Molnar and his colleagues pointed out that "these differences were larger than class-size reductions in the Tennessee experiment and would be predicted to have measurable effects based on the Tennessee evidence."[46] In fact, the results of the early SAGE evaluations mirrored the STAR findings. In 1997–98, first-graders in SAGE classrooms scored approximately one-fifth of a standard deviation higher than the control group. The effects were largest for black children and for students attending the Milwaukee public schools, an urban district with a large percentage of low-income children.[47]

The promising findings from the first- and second-year evaluation prompted the Wisconsin legislature to expand the SAGE program to include more than 500 schools by year 3 (2000–01). Critics of the rapid scale-up of SAGE have argued that class-size reduction is now too broad and expensive, that the benefits will be diffused, and that the goal of assisting disadvantaged children will be undermined. According to the Wisconsin Policy Research Institute, the new and expanded version of the SAGE program "has lost its primary focus and, arguably, its initial justification."[48] The report concluded that a more accurate interpretation of existing evaluations would support a limited and cost-effective policy since "only African-American students in SAGE do better than African-American students in larger classes, and they do so only in first grade, and only in certain subjects and classrooms."[49] More recently, researchers at the University of Wisconsin–Madison conducted an analysis of long-term effects of the SAGE programs on kindergarten and first-grade students who were part of the original evaluation. The analysis confirmed significant program effects on standardized tests in grades 1 through 3 and replicated earlier analyses showing larger effects of SAGE on black students. However, there were no significant differences between SAGE and comparison students on a fourth-grade standardized test in reading comprehension, language arts, and mathematics.[50] Thus, two recent studies imply that a targeted class-size reduction policy would be more cost-effective than an untargeted policy in the early grades.

As with the evaluation of Tennessee's Project Challenge, evaluation of Wisconsin's SAGE program was planned before statewide implementation. That decision increased the odds that the results would be meaningful to researchers and policymakers. The availability of data from a well-designed quasi-experimental study enabled three independent organizations to evaluate SAGE in terms of its demonstrated impact on student learning—the initial goal of the program.[51] The results did not prescribe a policy, but they helped focus policy on specific educational goals.

California's Class-Size Reduction Policy

In many ways, the 1996 class-size reduction policy in California was motivated by an educational crisis that demanded immediate political action. The crisis was prompted in 1994 by a combination of factors: California fourth-graders had tied for last place on the NAEP reading test; schools had an average elementary school class size of 29 students, which was the largest in the nation; and large achievement gaps persisted between white and minority students. In response to the perceived crisis in education, the California State Department of Education, led by then superintendent Delaine Eastin, convened the California Reading Task Force, whose goal was to identify possible solutions for improving reading among elementary school children. The task force identified small class sizes as a promising remedy for raising achievement in the elementary grades. In addition, California legislators began to scrutinize the results of the Tennessee STAR study, which showed significant benefits of reduced class sizes on the achievement of minority and inner-city children in the early grades. To obtain additional information on the effects of class-size reduction and develop different strategies for implementing such a policy, the state legislature requested an analysis by the California Research Bureau (CRB), a nonpartisan state research organization modeled after the federal government's Government Accountability Office.

In a June 1996 report entitled "Reducing Class Size: A Review of the Literature and Options for Consideration," David Illig, an analyst with the CRB, conducted a comprehensive review of the available research and recommended a range of policy options for lawmakers. The CRB report provided state legislators with a clear analysis of the research on class size and policy options.[52] It noted that California's interest in class-size reduction "was motivated in part by the findings reported by the Tennessee Project STAR research team."[53] The report highlighted the findings of STAR, underscoring the conditions under which smaller classes improved achievement. Notably, the report discouraged an across-the-board reduction in class sizes. It also discounted the Glass and Smith findings in favor of the Tennessee STAR findings, used the STAR results to encourage a targeted class-size reduction policy in kindergarten and first grade and in high-poverty schools, and urged an independent evaluation of the state policy. Finally, the report raised questions about the generalizability of the Tennessee findings to California, which had a large percentage of English learners, limited space in overcrowded schools, and a shortage of credentialed teachers in urban schools.

The CRB report had very little impact on state policymakers. In July 1996, the Class-Size Reduction Program reduced class size to 20 students per teacher in kindergarten through third grade and was passed into law in one day.[54] The purpose of the state policy was "to increase student achievement, particularly in reading and mathematics, by decreasing the size of the K-3 classes to 20 or fewer students per certified teacher."[55] It was difficult to determine whether this goal was met because the rapid scale-up of the class-size policy made it virtually impossible to conduct a carefully controlled study. Evaluations funded after implementation provided weak and inconclusive evidence that class-size reduction improved achievement.[56] The authors of a final evaluation completed in 2001 concluded that class-size reduction "was nearly complete, and as a result we could not examine differences in SAT-9 scores between students who were and were not in reduced size classes."[57] The policy also had several negative and unintended consequences for urban districts and high-poverty schools. California's class-size reduction initiative was "associated with declines in teacher qualifications and a more inequitable distribution of credentialed teachers."[58] In light of the unclear results from evaluations of the California class-size policy, researchers have encouraged more controlled experiments that would address a lingering question: Is class-size reduction a cost-effective strategy for improving student achievement, and if so, under what conditions?[59]

Such questions assume that the California policy was designed primarily to produce measurable improvements in reading and mathematics achievement—an explicitly educational goal. In many ways, however, California's politicians viewed a massive, statewide effort to reduce class sizes as a response to an educational crisis—low NAEP scores in reading. Moreover, an untargeted policy satisfied the interests of a large number of groups. The perceived benefits were broadly distributed among state leaders wanting to demonstrate action in response to an educational crisis; parents, teachers, and union leaders wishing to reduce overcrowding in classrooms; and political leaders hoping to mollify various interest groups.[60]

Sociologist Carol Weiss notes that in an atmosphere of crisis, research becomes ammunition to support predetermined positions "even if conclusions have to be ripped out of context."[61] For California legislators, reducing class size in all schools seemed like the best strategy for improving academic achievement for all subgroups of students. Yet the Tennessee experiment's evidence was strongest for a class-size policy that targeted minority and inner-city children, and state policy analysts further underscored the cost-effectiveness of a targeted policy. However, it is unlikely that research will be called on to restrain the growth of a policy that distributes perceived benefits among voters in every California school district.

Discussion

The case studies suggest that the politics of the class-size debate often determine what, if any, effect research has on policymakers. Rather than asking why research does or does not influence policy, it seems equally important to consider how politics shapes the many uses of research in the policy arena. In doing so, I elaborate on five lessons that are relevant for the class-size policy in particular and education policy in general.

Lesson 1: When a policy enjoys a broad base of political support, there is virtually no incentive for state legislators to commission research on the pol-

icy or to evaluate it in terms of its demonstrated effect on student achievement. Since untargeted class-size reduction policies distribute benefits and costs, they inspire support among large numbers of voters and diverse constituencies. Popular policies can thrive in the absence of research evidence. The imperative to evaluate an untargeted class-size policy is weak because its primary goal is to advance political interests rather than to meet preset educational goals. Most state policies include statutory language stating that the goal of smaller class sizes is to improve reading and mathematics skills. Whether that goal is met or an evaluation is planned to measure performance is largely irrelevant. What matters most is whether the policy captures enough political support to survive. Votes, not evidence, are the touchstone for judging success. Therefore, the politics of a majoritarian issue often relegate social science to the periphery of the policy arena. That fact partly explains why research is often powerless to restrain legislators from enacting multimillion-dollar class-size reduction policies. The California and Indiana cases are representative of the many untargeted class-size policies that have proliferated in the past decade.

Lesson 2: When legislators enact untargeted class-size policies, careful evaluation of the policy is usually an afterthought and requires the use of methodological tools that produce ambiguous findings. When research is commissioned to study the impact of a class-size policy that includes all schools, evaluation suffers. For example, the most comprehensive evaluation of Indiana's policy occurred nearly twenty years after the original Prime Time policy was implemented. Because the Prime Time policy reduced pupil-teacher ratios in all public school districts, researchers conducted multivariate analyses of observational data that revealed ambiguous correlations between small classes and student outcomes rather than clear causal links. By 2002, Indiana's policy was a deeply popular policy resting on little rigorous empirical evidence.

The familiar pattern of research following policy expansion has been replicated in other states with untargeted class-size policies. For example, Nevada spent more than $500 million during the 1990s to cap class sizes at twenty students in the early grades. Despite the impressive amount of money devoted to reducing pupil-teacher ratios, state legislators have not funded an evaluation of the program. Instead, local districts have paid for limited evaluations, and most studies have revealed little consistent positive effect on student achievement. Therefore, a 1997 report recommended that the state legislature "fund a comprehensive evaluation of the Class-Size Reduction Program," but to date, Nevada legislators have not done so.[62] In 2002, Florida voters passed an amendment to cap class sizes from pre-kindergarten to twelfth grade by 2010, leaving little opportunity to conduct a rigorous evaluation of the policy. Although some educators and politicians have used research to encourage a more targeted policy, one sponsor of the Florida amendment dismissed the idea: "People can twist it. They can turn it upside down. But the voters want smaller class sizes one way or other."[63] Untargeted class-size policies may be evaluated at some later date, but they yield unclear findings that usually support only one confident conclusion—the need for better research. Yet that recommendation assumes that good research would be used to determine the scope and size of a public policy and that elected officials would be willing to tame the growth of a popular policy.

Lesson 3: Social science research may play a more direct role in helping legislators design targeted class-size policies where the "clients" of government are viewed as legitimate beneficiaries. James Q. Wilson points out that, in making decisions, politicians and their constituencies "take into account not only who benefits but whether is it *legitimate* for that group to benefit."[64] In *The Black-White Test Score Gap,* Christopher Jencks and Meredith Phillips contend that compensatory educational policies for young children are politically popular precisely because "the beneficiaries appear so deserving. Hardly anyone blames first graders' limited vocabulary on defects of character or lack of ambition. First graders of every race seem eager to please."[65] However, targeted class-size policies do not benefit everyone; they concentrate benefits among a subgroup of minority and low-income children and high-poverty schools and districts. Although proponents of such policies often invoke normative claims about the value of young children, they cannot assume that political support will form a reliable and broad foundation for legislative action.

The political predicament facing targeted class-size policies opens the door for research to enter the policy arena. Research is welcome because it is needed to garner political support. A targeted class-size reduction policy such as Tennessee's Project Challenge and Wisconsin's SAGE must rely more heavily on empirical evidence as a source of legitimacy because the benefits are concentrated among a small subgroup of disadvantaged children—that is, clients who do not vote, have no money, and often attend racially and economically segregated schools. Good research, then, may increase the odds that a targeted policy will become more popular if there is proof of a clear benefit to clients receiving some form of preferential treatment. In that case, empirical findings can have political consequences: if an evaluation indicates that the treatment had larger effects on the achievement of lower-performing students, then there is evidence that the policy works best for the clients most in need. Statistical interactions should be heeded and main effects ignored. Evidence from Tennessee's STAR experiment most strongly supported a targeted policy, which is precisely what state leaders adopted when they approved Project Challenge.

Although targeted class-size reduction policies are admittedly rare, they do exist and often rely on evidence as a source of legitimacy. For example, in Virginia, the Fairfax County Public Schools, the nation's twelfth-largest school system, has continued to implement a targeted policy based on evaluations of its reduced pupil-teacher ratio initiative, which reduced class sizes to 15 students in first grade in fifteen schools with the highest concentration of low-income and low-achieving students. A 1997 local evaluation concluded that the "Reduced-Ratio Program is more effective for students from low socioeconomic backgrounds." Based on that finding, the authors recommended that resources "be focused in a smaller number of schools in the poorest communities."[66] In the past decade, the district has continued to allocate money for limited class-size reductions and other policy innovations in twenty low-performing schools that represent less than 10 percent of the district's elementary schools.[67] Results from local evaluations helped justify the targeted class-size policy, much the same way that research influenced the Tennessee and Wisconsin policies.

Lesson 4: Although different incentives govern the work of scholars and politicians, political decisions can directly influence the quality of social science research. Lawmakers work to satisfy their constituencies, and social scientists work to publish papers in peer-reviewed journals. Ostensibly, there is a clear division between the world of ideas and the world of action. However, the case studies suggest that political decisions can directly affect the methodological quality of social science research. Evaluations of targeted class-size policies may yield more publishable findings, because they usually meet a minimum requirement of quantitative policy analysis—the presence of a control group.[68] When class reduction is targeted, the treatment is withheld from some students and schools, and it is possible to create a well-matched control group formed through random assignment or a rigorous matching procedure. The availability of an untreated control group is a prerequisite of all evaluation designs that attempt to infer a link between smaller class sizes and student outcomes.

This is one reason why many social scientists—in particular, economists, statisticians, and quantitative sociologists—have exploited data generated by the Tennessee and Wisconsin studies to conduct a number of creative secondary analyses.[69] Scholars have reaped enormous benefits from these two state policies, published dozens of empirical and theoretical papers based on data, and engaged in open and honest debate about the implications of the findings for research and policy.[70] By passing legislation to evaluate targeted class-size policies, lawmakers in Tennessee and Wisconsin contributed to the work of social scientists. The reverse was true in California and Indiana, where the massive scale-up of class-size policies created major hurdles in evaluating the effects of policy on student achievement. The case studies suggest that there is a reciprocal relationship between research and policy: just as social science can inform education policy, so political decisions can shape the rigor and quality of research.

Lesson 5: Once in the policy arena, social scientists do not provide definitive solutions to complex problems like the racial achievement gap; rather, they assume a critical perspective that encourages evaluation of educational policies in terms of their effects on student achievement. Mary Jo Bane has argued that social scientists should be viewed less as "expert problem solvers" than as "participants in democratic deliberation . . . making contributions to public discussions in which we do not control either the outcomes or the use of our findings."[71] Regardless of their disciplinary training and political perspectives, social scientists share a method—a way of thinking about problems—that performs a valuable function in the policy arena by helping to clarify questions and narrow policy options. They are trained to frame questions that can be addressed with appropriate methods; to test theories that can be falsified with data; to use reliable albeit imperfect measures of complex constructs; to interpret and report results accurately; to highlight alternative explanations of the findings; and never to claim 100 percent confidence about any finding—except the need for more and better research. The goal of social science research is not to prove a point or to rationalize a political decision. Rather, the social science perspective represents a kind of countervailing pressure that may help to restrain policy, focus its goals, and encourage measurement of policy impacts.

When research findings accord with the political views of a large number of citizens and elected officials, they have greater relevance and currency in the policy arena. That is one reason why the results from the Tennessee STAR project have influenced a number of state and district policies. According to economist Gary Burtless, "even though the trend toward smaller class size was under way for decades before Tennessee experimentally tested the impact of class-size reductions, the STAR experiment results were among the first to be widely cited in the popular press as persuasive evidence that smaller classes could be helpful."[72] Given the current national effort to "leave no child behind," policies that improve the achievement of minority children are likely to capture the attention of scholars, legislators, and lay audiences. Better collaborations between politicians and professors might improve the capacity of state government to fund and support experimental evaluations that produce clear findings to guide efforts to address the achievement gap.[73]

Future Prospects

That targeted class-size reduction policies are seemingly so rare may deepen pessimism about the role that research can play in shaping education policy. But there are also hopeful signs that compensatory education policies reserved primarily for young children from minority and low-income families are politically feasible and scientifically defensible. As clients of government, young children are viewed as legitimate and worthy recipients of additional resources and preferential treatment. The goal of narrowing achievement disparities is etched into the No Child Left Behind Act. Spending money to reduce class sizes for minority students at the beginning of their schooling careers represents a narrowly tailored public policy that serves compelling interests in U.S. society—most notably, the national effort to address achievement disparities. Ideally, intellectual and moral commitment to this task should motivate scholars to encourage good research and effective policies that enhance the quality of education for the most vulnerable members of our democracy.

Notes

1. International evidence also shows little significant relationship between class size and achievement in the middle grades. See, for example, the paper in this volume by Ludger Wößmann. See also, "Special Issue—Class Size: Issues and New Findings," *Educational Evaluation and Policy* (Summer 1999). More recent reviews of the empirical research on class size also are provided by Alan B. Krueger, "Economic Considerations and Class Size," *Economic Journal* 113, no. 485 (2003): 34–63; Eric A. Hanushek, "The Failure of Input-Based Schooling Policies," *Economic Journal* 113, no. 485 (2003): 64–98.

2. Quoted in Lawrence Mishel and Richard Rothstein, eds., *The Class Size Debate* (Washington: Economic Policy Institute, 2002), p. 3.

3. Ibid.

4. Criticisms of across-the-board class-size reduction policies and analyses of costs can be found in Eric Hanushek, "Evidence, Politics, and the Class Size Debate" in *The Class Size Debate*, edited by Mishel and Rothstein; John Folger, "Lessons from Class Size Policy and Research," *Peabody Journal of Education* 67, no. 1 (Fall 1989); Dominic Brewer and others, "Estimating the Cost of National Class Size Reductions under Different Policy Alternatives," *Educational Evaluation and Policy Analysis* 21, no. 2 (Summer 1999): 179–92; Caroline Hoxby, "The Effects of Class Size on Student Achievement: New Evidence from Population Variation," *Quarterly Journal of Economics* 115, no. 4 (2000): 1239–285.

5. In a 2006 poll conducted by Public Agenda, 85 percent of superintendents and principals indicated that they would vote for a local school board candidate who believed that "if the public schools finally got more money and smaller classes, they could do a better job." See Public Agenda, *Reality Check 2006* (New York, 2006), p. 20. In addition, 86 percent of new teachers believed that a "very effective" way to improve quality is to "reduce class size." See Public Agenda, *Where We Are Now: Twelve Things You Need to Know about Public Opinion and Public Schools* (New York, 2003), p. 31. In a 1999 survey involving a random sample of 1,422 adults nationwide, a majority

of parents (61 percent) and nonparents (64 percent) thought that overcrowded classrooms were a "major" problem facing the local public schools. When given a list of policies to improve their local schools, 75 percent of parents and 66 percent of nonparents "strongly" favored "reducing class sizes" even if the changes "cost more money and required additional tax dollars." See poll data for NPR/Kaiser/Kennedy School Education Survey (www.npr.org/programs/specials/poll/education/education.results.html 1999).

6. James Q. Wilson, *American Government, Institutions, and Policies,* 3rd ed. (Lexington, Mass.: D. C. Heath, 1986), p. 431.

7. Ibid., p. 432.

8. H. Hugh Heclo, "Values Underpinning Poverty Programs for Children," *Future of Children* 7 (Summer/Fall 1997):141–48.

9. James S. Coleman and others, *Equality of Educational Opportunity* (Washington: U. S. Government Printing Office), p. 312.

10. Christopher Jencks, "The Coleman Report and the Conventional Wisdom," in *On Equality of Educational Opportunity*, edited by Frederick Mosteller and Daniel P. Moynihan (New York: Random House, 1972), p. 98.

11. John P. Gilbert and Frederick Mosteller, "The Urgent Need for Experimentation," in *On Equality of Educational Opportunity*, edited by Mosteller and Moynihan, p. 375.

12. Gene Glass and Mary L. Smith, *Meta-Analysis of the Relationship of Class Size and Student Achievement* (San Francisco: Far West Laboratory for Educational Research, 1978); Gene Glass and Mary L. Smith, "Meta-Analysis of Research on Relationship of Class Size and Achievement," *Educational Evaluation and Policy Analysis* 1, no.1 (1978): 2–16.

13. Glass and Smith, *Meta-Analysis of the Relationship of Class Size and Student Achievement*, p. ii.

14. Ibid.

15. Educational Research Services, *Class Size Research: A Critique of Recent Analyses* (Arlington, Va.: 1980).

16. Robert Slavin, "Class Size and Student Achievement: Is Smaller Better?" *Contemporary Education* 62 (Fall 1990): 6–12.

17. Hans J. Eysenck, "An Exercise in Mega-Silliness," *American Psychologist* 33, no. 5 (1978): 517.

18. Gene Glass, "On Criticisms of Our Class Size/Student Achievement Research: No Points Conceded," *Phi Delta Kappan* 62, no. 4 (1980): 244.

19. Henry J. Aaron, *Politics and the Professors* (Brookings, 1978).

20. According to a review of state class-size policies, the Education Commission of the States found that a total of six class-size reduction policies were implemented from 1977 to 1988. From 1989 to 2005, there were a total of twenty-three class size reduction initiatives. See Kyle Zinth, "State Class-Size Reduction Measures" (Denver: Education Commission of the States, March 2005).

21. Gary W. Ritter and Robert F. Boruch, "The Political and Institutional Origins of a Randomized Controlled Trial on Elementary School Class Size: Tennessee's Project STAR," *Educational Evaluation and Policy Analysis* 21 (Summer 1999): 115–16.

22. "On May 22, 1985, House Bill 544 (HB0544) to implement Project STAR was passed in the Tennessee House of Representatives by a vote of 94 to 1; the Tennessee Senate passed the bill on the following day by a vote of 27 to 0." Cited in Ritter and Boruch, "The Political and Institutional Origins of a Randomized Controlled Trial on Elementary School Class Size," p. 117.

23. Ibid., p. 123.

24. According to Frederick Mosteller, the Project STAR study is "one of the most important educational investigations ever carried out and illustrates the kind and magnitude of research needed in the field of education to strengthen schools." Frederick Mosteller, "The Tennessee Study

of Class Size in the Early Grades," *Future of Children,* vol. 5, *Critical Issues for Children and Youths* (Summer/Fall 1995): 113–26, quote on p. 113.

25. The most relevant findings are reported in publications by Charles Achilles, Jeremy Finn, Eric Hanushek, Alan Krueger, and Frederick Mosteller. See Mosteller, "The Tennessee Study of Class Size in the Early Grades"; Jeremy D. Finn and Charles M. Achilles, "Answers and Questions about Class Size: A Statewide Experiment," *American Educational Research Journal* 27, no. 3 (1990): 557–77; Eric A. Hanushek, "Some Findings from an Independent Investigation of the Tennessee STAR Experiment and from Other Investigations of Class Size Effects," *Educational Evaluation and Policy Analysis* 21, no. 2 (1999): 143–64; Alan B. Krueger, "Experimental Estimates of Education Production Functions," *Quarterly Journal of Economics* 114, no. 2 (1999): 497–532; Alan B. Krueger and Diane M. Whitmore, "The Effect of Attending a Small Class in the Early Grades on College Test Taking and Middle School Test Results: Evidence from Project STAR," *Economic Journal* 111, no. 468 (2001): 1–28; Jeremy D. Finn, Susan B. Gerber, and Jayne Boyd-Zaharias, "Small Classes in the Early Grades, Academic Achievement, and Graduating from High School," *Journal of Educational Psychology* 97, no.2 (2005): 214–23.

26. For example, see the paper in this volume by Diane Whitmore Schanzenbach.

27. It is important to note that Governor Ned McWherter, a Democrat, and his appointed state education commissioner, Charles Smith supported the Project Challenge policy. Despite a change in political leadership from the Alexander to McWherter administration, the class size policy continued the legacy of STAR by using its findings to design a targeted class-size policy. Randy Kenner, "Teachers Given Smaller Classes Call Students Big Winners," *Knoxville News-Sentinel*, November, 11, 1990, p. A1.

28. Personal correspondence from Charles M. Achilles, professor emeritus, School of Education, Eastern Michigan University and Seton Hall University, August 10, 2006.

29. Charles M. Achilles, Jayne B. Zaharias, and Barbara Nye, "Policy Use of Research Results: Tennessee's Project Challenge," paper presented at the annual meeting of the American Educational Research Association, San Francisco (April 1995).

30. Frederick Mosteller, "How Does Class Size Relate to Achievement in Schools?" in *Earning and Learning,* edited by Susan E. Mayer and Paul E. Peterson (Brookings, 1999), pp. 117–30.

31. Charles M. Achilles, Barbara A. Nye, and Jayne Boyd-Zaharias, *Policy Use of Research Results: Tennessee's Project Challenge,* paper presented at the annual meeting of the American Educational Research Association, San Francisco, April 1995.

32. Frederick Mosteller, "How Does Class Size Relate to Achievement in Schools?" p. 123.

33. Ibid., p. 18.

34. Jennifer McGiverin, David Gilman, and Chris Tillitski, "A Meta-Analysis of the Relation between Class Size and Achievement," *Elementary School Journal* 90, no. 1 (1989): 47–56.

35. Ritter and Boruch, "The Political and Institutional Origins of a Randomized Controlled Trial on Elementary School Class Size," p. 115.

36. Ibid, pp. 18–29.

37. "Early Grades: Actions to Reduce Class Size," *Education Week*, October 16, 1985.

38. Christopher Tillitski, "The Longitudinal Effect Size of Prime Time, Indiana's State-Sponsored Reduced Class Size Program," *Contemporary Education* 62, no. 1 (1990): 26.

39. Personal correspondence from Daniel K. Lapsley, professor of psychology, Department of Psychology, Notre Dame University, August 1, 2006.

40. Daniel K. Lapsley and others, *Instructional Assistants, Class Size, and Academic Achievement: An Evaluation of Indiana's Prime Time*, report submitted to the Indiana Department of Education (February 2002), p. vi.

41. Ibid., p. 60.

42. Personal correspondence from Jayma Ferguson, Division of Prime Time/Reading First, Indiana Department of Education, November 13, 2006.

43. Marshall S. Smith, "Assessment Trends in a Contemporary Policy Context," in *Analytic Issues in the Assessment of Student Achievement*, edited by David W. Grissmer and J. Michael Ross (U. S. Department of Education, National Center for Education Statistics, 2000), p. 273.

44. Alex Molnar and others, "Evaluating the SAGE Program: A Pilot Program in Targeted Pupil-Teacher Reduction in Wisconsin," *Educational Evaluation and Policy Analysis* 21 (Summer 1999): 165–78. The SAGE program was initially open to schools in which at least 30 percent of students were from families below the poverty line and from districts where at least 50 percent of students were below the poverty line. Moreover, SAGE consisted of four interventions, and in exchange for $2,000, districts were required to reduce the student-teacher ratio to 15 students per teacher, beginning with kindergarten and first grade in 1996–97; establish longer school days; develop a rigorous curriculum; and create staff development programs. However, the focus of SAGE became reducing class sizes because most schools claimed to have "rigorous curriculum" in place, longer school days, and staff development. For more details, see John A. Zahorik, Alex Molnar, and Philip Smith, *SAGE Advice: Research on Teaching in Reduced-Size Classes* (Educational Policy Studies Laboratory, College of Education, Arizona State University, 2003).

45. As in any quasi-experimental study, there are possible selection biases that threaten the internal validity of the treatment effects. In the SAGE studies, a number of comparison schools decided to opt out of the study due to the testing burdens and limited benefits of participation. Since 1996–97, seven of the original seventeen comparison schools left the study, and five of those seven applied for and became SAGE schools. According to Thomas Hruz, *The Costs and Benefits of Smaller Classes in Wisconsin* (Thiensville, Wis.: Wisconsin Policy Research Institute, 2000), p. 21: "This problem with the departure of comparison schools relates more generally to concerns of selection bias, which occurs when tested members of a study volunteer to participate because they have a vested interest in the program. The problem is particularly acute in SAGE, where schools apply to participate (and are publicly eager to do so) and where comparisons are made against schools that are forced, seemingly with contempt, into participating."

46. Alex Molnar and others, "Evaluating the SAGE Program," p. 166.

47. Ibid., p. 177. A more recent summary of SAGE results is in Phil Smith, Alex Molnar, and John Zahorik, "Class-Size Reduction, A Fresh Look at the Data," *Educational Leadership* 61, no. 1 (2003): 72–74.

48. Hruz, *The Costs and Benefits of Smaller Classes in Wisconsin*, p. 7.

49. Ibid., p. 34.

50. Norman L. Webb and others, *Participation in the Student Achievement Guarantee in Education (SAGE) Program and Performance on State Assessments at Grade 3 and Grade 4 for Three Cohorts of Students: Grade 1 Students in 1996–97, 1997–98, and 1998–99*, (Madison, Wis.: Wisconsin Center for Education Research, 2004).

51. The three evaluations were carried out by researchers at the University of Wisconsin–Milwaukee, the University of Wisconsin–Madison, and the Wisconsin Policy Research Institute.

52. David C. Illig, "Reducing Class Size: A Review of the Literature and Options for Consideration" (Sacrmento, Calif.: California Research Bureau, 1996). The California Research Bureau is akin to the federal Government Accountability Office. Its mission is to provide "nonpartisan research services to the Governor and his staff, to both houses of the legislature, and to other state elected officials."

53. Ibid., p. 2.

54. Thomas B. Timar, "The 'New Accountability' and School Governance in California," *Peabody Journal of Education* 78, no. 4 (2003): 189.

55. George W. Borhnstedt and Brian M. Stecher, eds., *What We Have Learned about Class Size Reduction in California* (Sacramento, Calif.: California Department of Education, 2002), p. 18.

56. Mixed results of the California policy on student outcomes are in Borhnstedt and Stecher, eds., *What We Have Learned about Class Size Reduction in California*. However, based on a

propensity score analysis, recent empirical research suggests that the California policy had a positive impact on math achievement. See Fatih Unlu, "California Class Size Reduction Reform: New Findings from the NAEP," Working Paper (Princeton University, Department of Economics, November 2005).

57. Borhnstedt and Stecher, eds., *What We Have Learned about Class Size Reduction in California*, p. 5.

58. Ibid., p. 6.

59. Ibid., p. 66.

60. For more on the political and institutional origins of the 1996 class size reduction policy, see Borhnstedt and Stecher, eds., *What We Have Learned about Class Size Reduction in California*, chapter 1.

61. Carol H. Weiss, "The Many Meanings of Research Utilization," *Public Administration Review* 39, no. 5 (1979): 427.62. Mary Snow, *An Evaluation of the Class Size Reduction Program* (Carson City, Nev.: Nevada Department of Education, 1997), p. 6.

62. Mary Snow, *An Evaluation of the Class Size Reduction Program* (Carson City, Nev.: Nevada Department of Education, 1997), p. 6.

63. Stephen Hegarty, "On Class Size, Question Is How," *St. Petersburg Times*, December 25, 2002, p. 1B.

64. Wilson, *American Government, Institutions, and Policies,* p. 428.

65. Christopher Jencks and Meredith Phillips, eds., *The Black-White Test Score Gap* (Brookings, 1998), p. 47.

66. James DiStefano, *Evaluation of the Reduced-Ratio Program Final Report* (Fairfax, Va.: Fairfax County Public Schools, Office of Program Evaluation, 1997), p. 30.

67. Michelle P. Serafin, *Project Excel, Final Report: Fall 1999–Spring 2003* (Fairfax County, Va.: Fairfax County Public Schools, Office of Program Evaluation, 2003), p. B-3.

68. Even more sophisticated methods, such as the use of propensity scores to match treatment and control cases, require the treatment to be withheld from some group of students. The logistic regression models used to create propensity scores are based on a binary outcome, which usually denotes whether or not the subject received the treatment. Absent a control group, there is no way to apply propensity score analyses to data. See Paul R. Rosenbaum and Donald B. Rubin, "The Central Role of the Propensity Score in Observational Studies for Causal Effects," *Biometrika* 70, no. 1 (1983): 41–55. For a recent extension of propensity score analysis to nonbinary treatments, see Kosuke Imai and David van Dyk, "Causal Inference with General Treatment Regimes: Generalizing the Propensity Score," *Journal of the American Statistical Association* 99, no. 467 (2004): 854–66.

69. For example, see the paper in this volume by Diane Whitmore Schanzenbach.

70. Psychologists and economists interested in studying how the quality of student-teacher interactions is related to improved social and cognitive outcomes have studied the mechanisms inside small classes to help explain improvements in student achievement in the early grades. For relevant research, see National Institute of Child Health and Human Development (NICHD) Early Child Care Research Network, "Does Class Size in First Grade Relate to Children's Academic and Social Performance or Observed Classroom Processes?" *Developmental Psychology* 40, no. 5 (2004): 651–64; Edward Lazear, "Education Production," *Quarterly Journal of Economics* 116, no. 3 (2001): 777–803; Jeremy D. Finn, Gina M. Pannozzo, and Charles M. Achilles, "The 'Why's' of Class Size: Student Behavior in Small Classes," *Review of Educational Research* 73 (Fall 2003): 321–68; Ronald F. Ferguson, "Can Schools Narrow the Black-White Test Score Gap?" in *The Black-White Test Score Gap,* edited by Jencks and Phillips. In "Can Schools Narrow the Black-White Test Score Gap?" (p. 368), economist Ronald Ferguson contends that the "interaction of class size and race is not an especially surprising finding. . . . If, as the evidence indicates, black children are more sensitive than whites to teachers' perceptions, and black children's work habits

and behavioral problems present greater challenges to teachers, smaller classes that are easier for teachers to manage may have more impact on improving black students' scores than whites'. It is probably correct that having fewer pupils per class can improve learning outcomes and reduce racial disparities."

71. Mary Jo Bane, "Presidential Address—Expertise, Advocacy, and Deliberation: Lessons from Welfare Reform," *Journal of Policy Analysis and Management* 20, no. 2 (2001): 191–97. Quote is from p. 195.

72. Gary Burtless, "Randomized Field Trials for Policy Evaluation: Why Not in Education?" in *Evidence Matters*, edited by Frederick Mosteller and Robert Boruch (Brookings, 2002), p. 196.

73. For a recent analysis of the role of nonpartisan research organizations on state policymaking, see John A. Hird, *Power, Knowledge, and Politics* (Georgetown University Press, 2005). According to Hird's analysis, very few state governments have the capacity to carry out complex analytical studies of public policy. With respect to education policy, some state governments (for example, Texas and Florida) have collaborated with university researchers to set up sophisticated longitudinal databases. However, planned experiments, such as those in Tennessee and Wisconsin, are also needed to obtain better data on the causal effects of education policies such as class-size reduction.